VASE PAINTING, GENDER, AND SOCIAL IDENTITY IN ARCHAIC ATHENS

Spectators at the sides of narrative vase paintings have long been at the margins of scholarship, but a study of their appearance shows that they provide a model for the ancient viewing experience. They also reflect social and gender roles in archaic Athens. This study explores the phenomenon of spectators through a database built from a census of the *Corpus Vasorum Antiquorum*, which reveals that the figures flourished in Athenian vase painting during the last two-thirds of the sixth century B.C.E. Using models developed from psychoanalysis and the theory of the gaze, ritual studies, and gender studies, Stansbury-O'Donnell shows how these "spectators" emerge as models for social and gender identification in the archaic city, encoding in their gestures and behavior archaic attitudes about gender and status.

Mark D. Stansbury-O'Donnell is professor of art history at the University of St. Thomas in St. Paul, Minnesota. A scholar of Greek art, he is the author of *Pictorial Narrative in Ancient Greek Art* and has published articles on the painter Polygnotos and issues of narrative and methodology in the *American Journal of Archaeology* and several edited volumes.

VASE PAINTING, GENDER, AND SOCIAL IDENTITY IN ARCHAIC ATHENS

MARK D. STANSBURY-O'DONNELL

University of St. Thomas

CAMBRIDGE
UNIVERSITY PRESS

CAMBRIDGE
UNIVERSITY PRESS

32 Avenue of the Americas, New York NY, 10013-2473, USA

Cambridge University Press is part of the University of Cambridge.

It furthers the University's mission by disseminating knowledge in the pursuit of education, learning, and research at the highest international levels of excellence.

www.cambridge.org
Information on this title: www.cambridge.org/9781107662803

First published 2006
First paperback edition 2014

Printed in the United States of America

A catalog record for this publication is available from the British Library.

Library of Congress Cataloging in Publication data
Stansbury-O'Donnell, Mark, 1956–
Vase painting, gender, and social identity in archaic Athens / Mark D. Stansbury-O'Donnell.
p. cm.
Includes bibliographical references and index.
ISBN-13: 978-0-521-85318-7 (hardback)
ISBN-10: 0-521-85318-4 (hardback)
1. Vase-painting, Greek – Greece – Athens. 2. Vases, Ancient – Greece – Athens.
3. Spectators in art. 4. Sex role in art. 5. Art and society – Greece – Athens.
I. Title.
NK4645.S73 2005
738.3'82'09385 – dc22 2005019531

ISBN 978-0-521-85318-7 Hardback
ISBN 978-1-107-66280-3 Paperback

To Wendy

CONTENTS

LIST OF ILLUSTRATIONS

ACKNOWLEDGMENTS

This project grew out of some unanswered questions regarding spectators in narrative images that lingered from my earlier study of narrative art. It was not clear in the beginning where these questions would lead, and I am thankful for the help and guidance of a number of people as my work has developed and changed over the past five years. Most particularly, I would like to thank Jerry Pollitt and Alan Shapiro, who have supported the project from its early stages with their comments and letters and who have provided models for me to follow. I am deeply grateful.

I would like to thank Beatrice Rehl and Cambridge University Press for their interest and support for this project, and particularly to acknowledge the comments of the anonymous readers for the Press. Their comments led to a number of refinements in the manuscript that strengthened it.

Pam Gordon invited me to speak about my work to the Department of Classics and the Hall Center for the Humanities at the University of Kansas in September 2002, and I am appreciative of the opportunity to present some of the more difficult elements of chapter 3 at an early stage and to hear the comments of the faculty and students. In addition, Professor Gordon read drafts of other portions of the work and made a number of suggestions that helped the development of the manuscript. I would also like to thank Judy Barringer, Sheramy Bundrick, Susan Matheson, Sarah Morris, and Ann Steiner for comments, discussion, suggestions, and support at various stages of the project that helped to focus and clarify it.

Portions of this work were presented at the meetings of the Archaeological Institute of America and the Society for American Archaeology. I am grateful for comments and discussion from members of those sessions.

The Minnesota Humanities Commission provided a timely grant in 2001 in support of this project that enabled the construction of an early version of the database that is one of the foundations for this study.

I am deeply grateful for several grants and releases from the University of St. Thomas during the past four years that provided the time for data collection as well as support for travel and the acquisition of photographs. Most particularly, my sabbatical in 2003–2004 allowed the manuscript to be completed and revised.

A number of colleagues at St. Thomas also provided a forum for presenting work in progress and offered helpful comments, including members of the Department of Art History, the Luann Dummer Center for Women, and, especially, Britain Scott, Jill Manske, Elaine Lilly, and Thomas Ressler.

Two graduate students were very helpful at the beginning and end of this project. Vanessa Rousseau tested several early models for the database and for sampling volumes of the *Corpus Vasorum Antiquorum* that led to improvements in my design and protocol for data collection. Amy Pence Brown read through the manuscript before final revisions and brought fresh eyes and judgment to its writing and organization.

The Minneapolis Institute of Arts not only had one of the vases that had raised questions about spectators in my mind (see figure 1), but also invited me to give several public lectures and classes on the viewing experience that helped to keep a larger perspective in my mind's eye throughout the project.

For their assistance and generosity in providing photographs and permissions for reproduction, I would like to thank the Antikensammlung in Munich; the Ashmolean Museum in Oxford; the Art Institute of Chicago; the Bibliothèque nationale de France; Jaclyn Burns of the J. Paul Getty Museum; the Cleveland Museum of Art; DeAnn Dankowski of the Minneapolis Institute of Arts; Dorothy Davila of the Harvard University Art Museums; the Department of Greek and Roman Antiquities at the British Museum; Andreas Dobler of the Hessische Hausstiftung, Museum Schloss Fasanerie; Megan Doyon of the Yale University Art Gallery; Professor Dr. Bettina Baronesse v. Freytag Löringhoff of the Institut für Klassische Archäologie, Eberhard Karls Universität Tübingen; Dr. Wilfred Geominy of the Akademisches Kunstmuseum-Antikensammlung der Universität Bonn; Claus Hattler of the Badisches Landesmuseum Karlsruhe; Dr. Klaus Junker of the Institut für Klassische Archäologie, Universität Mainz; the Los Angeles County Museum of Art; Susan Matheson of the Yale University Art Gallery in New Haven; Larry Mensching of the Joslyn Art Museum in Omaha; the Metropolitan Museum of Art in New York; the Museum of Fine Arts in Boston; the Nationalmuseet in Copenhagen; the Nelson-Atkins Museum of Art in Kansas City; Dr. Isabella Nobile, Curator, Museo Civico di Como; Claudia Ponton at Art Resource; the San Antonio Museum of Art; Dr. Rüdiger Splitter of the Staatliche Museen Kassel; Luisa Veneziano of the Deutsches Archäologisches Institut in Rome; the Walters Art Museum in Baltimore; and the Washington University in St. Louis Gallery of Art.

Finally, I would like to acknowledge my personal good fortune in being able to look at spectators. As a graduate student, I had the opportunity to study with extraordinary scholars/teachers in classical art and archaeology, who encouraged odd questions or perspectives and have continued to inspire me as both teacher and scholar. The support of my wife Wendy, my son Ben, and my family is inestimable.

ONE

SEEING SPECTATORS

When one looks at Greek pottery of the sixth and fifth centuries B.C.E., one finds a trove of figural scenes with all kinds of action, from mythological encounters to battles to scenes that seem drawn out of the rhythms of daily life. The sheer number of figural scenes in a medium that was in large-scale production is staggering when one looks at other pottery in the ancient world, and this richness has made vase painting an important source for our knowledge of Greek mythology and customs. For example, a black-figure amphora in the Minneapolis Institute of Arts shows a warrior wearing his helmet and cuirass, carrying a shield and striding toward the right away from a woman and an older man with beard ("Minneapolis amphora," figure 1).[1] He turns his head back to look at them, while the woman holds both of her hands in front of herself at different angles and the older man raises his left arm and hand in a gesture to acknowledge the warrior's actions. To the right is a beardless younger man wrapped in a mantle, his right hand in front of him but wrapped in the cloak so that he essentially makes no movement or gesture. Such scenes are typically labeled as the warrior leaving home and are common in both archaic and classical vase painting.

What is striking about the picture, however, is that three out of the four figures essentially watch the remaining figure perform an action. That many figures on vases watch others doing things is quite normal for Greek art, and each one on this vase has some plausible role for being there. The woman could be a wife or perhaps a mother of the warrior, reacting with some distress to his departure, while the older male is likely a father watching his son depart, saluting his performance of his duties as head of the household and as a member of the *polis* or city-state.[2] The role of the young man to the side is more difficult to construct. He could be a son of the warrior or a younger brother, but he observes the actions of the warrior, perhaps looking to the day when he, too, will do the same. Even though we can conjure a narrative role for each of the figures in the action, the striding warrior alone is the essential nucleus of the

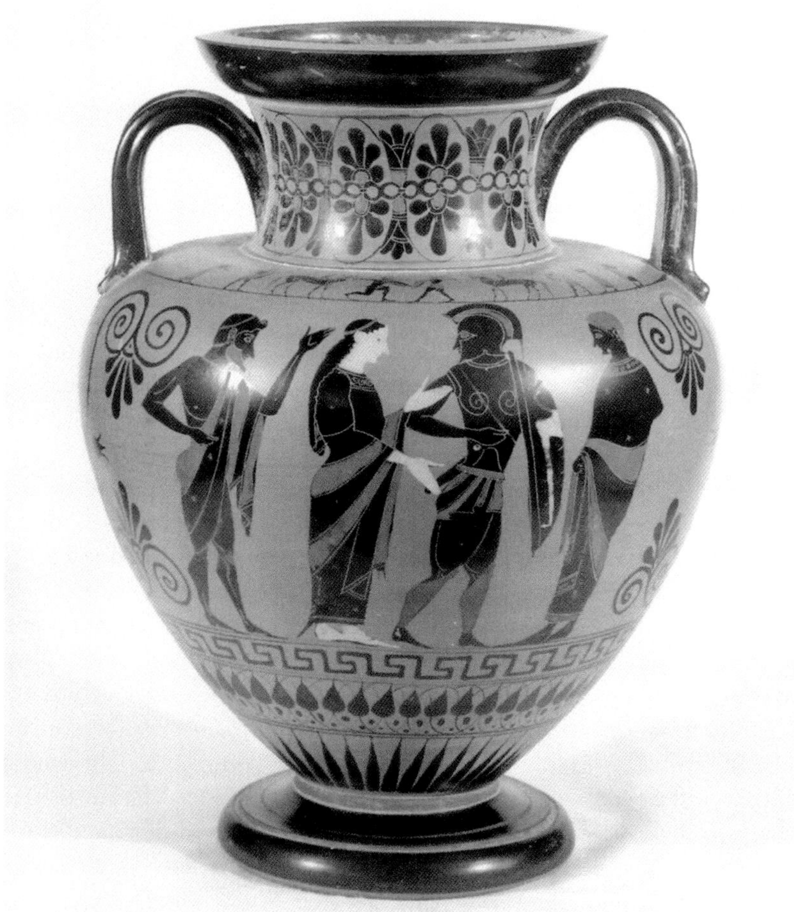

1. Attic black-figure amphora, attributed to the Painter of Vatican 359, c. 530. Side B: Departure of warrior. Minneapolis Institute of Arts, Ethel Morrison Van Derlip Fund, 57.1. (Photograph, The Minneapolis Institute of Arts)

scene. The remaining figures add depth to the action and provide it with a context, but the fact remains that they will do nothing that will change the course of the action or determine whether the warrior will come home with his shield or on it.

In essence, these figures watch the action, not unlike a viewer of the vase. If one considers the original viewer, the member of a household in which the amphora would have been used, or member of the family who would have left the vase as an offering in a tomb, then the reactions of these peripheral figures are like those of the viewer to the events in his or her own life. Men go to war; sometimes they come home and

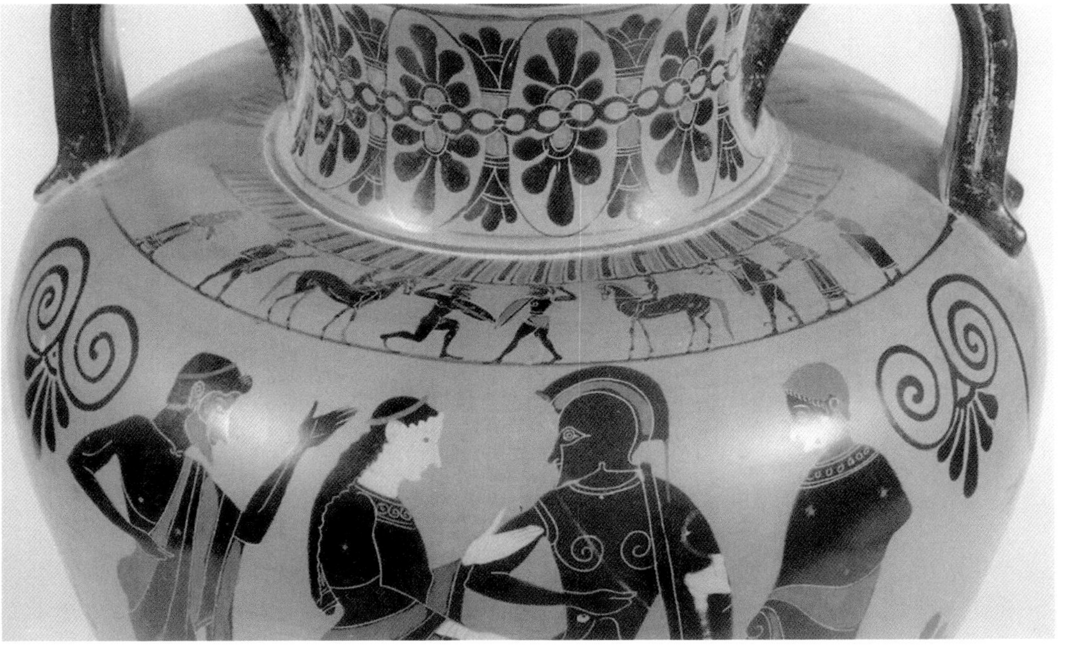

2. Attic black-figure amphora, attributed to the Painter of Vatican 359, c. 530. Side B: Detail of shoulder: warriors fighting. Minneapolis Institute of Arts, Ethel Morrison Van Derlip Fund, 57.1. (Photograph, The Minneapolis Institute of Arts)

sometimes they do not. The departure is stressful, but others can take pride in it for its social and civic importance. Undoubtedly the variety of reactions of these figures mirrors the variety of emotional responses by the different types of viewers of the vase, although it is highly improbable that the scene appeared just like this in real life. The scene is a construction that represents the events, ideas, and values of the period, of its maker and its viewers.

The division between actors and watchers becomes even more striking if we look at the picture on the shoulder of the same amphora (figure 2). In the center of the long frieze are two warriors fighting. The figure on the right has helmet, cuirass, skirt, and shield just like the departing warrior below, and the repetition of these features serves as an index to connect the two pictures in a sequence. The second warrior in the fight has a helmet and shield, but is otherwise nude as he crouches to attack. This shoulder scene forms a logical sequel to the action of departure on the body of the amphora, but whereas the former scene took place in a domestic/civic setting where one might expect non-warrior viewers, the battle frieze is even more populated with spectators. On either side of the warriors are horses ridden by nude, youthful riders. Usually called squires, their presence makes a certain amount of sense for the idea of the elite warrior, who might own or use a horse to get to the battlefield where he would fight on foot. The nudity of the rider, like that of the one warrior, would be a departure from what one would expect at a real battle, and his lack of a weapon makes his function in a battle dubious at best.[3] Still, his presence lends a heroic patina to the combat in the center. Indeed, the fight itself is a departure from the combat practices of the sixth century, which emphasized fighting in tightly organized, group formations, rather than in hand-to-hand duels, so the presence of a battlefield attendant is not so strange given that the picture is not reality. Behind the right horse appears Hermes, identified by his wide-brimmed hat or *petasos*, winged boots, and *kerykeion*. As conductor of the souls of the dead, his presence makes logical sense for a battle, although his appearance here is not meant to be taken any more literally than that of the squires or warriors themselves.

More striking, however, are the figures at the ends of the frieze: a woman and youth on both sides. On the left, behind the horse, a nude youth, with a cape or *chlamys* over his left arm, raises that arm in a gesture like the older man in the picture below. At the far left is a woman wearing a belted garment and holding her left hand before her body. Her pose and gesture recall those of the woman in the departure scene below. Behind Hermes on the other side of the frieze, we find a mirror image of the woman on the left. Behind her at the end of the frieze is a mantled youth, who holds out one hand wrapped within his mantle, like the youth in the picture below. Clearly the repetition of so many motifs and figures in the two sections of the vase must lead us to the conclusion that the two pictures are meant to be viewed as an ensemble. However, the logical possibility of women and youths on a battlefield watching the fight is far more remote and artificial than the presence of the same figures in the picture of the departure, or even of Hermes and the squires who could, in theory, become involved in the action. Structurally, the women and youths at the margins of the fight play a more detached role in the picture.

What are these figures doing in a picture of a battle where they would have no real or imaginary role? Certainly they fill out the long surface of the frieze, maintaining a steady rhythm of decorative accents matching the neck and body of the vase. However, the painter could easily have shown a series of warrior duels that would have served the same decorative function and would have had more internal narrative consistency as well, or might have used a non-figural pattern to fill out the surface, such as the scrolls that appear below the handles on the amphora. The careful repetition of the larger figures on the body in the smaller frieze above also argues for intentionality in the scheme beyond its decorative potential. What, though, are we to make of the figures, and what is the relationship between what they watch and what the actual viewer of the vase sees? Whereas these figures have usually been labeled as onlookers or spectators, and thereafter overlooked, they appear on hundreds of vases. In many cases they so intrude visually and compositionally upon the main action that their decorative role must be decidedly secondary to their narrative role. Indeed, these peripheral figures bear scrutiny in their own right. As one looks at a vase and thinks about the original viewing context, one should consider that these watchers provide a diagram of the viewing experience to guide us in looking at the images. Essentially, these figures can help us to understand the role of images, narratives, and actions in developing the identity of the ancient viewer.

1.1 EARLIER WORK ON SPECTATORS

There has been little systematic study of spectator figures on Greek vases, although their presence has long been noted. In an early article on the Amasis Painter, J. D. Beazley described a vase in the Guglielmi Collection in Rome, saying that:[4]

> As to the flanking figures, the young man with the spear is repeated almost unaltered on the other side of the vase, and elsewhere in our painter's work, and another favourite of his is the naked youth holding a round aryballos, of Corinthian type, by its cord. It would be ideal to seek names for these two: they are onlookers, courtiers, retinue: let us call them Rosincrantz and Guildenstern.

The term onlooker has become common for these figures, although it lacks the evocative quality of the Shakespearean characters as a label. Rosencrantz and Guildenstern, however, were involved in the action that they witnessed, even if witlessly, and were ultimately and extremely affected by it. This is not the situation in pictures such as the warriors fighting in figure 2.

D. von Bothmer continued the stage analogy in a later article on the Amasis Painter, saying that these "figures are like stock characters in a play lined up afresh for another curtain call . . . their part in the scene (and thus the scene itself) defies recognition."[5] He notes that the grouping of such figures is "almost haphazard and certainly unconventional" and is found in the work of other painters. Ultimately, these loose figures are "supernumeraries" that the Amasis Painter uses less and less as his career progresses. Certainly, in formal terms, the figures have a peripheral role in support of the main figures in the center of the composition and, with their regular spacing, play a decorative role by helping to fill up the surface of the vase. The occurrence of spectators, however, continues into the late archaic period after the Amasis Painter, and in many cases they intrude upon the main figures when their absence would hardly be felt from a decorative point of view (see, for example, figure 69).

More recent study has sought to provide a broader overview of the spectator phenomenon. S. Korte-Konte approached the subject from an iconographic point of view, and was the first to document and describe spectators, *theates*, in a range of scenes.[6] She cataloged 95 scenes of Theseus and the Minotaur that contain spectators, 43 of Herakles and the Lion, 23 of other labors of Herakles, and 46 combat duels like that on the Minneapolis amphora. Importantly, her catalog shows that most of the works are Attic black-figure, with only a small number of non-Attic works. Her catalog does not contain other mythological scenes with spectators, or scenes like athletic and other contests, but the number of vases that she included in her catalog suggested for the first time how widespread the phenomenon of spectators actually was. She also noted that in some cases the spectators had no discernible place in the story, whereas in scenes like Theseus and the Minotaur they had an iconographic identity.[7]

T. Carpenter focused in more detail on the use of spectators, which he termed "stock figures," in the work of the C, Heidelberg, and Amasis Painters and their associates.[8] He noted that these figures include men, youths, and women, and that they have repeated elements of pose and dress and often occur in groups of two and three. Such figures appear frequently in the work of the C Painter, but many of his works are without a narrative core, so they are not truly spectators or onlookers like those we have seen. The Heidelberg Painter does provide a narrative focus for the vase pictures, now providing something for the stock figures to see but without making any direct connection to the figures performing the action. Carpenter notes that:[9]

> It can probably be assumed that for both painters the stock figures simply represent types of upper class Greeks. The conspicuous fillets worn by the men, particularly in the Heidelberg Painter's works, suggest that they are not dressed in everyday clothing, but rather that they are prepared for some special occasion. The presence of clearly respectable women in public with men and youths also points to the special nature of the occasion.

Carpenter went further, however, in suggesting that the figures are not merely decorative but contain some kind of meaning:

> Since the Heidelberg Painter seems to have borrowed these figures from the perfectly logical scenes by the C Painter, it is possible that he intended a symbolic connection between the stock figures and the central scene. In other words, the central scene may in some way be symbolic of the occasion for which the festive Greeks are dressed, but this, of course, must remain surmise.

Carpenter's suggestion that the figures reflect public, festival types of dress is noteworthy, and draws a firmer connection between the spectator and the life of the city.

I. Scheibler raised further this question of the meaning and value of the spectator (*Zuschauer*) for the ancient viewer.[10] She observed that archaic pictures are not a coherent field of space and time and have their own logic. She noted, for example, the deliberate variety of observers in a scene like the warrior leaving home; like the Minneapolis amphora, these pictures often contain an older man, a younger male, and a female figure whose identities are ambiguous and variable. She suggested that the variety is not simply an aesthetic preference or delight, but that artists such as the Amasis Painter are taking care to distinguish different forms of youth and men that represent different stages of life, from boy to ephebe (with first growth of beard) to adult man. Thus the variety of the figures reflects the variety of ancient viewers, particularly in the more detailed work of the Amasis Painter.

Carpenter and Scheibler focus on the work of a very few painters, but the inquiry into spectators broadened as part of the Munich exhibition *Kunst der Schale, Kultur des Trinkens*. B. Kaeser's short article on spectators noted that they are very common on band cups and they were already employed on earlier Little Master cups.[11] He remarked on their formal constancy, like the stock figures of the Heidelberg and C Painters, despite changes in subject matter ranging from Theseus and the Minotaur to Peleus and Atalanta to erotic scenes. Their presence in the picture is important, and in general they are witnesses to the reality and importance of the action that they observe. In particular, he suggests that the active spectators are models for the activity of the viewer of the vase, and that the men and youths on the cups represent the citizens of the community.

H. A. G. Brijder provided a new dimension to the study of spectators in his work on Siana cups, particularly by the Heidelberg Painter.[12] He observed that some activities, such as athletic events, komos, and symposion, are exclusively for male spectators. Women are present at combats and in scenes with Herakles, but have no exclusive subjects that they witness, as do male spectators. Women's behavior typically follows the *aidos* gesture of drawing the veil, and, following the suggestion of A. Steiner, he suggests that these women may be potential brides.[13] He also notes that it is sometimes hard to decide whether a figure, particularly a more active type, is part of the central action or belongs to the onlookers. He compiles a catalogue of spectator types, noting five examples of adult men, three types of male youths, and six types of women, who, unlike the male spectators, are not distinguished by age.

The result of this body of work indicates the potential for seeing spectators as models for the contemporary viewers of the vase and makes a strong case that the figures are not marginal and simply decorative in their intent. H. van Wees draws upon this to look at spectators as documenting social behavior, particularly among upper class Athenians, based on their dress and adornment.[14] He notes that many of them carry spears, indicating their status; because many of these scenes with spear-bearers are of contemporary events such as athletic contests, the presence of the spears is remarkable and reflects actual social practice. Thus, the spectators represent the habit of "bearing iron" or carrying weapons in public until the end of the sixth century. The difficulty here, however, is that the picture is regarded as a literal recording of contemporary events. It is important to remember that these pictures are constructions and not snapshots, and that the logic within them may be conceptual rather than literal. Indeed, spectators were not part of the scene at warrior duels, and it is unlikely that a scene of contemporary action is any more real. As J. Barringer has stated more broadly, "...the vase paintings are not scrupulous records of real life either and are instead, selective constructs of a culture's ideas about itself."[15] It is on these terms that we need to look more closely at spectators.

The recent studies on spectators collectively make several points. First, the number of vases with spectators is potentially large, and includes a number of different artists, vase types, and subjects. Second, the figures reflect in some manner the members of contemporary society, especially their civic and public life. Third, it is likely that the figures have some meaning, given the intentionality in their depiction and variety. There is some recognition of the variety of spectator types and of differences by gender and age, and that the relationship between the spectators and the central action is complex. The studies are limited, however, by their narrow focus. Many look at the work of only a few select painters or scenes and none makes a comprehensive effort to document the range of spectator and vase types and their context. It is also clear that an iconographic approach is limited by the lack of literary sources that mention these spectators.

There remain, then, a number of unanswered questions that these studies have raised in part. How can one define and categorize the range of spectator types and the relationship of spectators to the central action? Can one develop some sense of the number of vases with spectators, and of patterns in their occurrence, such as vase shape, chronology, and point of production? Can one develop interpretive models that will provide a stronger foundation for discerning the meaning of the figures within the picture for the original viewer? Are there differences in the behavior of spectators based on their gender or on the type of scene that they witness, and what do these tell us about norms of behavior and social stereotypes?

1.2 APPROACHING SPECTATORS

To answer these questions requires a systematic approach because there is no guidebook or discussion from antiquity that helps us to understand them. First, it will be necessary to define what a spectator is, and to distinguish different categories of onlookers from each other. This, then, would allow one to gather data on their appearance on vases, thereby contextualizing their deployment. Finally, from this data one can determine how to approach the question of interpretation, and what models and methods to use in developing that discussion.

Interpretation thus raises the issue of theoretical models, and whether there are alternatives to the approaches discussed in the previous section that should be used. Before outlining the methodologies that will be used in this study, we should consider briefly the question of the use of theory.[16] On the one hand, there are scholars who advocate the importance of theory for scholarly inquiry, particularly the injection of theories developed in the study of literature or of the social sciences. On the other hand, theory itself has been criticized as too abstract, non-empirical, and difficult to engage. The symposium hosted by the journal *Critical Inquiry* on April 11, 2003 and the essays subsequently published in the winter 2004 issue highlight some of the turmoil and disagreements in the academic community regarding the nature and future of theory.[17] For the study of ancient art, there are questions about the interjection of a modern perspective back onto ancient material, the producers and users of which did not concern themselves with theory.[18] Some would question whether theoretical approaches are too abstract in nature, and whether they predetermine the interpretation of an artifact or question. Students frequently desire "facts" rather than methodology, and resist the frequently difficult writing style of theoretical texts. The deployment of theory can be intensely political, seeking to nullify other, usually more traditional, interpretive models. Is the use of theory, then, just a way to say much and little at the same time, and is it of any concern outside of academia?[19]

The critiques of theory are often justified, but this does not negate the importance of developing a range of theoretical models to use in the study of ancient art. Any form of scholarly study has its theoretical foundation and assumptions. We assume, for example, that vases with very similar stylistic features were produced around the same time and place, and possibly even by the same potter and painter. We assume that literary sources can aid us in the identification and interpretation of pictorial scenes and that poet and painter shared a common culture. Although both of these assumptions have validity, both stylistic analysis and iconography have relegated spectators to the margins of scholarly interest because, according to these approaches, they are secondary in importance and only vaguely contribute to the meaning of the picture, despite the signs of their intentionality. To develop the picture of spectators, one needs to consider alternative approaches, not because the more traditional approaches are incorrect, but because one needs additional tools to see the evidence of spectators fully.

Theory, however, should not be thrown wantonly at a subject. Indeed, as M. Povey articulated at the *Critical Inquiry* symposium, "Theory and practice must somehow be brought together so that the construction of theoretical paradigms draws more closely upon observable evidence."[20] In other words, theory does not have to be iconoclastic and abstract; indeed, it should be practical and functional. Its application should be grounded in the testimony and outlook of the time period, and adapted to the circumstances of the culture. Its use should build upon the material evidence itself, and be the result of detailed observation and description. For the study of ancient art, this means that one should rely upon a range of interpretive models and look toward the convergence of lines of inquiry and analysis. In some cases, a different theoretical model will contradict scholarly opinion, but in many cases a new approach can provide an alternative means for confirming and offering nuances to established interpretations. Given the fragmentary nature of our knowledge of the ancient world, subjecting its art and other remains to multiple approaches and tests can provide a larger framework for our understanding. Thus, to view spectators, I would propose taking a multidimensional approach in the hope that a combination of viewing points can shed some light on the context and interpretation of the vase paintings.

To begin, we must define and differentiate spectators based on their role within the picture and their behavior, as will be seen in chapter 2.1. Here, we can draw upon structural analysis in narrative to offer definitions for different kinds of spectators. Based on these definitions, it is then possible to develop some sense of the extent of spectators in vase painting by gathering data on their occurrence, using primarily the volumes of the *Corpus Vasorum Antiquorum*, but also data derived from excavation reports from sites in Athens as well as a sample of vases in the online Beazley Archive (chapters 2.2–2.4). The data show that spectators are a phenomenon that is not a widespread feature of Greek art generally; they are localized by time and place, distinctly Athenian in their appearance and belonging mostly to the period 565–490. Therefore, any interpretation of their meaning must consider this specific historical context.[21]

Following this general definition and survey of spectators, in chapter 3 we consider broadly the question of seeing and how what one observes is important in defining one's self and place within society. Lacanian psychoanalytic theory offers a general model for considering the function of the gaze and object in the construction of identity, as will be reviewed in chapter 3.1; we will also see that the physical and psycho-physiological nature of Greek theories of vision offer grounds for using this type of approach (chapter 3.2). To the degree that the modern approach to vision and identity corresponds to ancient Greek theories of vision, one can perceive that seeing mattered, and that what one saw became part of one's self. As a result, we will consider the dynamics of the viewing experience and identification in the final section (chapter 3.3), using the model of a viewing matrix that describes the components of the image, viewer, and viewing context.

In the remaining three chapters, we will focus on archaic Athens and how the spectators model the construction of civic and gender identity. Significantly, it is during this period that the major festivals of Athens were reorganized and expanded, that there was new construction in the sanctuaries, and that Athens greatly expanded its political and economic ambitions in Greece. As we shall explore in chapter 4, it is this expansion of ritualistic activity that illuminates one aspect for the meaning of spectators, in that the figures become models for choral performance and for civic observation, and in so doing help to forge an identity for the viewer as an Athenian, or what it meant to be an Athenian. A brief review of ritualistic theory will provide a context for analyzing the relationship between spectators and the central narrative, and between the ritual performers and observers in the city on the one hand and the image on the vase on the other.

The data also show that gender is not a neutral aspect in the determination of where spectators are found and how they behave. Gender, indeed, is a critical element of social and civic identity, and so we need to consider in more detail the varieties of spectator reactions and what they convey about gendered social expectations. In chapter 5 we will utilize a coding scheme for the categories and types of gestures and actions of spectators that is applied to the database. Looking first at adult men and then at male youths, we will consider what the frequencies of different types of spectator behavior imply about their relationship to the central narrative scene and its importance. We will develop this further by looking at the behavior of men and youths to specific subject matter to see whether different and patterned reactions and attitudes are encoded into the behavior of the spectators depending on the type of action that they witness. In the final chapter, we will apply the same approach to women spectators, exploring the nature of archaic stereotypes as they are encoded in the behavior of the onlookers. We will also consider whether the stereotyped behavior of women is consistent during the period, or if it undergoes changes that perhaps reflect a changing social position for women.

In summary, spectators are guides to the construction of social identity in sixth-century Athens as that city began to play a more important role on the stage of the Greek world. Ultimately, seeing matters.

TWO

DEFINING SPECTATORS

2.1 DEFINITIONS AND CLASSIFICATION OF SPECTATORS

To begin looking at spectators, we can return to the figures on the Minneapolis amphora discussed in the previous chapter (figure 3). As noted earlier, the figures watching the warrior leave on the body of the vessel have a plausible reason for being in the picture, being members of the household that the warrior leaves. Thus, they are witnesses to an action that is taking place in their time and space. For the women and youth who observe the battle scene on the shoulder of the vase, however, it is less plausible that they are on the battlefield in their best clothing, witnessing the fight directly. This contrast between the relationship of the spectators to the narrative action in the two scenes shows that we must not only define spectators generally, but also differentiate them.

To define spectators, we can use structural analysis. As originally developed by R. Barthes, this identifies four components or functions of the narrative picture: nucleus, catalyst, index, and informant (these and subsequent terms are summarized in the glossary).[1] For example, in the picture of Herakles wrestling the lion on an amphora in Chicago, Herakles and the lion form the nucleus of the narrative – that is, those elements that constitute the kernel of an action that is open-ended (figure 4).[2] Although the viewer knows how the story will end, there are hypothetically various courses the action could take. The figures of Athena and Hermes to the right are identified by their attributes; these serve as informants, a function that serves to identify figures, places, and time in the narrative picture. These figures are not, however, essential to the main action or nucleus and could be removed from the picture without altering its basic sequence of events. This type of function is labeled a catalyst, moving the narrative forward and amplifying its context but not being essential to its core. The gods also link the action of the picture to the concerns of the gods in general; this type

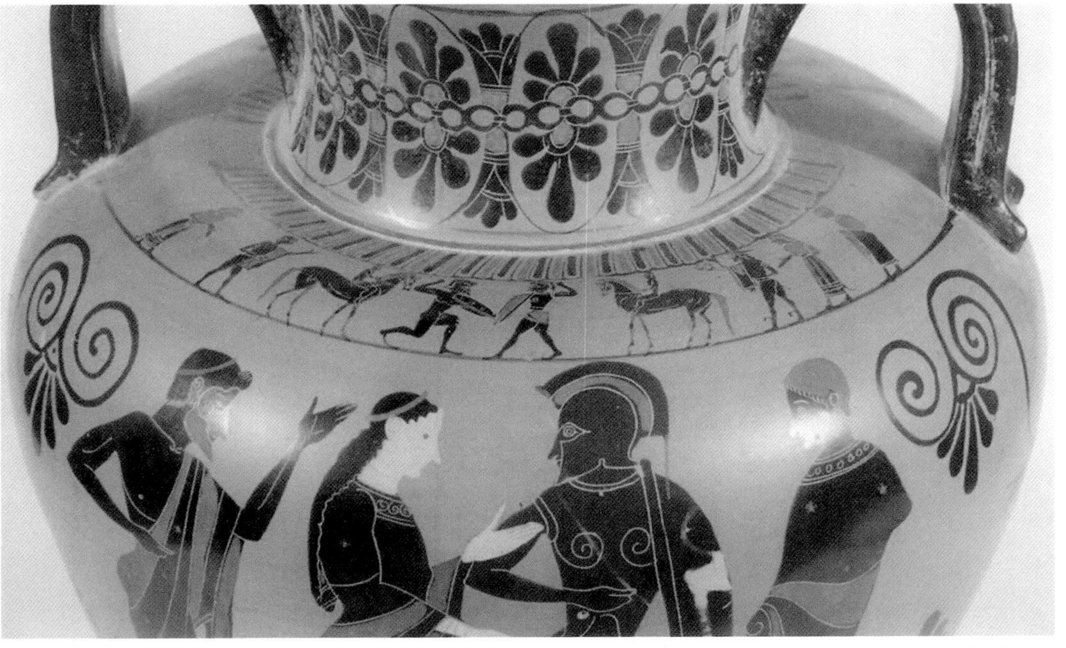

3. Attic black-figure amphora, attributed to the Painter of Vatican 359, c. 530. Side B: Detail of shoulder: warriors fighting. Minneapolis Institute of Arts, Ethel Morrison Van Derlip Fund, 57.1. (Photograph, The Minneapolis Institute of Arts)

of symbolic connection is an index – i.e., an element linking the action of the picture to other actions or ideas. The figure of Athena, for example, appears in other pictures of heroes, and this repetition in different contexts links Herakles to a larger group of heroes and their deeds through her role as an index in the picture.

The figures on the left side of the picture are more difficult to place. They have been identified as Iolaos, who frequently appears holding the club of Herakles in these scenes, and Nemea, who would serve as a place personification. However, the man does not hold a club, as would Iolaos as the attendant of Herakles, but, rather, a spear.[3] The woman has no attribute at all, so that neither of these figures displays any direct connection to Herakles. Like Athena and Hermes, they, too, are catalysts in the picture, but their role here would seem to be different from that of the gods given that they have apparently no additional function as an index.

All four peripheral figures are observers of the nucleus, but are they spectators? For general purposes, we may define a spectator as a figure who observes the action of the nucleus but is not involved in it, or will not immediately be affected by it physically. For instance, in pictures of Herakles and the lion where Iolaos holds the club or other implement of Herakles, Iolaos is involved in the action as a helper, even if his action is not essential, and therefore is not a spectator. Similarly, in pictures of Peleus pursuing Thetis, we frequently see Nereids fleeing from the scene while looking back at the

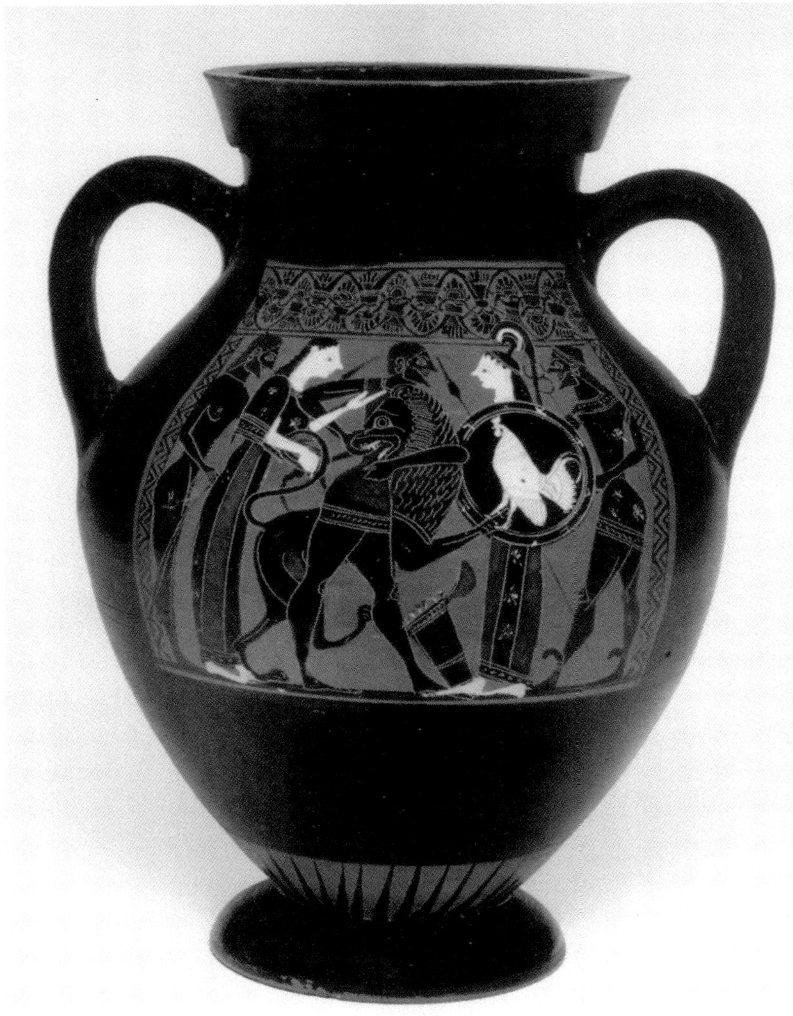

4. Attic black-figure amphora, attributed to the Painter of Tarquinia RC 3984, c. 550–525. Terracotta, black-figure technique, 28.2 cm. Katherine K. Adler Endowment, The Art Institute of Chicago, 1978.114. Side A: Herakles and the Nemean Lion. (Photography © The Art Institute of Chicago)

action. These women observe, but they also react to the action because there is the logical potential that the aggressor will pursue them if they remain at the scene. Structurally, Peleus's action of grabbing could be applied to the other female figures in the scene to make a plausible next stage of the episode.[4] The primary criterion for defining spectators, then, is that there needs to be some kind of boundary, whether temporal, spatial, or conceptual, between them and the nucleus. As a secondary criterion, we can

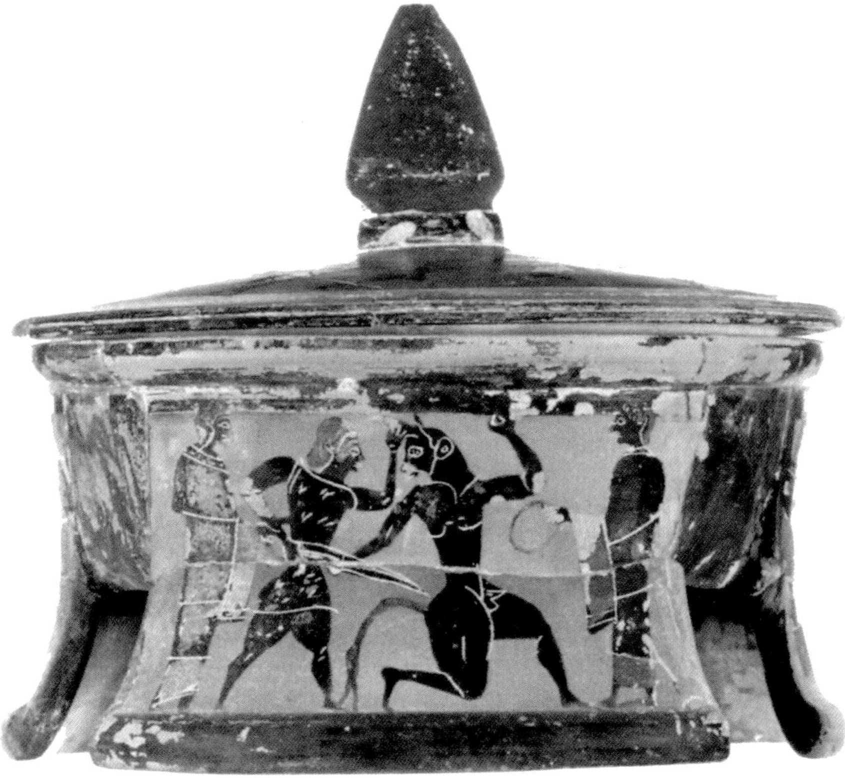

5. Attic black-figure tripod pyxis, near the Painter of Munich 1842, c. 540. Side C: Theseus and the Minotaur. Malibu, California, The J. Paul Getty Museum, 86.AE.142.1–2. (Photograph © The J. Paul Getty Museum)

look at the role the spectator plays as a catalyst and index in the picture to distinguish four different *classes* of spectators.

Using these criteria, Athena is a spectator in this picture. While she frequently appears in images of the deeds of Herakles, she is generally understood to be there as a protector and background guide, but does not physically intervene in the struggle. Indeed, if we think of the appearances of the gods in the *Iliad*, it is often in disguise and their presence is only realized after their departure.[5] Their role is to instill resolve for carrying out an action, rather than acting themselves. This lack of direct action distinguishes Athena's role from that of a helper like Iolaos, and one should consider that her presence in the picture is understood more conceptually than physically in the narrative space. Undeniably, however, Athena has a strongly vested interest in the result of the action and the fortunes of the hero. This comes out through her function as an index, linking the action here to other episodes where she similarly appears. The appearance of Hermes, too, has a strong indexical function, given that, as messenger of the gods, he often makes their will manifest to mortals. The armor of Athena and the implements of Hermes also evoke their potential power to act upon the scene as gods. As indexes, these divine figures refer to the close interest of the gods in the action of the hero and its general impact on their affairs. We can call this an *invested spectator*, in that the spectator has a stake in the result of the narrative and may become involved in future action depending on its result. The invested spectator plays a very strong role as an index and comes closest to crossing the boundary into the action because of this involvement and an implicit power to affect the outcome. Thus the figure of Hermes on the shoulder of the Minneapolis amphora (figure 3) is an invested spectator, observing the fate of the doomed warrior and later conducting his soul or *psyche* to the underworld.

We will leave aside the two other figures on the Chicago amphora for the moment to define a second class of spectators. On a pyxis in the Getty Museum, we see a scene of Theseus fighting the Minotaur as the nucleus of the picture (figure 5).[6] On either side stand two youths wearing mantles; each holds out a wreath toward the central figures. These figures are catalysts in the picture and are metonymical references to the seven boys and seven girls that were sent to be victims of the Minotaur. Their dress distinguishes them from the hero, and helps to create a boundary between the central action and themselves. They make no movement that would link them logically to the Minotaur or to the hero as part of the immediate sequence of action, but they do serve as indexes to refer to the broader Athenian context of the story. Unlike Athena and Hermes on the Chicago amphora, however, these youths manifest visually no power to influence the course of action. By presenting wreaths, they can only acknowledge the importance of the action after the fact. They do have a strong interest in the course of the action because if Theseus is unsuccessful in his struggle, they will assume roles in the next stage of the story as victims. These figures, then, have a clear indexical function in the picture, but have a lower degree of involvement and power to affect future events and change than invested spectators. We may label the figures as *interested spectators*, signifying the more modest role of the figure in the narrative structure and involvement in its result.

Another example of the interested spectator is found on a Tyrrhenian amphora in the Metropolitan Museum of Art (figure 6).[7] In the center of the shoulder are two warriors fighting with spears. An inscription identifies the figure on the right as Achilles. The presence of two women on a battlefield is unusual, as we noted for the Minneapolis amphora earlier, but in this case they additionally serve as informants to identify the scene as Achilles fighting Memnon, with their divine mothers, Thetis and Eos, watching. These goddesses do not have the direct power to influence the action. In the *Iliad*, Thetis persuades Zeus to support her son in his argument with Agamemnon, but it is clear that Zeus has the real power to sway events.[8] Unlike Athena, neither of these figures has any implement or device that conveys her power to intervene; rather, they gesture with empty and separated hands toward the scene, an action that conveys an inability to control the situation, as we shall see in chapter 6.[9] Still, their presence in the

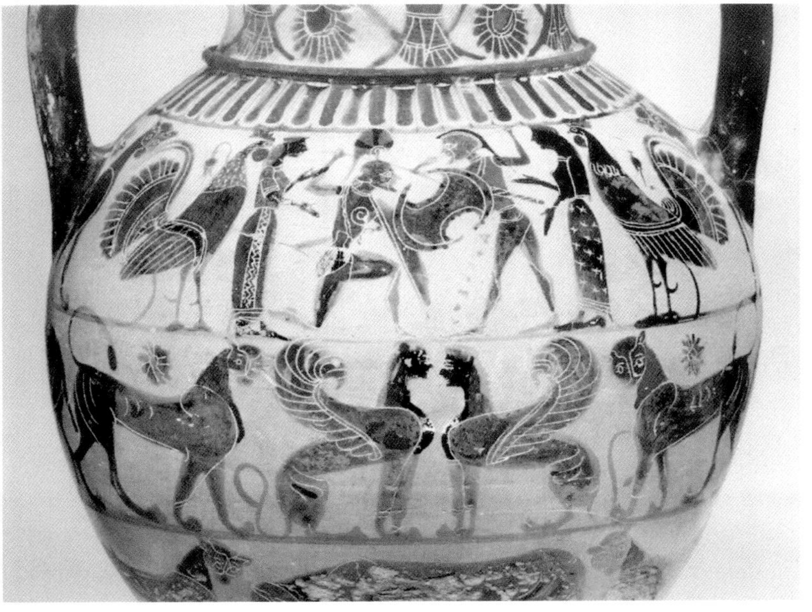

6. Attic black-figure neck amphora, attributed to the Prometheus Painter, c. 570. Side A: Achilles and Memnon. New York, The Metropolitan Museum of Art, Purchase, Christos G. Bastis Gift, 1959 (59.11.25). (Photograph, all rights reserved, The Metropolitan Museum of Art)

picture indexes the will of the gods in the fight. These figures, too, are interested spectators, signifying their role as indexes and their more indirect involvement in the action.

Looking back at the departing warrior scene on the Minneapolis amphora (figures 1 and 3), the observing figures are also interested spectators. They serve as catalysts in the picture, providing the social context of the warrior's action. Each figure indexes a different group within the household and also a different element of Athenian society, all of whom have a stake in the orderly function and defense of the city. The figures have a clear interest in the ultimate result of the warrior's actions, but this conclusion is relegated to the future and the spectators are powerless to intervene.

A different class of spectators exists who still serve as catalysts within the picture, but their connection to the participants in the action is negligible. On a black-figure amphora in the Cabinet des Médailles in Paris we see an unusual scene of a man wearing a helmet and bearing two shields jumping on the back of horse (figure 7).[10] A nude youth rides the horse, while an aulist plays behind him. The scene has been frequently discussed in the literature and has been linked loosely to the *apobatai* competition in the Panathenaic games, in which hoplites jumped on and off of chariots.[11] The performative nature of the action is made explicit by the representations of spectators in stands on the left. Here we see three men with beards and wearing cloaks watching the performer and raising both arms out toward him. On the top step is a smaller nude youth, who also holds out both arms. An inscription runs from the top toward

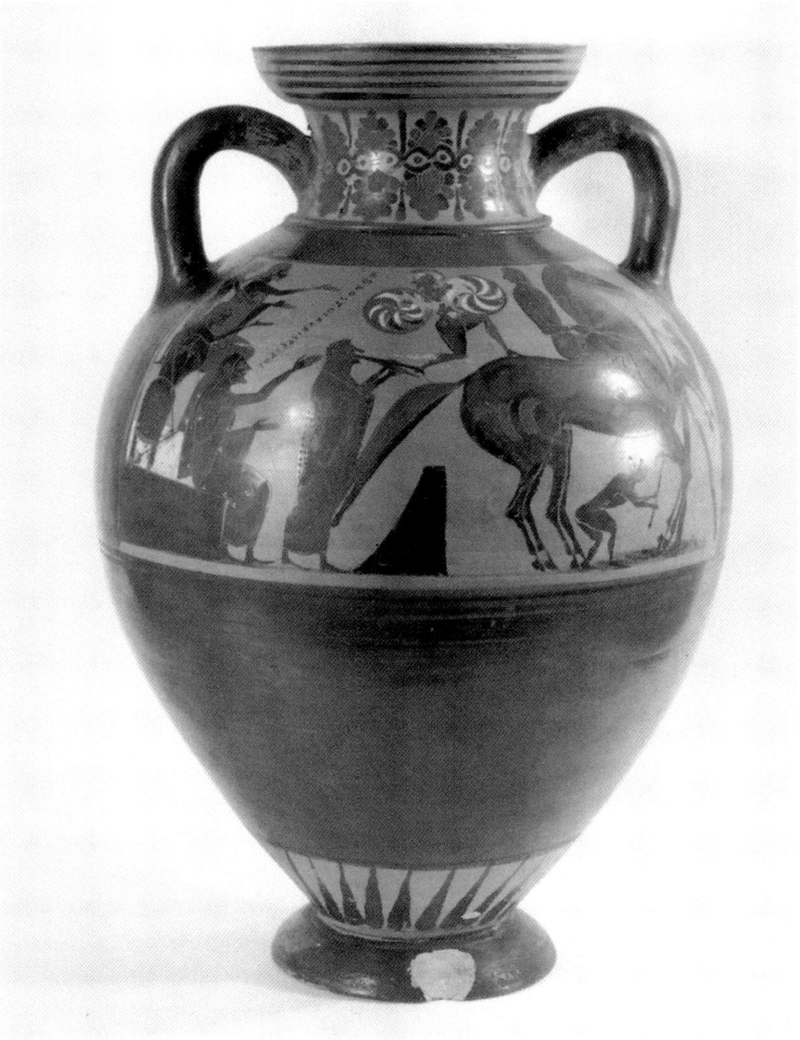

7. Attic black-figure pseudo-Panathenaic amphora. Side B: Man with armor jumping onto horse. Paris, Cabinet des Médailles 243. (Photograph courtesy Bibliothèque nationale de France. Service reproduction)

the mouth of the bottommost spectator: ΚΑΛΟΣ ΣΤΟΙ ΚΥΒΙΣΤΕΤΟΙ, or "good for the tumbler."[12] The words work like a speech balloon, signifying the spectator's approval and providing a cue for interpreting the gesture of the raised and extended right arm and hand, a gesture of acclamation and praise. These spectators, who serve as catalysts in the picture but with only a minimal role as indexes and who would seem to be present at the action, we may classify *detached spectators*, signifying their separation and lack of individual connection to the participants. Detachment does not, however, mean a lack of emotion or reaction, as the spectators in the stands indicate.

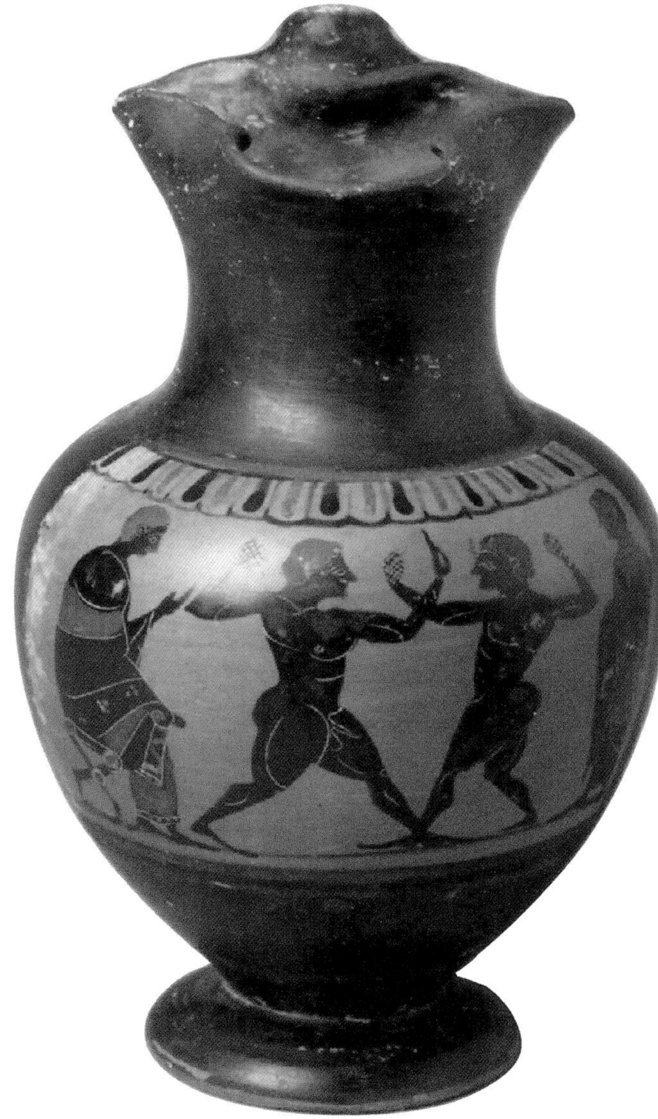

8. Attic black-figure oinochoe attributed to the Class of London B524, c. 550–40. Cleveland Museum of Art, Gift of Amadio Canessa, 16.1062. (Photograph © The Cleveland Museum of Art)

The spectators in this picture are clearly distinguished from the nucleus by their dress, position in the picture, pose, and placement in stands. Such explicit representations of a contemporary spectator event and seating are, however, very rare.[13] More typical is a scene like that on an oinochoe in the Cleveland Museum of Art (figure 8).[14] In the center of the panel are two nude youths boxing. To the left is a seated youth wrapped in a mantle who raises up his left hand with the palm facing up, the same gesture as made by the men on the stands in figure 7. On the right side of the picture is a standing, mantled youth who keeps his hands wrapped inside his garment. Although the picture space here is not as carefully articulated as it is in the Cabinet amphora, there is still a distinction of dress, pose, and action between the spectators and the boxers. This picture is not meant as a literal representation of a specific athletic competition or occasion, but generally of athletes who could perform in a public setting such as the Panathenaic games or at a less open venue such as a *palaistra* or gymnasium. The spectators here are catalysts, making the match a public event at some level and worthy of observation, but they do not have any apparent connection to the boxers, nor do they have a strong indexical role except to a broad class of members of the polis. In some pictures like this, one or both spectators may also hold forked sticks, which would place them into the role of trainers or judges, but in such cases the onlookers are participants in the action and not spectators.

We can observe a fourth and final class of spectator on a neck amphora in New York showing two warriors battling (figure 9).[15] On either side are women wearing patterned chitons and mantles; the woman on the left also has a diadem on her head. Both women raise their hands and gesture toward the central action. The composition is nearly identical, but more crowded than that of the amphora in figure 6, but here the warriors and women have no attributes or informants to identify them and the scene is one of many such duels with onlookers that we must consider more generically as battle scenes.[16] The presence of the women spectators here cannot be dismissed as decorative; there is no real picture surface needing to be filled, and they intrude into the central action itself. Still, it is not logical that women would be there on the battlefield, standing between the legs of the warriors, and we have to consider that their presence here as spectators is conceptual rather than actual. The scene that they witness takes place away from the household and the city where they would be, but its importance to them is no less for its being removed in space and time. In many ways, the picture is an extension of the warrior-departing scene we saw in figure 1, but in this case the connection of the women to the men is less specific because the domestic context is missing. However, members of a household would react to the news of a battle involving a warrior/relative, and the reaction of the women here becomes an index for the reaction of a viewer or of a contemporary Athenian to such news. We will term this class of figure as a *pure spectator*, one who is not part of the narrative as a catalyst and who does not belong in the time and/or place of the central action.

A similar situation exists with spectators in mythological scenes, such as the picture of Herakles and the lion in Chicago that we examined earlier (figure 4). Athena and Hermes are invested spectators, but the man and woman on the left side of the picture are more problematic. The man holds a spear, a common object for a spectator, as we shall see in chapter 5, but he does not hold anything that could be associated with Herakles in the center. Similarly, the woman extends one hand and appears to hold a wreath in the other. Nothing links either figure directly to Herakles and their presence would certainly complicate his action if it were literal. Because they have no specific identity, nor a role in the action, they are not catalysts in the narrative. Rather, they

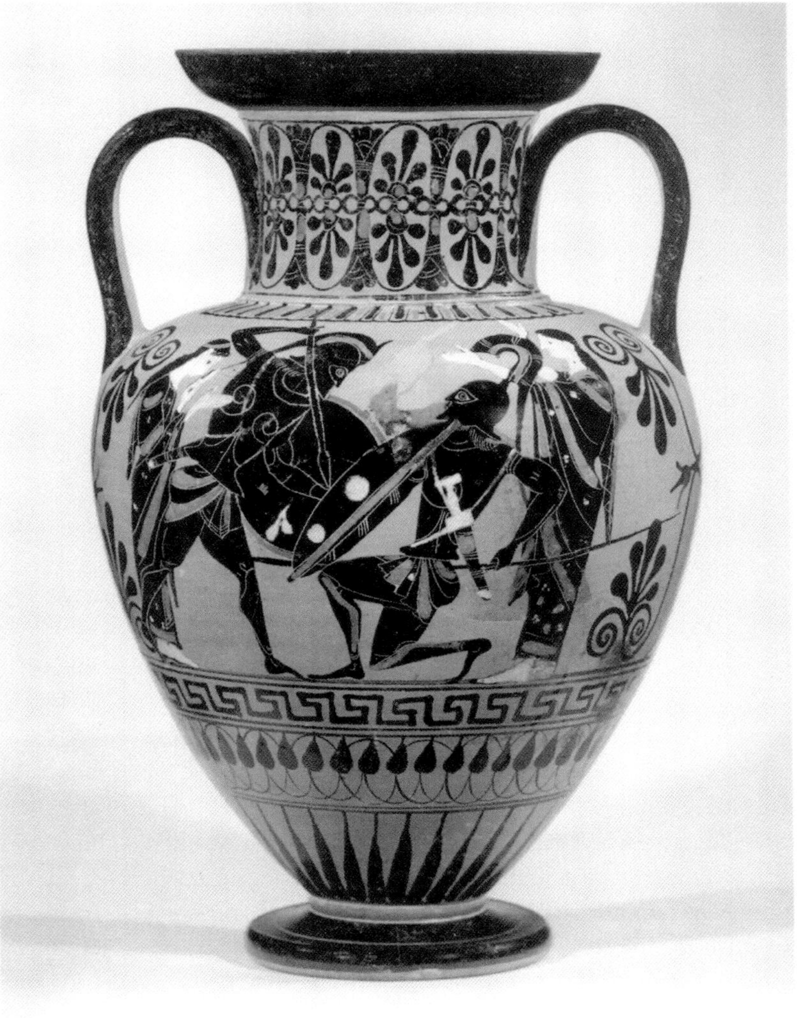

9. Attic black-figure neck amphora attributed to the Medea Group, c. 520. Side B: Warriors fighting. New York, The Metropolitan Museum of Art, Christos Bastis Gift Fund, 1961 (61.11.16). (Photograph, all rights reserved, The Metropolitan Museum of Art)

are spectators who are only conceptually present at the scene, and therefore are pure spectators. Their dress, or lack thereof, is consistent with their being in the time and space of the viewer, and so they serve as indexes for the viewer of the vase. The mythological past, like the contemporary battle, is physically removed from the time and place of the viewer, but its impact is real and immediate as part of the fabric of civic life and belief.

As Brijder noted in his analysis of onlooker types, it is sometimes hard to tell when such a figure is a spectator and when a participant.[17] Generally speaking, the first

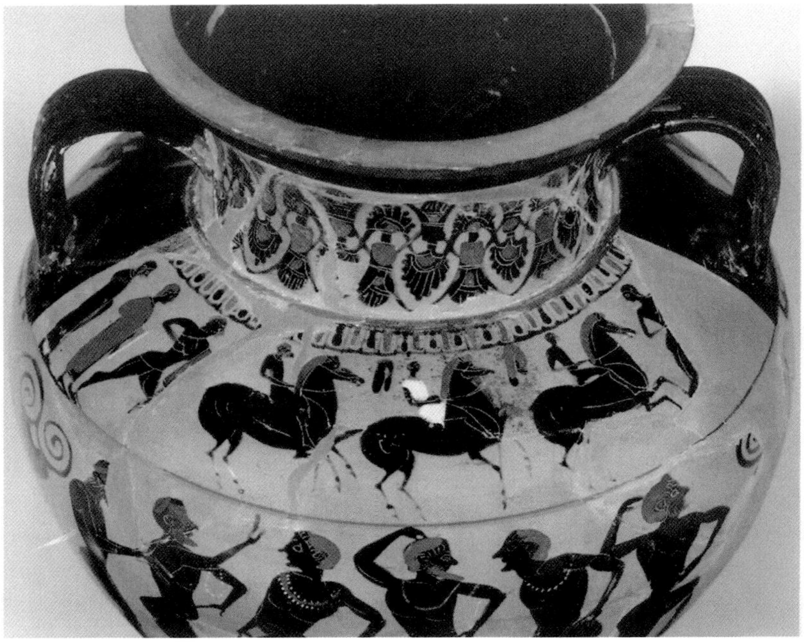

10. Attic black-figure neck amphora attributed to Group E, c. 550–540. Side B: Shoulder: Riders. New York, The Metropolitan Museum of Art, Fletcher Fund, 1956 (56.171.18). (Photograph, all rights reserved, The Metropolitan Museum of Art)

three classes of spectators belong in the general time and arena of the action that they observe, hence their status as catalysts in the narrative, but also their occasional ambiguity as secondary participants in the nucleus. For example, on the shoulder of a hydria in the Metropolitan Museum, we see three youths on horses. The middle rider wears a short white chiton, whereas the other two appear to be wearing chitons without added color (figure 10).[18] On the far left are two mantled youths watching the action quietly as detached spectators. More difficult to define are the two nude youths who appear directly in front of and behind the riders. Portions of both figures are missing, but the edge of a chlamys (cloak) can be seen hanging from the upper left arm of the back runner. Are these spectators to a race reacting in a highly animated manner, or are they participants in a parade and hence a secondary part of the nucleus?

The nudity of the runners distinguishes them from both the riders and the standing spectators, and, as we shall see, it is not unusual for the responses of spectators to be vigorous or to imitate the actions of the central figures. If the scene were a horserace, then it is not logical for the runners to be participants, but such pictures were not meant to be literal and instead evoke the spectacle of the race generally and its importance to civic life. The riders do not use crops to spur on their horses, as they do in race scenes on Panathenaic amphora in the later sixth century.[19] Of particular note is that the rider distinguished so sharply by his white costume is in the middle of the frieze and in the middle position of the riders. He would seem to be honored, but would only be in second place if this were a literal representation of a race. What we have here is more equivalent to the parade to the gate, or perhaps a post-race parade, with the riders evoking the race itself as well as the ceremonies surrounding it. This would make the near nudity of the runners more appropriate as participants in the parade, supporting the riders, perhaps as grooms, and adding an idealized, athletic dimension to the imagery.[20] The fact that they wear their chlamys over their arm recalls the similar dress and behavior of many figures in hunting scenes on vases, where it is clear that the figures are participants in the hunt, ephebes signaling their status as heroic and future adult members of the community.[21]

The same type of striding, acclaiming, nude figure can also appear in conjunction with mythological or battle scenes, where their presence is less logical, as was noted earlier on the shoulder of the Minneapolis amphora (see figure 3). Although the distinction between this figure at a horse race and at a battle may not have occurred actively to the original viewer, the distinction needs to be made for the purposes of developing definitions and a database. Therefore, we will not regard striding nudes as spectators in cases in which the scene is contemporary in time and the figure could logically be part of the action. A modern analogy might be the presentations at the end of each stage in the Tour de France, where attractive women hand flowers to the winners and direct the audience's attention. Being on a stage, they would still be a point of attention even if the winner were not there, although of less immediate interest, at least to a cycling enthusiast. In other words, if removing the central figure would still yield a plausible separation of performer and spectator, we will not count them as spectators. In cases in which the central action belongs in another realm, like a battle, then we will regard them as spectators.

To summarize, there are four classes of spectators that we can identify:

I. *invested spectators*: catalysts in the narrative, having a strong indexical role and potential to intervene in the action
II. *interested spectators*: catalysts in the narrative, having a strong indexical role, but no real potential to affect the result (but themselves able to be affected secondarily)
III. *detached spectators*: catalysts in the narrative, having a weaker indexical function; usually "contemporary" scenes
IV. *pure spectators*: not catalysts in the narrative, having a weaker indexical role; usually scenes removed in time and/or place

As we have already observed, there is a large range of actions that spectators perform. We will analyze these in more detail in chapters 5 and 6, but here we may note and define three broad sorts of spectator actions/reactions. We will call these *moods*, to distinguish them from the *classes* that we have just defined. It is important to note that any of the moods can be found within any class of spectator. Perhaps the easiest to distinguish are the quiet, standing types that we have seen in figures 3, 5, 8, and 10. The prototypical, mantled youth, Beazley's Rosencrantz and Guildenstern, belongs to this mood, as do quietly standing, spear-bearing figures. This mood we will call *inert*, signifying their lack of action.

Many spectators are more animated in their response, as we saw in figures 3, 4, 6, 7, 8, and 9. Their responses mostly consist of arm and hand movements, but might also involve the tilt of the head and movement with the legs. Their reactions can range from praise or acclamation, as we saw in figures 4, 7, and 8, to distress or agitation, as in figures 6 and 9. This sort of mood we will call *reactive*, signifying the animated response of the spectators to what they witness.

A distinct variation on the reactive sort, however, deserves a specific note. For example, on a Euboean lekythos in the Yale University Art Gallery we see Herakles fighting Kyknos in the center of the vessel (figure 11a).[22] Behind Kyknos are two youths, the nearest of whom is a mantled spear-bearer who is both a pure and inert spectator (figure 11b). The other youth is nude and holds a spear with his bent right arm; he extends his left arm straight out and holds a chlamys over it. The pose of this figure mimics elements of Herakles's action in the center, particularly by in the position of the extended left arm and the sharply bent position of the elbow that projects from the other side of the torso. Whereas Herakles's hand is raised up and the youth's is held lower, the general demeanor of this figure is one that projects a weapon, as indeed we can see in the posture of the right arm of Kyknos. This mood of action we will label separately as a *mimetic*, signifying a closer behavioral relationship between the spectator and the nucleus.[23]

To summarize, we have defined four classes of spectators based on their structural role within the image: invested, interested, detached, and pure. We have also seen briefly that spectator actions are not one-dimensional, and have noted three moods to describe their behavior: inert, reactive, and mimetic. Using these definitions, it is possible then to survey the appearance of spectators in Greek vase painting, as we shall do in the next section.

2.2 DEVELOPING DATA ON SPECTATORS

It is clear from previous looks at spectators that they occur in the work of a number of different artists over an extended period of time, and that they accompany a range of narrative scenes.[24] In the absence of testimony about their meaning, we must develop more specific information about their appearance in order to approach the question of their interpretation. In this section, we shall consider the sources for developing a database on spectators, before turning to the data and their analysis in the following section.

A census would be the most reliable means for gathering data on spectators because it would provide a large number of examples from which we could detect patterns in distribution by variable. However, the requirements of a data source for a census are difficult to meet.[25] First, the source must include vases from all periods and fabrics so that we can determine whether the appearance of spectators is widespread, or localized

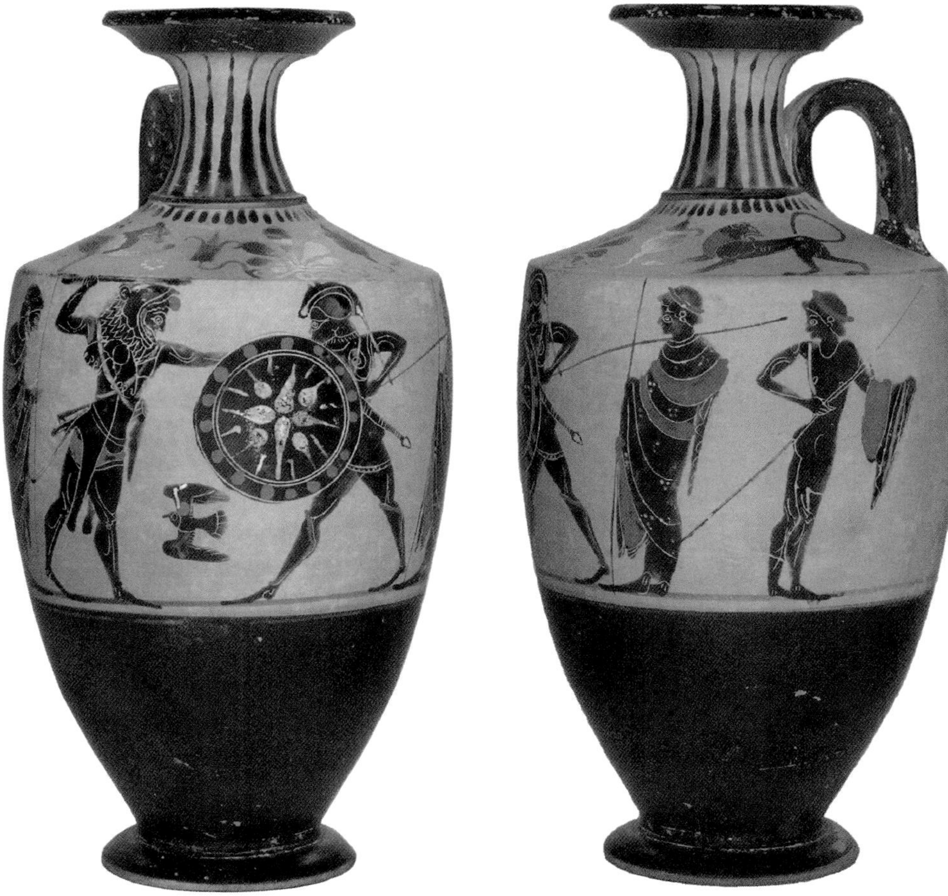

11. Euboean black-figure lekythos, mid-6th century. Herakles and Kyknos. New Haven, Stoddard Collection, Yale University Art Gallery, 1913.110. (Photograph, Yale University Art Gallery)

by time and place. Second, the source should include unattributed as well as attributed vases, and provide information, when known, about provenance. Third, the source must include illustrations of the work that show both the narrative nucleus and the spectators, so that not only the class and mood of the spectators can be determined, but also information on their arrangement, gender, and action.

Unfortunately, there is no single source for these data that does not have one or more serious limitations. The lists of Beazley have been a source for many statistical studies on vase painting, including iconographic and trade and distribution patterns.[26] However, the Beazley lists include only Attic vases, and therefore cannot answer the question as to whether spectators are a Greek or an Attic phenomenon. The lists also include only attributed works. Although substantial, the number of attributed black-figure vases is much smaller than red-figure vases, skewing the lists toward the latter fabric.[27] Although the lists do refer to published photographs of the vases, in many cases there are no sources for pictures. Beazley's use of the term onlooker is also inconsistent; many spectators are described simply as draped man, draped youth, or simply youth, man, or woman. In spite of these limitations, however, Beazley's organization of Attic vase-painting into artists and groups remains fundamental for the study and discussion of these vases, particularly for chronological sequence, and we will need to make use of his lists when discussing Attic vases.

The online Beazley Archive at Oxford remedies many of the limitations of the Beazley lists by vastly expanding the number of vases, including unattributed works.[28] As of August 2004, it contains almost 55,000 examples, including vases in the Beazley lists as well as vases published in journals, excavation reports, and volumes of the *Corpus Vasorum Antiquorum*. Many of the pages for individual vases include detailed pictures, and additions to the database have considerably expanded its size in the last few years. Being able to search by a number of different fields, such as artist, shape, provenance, and subject matter, make it a powerful resource for the study of vase painting. However, to date, the Beazley Archive only includes Attic vases. It also follows Beazley's approach to the labeling of onlookers and draped or other peripheral figures, creating difficulties in searching for examples of spectators on vases. Because only a minority of vases have illustrations at present, conducting a census would be difficult, although the searchable nature of the archive makes it valuable as a source for sampling and for reference, as we shall discuss further.

Excavation reports form another source for data. These are usually very good for including illustrations of the vases, and offer detailed information on provenance that is frequently absent in other sources.[29] However, many important sites in Greece and Italy were robbed of their vases before they were systematically excavated and reported. The distribution and publication of excavation sites are also uneven. The fragmentary quality of much of excavated pottery also means that finding vases that include both the narrative nucleus as well as the spectators is frequently difficult.

A fourth potential source is the *Corpus Vasorum Antiquorum*. Initiated by E. Pottier in 1919 as an international project to publish the thousands of vases in museum collections, the CVA meets several of the requirements for a data source.[30] They include all fabrics of vases, although the number of Attic vases is far higher than the others. They frequently include all vases within a category of specific fabric and shape, so that unattributed and lesser quality works appear along with the better-known pieces of the collection. Information on the vases is detailed and generally consistent, and includes illustrations of each vase, especially in the later volumes. Unfortunately, most of the vases lack a provenance, and because many of the major European collections were built on vases taken early from tombs in Italy, the number of vases from Greek findspots is very much underrepresented. Only eight fascicules of the CVA have been published for Greek collections, compared with 76 for German museums and 71 for Italian museums through 2003, skewing the population.

To summarize, there is no single source that is simultaneously comprehensive, representative, and adequate to the task of gathering data. The accessibility and growth of the Beazley Archive offers the greatest potential for meeting these requirements, and it is to be strongly hoped and encouraged that the resources will continue to be available for its continued refinement and expansion, especially into non-Attic pottery. The inclusion of excavation and CVA material within the Beazley Archive is important for meeting the needs for finding spectators, but it is not possible at this time to undertake a large-scale census on a subject like spectators without consistent labeling of peripheral figures. The thesaurus for the archive is excellent for mythological and other identifiable figures, but many onlookers are not described as such. For example, a search in the subject field for "onlooker(s)" yields 478 vases, but this list included only three of the nine vases discussed in this chapter.[31] Without illustrations of a significant majority of vases at this time, it is difficult to conduct a record-by-record census without leaving out significant numbers of vases because of insufficient visual evidence.

Given these limitations, it would appear that the best choice of a data source for a census would be the CVA because it includes non-Attic work as well as unattributed vases, and provides illustrations of each vase.[32] The volumes of the CVA constitute a well-defined population, allowing for replication. Conducting a census of the CVA would yield a large database that would include at least one-fourth of the vases in the Beazley Archive, making it sufficiently comprehensive to produce descriptive data on spectators. However, because of the limitations mentioned earlier, we should also include two smaller samples to supplement and test the credibility of the data.[33] First, to compensate for the lack of vases found in Greece, particularly from Athens, in the CVA, we will include a census of spectator vases published in the excavation reports from the Kerameikos, Agora, and Acropolis.[34] These data, which will be called the "Athens census," will be kept separate in its presentation from the "CVA census." Second, we will test the results of the CVA census by conducting a random sample of the Beazley Archive, as will be described in more detail in chapter 2.4. A random sample presents a more manageable means of searching for spectators outside the limits of the subject field search, and can confirm or nullify some of the hypotheses developed by the CVA census. A sample, rather than a census, realistically allows for tracking down illustrations in a way that a census would not.

Using the CVA as the primary source for data on spectators is not an ideal solution, but it does seem to be the best choice available under the current circumstances. The difficulty of using one main source, whether the Beazley lists, the CVA, or the Beazley Archive, should not, however, limit the effort to use descriptive data to find patterns in vase-painting and to interpret its themes.[35] Within their limitations, such studies provide information about the incidence of iconographic subjects on a broad scale and give us a glimpse of the visual language of images, focusing as much on viewers as on artists.[36] All such efforts, however, should eventually be tested against a more comprehensive, representative, and searchable database as it emerges in the future.

If one were to cast a broad net that included all four classes of spectators, one would easily have thousands of examples to examine. Indeed, pictures of Athena at the deeds of heroes, like figure 4, would alone furnish a lengthy list. Doing this, however, would not accomplish much except to convey the impression that someone is always watching something in Greek pictures. If we are to consider the role of spectators in the picture and their meaning, we have first to account for their identity. To explore Athena's or another god's role as an interested spectator, we must account for all that she represents as a goddess, both to the hero of the narrative as well as to the viewer. Similarly, if we look at the members of a household watching a warrior depart, these figures have an identifiable relationship to the central subject and we have to see them first within the context of their roles and identity within the house. The situation is different for detached and pure spectators because these figures have the smallest amount of involvement in the nucleus and the least amount of ability to affect or be affected by its action. They are without directly manifested familial or personal ties to the narrative subject and only the broadest relationship to the central subject. Their identity is general rather than defined, civic and communal rather than personal. Because of this, they offer an opportunity to explore vision and social identity generally.

For this reason, we shall limit the examples of spectators for the current study to the classes of *detached* and *pure* spectators only. This automatically excludes some significant types of scenes with spectators that appear frequently in Greek art, including the departure and arming of the warrior (figure 1), Athena or other gods as sole spectators to most of the actions of heroes (figure 4), Theseus and the Minotaur (figure 5), and Achilles fighting Memnon (figure 6). The behavior of the spectators in these scenes is similar to detached and pure spectators, but the general importance of spectacle and spectator can be better understood if a highly personal interest on the part of the spectator is not a factor.

To develop the database, a data sheet for each vase was created using Filemaker-Pro. This sheet included the following information: museum and accession number, object type/shape, artist, fabric, date, CVA reference as well as additional bibliography and references to the Beazley lists and Beazley Archive as appropriate, subject of the nucleus, placement on the vase, context or provenance of the vase, the number of spectators, their deployment in the composition, their mood (inert, reactive, mimetic), their gender (man, youth, woman), and finally a coding for the gender, action, and gesture (explained in more detail in chapters 5 and 6).[37] If the illustrations for a vase did not show the spectators, it was not included in the database, unless alternate pictures could be found. Fragments that did not show at least parts of both the nucleus and the spectator were also not included. Digital pictures for each entry were made and cross-referenced in the program iPhoto to the database. In many cases, an individual vase had more than one scene with spectators, either in different zones such as the shoulder and body, and/or on different sides. In such cases, each vase was considered as a single entry; each scene with spectators was recorded separately so that for some vases there were two or three different scenes with spectators. The result was a database of 742 vases containing detached and pure spectators, which we will analyze.

Because some of the vases have multiple types of spectators and more than one scene, the percentages for relative frequency often exceed 100.

2.3 CVA CENSUS: RESULTS AND ANALYSIS

In this section we will review the data about spectators from the CVA census. The value of a large database for analysis, as I. Scheibler's important study of a single shape, the belly amphora, demonstrated, is that one can spot trends or clustering of qualities that point to social context and meaning.[38] In this study, we are looking at a subject rather than a shape, but by looking at the occurrence of spectators by variables such as vase shape, date, and gender, we can find areas in which spectators are especially important or are relatively absent.

We will begin by looking at the chronological distribution of all 742 vases in the CVA census, with a comparison to the vases in the Athens census. Following this, we will look at other variables: fabric, findspot, artist, shape, gender, and mood. In some cases, we will look at the distribution of two variables, such as distribution of vase shapes by chronological period, or gender by vase shape. The result of this examination is a recognition that the appearance of spectators on vases is not a steady and diffuse phenomenon, but instead is concentrated in archaic Athens. Within this place and period, however, the appearance of spectators ebbs and flows and shifts its function.

Chronology and Fabric

One of the more difficult issues to resolve in surveying spectator vases is chronology, because there have been controversies over the past two decades regarding the dates for pre-classical Greek art.[39] Many early volumes of the CVA did not assign dates, and the entire approach to dating changed significantly with respect to attributed vases since the publication of the Beazley lists. For the CVA census, the following compromise was adopted. Dates for vases listed in the CVA were recorded in the database as given in the publication, but each vase was assigned to a quarter-century period (600–575; 575–550, etc.). Because a very large number of sixth-century vases were placed in a range straddling two periods, three additional periods, 560–540, 535–515, and 510–490, were added to cover those works and artists, creating, in the process, a succession of overlapping periods.[40] To produce internal consistency in the period assignments, a comparison of dates for vases assigned to the same artist or group in the database was made. Dates from volumes of the CVA published during the last twenty years were given special weight, and based on this process, a single period was assigned for each artist (a list of selected artists and groups and their assigned periods is found in table 5).[41] Admittedly, this is not a perfect solution, but it does preserve the relative chronological sequence and tends to focus on periods rather than absolute dates.

Table 1. *Chronological Distribution of Spectator Vases*

Period	# of CVA Vases	% of CVA Census (742)	# of Athens Excavation Vases	% of Athenian Census (103)
750–600	3	0.4	0	0
600–575	1	0.1	0	0
575–550	43	5.8	3	2.9
560–540	77	10.4	3	2.9
550–525	193	26.0	25	24.3
535–515	66	8.9	2	1.9
525–500	178	24.0	9	8.7
510–490	88	11.9	46	44.7
500–475	43	5.8	11	10.7
475–450	25	3.4	2	1.9
450–425	10	1.3	2	1.9
425–400	7	0.9	0	0
400–300	8	1.1	0	0

The number of vases with spectators for each period is shown in table 1, along with the percentage of total vases in the CVA census. Data from the Athens census are similarly listed in the last two columns and will be discussed later in conjunction with fabric.

As can be seen from these results, there are very few examples from the eighth and seventh centuries. For the Geometric period, there is a problem distinguishing spectators visually from participants. There are a few very early examples, especially outside of the CVA, such as the Dipylon warriors flanking a ship on the Middle Geometric skyphos from the Eleusis cemetery, where the shields, inaction, and scale distinguish these figures from those on the ship.[42] An Orientalizing krater from Melos with the combat between Achilles and Memnon shows Thetis and Eos watching their sons, as on the later vase in figure 6.[43] Although this is an example of the interested spectator, and therefore outside of the data gathered here, these early vases show that, conceptually, the idea of spectators watching a battle fits the logic of the picture at an early stage, before the advent of spectators as a common phenomenon. There is, however, no pattern that begins to emerge from the early examples in the CVA or elsewhere, and one has to conclude that the inclusion of spectators was an individual decision by a vase painter and not an established part of the visual language for narrative images. That many of these early examples are not Attic in fabric also shows that the earliest spectators were a widely occurring, if rare, concept, and not localized.[44]

This pattern changes sharply in the second quarter of the sixth century, when we find 43 examples of spectator vases, up from just one example in the quarter century before. From this point, the phenomenon continues to grow through the mid-century and reaches a peak during the third quarter. The numbers begin to decline slightly in the last quarter of the century, and taper even more sharply after 490. By the end

Table 2. *Fabric of Spectator Vases*

Fabric	# of CVA Vases	% of CVA Census (742)	# of Athens Excavation Vases	% of Athenian Census (103)
Attic	722	97.3	100.5	97.6
Geometric/Orientalizing	1	0.1	0	0
Black-figure	650	87.6	97.5	94.7
Red-figure	71	9.6	3	2.9
Boeotian	5	0.7	0	0
Chalkidian	1	0.1	0	0
Corinthian	4	0.5	0	0
Etruscan	1	0.1	0	0
Euboean	3	0.4	2.5	2.4
Lucanian	2	0.3	0	0
North Ionian	1	0.1	0	0
Pseudo-Chalkidian	1	0.1	0	0
Unspecified non-Attic	2	0.3	0	0

Note: One excavation vase was identified as Euboean or Attic. This has been counted as 0.5 in each category.

of the archaic period in 490/480, the number of vases with spectators is fewer than it had been almost a century earlier, and as a percentage of all vases produced at that time, even smaller. Isolated examples continue to occur during the fifth century, but the spatial, temporal, or participatory differentiation that distinguishes detached and pure spectators is not common, and most spectators fall into the invested or interested classes in the classical period.

These numbers for detached and pure spectators suggest that their popularity in vase painting belongs primarily to the middle to late archaic period. Almost three-fifths of all spectator vases are found between 550 and 500, and 87 percent date to the periods encompassing 575 to 490. Any investigation of spectators, then, should focus on this era.

The data also show that an overwhelming majority of vases were produced in Athens, as can be seen in table 2. As can be seen, only 20 vases in the CVA census, 2.7 percent of the total, were made outside of Athens. Some of these, especially the Euboean and Boeotian examples, are listed as of questionable fabric in the CVA, and even if they are non-Attic, they are heavily influenced by Attic representations, as was the Euboean lekythos discussed earlier (see figure 11). Furthermore, 87.6 percent of all vases are Attic black-figure, suggesting that the focus on the archaic period in Athens as the context for the development of spectators is justified. The conclusion is that spectators seem to be a particularly archaic Attic phenomenon.

The data from the Athens census generally follow the trends of the CVA census: 85.4 percent of the vases were produced between 575 and 490, compared with 87 percent for the CVA census, but with a later peak, during the period 510–490. As we shall see, the dominance of the lekythos shape in the Agora and Kerameikos excavations during this period is the reason for this spike, a jump in the popularity

Table 3. *Distribution of Spectator Vases by Shape*

Shape	# of CVA Vases	% of CVA Census (742)	# of Vases in Athenian Census	% of Athenian Census (103)
Amphora	198	26.7	5	4.9
Pelike	11	1.5	0	0
Hydria	72	9.7	1	1.0
Krater	25	3.4	6	5.8
Pitcher	33	4.4	5	4.9
Cup	175	23.6	10	9.7
Skyphos	21	2.8	5	4.9
Lekythos	173	23.3	64	62.1
Pyxis	11	1.5	2	1.9
Other shapes/uncertain	23	3.1	5	4.9

of the shape that is also observed in the CVA census, as we shall see later. Although one would expect that spectator vases found in Athens would be Attic, there were two vases found in the Kerameikos that were Euboean, and one that was either Euboean or Attic. In one case, the excavator speculated that the grave with the Euboean lekythos was of a Euboean rather than an Athenian citizen.[45] Overall, the incidence of Attic fabric is similar to that of the CVA census.

Vase Shape and Function: General Considerations and Chronological Distribution

An analysis of the types of vases with spectators shows that amphorae, cups, lekythoi, and hydriai are the most frequent shapes in the CVA census, as can be seen in table 3.[46] The remaining shapes each constitute less than five percent of the total, and vase shapes with fewer than 10 examples have not been listed separately. Lekythoi from the Kerameikos and Agora account for three-fifths of the vases in the Athens census, with cups a distant second in frequency, reflecting the predominance of late archaic grave contexts for spectator vases in Athens. Before examining in greater detail the chronological distribution of the four most common vase shapes in the CVA census, we can look briefly at some of the notable qualities about the other vase shapes.

Pitchers, including the oinochoe and the olpe, have the largest number of examples among these secondary shapes; their chronological distribution generally follows the overall pattern for the CVA census found in table 1, so that they do not seem to have been favored or neglected within a specific period.[47] The krater, on the other hand, is a negligible shape for spectators until after 475, when a number of red-figure kraters with symposion music scenes occur.[48] The pelike, although small in number overall, is concentrated in the half-century between 525 and 475.[49] It is a relatively late shape to develop in Attic vase painting; about half of the examples show music performances.

Table 4. *Relative Frequency of Selected Vases in the CVA Census by Chronological Period*

Shape	All Periods	575–550	560–540	550–525	535–515	525–500	510–490	500–475
All vases	742	43	77	193	66	178	88	43
Amphora	26.7%	25.6%	57.1%	38.9%	21.2%	23.6%	8.0%	9.3%
	198	11	44	75	14	42	7	4
Hydria	9.7%	0	6.5%	10.4%	16.7%	14.6%	6.8%	0
	72	0	5	20	11	26	6	0
Cup	23.6%	60.5%	18.2%	33.2%	37.9%	6.7%	1.1%	37.2%
	175	26	14	64	25	12	1	16
Lekythos	23.3%	4.7%	9.1%	3.6%	18.2%	38.2%	71.6%	27.9%
	172	2	7	7	12	68	63	12

The skyphos, like the pitcher, follows the overall pattern of distribution of the CVA census, except for an upsurge in the period around 500. These skyphoi belong to a sub-group of large skyphoi, the Heron Class, which Scheibler has studied and linked to their possible use in cult practices and rites of initiation.[50] One other shape, the pyxis, is also small in number, but its distribution occurs early on. These are primarily the tripod type of pyxis, a shape developed in Corinth and adopted briefly in Attic vase painting.[51]

A chronological breakdown by the four most frequent vase types also shows that different shapes were favored in various periods, as can be seen in table 4. In each case, the relative frequency for each shape is computed as a percentage of the total number of vases for that period. From these data, one can see that for most shapes there are periods during which they are more prevalent. Spectators appear first on amphora and especially cups; the earliest cups are primarily of the Siana type, whereas the amphora are ovoid and associated with the Tyrrhenian Group.[52] The cup and amphora continue to dominate production through the third quarter of the sixth century. The relative frequency of the lekythos begins to rise sharply after 535, and dominates between 525 and 490. Thus, we see a marked shift during the last third of the sixth century from the amphora and cup to the lekythos as the predominant shape for spectator vases. Because the cup is associated with the symposion and the lekythos with funerary practices, this pattern of chronological distribution suggests a change in the context for vases with spectators during the course of the sixth century; we will consider further this question of context subsequently, following a review of data on artists and findspots. The hydria is never the most common shape, but it does flourish between 550 and 500, maintaining its position during the transition to the lekythos. These results can be seen more graphically in chart 1.

Production and Distribution

The data on chronology and fabric pointed to archaic Athens as the locus for the production of images with spectators. In this section, we explore data on the Athenian

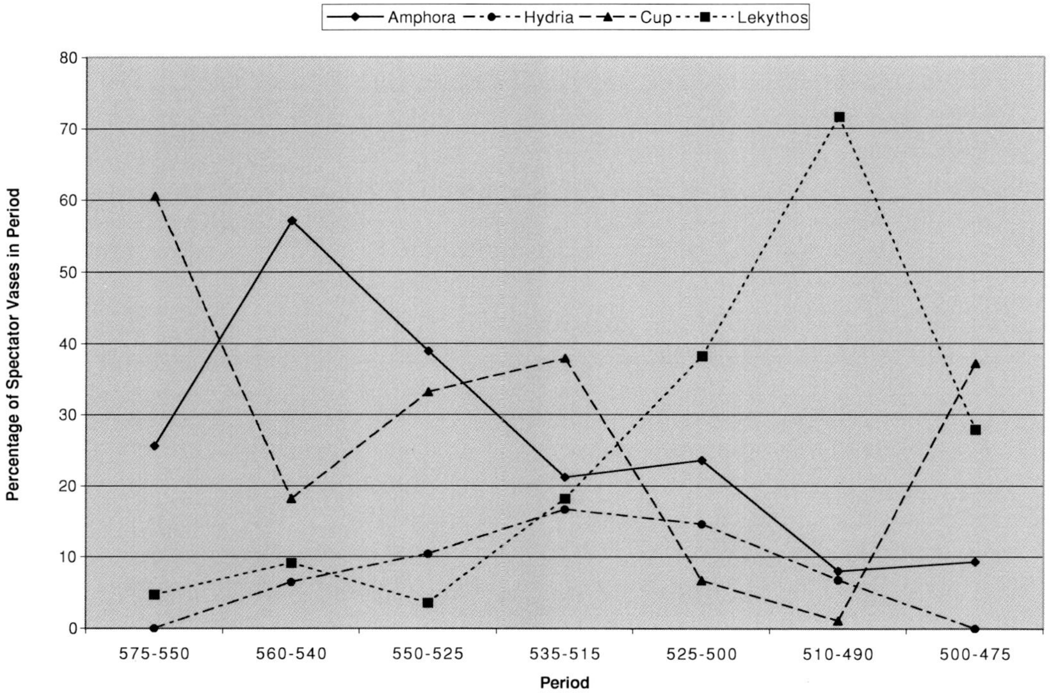

Chart 1. Relative Frequency of Selected Vase Shapes within Periods.

context in more detail, looking first at their production in terms of the artists and workshops making them, and then at the distribution of spectator vases by their findspot.

Most of the vases in the CVA census have been attributed to artists or groups. The data, shown in table 5, list those groups or artists to whom five or more vases in the CVA census have been attributed. In a number of cases, a vase is said to be "near" or "in the manner of" the artist or group; for the data here, these vases have been included in the totals under each artist. In addition, there is a large group of unattributed band cups that have been included under their shape name; there are two bodies of these, a main group in the period 550–525, and a later group falling into the years 535–515. The artists are listed according to the period to which they have been assigned for this study, and then alphabetically within that period.

As can be seen from these data, spectators appear in the work of a wide range of artists and groups, including those who specialize in a particular shape or market, such as the Tyrrhenian Group or the Nikosthenes Painter, or those whose wares are more broadly distributed, such as Lydos and the Amasis Painter.[53] For the second quarter of the sixth century, the data also show that there were two main groups of artists who first produced spectator vases in large numbers, the Tyrrhenian Group and a cluster of artists producing Siana Cups (C Painter, Heidelberg Painter, Sandal Painter, Taras Painter). We will consider these two groups in more detail in the next section.

Table 5. *Distribution of Vases in the CVA Census by Artist or Group*

Artist/Group	Number
575–550	
C Painter	6
Heidelberg Painter	7
Sandal Painter	5
Earlier Tyrrhenian Painters	6
560–540	
Amasis Painter	10
Group E	22
Lydos	15
Later Tyrrhenian Painters (not Castellani Painter)	8
Later Tyrrhenian Painters: Castellani Painter	9
550–525	
Affecter	10
Earlier Band Cups	49
BMN Painter	6
Painter of Louvre F6	8
Princeton Group	5
Princeton Painter	6
Ready Painter	6
Swing Painter	17
535–515	
Dolphin Group	9
Later Band Cups	25
Lysippides Painter	11
Nikosthenes Painter	5
525–500	
Antimenes Painter	17
Fat Runner Group	12
Hoplite Leaving Home Group	13
Phanyllis Group	14
Group of Vatican G52	21
510–490	
CHC Group	6
Class of Athens 581	18
Cock Group	27
Edinburgh Painter	5
Hound and Hare Group	7
500–475	
Haimon Painter	5

About one-half of the vases in the CVA census have some kind of provenance listed (363/742), although in many cases the provenance is limited to a country rather than to a specific region or site and is often listed as speculative.[54] Still, a review of these data shows that the spectators were featured on wares that were consumed in Attica

Table 6. *Distribution of Findspots for Vases in the CVA and Athen Censuses*

Location	Number
CVA Census	
Greece	81
Athens/Attica	19
Boeotia	19
Rhodes	17
Italy	276
Etruria	175
Vulci	95
Cerveteri	20
Tarquinia	17
Bologna	7
Falerii	6
Veii	3
Nola	6
Sicily	20
Taranto	29
Cyprus	4
Russia	2
Libya	1
Spain	1
Turkey	1
Athens Census	103
Agora	54
Kerameikos	36
Acropolis	13

Note: Not all individual findspots have been listed under Greece and Italy.

and Greece and also were exported to other sites in western Greece and especially Etruria, as can be seen in table 6.

The CVA census shows that 23.6 percent of all spectator vases come from Etruria, and another 13.6 percent from other sites in Italy, particularly Greek settlements in southern Italy and Sicily. Findspots in Greece account for 10.9 percent of the vases, with about equal numbers from Attica, Boeotia, and Rhodes. It is clear that the number of vases from Etruria is more than double that from modern Greece, and still larger than the number from all sites in greater Greece. Given that relatively few volumes of the CVA have been published for Greece compared with Italy (8 to 71) and that many European and American collections were based on vases acquired in Italy rather than Greece, the greater number coming from Italy is not surprising. Nevertheless, the data do show that spectators were not produced simply for local consumption, but were prominent on vases exported to both Greek and non-Greek sites in the Mediterranean. As can be seen at the bottom of the table, the Athens census adds another 103 vases from the city. This is still fewer than the number from Etruria in the CVA census, but it does show that there was a local market for spectator vases, too.

The data on findspot show that spectator vases were widely distributed; this raises the question as to whether they should be seen as part of an Athenian context, or as an export phenomenon. When considered with data on vase shape and attribution, it is apparent that we need to give some discussion to the idea of the context in which spectator vases appear, as we shall do in the next section.

Context

Trying to unravel the context in which spectator vases appear is complicated by the lack of provenance for many vases, and debates over the interpretation of a vase's function by its shape and findspot. For example, was a drinking cup found within a tomb intended solely as a grave good, or should it be understood primarily by its function for drinking wine, and hence within a sympotic rather than a funerary context? Was a vase found in an Etruscan tomb intended specifically for that destination, and is the selection of subject matter geared to the interests of the Etruscan purchaser, or does the vase reflect an Athenian sensibility? For context we have to consider what impact the final destination of a vase – broadly speaking, a domestic, sanctuary, or burial context – has on its interpretation, and whether we should focus on the point of origin or the destination as more important for understanding the images.

There is much scholarly debate over these issues, and the lack of archaeological context for so many Greek vases, as well as the uncertainty over the original scale of production, make the consideration of trade and production difficult.[55] The point of view adopted here is that most workshops in Athens produced for a broad market that would include wares for export, particularly in the selection of shape. In most cases, there was not a direct connection to these export markets, but rather to traders who mediated between origin and destination. In terms of subject matter, workshops do not appear to have developed themes specifically for an export market; rather, a selection of themes from a broader repertory operated, either through the workshop or through the trader. Since the distribution pattern of vases was broad in most cases, we should generally look at the point of origin, Athens, as the source for the development and deployment of a widely dispersed subject like spectators. Further, since the market was broad and the vases were likely produced without a single, distinct purchaser in mind, we need to think of vases as being multifunctional. That is, we should consider that a shape like a drinking cup could be used within a variety of contexts: symposion, votive offering, grave ritual, or grave good; it might be used for more than one purpose before it was placed in its eventual findspot. When considering the meaning of the spectator for the viewer in later chapters, then, we need to consider the potential for multiple contexts in looking at the imagery.[56]

To elaborate on this viewpoint, we can begin by looking at the question of Etruscan findspots. Is there evidence that spectator vases are specifically funerary in their intent and are intended for Etruscan tombs, where the largest number of those vases with findspots were found? In a few cases, the overwhelming number of findspots for vases by a few workshops indicates that most of their wares were destined for export to Etruria; the Tyrrhenian Group, the Nikosthenes Workshop, and the Affecter would seem to have specialized for this market, including shapes borrowed from Etruscan pottery.[57] Beyond these specific examples, however, it would seem that most workshops did not concentrate on a single market like Etruria, but may have had a more limited connection to markets in one area as part of a much broader distribution that included the local market.[58] For example, according to Tuna-Nörling's compilations, 34.57 percent of the works of the Amasis Painter have Etruscan findspots, compared with 18.52 percent for Athens, 11.11 percent for mainland Greece, 17.28 percent for eastern Greece, and 2.47 percent for western Greece. For the work of Lydos and his circle, 21.30 percent are from Etruria, 40 percent are from Athens, 14.35 percent from mainland Greece, 10.87 percent from eastern Greece, and 7.39 percent from western Greece.[59] C. Scheffer has shown that late black-figure workshops seem to have had a special interest in one or two areas of distribution, so that 69.6 percent of the Gela Painter's lekythoi are found in western Greece, but 63.3 percent of the Cock Group's production of lekythoi is found in Athens and mainland Greece.[60] Almost all workshops, however, have a good portion of their work distributed throughout the Mediterranean. Based on the distribution patterns of workshop wares and on A. W. Johnston's work on trademarks, several scholars have concluded that many workshops would have been associated with one or more specific traders who would collect wares in Athens for export.[61] This would mean that although the trade patterns are not random and some selectivity is at work, the end users were not involved in the production and early stages of distribution.

It would appear that shape was the most important element in the selection process because the distribution of shapes was not random. For Etruria, banqueting was the primary interest for the user, so sympotic vessels are highly represented among the finds from there, whereas shapes like the lekythos are much less common.[62] In contrast, the lekythos was far more popular as a ware in the Greek colonies. The Etruscans also seemed to prefer large pots, and Johnston has argued that for some shapes, like the neck amphora, most of the production must have been destined for export.[63] The supposition was once that Etruscans collected "sets" of Greek vessels, but more recent analysis suggests that they picked up just a few examples of a certain shape and had an eclectic taste in vessels. The recent work of C. Reusser has tried to consider the question of Etruscan selection of Attic vases, and whether they were for a domestic, votive, or primarily funerary purpose, based on an immense compilation of material from major and minor sites within Etruria.[64] His conclusions are that Attic vases were acquired for all three contexts, but they were initially purchased either for domestic use or for offerings in sanctuaries. They were purchased by a broad clientele, urban and rural, richer and poorer, and were used for defined occasions, including rituals and banquets, but not strictly for tombs.

Based on these analyses, it would seem that the Etruscan market was a slice from a large network of markets to which Attic workshops catered. Shape was an overriding concern for production, but there is little evidence to suggest that there was a large degree of selectivity in terms of subject matter, to the degree that some themes were exclusive to an export market or a specific destination.[65] Workshops apparently produced for a predominantly Greek sensibility. This would be especially practical given that their wares could end up in a wide range of markets, Greek and non-Greek. Most scenes would have been "readable" by a non-Athenian viewer, particularly since archaic narrative images had to leave much of the story to the imagination of the viewer in any case.[66] Producing images for a large audience, Athenian or otherwise, required that action be clear and evocative for a viewer. Although misreading an image would be possible, if a theme were too incomprehensible, it is not likely that it would have found a repeat market. Thus, we need to consider that the imagery of the vases is local in origin if it is repeated in a widely dispersed area. As J. Barringer has stated about the diffusion of hunt scenes in the sixth century, the "artists who created the vases painted them with images familiar to an Athenian audience," even if the vases are found very far from city.[67] These vases should, then, be seen as reflecting local, Attic concerns and values.

We can confirm this pattern by looking at the spectator vases produced in the second quarter of the sixth century, the first period in which they appear in large numbers. Of the 43 spectator vases from that period listed in table 1, there are two distinct groups of artists who produced them. The artists who specialized in the Siana cup, such as the C Painter, the Taras Painter, the Heidelberg Painter, and the Sandal Painter, produced 23 spectator vases, as can be seen in table 7.[68] The early Tyrrhenian Group, whose wares are predominantly associated with Etruria, produced six vases.[69] There are findspots for 11 out of the 23 Siana group vases; eight are from Greece and three from the western Greek colony at Taranto.[70] All five of the six Tyrrhenian Group vases for which we have findspots are from Italy, three specifically from Etruria and two simply listed as Italy, but likely Etruria. Overall, the distribution of spectator vases in the earliest phase of production is about evenly split between present-day Greece and Italy, but almost two-thirds ended up in greater Greece. This would indicate that spectators were not developed for one particular market, but were employed by different groups of Athenian painters and exported to a variety of geographic destinations, Greek and non-Greek.

As can be seen in table 7, the subject matter on the Siana cups is broader than that of the Tyrrhenian group, and includes a number of civic scenes that continue in popularity throughout the sixth century. Both groups feature Herakles as their predominant mythological subject, but the most popular scene for both groups is the more formulaic representation of warriors fighting. Indeed, in comparing the subject lists for the two groups, it would appear that the Tyrrhenian Group selected a narrower

Table 7. *Comparison of Context and Subjects of the Siana Group and the Tyrrhenian Group*

Siana Group		Early Tyrrhenian Group
23	**Total vases**	6
	Findspot	
8	Greece (all)	0
3	Greece: Boeotia	–
3	Greece: Rhodes	–
3	Italy (all)	5
–	Italy: Etruria	3
3	Italy: Taranto	–
	Subjects	
2	Athletes	–
3	Parades & Processions	–
2	Riders	–
2	Komos	–
2	Youth	–
1	Herakles & lion	–
1	Herakles & Nessos	2
–	Herakles & other	1
1	Other myth	–
8	Warriors fighting	3
–	Racing	1
1	Nike (winged female)	–
1	Hunt	–

range of scenes featured in Attic vase-painting for their wares, but that these scenes were all found in the Attic repertory. These factors confirm the belief that we should look at the Athenian context to study the development and meaning of spectators.

This discussion of contexts leads us back to Athens in terms of the geographic distribution of spectator vases, but we also need to consider the functional context of the vase – that is, whether it is intended for a specific environment such as the symposion, the home, the sanctuary, or the grave. For example, is a cup found in a grave to be viewed primarily as a grave good or, more functionally, as a drinking vessel? This debate, recently reviewed by K. Junker, is not such a simple dichotomy as it first appears.[71] As Junker points out, there are also funerary offerings and rituals performed at the gravesite by the living, which included drinking wine, so that nonsympotic drinking is also a context in which we can consider vases from a funerary viewpoint. Such vases would not have to be produced specifically for funerary ritual, but their selection in terms of subject matter might be influenced by that purpose, and they might be left in an offering trench or at the tomb afterward, even if they were not produced specifically as grave goods. Unlike the drinking cup, the lekythos is usually regarded as a funerary vase and, indeed, large numbers of lekythoi appear both in

Table 8. *Contexts of Vases in Athens Census*

Context	Number	% of Athenian Census (103)
Grave	42	40.8
Trench	3	2.9
Well	28	27.2
Domestic	1	1.0
Sanctuary	13	12.6
Fill	5	4.9
Other/Uncertain	11	10.7

tombs and around graves as offerings. However, as L. Hannestad has pointed out, large numbers of lekythoi were found in nonfunerary contexts in Athens; she has suggested that the vessel would also have been used within a domestic context.[72]

As a case study for the context of spectator vases, we can look in more detail at the major shape found in the excavations of the Agora and Kerameikos, the lekythos. Of the 103 spectator vases in the Athenian census, three-fifths were lekythoi (see table 3). Of these 64 lekythoi, 42 were found in graves or in offering trenches. Of the remaining 22 vases, 17 were from wells in the Agora, one from a house level, one from a pit, and three with no context recorded. Although the association of the lekythos with grave offerings is strong in these figures, it is by no means exclusive and about one-third of spectator lekythoi were found outside of that context. It is possible that these were used in the household for placement around a body during the prothesis, but they could also have been used as oil containers more generally, or both.[73] The point is that even a shape so closely associated with a single context is not uniformly found in that context. The flexibility of context for vases also extends to the next most common shapes from the Athenian census, the cup, the krater, the oinochoe, and the amphora. Of the ten spectator cups, one came from a grave in the Kerameikos whereas four came from fill areas in the Agora and five from the sanctuary of the Acropolis and therefore were presumably nonfunerary. Similarly, one out of the five oinochoai in the Athenian census came from a grave in the Kerameikos, but three came from wells in the Agora and one from a pit. Of the six kraters, none came from a grave, as is also true of the five amphora. In general, the context of spectator vases in Athens shows that fewer than half were used in graves and that the vases were found in a variety of settings (see table 8).

In conclusion, we cannot usually know for what purpose a vase was purchased, only where it found a final destination. During its life, a vase might have been used in more than one context, and so we will have to look at spectators in a multifunctional way, taking into account the function of the vase based on its shape, as well as its possible contexts. A cup could be used in a symposion as part of a small and select group of men in a domestic setting, or it could be used more communally while feasting at a sanctuary. As a votive offering, it loses its function as a drinking cup; as a

Table 9. *Relative Frequency (%) of Spectators by Gender and Period*

	All Vases	575–550	560–540	550–525	535–515	525–500	510–490	500–475
Youth	71.0	48.8	67.5	72.5	81.8	69.7	77.3	62.8
Men	30.1	69.8	37.7	37.3	7.6	21.3	19.3	30.2
Women	23.6	46.5	42.9	18.7	22.7	25.3	11.4	18.6

grave offering it continues to be symbolically useful for the deceased or ritually useful for the remembrance of the dead.[74] The lekythos would be used as a grave good, but it would also be used in the house, either as part of the prothesis or perhaps simply as an oil container that might later end up in a tomb. The amphora was primarily a storage container, but could similarly be used within the house or in a tomb. Finally, the hydria could be sympotic, but it also served more everyday household needs; it also had an important role in funerary ritual, both for washing the body and ceremonies at the tomb, in addition to being placed at the entrance of the house during the prothesis for purification and as a sign to visitors.[75] The fact that spectators are found among a range of vase shapes and contexts suggests that they had a broad social appeal in Athens and need to be considered in that light.

Gender and Spectators

We can also examine the CVA census by looking at the selection of spectators by gender and age. Most broadly, spectators can be classified into three gender groups: young men without a beard, hereafter described as *youths*; adult men with a beard, hereafter *men*, with the term *male* reserved for both youths and adults; and *women*.[76] As we shall see in chapters 5 and 6, we can further place spectators into categories based on their level of activity, and then individual types based on their gestures. As we can see in table 9, youths are found on 527 of the 742 vessels in the CVA census, for 71 percent of the total. Men and women occur less than half as frequently, on 30.1 percent and 23.6 percent of all vessels respectively (because many vases have more than one of each gender of spectator, the percentages will total more than 100). Although the numbers for gender on all vases establishes an aggregate "base," it is clear that there is considerable variation from these figures within each chronological period. Women spectators, for example, appear at a higher level during the first two periods of spectator vases, 575–550 and 560–540, but then drop noticeably during the second half of the century. At the turn of the sixth century, their appearance diminishes even further. Like women spectators, men also appear in very high numbers during the second quarter of the sixth century, leveling off in the middle of the century and then dropping significantly during the last third. Conversely, youth appear in smaller proportions during the first period, but become the predominant spectator thereafter. Thus, it would appear that men and women had more appeal as spectators during the

Table 10. *Distribution of Spectator Gender by Vase Shape*

shape	# Vases	# Vases with Youths	# Vases with Men	# Vases with Women	% Shape with Youths	% Shape with Men	% Shape with Women
All vases	**742**	**527**	**223**	**175**	**71.0**	**30.1**	**23.6**
Amphora	198	99	85	86	50.0	42.9	43.4
Pelike	11	2	6	3	18.2	54.5	27.3
Hydria	72	43	26	33	59.7	36.1	45.8
Krater	25	21	9	5	84.0	36.0	20.0
Pitcher	33	22	10	6	66.7	30.3	18.2
Cup	175	149	42	18	85.1	24.0	10.3
Skyphos	21	18	5	5	85.7	23.8	23.8
Lekythos	173	150	30	9	86.7	17.3	5.2
Pyxis	11	7	4	4	63.6	36.4	36.4

earliest periods of their appearance on vases, but diminished during the later phases. It also would appear from the amount by which the sum of the percentages exceeds 100, that there was less mixture of genders among spectators in the later vases than in the two earlier periods.

This picture of a shift between the earliest phases of spectator vases and the later periods conforms to the change in vase shape that we saw earlier, in chart 1 and table 4. In looking at the appearance of youth, men, and women by vase type, we can see that youths appear with a far greater frequency on lekythoi (86.7 percent of lekythoi, compared to 71.0 percent of all vases in the CVA census), whereas men appear at reduced levels and women at very low levels, as can be seen in table 10. This preponderance of youths as spectators on lekythoi is somewhat surprising, given that one would associate the use of a lekythos with women attending to the grave, and their frequent representation in such duties in later white-ground lekythoi.[77] As we shall discuss further in chapter 4, the lekythos serves like an elegy, with the deceased represented by the exploits of the hero, athlete, or rider and his commemoration by the spectators representing the members of the polis. The heroization becomes a model for the young spectator, who, by noting and emulating the accomplishment of the deceased can, in turn, take his place within the community, and be remembered for it. The clear concentration on male and especially youthful spectators on lekythoi suggests that spectators may be taking on more of a commemorative role in the last part of the sixth century and first decade of the fifth.

In contrast to lekythoi, in which youths appear on six out of every seven examples, youths are found on only half of all amphorae. Men and women, however, appear at much higher frequencies than in the CVA census generally. Men are found on 42.9 percent of amphorae, about 13 points higher than their overall frequency, whereas women even exceed men as spectators, being found on 43.4 percent of all amphora, 20 points higher than for the CVA census as a whole. We can also see that the frequency of women spectators on hydria is similarly high, 45.8 percent, and far exceeds the frequency for men as spectators, at 36.1 percent. This sharply contrasts with the small number of women on lekythoi (about 1 out of 20), and suggests that the depiction of women spectators is most closely tied to these two shapes. As we have seen, both vessels are multifunctional. The amphora can have a sympotic use, but it can also be used for a variety of storage purposes in the house or as part of grave goods, where it might be used as a cinerary urn. The hydria can also serve a domestic, sympotic, or funerary purpose. The implication of this is that women would have been potential viewers and users of the vases, and we see them represented more frequently on these shapes.

A very different pattern is found on cups, where women appear as spectators on only one-tenth of all cups in the CVA census. The cup is a shape that would be associated more with a male user, whether in a sympotic, ritualistic, or funerary setting. Men are found on approximately one-fourth of all cups, but youths appear on 85.1 percent of these vessels, only a little less than their frequency on lekythoi. Within the context of the male symposion, the high frequency for youthful spectators on cups would indicate that the youths at these symposia were an important model and/or reflection of the spectators on the cups. This suggests that spectators had a role in the symposion and its function in forging social links and identity. As we shall see in the next chapter, the relationship between the viewer of the cup and other members of the symposion models that relationship of the spectators in the vase and the narrative nucleus. As an object that was held close to the face, not unlike a mirror, the imagery on the cup has a potentially more reflective quality of the gaze and its role in the construction of individual and social identity.

It would appear from the pattern of gender distribution on vase shapes that there is a definite focus upon gender as a primary target audience for the spectators; when we consider the importance of public rituals that mark the transformation of youths into adult male citizens of the community, it is not surprising that we would see this reflected in the gender distribution of spectators.[78] Still, the numbers of men and women as spectators show that they, too, are important, if less common, and that gender is an issue to be considered in the study of spectators.

Gender and Mood

As we noted in section 2.1, one can classify spectators not only according to their structural role within the picture, but also in terms of their reactions to the scene. Spectators can be *inert*, reacting minimally or not at all to the scene; *reactive*, responding through gestures and body position to the action; and *mimetic*, a special type of reaction in which the figure mimics the behavior of the central figures. We will study in more detail the variety of reactions of spectators in chapters 5 and 6, but for now we should also look at the general patterns of gender and mood in spectators. The results are listed in table 11; because many vases have more than one mood and gender of spectator, the results for each gender exceed 100 percent, especially for youths:[79]

Table 11. *Relative Frequency (%) of Behavioral Moods of Spectators on Vases by Gender*

	Inert	Reactive	Mimetic
Men	56.1 (125/223)	41.7 (93/223)	6.7 (15/223)
Youth	78.0 (411/527)	30.0 (157/527)	10.4 (55/527)
Women	27.4 (48/175)	78.9 (138/175)	1.1 (2/175)

This distribution shows a striking behavioral contrast between men, and particularly youths, on the one hand, and women on the other. Almost four-fifths of the vases with youthful spectators feature the quiet, standing figure of the youth, with or without a spear or staff, like the figure on the far right of figure 3. Only 30 percent of the vases have youths with reactive behavior, such as the youth on the left side of the same vase. It is clear that the expected behavior of youths as spectators is poised, calm, and focused. For men, the discrepancy between inert and reactive moods is much smaller. Slightly more than half of all vases with male spectators are inert in mood, and about two-fifths of the vases have reactive men. This would suggest that men are more expected to react to scenes than youths, although the poised, inert spectator is still the more popular type.

For women, this type of inert spectator is found on just over one-fourth of the vases (27.4 percent), a frequency that is almost one-third that of youths and less than half that of men. In contrast, nearly four-fifths (78.9 percent) of all vases with women spectators show reactive types, almost exactly the reverse of the pattern for youths. The expectation that women spectators will respond actively to the situation in the narrative is, then, in sharp reversal from the expectations for youths.

There is also a disparity among the three gender groups in mimetic behavior. For youths, 10.4 percent of vases show this behavior, whereas the number for men is somewhat smaller at 6.7 percent. The frequency for women is smaller still, with only two vases displaying mimetic behavior.[80] In both cases of mimetic women spectators, the mimicry is not of a figure in the nucleus of the picture, but of one of the catalysts. The numbers of mimetic spectators are small compared with the other two categories, but the fact that mimetic youths occur at almost ten times the frequency of women shows that emulation as a behavior was more prevalent for youths than for women.

This distribution suggests differing expectations of behavior among youths, men, and women that reflect the gender stereotypes of archaic Athenian culture. There are subtleties about the behavior of all three groups that can be discerned by looking at the specific forms of response in each behavioral mood, and we will return to that discussion in chapters 5 and 6. For now, however, it should be noted that spectators reflect a gendered division of the social world of Athens. They provide an opportunity to supplement the documentary sources for the archaic period and to see how the expectations for social behavior can be coded in these representations.

Table 12. *Scenes with Spectators*

Mythological Scenes	**226**	
Herakles	154	Lion (75), Nessos (35), Triton (12)
Theseus	8	
Amazonomachy	17	
Gigantomachy	11	
Trojan War	20	
Dionysiac	4	
Other Myth	12	Peleus & Atalanta, single Amazon, Oedipus
Divine Figures/Creatures	**45**	
Nike	18	
Siren	9	
Sphinx	14	
Other	4	
Warrior/Heroic Scenes	**212**	
Warriors fighting	168	
Non-fighting action	31	Running, jumping, somersault, carrying body, marching, with horse
Related Scenes	12	Hunt, chariot, pursuit
Athletic Scenes	**127**	
General/various	33	
Boxers	18	
Wrestlers	14	
Runner(s)	59	
Race (horse)	3	
Ritualistic/Processional Scenes	**129**	
Rider	76	Frequently with nude youths as procession
Music	36	Public and sympotic
Dancers	10	Various types
Other	7	Procession, wedding, assembly
Other Scenes	**64**	
Animals	15	Lions, cocks, horse, swan
Craft	4	Pottery, agriculture
Erotic	12	
Women	3	
Youth	30	Single figure (usually nude), in line, various actions

Subject Matter

We will have a more detailed discussion of some of the major scenes found with spectators in chapters 5 and 6, where we will consider how men, youths, and women react differently or similarly to the same narrative nucleus. The overall subject matter is very wide ranging, but can be broken down in table 12. Because some vases feature multiple scenes with spectators, the total number exceeds the 742 vases of the CVA census.

There is a roughly even distribution of scenes among myth, heroic genre scenes, and scenes drawn from the contemporary city. Herakles is by far the most popular

Table 13. *Spectator Vases in the Beazley Archive Sample*

	Total # in Beazley Archive Sample	# of Spectator Vases	% of Spectator Vases in Sample
Black-figure	163	18	11.0
Red-figure	175	3	1.7
White-ground	16	0	0.0
Total	354	21	5.9

hero, although it should be remembered that we have excluded scenes of Theseus and the Minotaur from this because of the *invested* classification of the spectator in those scenes. There are a number of different mythological combat scenes, but these are dwarfed in comparison to the number of scenes in which two anonymous warriors fight each other with spectators watching, by far the largest single subject on vases with onlookers. Warriors are the subject of a few other noncombat scenes like running, marching, and dancing/athletic performances, but these, in turn, are surpassed by more generic figures of athletes and nude youths performing the same actions. Youthful runners are especially common for athletic scenes, followed by boxing and wrestling. There are also a number of processional scenes featuring a rider, very often flanked by two nude youths walking in line with him and serving as catalysts in the picture. Music is a common civic scene, with public performances earlier and sympotic performances on later vessels. Finally, there are a series of miscellaneous scenes, including erotic encounters and animals, in addition to single figures of youths and women.

What this variety demonstrates is that the use of spectators was not limited by the subject matter of the narrative nucleus and, indeed, that spectators were thought to be appropriate as witnesses to all manner of events, past and present, that were of importance to the city. This being said, the reactions of spectators to different types of scenes is not uniform, either by scene or by gender, which is the subject of the last two chapters.

2.4 BEAZLEY ARCHIVE SAMPLE

Before summarizing the data discussed in section 2.3, we shall compare some of the data found in the CVA census with the results of a random sample from the Beazley Archive. Each vase in the Archive has a unique "vase number," although the numbers are not assigned sequentially from a single starting point. Therefore, 2,000 randomly generated numbers between 1 and 400,000 were entered into the "vase number" field on the search page of the Beazley Archive between August 2 and 24, 2004.[81] Because the Beazley Archive had a total of 54,834 black- and red-figure vases during August 2004, about five-sixths of the random numbers returned no record. The result was a sample of 354 vases, as seen in table 13. When the description of the vase included both

Table 14. *Fabric of Spectator Vases in the Beazley Archive Sample*

	# in Beazley Archive Sample	% in Beazley Archive Sample	% in CVA Census
Black-figure	18	85.7	90.2
Red-figure	3	14.3	9.8

an action and peripheral figures such as "onlookers," "draped man," "draped youth," "man," "youth," "woman," etc., the vase was investigated to determine whether or not the figures met the definitions for detached or pure spectators, as outlined in section 2.2, either using photos made available on the web record for the vase or in one of the entries in the publication record. In the event that a suitable image could not be found, the vase was not included among the sub-group of spectator vases, but was maintained in the sample as a non-spectator vase.

In order to consider the reliability of the figures from the CVA census, three sets of hypotheses were formulated for testing using the Beazley Archive sample.[82] Because the proportion of spectator vases within the sample population was relatively small (5.9 percent), the hypotheses were formulated to test variables for which only two or three values were possible (for example, spectator vases could be either black-figure or red-figure). Variables for which more values were possible, such as chronological period, subject matter, and artist, would require a far larger sample than was undertaken here. In general, the goal was to see whether or not the frequency found in the Beazley Archive sample was within ten percentage points of the frequency for the same variable in the CVA census. If so, this would corroborate the relative proportions of some of the data discussed in chapter 2.3 as reasonable.

Spectator Vases as Predominantly Attic Black-Figure

As was seen previously in table 2, there were 650 Attic black-figure vases in the CVA census and 71 red-figure vases. Thus, black-figure accounts for 90.2 percent of Attic spectator vases in the CVA census. For hypothesis 1, therefore, we want to determine whether this predominance of black-figure over red-figure vases is also true for spectator vases in the Beazley Archive sample:

> Hypothesis 1: Because 90.2 percent of all Attic vases in the CVA census are black-figure, *at least 80 percent of all vases with spectators in the Beazley Archive sample are black-figure.*

As can be seen in table 14, sixth-sevenths of the spectator vases in the Beazley Archive sample are black-figure; this frequency of 85.7 percent is only slightly less than the frequency of 90.2 percent of the CVA census, and indicates that the association of spectators with black-figure vases is warranted.

Table 15. *Shape of Spectator Vases in the Beazley Archive Sample*

	# in Beazley Archive Sample	% in Beazley Archive Sample	% in CVA Census
Amphora	7	33.3	26.7
Cup	6	28.6	26.7
Lekythos	3	14.3	23.3
Sub-total	16	76.2	73.5
Hydria	1	4.8	9.7
Other	4	19.0	16.8

Vase Shape in the Beazley Archive Sample

In table 10 we saw that there were three predominant shapes for spectator vases: amphorae, cups, and lekythoi.[83] Together, they account for nearly three-fourths of all spectator vases in the CVA census, leading to the second hypothesis:

> Hypothesis 2: Because 73.6 percent of all vases in the CVA census were either an amphora, cup, or lekythos, *at least 64 percent of all vases in the Beazley Archive sample will be either an amphora, cup, or lekythos.*

In table 15, we see that 16 of the 21 spectator vases belong to one of these three shapes, slightly exceeding the frequency for these shapes in the CVA census. The frequency for the amphora and cup were slightly higher than those for the CVA census, whereas the lekythos was somewhat lower, but still within a range of ten percentage points. The variations for the individual shapes remind us that the CVA census may over- or underrepresent certain shapes, but that the larger patterns hold up in the sampling of the Beazley Archive.

Gender of Spectators

The gender of spectators has three possible values as it was set out for the CVA census: man, youth, or woman. Because more than one gender of spectator can occur on a single vase, three hypotheses were formulated for testing:

> Hypothesis 3a: Because 71 percent of all vases in the CVA census have a youth as spectator, *at least 61 percent of all vases with spectators in the Beazley Archive sample will have a youth as spectator.*
> Hypothesis 3b: Because 30.1 percent of all vases in the CVA census have a man as spectator, *at least 20 percent of all vases with spectators in the Beazley Archive sample will have a man as spectator.*
> Hypothesis 3c: Because 23.6 percent of all vases in the CVA census have a woman as spectator, *at least 14 percent of all vases with spectators in the Beazley Archive sample will have a woman as spectator.*

Table 16. *Gender of Spectators on Spectator Vases in the Beazley Archive Sample*

	# in Beazley Archive Sample	% in Beazley Archive Sample	% in CVA Census
Youth	12	57.1	71.0
Men	9	42.9	30.1
Women	5	23.8	23.6

As summarized in table 16, the number of men as spectators in the sample was more than ten percentage points higher than the CVA census, whereas the hypothesis for youth fell four percentage points short of being probable, and therefore should be rejected. This lower frequency for youth in the sample is not surprising, however, given the lower frequency of occurrence for lekythoi in the sample compared with the CVA census. Indeed, given the strong link between the lekythos and the youth as spectator, one would expect that a decrease in the number of lekythos examples would lower the frequency of youths as spectators. The gender frequencies for the Beazley Archive sample do confirm that males collectively are far more common than women as spectators, and that the largest single group of spectators is, in fact, youth, with men as the second largest group, and women as the smallest.

Overall, the data from the Beazley Archive sample corroborate the general pattern of fabric and vase type, and although it warns us that the frequency of youth as spectators in the CVA census may be exaggerated somewhat, it suggests that the order of popularity of youth, men, and women as spectators is valid. Indeed, the results of the sample confirm that even if a census as large as the CVA may not provide a completely representative sample of all surviving Greek vases, its size does provide some reliability as a source for studying a subject like spectators.

2.5 DISCUSSION

We began this chapter by using structural analysis to define four classes of spectators (invested, interested, detached, and pure) and three moods of action (inert, reactive, and mimetic). Using these definitions, we were able to establish the parameters for a database, choosing a census of the CVA as the primary source, supplemented by a census of three Athenian excavations and a sampling of the Beazley Archive. Until such time as a comprehensive and readily accessible database exists, there is no perfect source for defining data, but this multifaceted approach did show some consistent patterns that can help us direct an investigation of spectators.

From the CVA census, it was very clear that spectators were not a general feature of Greek art, but were mostly limited to Attic black-figure vase painting between 575 and 490. The predominance of black-figure over red-figure was confirmed by both the Athenian excavation census and the Beazley Archive sample, and the latter suggested that spectator vases might account for one-tenth of black-figure production, a considerable proportion for a single subject. Therefore, any interpretation of their meaning must consider this context.[84]

The wide geographic dispersal of the vases according to their findspot means that the production of spectator vases was not intended for a narrowly defined market. To understand their significance and meaning, therefore, we need to look at their point of origin in Athens. An examination of the contexts for vases in the Athenian excavation census showed that spectator vases were not limited to tombs, and that even a shape like the lekythos, with strong funereal associations, was often found in non-grave contexts. An examination of the vases produced during the first major period of production during the second quarter of the sixth century showed that two distinctly different groups produced spectator vases of different shapes and headed for different markets, but that their subject matter drew from the same pool of scenes: mythological, heroic, and civic. Combined with recent studies of the production and acquisition of vases in Etruria and the Mediterranean, these data indicate that we should approach spectator vases as multifunctional objects that were suitable to an array of different contexts: sympotic, votive, domestic, funereal, and grave offerings.

When looking at the details of the images on the vases, we saw that gender is an issue that needs to be considered in more detail. The CVA census showed a clear hierarchical order of popularity for spectators by gender and age: youth, men, and finally women. The Beazley Archive sample did not confirm the specific proportions of spectators by gender in the CVA census, but it did confirm the hierarchical ranking. The CVA census also showed that some shapes were particularly associated with a specific gender, such as lekythoi and cups with youth, and amphora and hydria with women and men. The lekythos was one of the most popular shapes for spectator vases, but only during the last half of the main period of production. Its rise as the favored shape may, then, coincide with an increased popularity for burial customs and goods as a venue for spectator vases.

Not only was there a definite pattern in the selection of gender for spectators, there was also a dichotomy in their behavior. The predominant mood for youthful spectators was inert, at a ratio of about 2:1 compared with vases with reactive spectators. For women, the ratio was reversed to 1:3. The majority of vases with men as spectators has inert types, but the ratio was much closer to equal, about 4:3. This pattern suggests that the representation of males and females as spectators encoded views about their behavior and character. Gender indeed is a critical element of social and civic identity, and so we will need to consider in more detail the varieties of spectator reactions and what they convey about social expectations and gender stereotypes in sixth-century Athens.

The data on spectators show that they are a complicated phenomenon, but one that provides an opportunity to explore how representations help construct a social and civic identity for the viewer. Before turning to spectators as a case study for social and gender identification in Athens, we need to consider the importance of viewing and how the images of spectators can help model the experience of the viewer.

THREE

VISION AND THE CONSTRUCTION OF IDENTITY

If we take another look at the spectators on the Minneapolis amphora (figure 12), we can consider the visual dynamics surrounding the narrative by incorporating the viewers of the vase with the spectators in the picture.[1] As we saw in chapter 2, the narrative nucleus consists of the two warriors fighting. The squires with horses serve as catalysts and interested spectators to the duel. Five more spectators watch from the side, separated conceptually from the narrative scene, including Hermes, whom we would identify as an invested spectator. The two pairs of youth and woman on either end of the picture are pure spectators of the fight. All face the action at the center of the frieze, and their reactions indicate its importance. Stepping back a bit from the vase, we find the viewer, who is also a pure spectator of this narrative nucleus, removed from it in time and space and having no impact on its result. Additionally, we can readily imagine additional viewers in a setting who could see the picture, although perhaps not as well as the person holding the vase given its scale and placement on the shoulder. Thus we have two sets of spectators, one inside and one outside the picture. The latter set of viewers sees not only the action, but also the spectators within the picture. There emerges, then, not only the sensation of seeing something, but also the state of being seen. The only figures who do not see beyond their immediate group are the two warriors in the center, who presumably have eyes only for one another and not the various observers.

This web of vision, of seeing and being seen, provides an opportunity to consider how narrative images with spectators play a role in shaping the identity and self-conception of the viewer. We will focus on more specific aspects of social and gender identity in Athens in the following chapters, but here we should consider the broader dimensions of the viewing experience. How does looking at an object or image affect the viewer? What is the relationship between what one sees and what one does, between images and self-image?

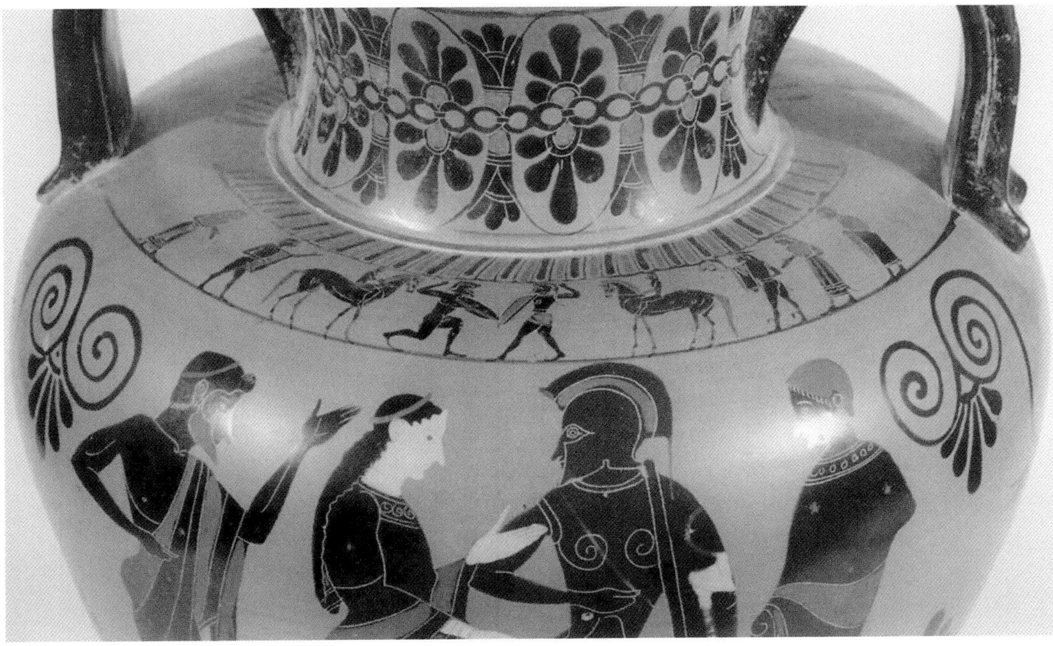

12. Attic black-figure amphora, attributed to the Painter of Vatican 359, c. 530. Side B: Detail of shoulder: warriors fighting. Minneapolis Institute of Arts, Ethel Morrison Van Derlip Fund, 57.1. (Photograph, The Minneapolis Institute of Arts)

One way of approaching this issue of the viewing experience is to look at some aspects of psychoanalytic theory that can shed light upon the web of seeing and being seen constructed by these spectators. In particular, if we look at psychoanalysis as a method that examines the construction of personal and social identity, then we can look at these spectators as examples for a model of the construction of identity in ancient Greece. Jacques Lacan's theories on vision and imagery, especially on such topics as the mirror stage and the gaze, have been particularly appealing to art historians in this regard, in that they provide a framework for discussing the picture and its relationship to the subject or viewer.[2]

Lacan's theory and writing are, however, difficult to access and he does not lay them out in a comprehensive, definitive way. Furthermore, he also regards verbal language rather than the visual field as the means by which identity and self are formed and in which the subject and object, the self and the other, are defined. One can argue, justifiably, that psychoanalysis itself is historically rooted and is not a universal theory that can be applied to a past culture.[3] To ground these ideas for the analysis of Greek art, we will also look at aspects of Greek theories of vision. These posited a more physical and direct connection between the viewer and the viewed than modern optical theory, and made sight an important element of the social fabric. With this combined perspective of psychoanalytic theory and Greek theories of vision, we will then construct a model for the viewing experience that considers who and what is seen by whom, and, through this process, explore in general terms the construction of identity through visual images.

3.1 LACAN AND PSYCHOANALYTIC THEORY

The appeal of a psychoanalytic approach to ancient art lies not in the opportunity to analyze the psyche of the artist or the subject matter of the images, but to consider how individual and social identity is constructed in a culture as it is revealed in its works of art.[4] The application of psychoanalysis to historical settings has precedents in the work of Freud, Lacan, and others, but the main components of psychoanalytic theory are focused on the formation of the modern individual's psychology. With this in mind, the effort in this chapter is not to produce a specifically Lacanian or psychoanalytic interpretation of Greek art and sexuality.[5] Rather, we seek to summarize some of the concepts that Lacan and others have put forward as a starting point for considering how spectators and sight affect the construction of individual and social identity in the viewer. This effort depends not only upon Lacan's writing, but also the work of others who have produced more comprehensive reviews of his theories and ideas, particularly A. Wilden, J. Rose, M. Jay, and T. Eagleton.[6]

The Real, the Imaginary, the Symbolic

Like Freud, Lacan views the human psyche as a tripartite structure. Whereas Freud divides the mind into three components based on the level of consciousness and uses pronouns to distinguish its components (*es*, *Ich*, *über-Ich* in German; id, ego, and super-ego in their familiar English translations), Lacan considers these components more in terms of the interaction of the subject with his or her environment and others (objects). Lacan uses the terms the Real, the Imaginary, and the Symbolic (*réel*, *imaginaire*, *symbolique*) to develop his tripartite structure as three overlapping and heterogeneous realms. The Real is perhaps the least discussed and developed of these areas, and is defined mostly in negative terms as that which is neither the Symbolic or the Imaginary, nor the "raw" state of existence as it is manifested biologically in a newborn infant.[7] In a sense the Real is the unprocessed world, before differentiation and distinction. The subject or individual does not yet exist because there is no perceived boundary between self and other.

In the next stage of development, between 6 and 18 months, the infant begins to develop a bipartite conception of the world.[8] This is seen most clearly in Lacan's definition of the mirror stage, to which we shall turn in more detail shortly. In this stage, the individual perceives the world as a series of images, both real and fantasy, which lends the term Imaginary, as in the realm of imagery, to this stage of development. It is at this stage that the subject becomes defined by the recognition that others exist in its world. At this stage, however, the subject sees these images, such as the mother, as extensions of itself that it controls.[9] It is also at this stage that the individual begins to construct an image of himself or herself. Looking in the mirror, the infant sees itself, and uses this image to construct an idealized representation of itself. While increasingly aware of its inability to control its environment and its own functions perfectly, the mirror image offers to the infant an idealized representation that appears to be integrated and in control of its environment. Because this image mirrors the self, there is a sense of control exercised by the infant since its reflection responds precisely to its actions.

At the stage during which the infant begins to speak, language becomes the foundation for the third realm of the psyche, the Symbolic.[10] For Lacan, words provide a means not only for naming what is present, but also for what is absent. This entails recognition by the individual of the other, of the object, as that which exists separately from itself and which, in some degree, it can never possess. Language, for Lacan, replaces imagery as the means for constructing identity by the way in which it recognizes otherness and denies the identity formed in the mirror. By recognizing absence, the Symbolic also defines desire as wanting that which is absent. Lacan used the term *objet a* (object small a) to denote this absent object that would satisfy the desire.[11]

It is at this stage that social factors begin to intervene, in Lacan's version of the Oedipal drama.[12] The phallus becomes a symbol that serves to differentiate men and women, and brings the realization of the mother's difference from the father. The child desires to provide the missing phallus for the mother, but the rules of society, identified by Lacan as the *nom du père*, intervene to control its action.[13] It is by learning to obtain the phallus through their relationships that the boy or girl develops gender identification. This is an important point of psychoanalytic theory, for Freud as well as Lacan. Gender is not based on biological drives or needs, as found in the Real, but in the construction of identity formed in the Symbolic realm through the acquisition of language and the development of social relationships.[14] The importance of the phallus, although it dominates the thinking of Freud and Lacan and reveals their prejudices, is not based on a fundamental reality of its inherent superiority, but is a choice of symbol made by the culture.[15] The result is the subjugation of those without – i.e., women. However, another symbol, such as the womb, vagina, or breasts, emphasizing birth, would, in theory, yield a different type of gender identification for a culture. Biology and anatomy, then, are not necessarily social destiny.

To summarize, the Real is the realm into which we all are born and which represents our most basic, undifferentiated needs and actions. For social creatures, this realm must be controlled as maturation proceeds. The first step is the Imaginary, which organizes the perceptions into images of self and of the world as extensions of that self. The initial sense of control exercised through these perceptions, both real and fantastic, is undermined by a growing awareness of the separateness and independence of other beings and objects. With the acquisition of language there emerges a sense of the individual subject and of the other, of the object, and an awareness of absence as well as presence. With language also come social codes that become the basis for constructing social identity. This distinction of the Symbolic can be thought of more broadly in terms of other forms of social identification beyond gender. Nationality, ethnicity, religion, and social class all provide symbols that can be and are used to differentiate layers of society. These, however, are layers that are usually placed on top of the distinction of gender, which forms, for modern western culture and many others, the first major division of a social group.

The Mirror Phase

Of particular interest in the formulation of the realm of the Imaginary is Lacan's definition of the *mirror phase*. As he describes, the infant at around six months perceives itself in the mirror, which results "in a series of gestures in which he experiences in play the relation between the movements assumed in the image and the reflected environment."[16] According to Lacan, we have to understand this mirror stage "as an identification, in the full sense that analysis gives to the term: namely, the transformation that takes place in the subject when he assumes an image." This is the first construction of the sense of self and subject, "before it is objectified in the dialectic of identification with the other." As mentioned earlier, at this stage the images that the infant sees, including the mirror reflection, are an extension of itself, so that seeing another baby, that child is regarded as a reflection of the self, rather than as another individual.

The result of the mirror stage identification is the construction of an "I," of an ego function. Rose explains the significance of this stage for the creation of identity, in that the child first becomes aware of the separateness between itself and the objects in the world around it:[17]

> As a result of identifying itself with a discrete image, the child will be able to postulate a series of equivalencies between the objects of the surrounding world, based on the conviction that each has a recognisable permanence. Identification of an object world is therefore grounded in the moment when the child's image was alienated from itself as an imaginary object and sent back to it the message of its own subjecthood.

The mirror further provides to the child an ideal image of itself, an Ideal-I. In its reflection, the child sees itself as in control of its world. But, as Rose points out:[18]

> This image is a fiction because it conceals, or freezes, the infant's lack of motor co-ordination and the fragmentation of its drives. But it is salutary for the child, since it gives it the first sense of a coherent identity in which it can recognise itself. For Lacan, however, this is already a fantasy – the very image which places the child divides its identity into two.

This narcissistic self-image will be undermined by the advent of the Symbolic order and will require reformulation.

The mirror stage is a function of infancy, and the source of a narcissism that can result from the continued adherence of the ego to its self-image beyond early childhood. The mirror stage itself is not of direct concern for our discussion, but the important point to consider for our purpose is the emphasis that Lacan places on sight and reflection in this first construction of identity in the individual. What the eye sees, it possesses in some measure at this stage, but in the next stage, in the realm of the Symbolic, the individual becomes aware of the limitations of this singular point of view.[19]

The Eye and the Gaze

We have already seen the importance of language in the continued development of the individual and in the distinction that it establishes between subject and object. The importance of sight in the definition of the Imaginary, exemplified in the mirror stage, becomes, in the realm of the Symbolic, a distinction between the eye and the gaze.[20] The eye, in this dichotomy, is what the individual subject sees; the gaze is the sense of being seen by others, in other words, the collective sight of other people, the social group. According to Lacan, the individual becomes aware that "I am looked at from all sides." Just as language in the Symbolic realm creates a division between subject and object in the individual, this awareness of the gaze, of being seen by others, creates a split between the individual and the surrounding environment and an awareness that the gaze is not only all-seeing but, by being all-encompassing, is in some sense more powerful than the singular point of vision, the eye of the individual.[21] The ideal image of oneself constructed in the mirror stage must now be set against the image that the gaze forms of oneself.

The construction of a new self-image is not, however, a matter of re-imagining oneself as outside the gaze, or "as seeing oneself seeing oneself."[22] Lacan points out that not only does the gaze see, it also shows. Being aware of the gaze, the individual is also aware of what others see and the gap between that image and the self-image. The individual also sees other objects in the field of the gaze with his or her own eye, and is made aware of what is lacking in oneself and therefore desires it. This can take the form of an object, what Lacan labeled in the Symbolic realm as the *objet a* (object small a). In seeing this object, the subject sees what he or she lacks, attempts to acquire its qualities, and measures his or her success against it. In so doing, the subject attempts to become that object in the collective gaze, acquiring an identity. According to Lacan, "from the moment that this gaze appears, the subject tries to adapt himself to it, he becomes that punctiform object, that point of vanishing being with which the subject confuses his own failure."[23]

This has several implications for the construction of identity. As Rose has summarized, both Freud and Lacan saw three levels or types of identification. The first two are rooted in the inability of the individual to negotiate the transition out of the

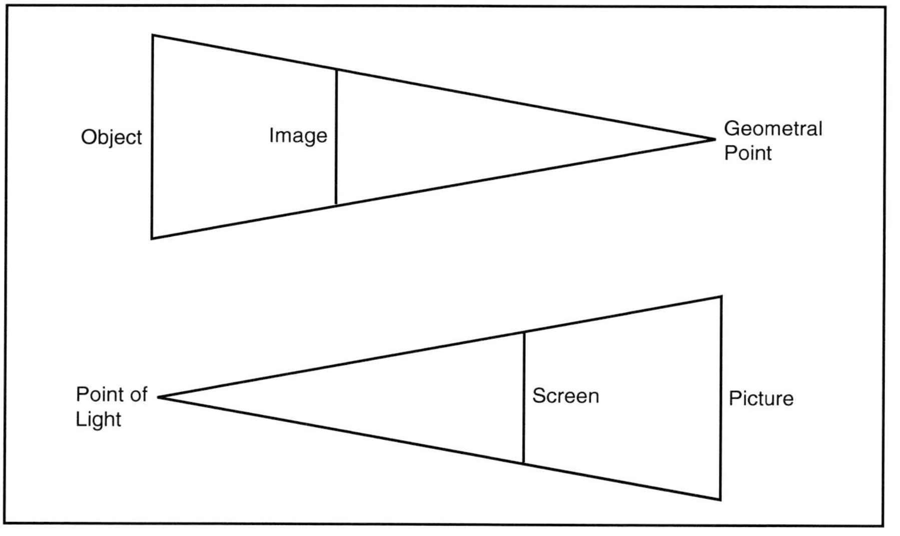

Diagram 1. Lacan's Visual Triangles (author, after Lacan [1978] 91).

earliest stages of childhood, but the third is rooted in the realm of the Symbolic and the construction of social identity. For Freud, there is a third level of "identification which arises with a new perception of a (repressed) common quality shared with some other person who is not the object of the sexual instinct."[24] Lacan reformulated this as *privation*, or the demand directed to an object that is separate from oneself and is missing (*objet a*). What ensues is a metonymic shift from the object to the subject, in which the individual adopts or repeats some aspect or trait of the object, and by so doing identifies with that object and shifts the gaze from that object to herself or himself.[25] This "double movement" links knowledge and action, allowing the individual to form a social identity and then act upon it.[26]

Lacan summarized visually the relationship of the eye and the gaze as two independent triangles (diagram 1).[27] The first triangle summarizes the eye and vision of the individual subject, which is located at the point of the triangle. What the eye sees at the base of the triangle is the object, and between these two is the image that is formed of that object. The second triangle places the gaze at the apex as a point of light radiating out, but it should be remembered that the gaze operates from multiple points simultaneously, unlike the eye. The base is the entire perceptual field, and midway is the individual subject – what Lacan termed the screen. If the two triangles are overlapped (diagram 2), one sees the coincidence between the image of the object formed by the eye and the image of the individual subject formed by the gaze. To the extent that these align diagrammatically, one might consider the degree of successful identification of subject with object and the construction of social identity. These diagrams are useful to consider, but we will develop an alternative schema later in this chapter that focuses on images with spectators and multiple viewers.

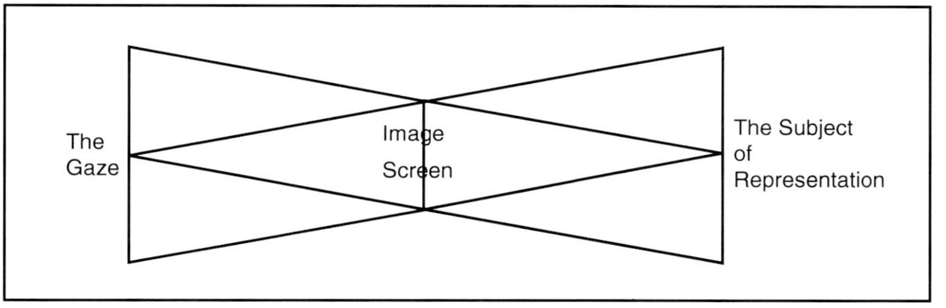

Diagram 2. Lacan's Superimposed Triangles (author, adapted from Lacan [1978] 106).

Lacan and Painting

Language asserted primacy over vision in Lacan's theory.[28] The awareness of the separation between the subject/individual and the object/environment is built first upon words, which create a permanent symbol for something that is not present and that exists independently of the individual. Sight alone creates a continuity between the individual and others that is impossible, narcissistic, and misleading.

Painting posed a somewhat different problem to Lacan, because on one level it represents the eye and vision of the artist as subject, but it is also a constructed image and object in its own right. When seen by a viewer, it embodies the gaze doubly, both as something seen by another (the artist) and as an object that engages and looks back at the viewer. For Lacan, the painting is a trap for the observer as well as for the gaze, and so can be considered a point of intersection between the two, as both image and screen.[29] As he proposes:[30]

> I shall advance the following thesis – certainly, in the picture, something of the gaze is always manifested . . . you will see in the end, as in filigree, something so specific to each of the painters that you will feel the presence of the gaze.

Whereas Lacan generally spoke of vision and imagery in terms of the Imaginary realm, a constructed image such as that found in painting and sculpture, and as important, in a range of media such as gems, vessels, and fabric, properly belongs to the Symbolic rather than the Imaginary realm. Like language, the image stands for something that can be absent or only partially present, and it is an object that resists complete incorporation by the viewer, maintaining an otherness. Further, images depend upon a vocabulary and syntax if they are to be decoded and function as a visual language parallel to spoken language.[31] By depicting something, an image not only provides a "name," but can also offer a substitute image for that which is absent. In this manner, pictures can provide a powerful source for identification in the viewer.

Something of this symbolic power of images emerges in Lacan's discussion of the paintings in chambers of the Doge's Palace in Venice, in which he considers how the viewers "see the gaze of those persons who, when the audience are not there, deliberate in this hall. Behind the picture it is their gaze that is there."[32] He calls this stage communal, in which the view of the patron/ruler coincides with those of the governed. The picture in a sense asks the viewers to lay down their individual sight and to take up the gaze embodied in the picture: "It is to this register of the eye as made desperate by the gaze that we must go if we are to grasp the taming, civilizing and fascinating power of the function of the picture."[33]

These constructed images serve the same purpose as verbal narratives in constructing the individual and social identity. In the psychoanalytic process, Lacan refers to the individual account of an event as a rememoration that includes not only the subject/actor, but implies the presence of spectators like the chorus of a tragedy. This stands[34]

> in the same relation to the waking rememoration of what is curiously called in analysis 'the material,' as the drama in which the original myths of the City State are produced before its assembled citizens stands in relation to a history which may well be made up of materials, but in which a nation today learns to read the symbols of a destiny on the march.

In other words, narratives serve to construct beliefs and identification for the group as well as the individual. Narrative pictures, like these spoken narratives, serve the same purpose. By being shared like language, artist, patron, and viewer are linked through 'the material' and identify with the values and actions represented therein, using them to model their own individual and collective behavior.

To summarize, the Symbolic level is the arena of interaction between an individual and culture. The individual sees, and is aware of being seen. The gaze manifests this sense of being seen by the culture, and sees not only the individual but also other objects in the visual field. The individual subject, by adopting traits of those objects, can align herself or himself with those objects to be an identified subject. Art is also part of this dynamic of vision, gaze, and identification by simultaneously representing the gaze as well as being an object within it. By adopting traits of an image into the self-image, the individual can create a social identity that conforms to the culture and can see himself or herself reflected in the painted image. Narratives, both verbal and visual, also create this alignment of individual and culture by codifying actions and values that are acceptable.

All of this is well and good, but it remains to bridge the gap between, on the one hand, the theoretical models of Lacan based on the analysis of the individual and the norms of contemporary society, and, on the other hand, how vision and gaze served to construct individual and social identity in ancient Greece. To do this, it is necessary to consider Greek ideas about vision before turning to the task of developing a visual model for interpreting images of spectators.

3.2 GREEK THEORIES OF VISION

The Greek understanding of visual perception differs significantly from our own, in which light reflects off the surface of an object and enters into the eye.[35] The receptors in the retina transmit the impulses that light stimulates in the receptors via the optic nerves to the brain, which then combines and reverses the data from the eyes into a mental image. In this view, then, there is a universal and objective quality of vision that can be measured and constructed according to modern optical theory, against which human perception and misperception can be measured. The person's response to what is seen belongs to the realm of psychology and physiology, and not physics.

Greek theories of vision, however, did not make the same distinction between the physics and mechanics of perception and the response to it. Seeing was a much more active and important business than we generally consider in our time. Furthermore, light was not seen as the critical factor, with the result that the Greeks developed several different approaches to explaining how vision worked. Despite the divergent explanations that we will see subsequently, one common quality of Greek theories is that they unite the physical, physiological, and psychological aspects of vision to varying degrees. A second feature is that they presume a much more intimate contact between the viewer and the viewed object than modern optical theory. In the following section, we seek not to develop a comprehensive discussion of the Greek theories, but to highlight some key points that show the Greeks felt at a fundamental level that what they saw had a direct power to affect them, to stimulate their emotions, and to impact their thought and judgment.

Although most testimony regarding vision is later than the archaic period, by stressing this common ground and the earlier sources where possible, especially those of the fifth century, we shall seek to show a common sense of vision that would be appropriate for the sixth century as well.

Eidola, Visual Fire, and Pneuma

As D. Lindberg has set out, one may divide Greek theories of vision into several different groups based on the surviving testimony on vision and perception.[36] One of these, the mathematical approach, is more concerned with geometry and measurement than with perception. Most of its investigations are not of interest for the current discussion, except for the central postulate that defines the visual ray as emanating from the eye. Although this might be a convenient postulate for their theorems, it also places the eye as an active agent in vision, a position that it shares with the three other groups of theories.

The Atomists, led by one of their founders, Democritus (born c. 460), developed a distinct theory of vision by the fifth century.[37] According to them, vision, like all sensation, is a form of touch or contact with the perceived object.[38] Seeing something means being materially touched by a simulacrum of the object itself, generally termed an *eidolon*. Aetius later reports that several philosophers held to this view: "Leucippus, Democritus, and Epicurus say that perception and thought arise when images [*eidola*] enter from outside; neither occurs to anybody without an image impinging."[39] Theophrastus reports in more detail on Democritus's theory, that:[40]

> The visual image does not arise directly in the pupil, but the air between the eye and the object of sight is contracted and stamped by the object seen and the seer; for from everything there is always a sort of effluence proceeding. So this air, which is solid and variously colored, appears in the eye which is moist (?); the eye does not admit the dense part, but the moist part passes through.

Essentially, all objects give off these miniature replicas of themselves, which enter into the eye and are apprehended by the mind and stimulate thought. Thus, visual perception, like other senses such as touch and taste, is caused by the direct physical contact of the object with the eye of the subject. Proof of this is offered by the observation that when you look into the eye of someone, you see as you would in a mirror the image of the objects in the perceptual field.[41] Thus the *eidolon* enters into the eye and into the mind of the viewer, where it generates and affects thought. Clearly, there are problems with this theory, including one of scale, in that it was difficult to explain how something as large as a mountain would be reduced to such a small size within the eye.[42] Critics such as Aristotle resisted the idea of the *eidolon* and ridiculed much of the theory.

Another approach to vision was the theory of extramission. In contrast to intromission, in which the image enters into the eye, in this view there were rays that emanated from the eye itself to enable vision. As Alcmaeon (active early fifth century) noted, according to Theophrastus:[43]

> Eyes see through the water round about. And the eye obviously has fire within, for when one is struck [this fire] flashes out. Vision is due to the gleaming, – that is to say, the transparent – character of that which [in the eye] reflects the object; and sight is the more perfect, the greater the purity of this substance.

For sight to work, both the visual fire and external light need to be functioning so that a connection between the eye and the object can be made.

This approach was elaborated by Plato in the *Timaeus*. He explains that:[44]

> And of the organs they [the gods] constructed first light-bearing eyes, and these they fixed in the face for the reason following. They contrived that all such fire as had the property not of burning but of giving a mild light should form a body akin to the light of every day. For they caused the pure fire within us, which is akin to that of day, to flow through the eyes in a smooth and dense stream; and they compressed the whole substance, and especially the centre, of the eyes, so that they occluded all other fire that was coarser and allowed only this pure kind of fire to filter through. So whenever

> the stream of vision is surrounded by mid-day light, it flows out like unto like, and coalescing therewith it forms one kindred substance along the path of the eyes' vision, wheresoever the fire which streams from within collides with an obstructing object without. And this substance, having all become similar in its properties because of its similar nature, distributes the motions of every object it touches, or whereby it is touched, throughout all the body even unto the Soul, and brings about that sensation which we now term 'seeing.'

Thus the visual fire makes a connection with the object and conveys this perception directly into the mind. Like the Atomists, the eye screens out coarser elements, allowing only the pure and fine quality to flow into it. The residual motions from perception left in the eye and mind result in images being recalled in the mind after the eyelids are closed, again an indication for the Greek theorists that the power of sight is found internally, and not externally.

Aristotle rejected the ideas both of the *eidolon* and of visual fire in favor of a transparent visual medium that connects the viewer and the object:[45]

> For seeing takes place when that which can perceive [the eye] is affected by something. Now it is impossible for it to be affected by the actual colour which is seen; it remains for it to be affected by what is intervening. But if it were to become a void, not only should we not see accurately, but nothing would be seen at all.

Thus Aristotle rejects, wrongly, Democritus's claim that we would see more clearly in a vacuum because perception requires a medium, like sound requires air and touch requires physical contact. For Aristotle, light is the activating state of this transparent visual medium. Colors on the surfaces of objects stimulate and produce change in the transparent medium, which is carried through the medium and acts upon the eye. The watery property of the eye permits it to receive the sensations of light and color, making it continuous with the object through the visual medium. The motion generated by objects in the medium stimulates motions within the viewer to enable perception. As Aristotle explains the connection between sight and thought, sense-perception creates a *phantasia*, an image in the mind that is true to the original object, but an image that can change once the active perception is past. The *phantasia* is used by the mind and is a necessary condition of thought.[46]

The Stoics further developed the idea of a visual medium as the *pneuma*. As Alexander of Aphrodisias (second century C.E.) stated, "Some people explain vision by the stress of air. The air adjoining the pupil is excited by vision and formed into a cone which is stamped on its base by an impression of the object of vision, and thus perception is created similar to the touch of a stick."[47] For sensory perception like touch and taste to work, it is necessary in this view that there be some kind of contact between the source and the sensory organ. The *pneuma* provides such a physical connection between the viewer and the object.

The theories outlined here were developed during the classical period and afterward, but it is clear from all of them that the Greeks did not understand vision as the perception of reflected light as we do. Indeed, light plays a minimal role in their theories, and then mostly as a medium rather than as the agent of sight itself. There is also some overlap in the theories, and it is this common basis or sense of vision that we may examine to think about the character of visual perception for the Greeks as it existed at the beginning of the classical and the end of the archaic period. One common element in these theories is that there is direct contact between the viewer and the object and that some type of emanation proceeds between the object and the eye.[48] Whether an *eidolon* or merely the patches of color enter into the eye, or the eye reaches out and touches the object, the eye is intimately, actively, and physically involved with what is seen. The watery and moist quality of the eyeball is compared to that of the surrounding medium and allows the essences to enter and to imprint upon the eye, while stopping coarser elements from passing.

A second feature of Greek visual theories is that what is seen enters into the mind itself because its images continue to recur in the "mind's eye" even after the thing has been seen. Thus, what we see has the power to enter into our soul and to affect our behavior. Perception depends not simply on the qualities of the object, but also upon the qualities of the viewer's eye and mind, with the result that each perception is unique.[49] Although there may be strong general tendencies in perception, what a viewer brings to perception matters greatly and helps to explain differing reactions to the same phenomenon.

The Effective Power of Vision

To summarize, we might say that what is seen has a power to shape us directly in a very tangible way. This can happen negatively, as attitudes about the evil-eye attest, but can also happen in a positive, formative way. To return to Plato, he describes the process by which love is enflamed:[50]

> So the stream of beauty [generated by the lover's perception and desire] passes back into the beautiful one [the beloved] through the eyes, the natural inlet to the soul, where it reanimates the passages of the feathers, waters them and makes the feathers begin to grow, filling the soul of the loved one with love.

The beloved (*eromenos*) is at first unaware of the source of this longing, but in becoming aware of the gaze of his lover (*erastes*) identifies the cause and responds. By their mutual gaze, and by seeing their own reflections in each other's eye, the relationship between the two lovers coalesces and advances.[51] With regard to vision, we have to understand from this the power of the gaze and of vision. What we see enters into us and stimulates our emotions and our minds. To see something beautiful and inspiring is to enflame the same feelings inside of oneself, whereas to see something base or horrid will have the opposite effect.

As Plato makes clear, the act of seeing by the lover has the capacity to affect the beloved, even when the beloved is initially unaware of the gaze. This raises a second critical point about the Greek understanding of vision, and that is its reciprocity.[52] Not only are we affected by what we see, but also who sees us can influence our behavior even when we are unconscious or only marginally aware of being seen. The eye is an emitter as well as a receptor, so that we are affected not simply by what we see, but by who sees us. Thus the lover's gaze invokes love within its object; thus the jealousy of the spurned can poison the soul of its object and can bring danger upon it, as with the evil eye.

The intimate connection between the emotions on the one hand and sight on the other was elaborated by the rhetorician Gorgias (flourished later fifth century) in his *Encomium of Helen*:[53]

> For the things we see do not have the nature we want them to have, but the nature each one actually has, and through the organ of sight the mind receives an imprint even in its characteristics. For instance, when the organ of sight gazes on hostile figures and an array, hostile with hostile weaponry, of bronze and iron, some for attacking, some in the form of shields, it is disturbed and it disturbs the mind, and the upshot is that often people flee the danger which is looming as if it were actually present . . . So if Helen's eye found pleasure in Alexander's body and transmitted the eager flirtatiousness of love to her mind, why should that be found surprising?

In Gorgias's argument, what we see directly affects our thought and action, whether love or fear, so that rational decisions can be undermined by the power of sight. The result in his argument, therefore, is that Helen is blameless for the devastation of Troy and Greece. Whether or not one agrees with this reasoning, Gorgias's argument draws upon a prevailing attitude that sight has an immediate impact upon the emotions and upon action.

To summarize, for the ancient Greeks, viewing was an active process, both for the viewer and whomever the viewer sees. Viewing can excite and enflame, or terrify and repulse, making it potentially hazardous if comprehension and judgment are not exercised diligently. The priestess at Delphi, seeing the Furies inside the temple in Aeschylus's *Eumenides*, runs from the temple exclaiming:[54]

> Things terrible to tell and for the eyes to see
> terrible drove me out again from Loxias' house
> so that I have no strength and cannot stand on springing
> feet, but run with hands' help and my legs have no speed.

So affected by what she has seen, she has lost control of movement and decision. As she catches her breath, she tries to identify the creatures on the basis of pictures that she has seen, but none quite matches the specific horror that she has seen. Only Apollo is capable of dealing with them, not a mortal.

At the other extreme is the contemplation of beauty, as we saw in Plato. An example of this is the victor in athletic competitions, who is admired by the audience when he receives his crown. Indeed, the beauty of such a figure is as important as his athletic ability and inspires feelings of love, as Pindar suggests by comparing one victor to Ganymede:[55]

> I praised the lovely son of Archestratos, whom I saw prevailing by might of hand alongside the Olympian altar at that distant time, fair of form, mingled with that youthful prime which once, with the aid of the Cyprian goddess, warded off shameless death from Ganymede.

Both men and women, looking upon such a figure, can be inspired to love what they see and to aspire to possess it. Modesty, however, is called for in the athlete by turning his glance downward. Otherwise, the potential for enflaming the viewer would be doubled by the return of the gaze upon him to the viewer.[56]

Painted images and other mimetic objects work along the same principles. What we see in a narrative picture has the ability to affect us, but it is modified to the extent that the viewer is looking at an object rather than a real person. Thus this type of perception lacks the reciprocity of vision, of seeing and being seen, that seeing the actual event would have, and hence allows the viewer to see it in a more contemplative manner. For example, in his *Poetics*, Aristotle talks about how we learn from what we see:[57]

> we take pleasure in contemplating the most precise images of things whose sight in itself causes us pain – such as the appearance of the basest animals, or of corpses. Here too the explanation lies in the fact that great pleasure is derived from exercising the understanding, not just for philosophers but in the same way for all men, though their capacity for it may be limited. It is for this reason that men enjoy looking at images, because what happens is that, as they contemplate them, they apply their understanding and reasoning to each element (identifying this as an image of such-and-such a man, for instance).

Viewing real corpses causes great pain, but viewing a picture of a corpse blunts that pain and allows more readily for contemplation and understanding, which are more tolerable emotions. Although one might be physically sick in looking at a corpse on the battlefield, seeing it in a picture allows one to consider who the figure is, what he has done and what has happened to him. Although this perception may lack the strength that first-hand experience provides because of the difference in the quality and intensity of the vision striking one's soul, it still has the potential for transforming the individual and affecting behavior.

Statues, too, do not affect the viewer to the same degree as the original, but as Steiner's analysis of the viewing of statues demonstrates, the statue stands in for the original object and similarly lowers its eyes in modesty.[58] Consistently, inscriptions and other testimony conflate the experience of viewing the statue and viewing the original, living human form, while allowing perhaps a greater degree of contemplation and consideration that the original situation might not allow. Still, viewing the statue of a deceased individual or a victorious athlete is meant to inspire feelings of affection in the viewer, similar in kind if not in degree to those inspired by the original.

As important, images are meant to inspire behavior. As Thucydides recounts, Perikles asked the citizens of Athens to look upon their city, recently transformed with new buildings and, by looking, become lovers of the city, willing to sacrifice their lives on its behalf:

> you must daily fix your gaze upon the power of Athens and become lovers of her, and when the vision of her greatness has inspired you, reflect that all this has been acquired by men of courage who knew their duty and in the hour of conflict were moved by a high sense of honour . . . [59]

Clearly, the sight of Athens would not be all-powerful by itself, but the image of Athens has power by virtue of its religion, history, and social relationships, which can by symbolized in its buildings. The sight of these is a powerful stimulus to unleash all of these existing associations, and the swell of pride and resolve that Perikles would hope to induce in his audience are surely enhanced by the almost tangible connection in the mind between what is seen and the viewer.[60]

For the Greeks, what one sees enters directly into the soul or consciousness. To the degree that one lacks comprehension and judgment, it can affect one adversely; if one has understanding, it can stimulate noble action. Seeing matters greatly because it shapes actions and character.

3.3 A MODEL FOR SPECTATORS, NARRATIVE, AND THE VIEWING EXPERIENCE

The utility of a psychoanalytic approach to spectators and to images more broadly lies in focusing upon how they serve to construct the identity of the viewer. Unlike the unregulated landscape that the eyes see, images (and the dwellings and cities in which they exist) are constructions that by their design, fabrication, and form define certain ideas, actions, and types, to the exclusion of others. In combination, images can convey more complicated messages and, as narratives, provide patterns for behavior. As such, visual art is like a language; it is in this realm of the symbolic, as Lacan suggests, that the "law" of society is formed and relationships between its members are defined. Whereas the early stages of psychological development, like the mirror phase, describe a process of differentiation in the child, the interest here is in what we might call the process of integration of the subject into the social world, as part of but not center of that world, balancing "I" and "we."

Much of psychoanalytic theory and discussion is based upon pathology and the individual case, making its direct application to art difficult and its terminology not immediately transferable to visual images.[61] Psychoanalysis also deals extensively with earlier stages of development than the images and their users that we will consider. Our focus here, however, is upon the normative with regard to identity and social relations, and not the abnormal. For these reasons, we will develop a different type of terminology along with a viewing matrix that will, I hope, clarify the relationships between viewers and visual representations as they project an identity for the members of a culture.

By emphasizing the normative, however, it must always be remembered that social standards for human development are conventions and not a universal condition. Thus, gender, class, age, sexuality, and other categories are constructions and are not necessarily inevitable. Indeed, the cases in which individuals do not conform to the gender or other expectations placed upon them, where they defy the hierarchy, are of great interest in terms of this methodological approach, but are beyond the scope of the present discussion.

The Viewing Matrix

Looking back to chapter 2 at the range of subjects that spectators watch in table 12, we can see that in most cases the narratives constitute an ideal model. Heroes, such as Herakles, fight monsters and villains, while warriors battle each other, fulfilling their duty to the polis. Athletes were also admired figures, and even if one cannot always tell who will win the contest or fight, the performance requires skill and resolve, the qualities of a noble ethos or character. Processional and other ritualistic scenes also model ideal figures, whether of a rider, or musicians and dancers performing before the city. Winged figures or individual youths also signify an ideal, whether of divine favor or of beauty like the kouros statue. A few types of figures or scenes do not quite fit this mold: animals and erotic scenes, or figures of sirens and sphinxes; such examples, however, account for only about 10 percent of all spectator scenes. Thus, we can generally say that both spectator and viewer look at a scene that represents an ideal, whether of action or form or both.

In order to lay out the impact of the image in the construction of identity, we must consider not only the figures within the image and the viewer, but also the specific viewing circumstances. Most imagery in ancient Greece was not private, but viewed in some type of public or social context. The sanctuaries were filled not only with architectural reliefs and statues, but vessels, textiles, and other objects that, when seen, were part of a public and often ritualistic viewing experience.[62] So, too, the pottery, metalware, paintings, and other works found in a domestic setting were intended primarily to be seen within the context of the symposion, household activity, or religious observances. Because most of the media and formats on which images appear have a functional purpose, it is necessary to consider how the objects were used to see how their images were seen and understood. For the present discussion, it is also important to include as part of the viewing circumstances not only the viewer, but the

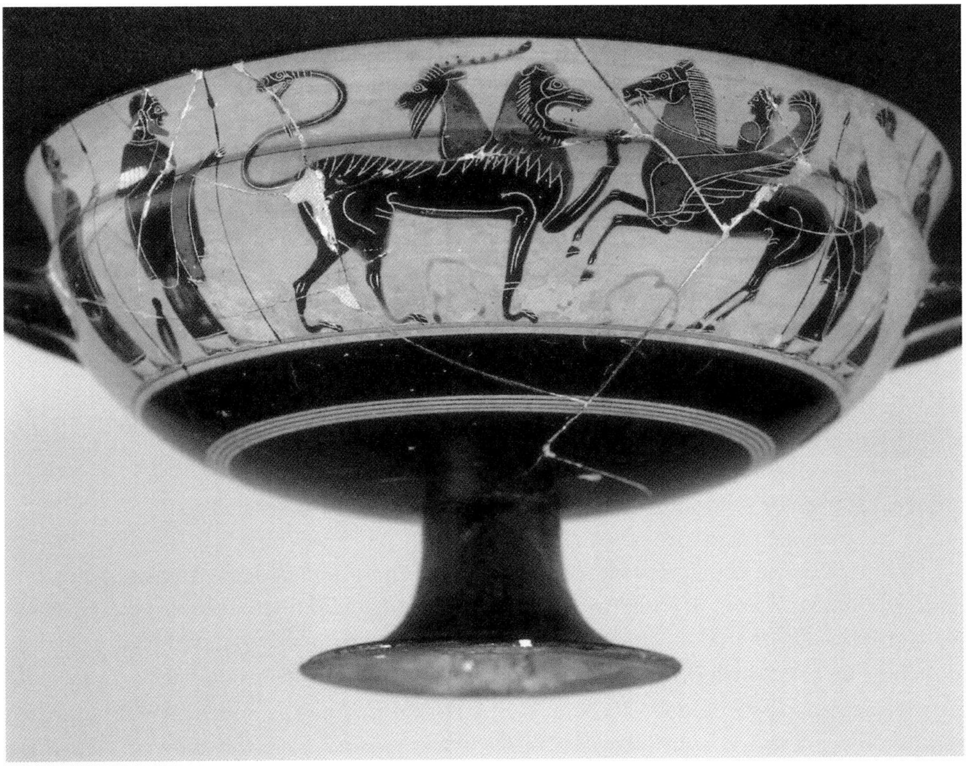

13. Attic black-figure Siana cup attributed to the Heidelberg Painter, c. 560. Side A: Bellerophon and Pegasus attack the Chimaera. Paris, Musée du Louvre A478. (Photograph, Réunion des Musées Nationaux/Art Resource, NY)

other members of the group sharing the experience of the occasion and seeing the same object.

In order to map out these elements and relationships, let us turn to a Siana cup in the Louvre by the Heidelberg Painter showing a scene of Bellerophon on Pegasus confronting the Chimaera (figure 13).[63] This scene is the nucleus of the composition, and its focus upon the nude youthful hero and his extraordinary action can lead us easily to label this scene as an idealized, heroic representation. Indeed, his pose, with both hands on the reins of Pegasus, is virtually identical to the numerous riders found on spectator vases (compare figure 10), marking equivalence between mythical hero and civic figure. There are pairs of adult male spectators to either side on the cup; all are similarly clad in chitons and himations and hold spears in front of them. Given their lack of any role as either nucleus or catalyst in the picture, we can identify these as pure and inert spectators. These spectators will allow us to map out the spectator as part of a visual matrix.

Bellerophon, like other mythological heroes, represents an ideal heroic type of Greek culture, possessing the quality of *arete* or excellence.[64] *Arete* consists of several different components, among them beauty (*kalos*), wisdom and self-control (*sophrosyne*), modesty (*aidos*), and courage (*andreia*). His resolve, prowess, and focus, as appropriate actions and ethical choices made by an individual, demonstrate *sophrosyne* and *aidos*. Bellerophon embodies Aristotle's later description of the good young men who are the blessing of the city: "good in bodily excellences, such as stature, beauty, strength, fitness for athletic contests; the moral excellences of a young man are self-control and courage."[65] Such ideals could be seen not just in mythological characters, but also in the exceptional figures of the contemporary world, among them athletes, soldiers, and leaders who embodied at least some of these ideals in a less extreme form.[66] Thus we can also see the spectators as embodying the qualities of Bellerophon, although in a more modest way.

Topoi, or flattering comparisons such as Pindar's comparison of a victorious athlete to the mythological Ganymede quoted earlier in the previous section, similarly cement the parallel in the mind between the contemporary world and the past. Just as words can represent something ideal and preserve it for posterity, so, too, can images embody and convey an ideal for viewers to emulate.[67]

To return to the image before us, we can label the nucleus of the picture with the capital letter "I," denoting its function as an ideal as well as its role as the focus of the picture and the model for identity. Spectators, of whatever type, we will designate as "Sp." The relationship between the spectators, whether on the left or right side of the picture, and the nucleus can be described graphically as a vector Sp→I, with the point of the arrow indicating the direction of the glance from the looking figure to the object (in the following discussion we will use the term glance to mean the act of looking by a figure or subject, and the term gaze to represent the collective vision and visual field). Because the spectators all look at the same figure, their collective vision or gaze focuses upon the hero and recognizes him as the ideal. Although inert, their formal dress and posture indicate their acknowledgment of the hero's status and of the importance of his actions. Standing in contemporary dress, their gaze also suggests the continuing respect and importance of the past action and its importance as an ideal for the present. By upholding the ideal of Bellerophon and his actions, they can hope to bring to themselves a similar respect for the achievements of their life.

The viewer of the vase we will designate with the letter "V." The viewer looks at the nucleus of the picture, which we can describe as the vector V→I. The viewer also sees the spectators within the visual field, so that we must add a second vector for the viewer, V→Sp. Because a vase like this drinking cup would likely have been used at some point in a public setting, whether a symposium, a funerary ritual, or a votive offering, we must consider that there were also a handful of other people in the viewing circumstances, which we will designate as "Gr" for group. The members of the group can see the cup and its composition as well as its holder, so there are three vectors to describe their collective gaze: Gr→I; Gr→Sp; Gr→V. Given the fact that the viewer would be holding the cup near the body, it is important to remember that

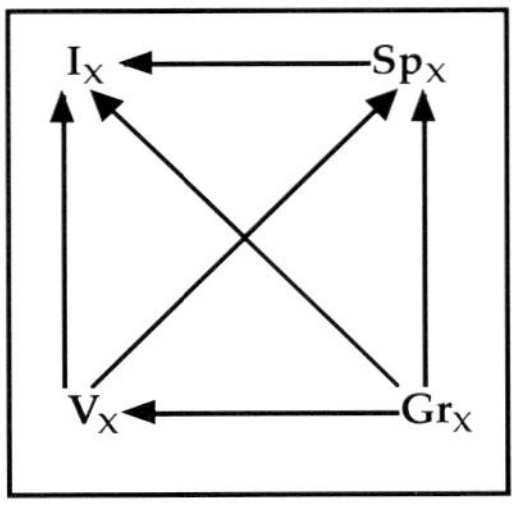

Diagram 3. General Viewing Matrix (author).

not all members of the group would be able to see clearly all of the three objects – narrative, spectator, viewer – at the same time. Collectively, however, each of the three objects would be under observation by the group, so that we can understand the view of the group as a function of the more abstract gaze of the collective society within this setting.

We can take these vectors and map them graphically as a model viewing matrix. Just as Lacan used diagrams to represent some of his ideas on the gaze, we can also use a graphic model to summarize the discussion just presented. It should be emphasized, however, that this diagram is only an abstraction and is intended not as a formula or law, but as a visualization of the discussion about viewing context and identification. The four constituents, the narrative ideal, the spectator, the viewer, and the group, can be laid out as a square, as seen in diagram 3. Because gender and age were important distinctions made among spectators, as we saw in the previous chapter, the subscript x here represents the type of figure, so that a youth will be designated as **y**, a man as **m**, and a woman as **w**.

If we assume for the moment that the viewer and the group for the Bellerophon cup are men, then its viewing matrix is as shown in diagram 4. The viewer, holding the cup, sees the narrative ideal as well as the spectators. As the diagram shows, the glance of the viewer toward the nucleus (I) is duplicated by that of the spectators, reinforcing its role as a collective focal point. A mature male viewer will also see in these spectators a reflection of himself, so that he shares the glance of the group of spectators and becomes part of their collective gaze. In the process, the ideal becomes shared among them,

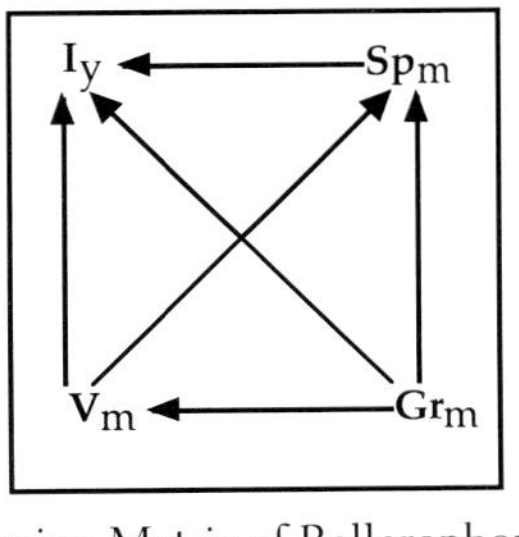

Diagram 4. Viewing Matrix of Bellerophon Cup (author).

confirming the importance of the narrative nucleus as an idealized representation for the viewer, not just as a private viewing pleasure, but as a collective experience.

In the diagram, one can also see that the glance of the spectators toward the ideal (Sp→I) is parallel to that of the group looking at the viewer (Gr→V). This is intended to show and remind us that just as the gaze of the spectators encompasses an object (I) and evaluates it (as an ideal), so, too, the gaze of a group sees the viewer and estimates his or her value against that ideal. This value will vary depending on the qualities of the viewer, but the more closely the viewer resembles the ideal, by displaying to the gaze of the group some of the ideal's qualities in a metonymic shift, the higher the group's estimation of the viewer will be and the stronger his or her social identity.[68] The group's gaze also encompasses the spectators in the picture, and just as the spectators function to recognize and regulate the ideal for the viewer, so, too, the group establishes and enforces the norms within the context of the viewing space.

As we have seen earlier, the ancient Greek viewer was aware of the gaze of the group. Furthermore, the viewer could see the gaze of the group toward himself or herself mirrored in the spectators looking at the nucleus. The viewer, in order to achieve the highest degree of social acceptance, prestige, and identity, would aspire to duplicate the gaze of the spectators toward the ideal with the gaze of the group toward the self. To do this, the viewer needs to realign the gaze of the group so that their image of the ideal becomes synonymous with their vision of the viewer. This means that the viewer must construct a self-identity through the assimilation of traits of the ideal expressed in the image and, by so doing, create a strong social identity. To the degree that the viewer can embody the values represented by the ideal, then the vectors Gr→I and Gr→V begin to converge and merge in the field of view. We can represent this graphically by moving the ideal and viewer closer to each other in the matrix, as represented in diagram 5. Because the viewer holds the image of the ideal close to himself, this shifting of the diagram begins to represent the alignment of the figures in the physical setting. We may refer to this process as *transposition*, by which the viewer places himself or herself next to the ideal visually and conceptually, so that the gaze of the group marks the ideal and the viewer as equivalent on some level and constructs a social identity for the viewer based on embodying some aspect of that ideal.

One consequence of a successful transposition of viewing vectors through the identification of the viewer with the ideal is that the spectators in the picture become less distinct from and more aligned with the group in the visual matrix. The result is that their role in the image becomes more oblique, both figuratively, in terms of their structural narrative function, and literally, in terms of the viewing angle that they occupy at the margins of the picture. Indeed, if we consider the sharply curving surface of the cup, or other vase shape, then the tangential line of sight from spectators actually shoots into space from the profile face and aims toward the viewer, as can be seen in diagram 6.[69]

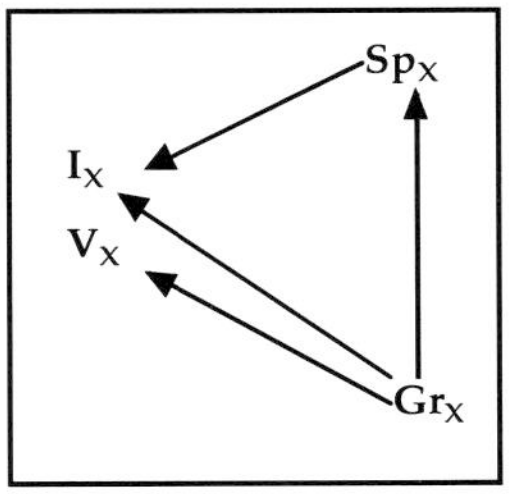

Diagram 5. General Transposition of Viewer to Ideal (author).

Thus, by transposing himself or herself with the ideal, the spectator serves to encourage the association and identification in the viewer's mind between the self and the ideal in the field of the spectator's gaze and, by extension, the group's gaze. Indeed, some members of the group, seeing the viewer in profile and holding the cup at a right angle with the handle pointing toward them, would also see the spectators looking at the viewer as if he were an ideal.

As discussed in chapter 2.3, we need to consider that the viewing context of a vase was variable, but the effect of the viewing circumstances and the interplay between viewer and group functions similarly across a range of contexts. In the case of a drinking cup such as the Bellerophon cup, the potential context could include a symposion, a funerary ritual, a grave good, or a votive offering. In the case of a symposion, the drinker would be with a group of other men and possibly youths as well. Because the cup would be held before the body more than it would held at the lips to drink, the figures on the cup would just be visible to some members of the group to either side of the drinker, whereas the drinker himself would be visible to virtually the entire group. The gaze of the spectators as they point toward the drinker mimics the collective gaze of the group.

The same type of dynamic would apply to a graveside ritual, except that it is then possible that one or more members of the group would be behind the drinker/holder of the cup, making its figures more visible to some members of the group. If we consider

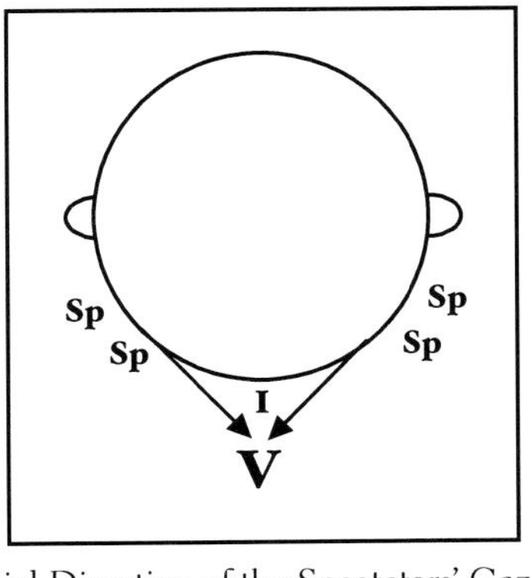

Diagram 6. Tangential Direction of the Spectators' Gaze on a Cup (author).

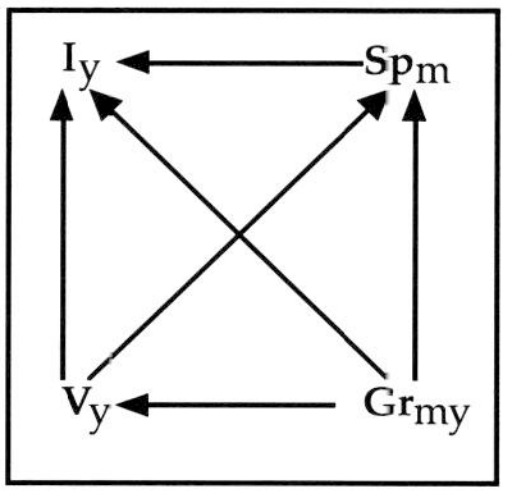

Diagram 7. Viewing Matrix of Bellerophon Cup with Youthful Viewer (author).

the grave as an object in the field of view, then the gaze of the group toward the grave is mimicked by the gaze of the spectators toward the hero, and in both cases the gaze of the observers signifies the worthiness of the spectacle. To the degree that an individual can emulate either the qualities of the deceased or those of the painted figure, one can assume aspects of that identity in the eyes of members of the group. Even in the case of a grave good, when we have to consider the deceased as the vase's user or viewer, the same dynamics of the gaze work. The act of setting a cup with the deceased is witnessed by the group at the graveside, some of whom can see the scene as the cup is handled and moved around. Any correspondence of qualities between the deceased and the hero marks the identification of the deceased and heroizes the dead. The spectators on the vase recognize both the hero and the deceased, as does the gaze of the group.

Finally, a cup might not be used for drinking when presented as a votive offering. Although an offering might not take place with a group of similarly focused individuals as at a drinking party or funeral, there would still be witnesses in a sanctuary to a gift. The placement of a gift would place the vase and giver together in the collective gaze; the action of the giver would be a worthy act and, if acknowledged by the group's gaze, places the offerer in a position like that of Bellerophon. In other words, the spectators on the cup serve to mirror the dynamic of the collective gaze of the group, and the acceptance that their gaze signals for the central figure in the picture is replicated in the gaze of the group toward the cup's donor.

If we change the viewer of the Bellerophon cup from a man to a youth, as would be appropriate in a variety of contexts, and also make the group a mix of youths and

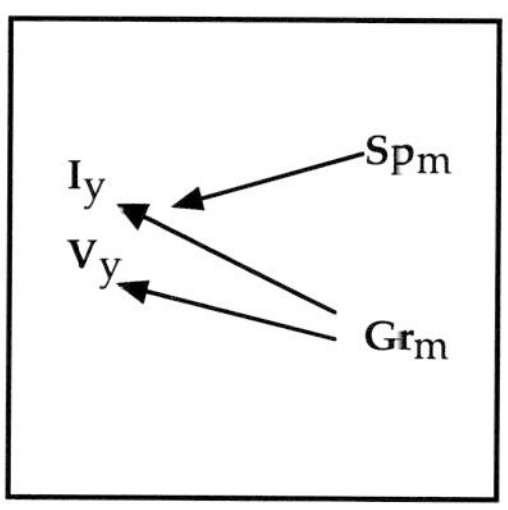

Diagram 8. Transposition of Viewing Matrix with Youthful Viewer (author).

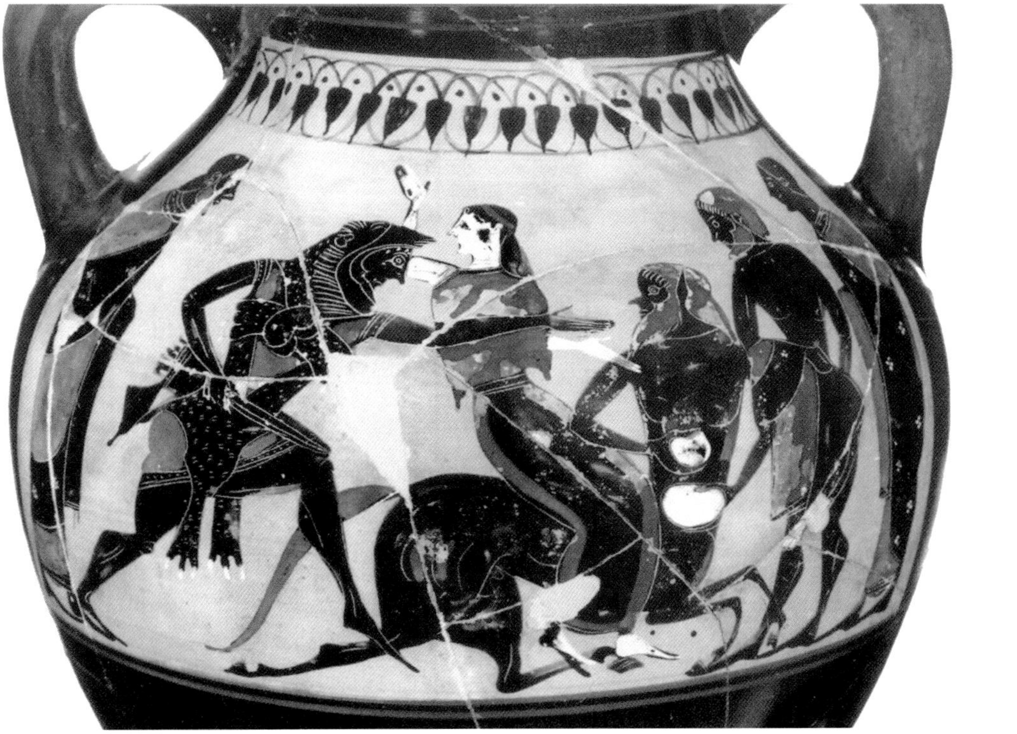

14. Attic black-figure amphora attributed to the Princeton Group, c. 530. Side B: Herakles, Nessos, and Deianeira. Munich, Antikensammlung 1384. (Photograph, Staatliche Antikensammlungen und Glyptothek München)

men, then the viewing matrix changes slightly (diagram 7). In this specific case, the youthful character of Bellerophon mirrors more directly the youthful nature of the viewer, so that the transposition onto the ideal involves aspirations for the future and present, rather than the present and the past, as it might for the mature viewer. The adult spectators, in this configuration, mirror the mature male members of the group. As the youth looks at the cup as shown in diagram 6, he sees the adult spectators looking directly at him, mirroring the gaze of the men in the symposion toward himself. In this sense, if the viewer also identifies the spectators as signs for the men of the group, then a more complete synchronization of spectator and group can occur than for the previous matrix linking the spectator and the group. The desired transposition of the matrix through identification would then place the youthful viewer as a focus for both imaginary spectators and real symposiasts, as represented in diagram 8.

Other images with spectators present more variables to consider as part of a viewing matrix. For example, a black-figure amphora in Munich related to the Princeton Painter shows two men and a youth as spectators (figure 14).[70] The nucleus consists of Herakles attacking Nessos, who carries Deianeira on his back. Unlike the Bellerophon picture, the heroic ideal here is an adult male. Not only is he attacking a monstrous figure, but he is also struggling against a threat to his household and generally to domestic order, for which Deianeira serves as an index structurally. At the far left of the picture is an adult male; at the far right is a youthful male. Both wear chiton and himation and stand attentively with their hands in their drapery. One additional man on the right is nude, with his cloak wrapped over his left arm and his right arm pulled back and bent. His nudity distinguishes him from both the other spectators as well as from Herakles, but it also gives him a more heroic form compared with the other spectators. His extended right elbow pulls the arm back into a position of readiness, like the position of the sword arm of Herakles, and both the hero and this spectator are placed at opposite ends of the centaur, like allies. These parallels make this spectator mimetic in mood, in contrast to the inert mood of the other spectators.

Although not part of the narrative nucleus, the mimetic spectator is positioned between the youthful spectator and the ideal of Herakles and demonstrates the dynamic of social identification through the metonymic acquisition of the traits of an ideal. Given his placement and parallels to the appearance of the ideal Herakles, the mimetic spectator stands as a secondary role model in the field of vision for the youthful spectator. The youth can see both him and Herakles, and can note the similarities in their form that allow them to be linked together. It is not necessary to fight a centaur to be like Herakles; the mimetic man shows the youth how to transpose oneself to the ideal by taking on some more limited aspect of the action and attributes of the ideal. Thus, the patina of heroic nudity and the movement of the limbs mimic the ideal. Because the mimetic spectator is an adult like Herakles, it is likely that he is also a householder with a wife, and so resembles Herakles in these aspects. The hero is defending his wife and household; the spectator's readiness to act, as suggested by the position of his right arm, shows that it may only be necessary for a figure to be vigilant in the protection of his house and family to emulate the heroic ideal. Deianeira also serves as an index for the emulation of this ideal; possession of a wife confers a similarity in status between Herakles and the married householder. Thus, the youthful spectator, if he follows in the footsteps of the mimetic adult spectator before him by marrying and vigilantly maintaining a house, can be like Herakles, too. In this picture, identification of the spectators with the ideal is more apparent than was the case of the spectators in the Bellerophon cup, and shows that it can be based on a variety of shared traits, and not exclusively on duplication of physique and physical action.

One effect of this inclusion of multiple types of spectators in the picture is to broaden the appeal of the ideal to the viewers of the vase and to offer several additional paths for transposition and identification. For example, the mixed group of spectators in the picture presents a likely reflection of the group setting in which the amphora itself would have been used. This would make it easier for an individual member of the group who looks at the vase to see himself in both a single spectator and as part of a larger group. The mimetic spectator offers to the viewer a model for how one can transpose oneself upon the ideal (as seen in diagram 5), not just by emulating heroic

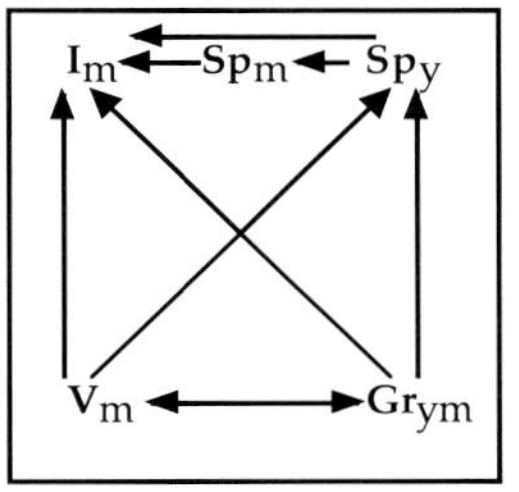

Diagram 9. Viewing Matrix of Munich 1384 (author).

action, but also by acquiring other signs belonging to the ideal. By having or obtaining a wife, a real viewer can transpose himself in the place of the hero, strengthening the linkage of viewer and ideal. Additionally, the older spectator showing a youth how to respond establishes him in the role of a teacher or mentor. As such, the mimetic spectator offers a secondary role model in the picture for the viewer, making a second transposition of the viewing matrix possible. The viewer can see himself in the role of mentor to a youth in the group and can assume this identity within the viewing context by instructing and modeling behavior for a youth.

To summarize, the possible transpositions offered in this vase include not only the emulation of heroic action or form in the ideal, but acquisition of signs belonging to that ideal (a wife) or imitation of the mentor role of the mimetic spectator. In this sense we have to consider that the adult male viewer not only looks at the object and picture, but also actively glances at selected youthful members of the group, returning their gaze and affecting the youth in turn, as seen in diagram 9 with the double-headed arrow in V←→Gr. As we saw earlier in Plato's description of the lover and beloved, the glance of the adult viewer can excite not only his own feelings, but can affect the feelings of the youth whom he sees. He can do this by adopting for himself the role of mentor and model at the symposion, like the mimetic spectator. To the degree that the adult male viewer can then attract the glance of a youth at the symposion to himself, he can transpose himself into the double role of ideal hero and ideal man, bringing the doubled glance of the youthful spectator ($Sp_y \rightarrow I$ and $Sp_y \rightarrow Sp_m$) onto himself. The convergence of glances is potentially powerful and may help to transform the adult male into the *erastes*/lover of a youth. We will return to this relationship later.

On an amphora in the Joslyn Art Museum in Omaha, we see a different set of visual dynamics (figure 15).[71] The nucleus here consists of a duel between an Amazon and a single warrior, who is probably protected by Athena, as indicated by the index of the owl. To either side are groups of three spectators. The figures next to the nucleus are women wearing chitons and himations, which they hold out in front of themselves. Behind them are youths in himations and chitons; the youth on the left also holds a spear upright whereas that on the right holds his hand inside his mantle. The last spectators are again women holding their mantles in front of themselves. All of the figures are pure and inert spectators.

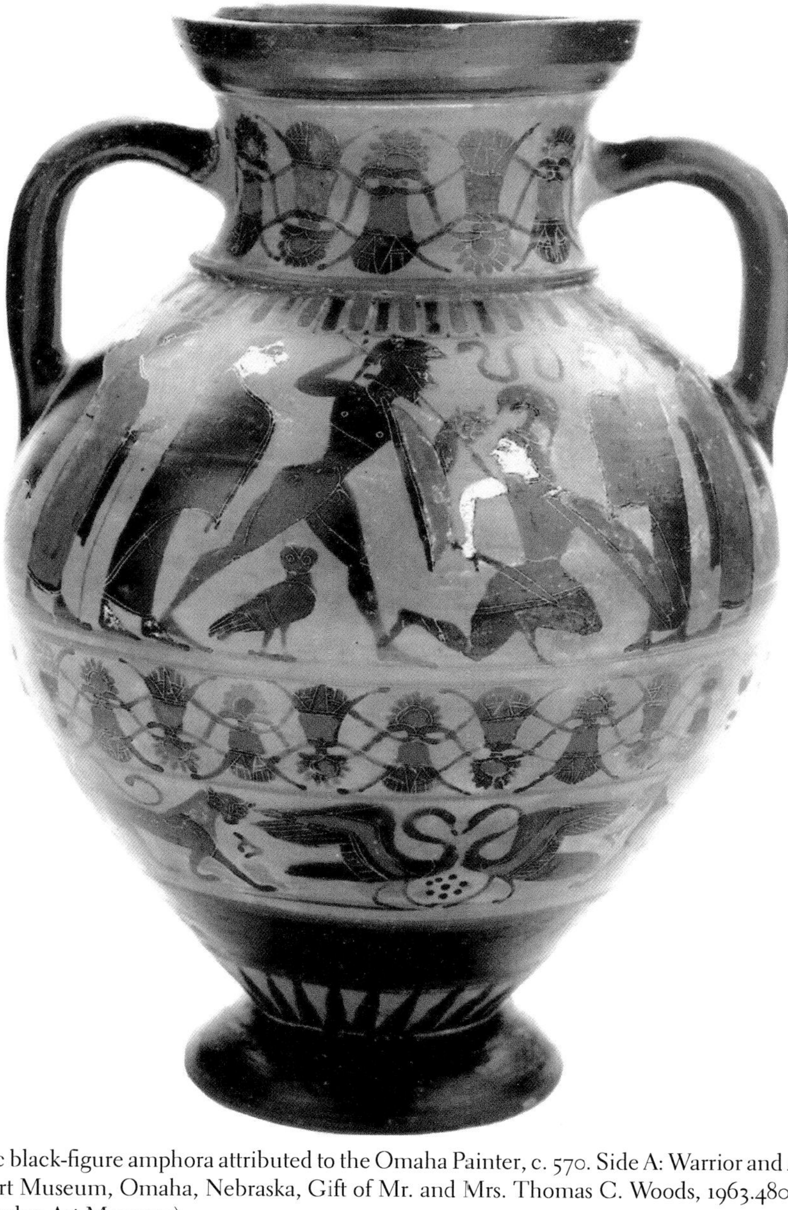

15. Attic black-figure amphora attributed to the Omaha Painter, c. 570. Side A: Warrior and Amazon. Joslyn Art Museum, Omaha, Nebraska, Gift of Mr. and Mrs. Thomas C. Woods, 1963.480. (Photograph, Joslyn Art Museum)

The inclusion of women as spectators in this picture adds a different dimension to the role of spectators from what we have seen so far. Within the specific context of a symposion, we would have to assume that the female members of the family would be absent, although female slaves or hired entertainers might be present in the room. However, as a household storage vessel, the vase would have been stored in the

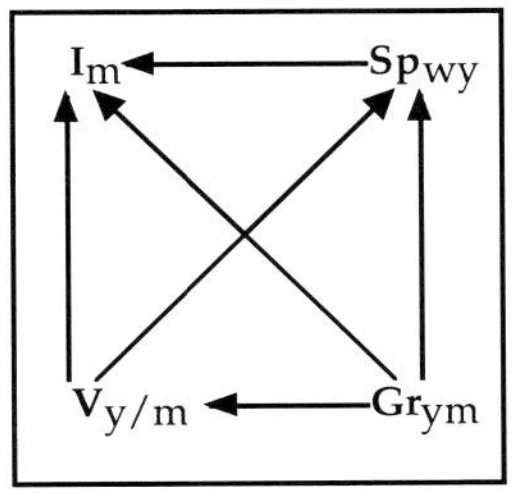

Diagram 10. Viewing Matrix of Omaha Amphora with a Male Viewer (author).

women's area of the house and carried by them. As a funerary vessel, it would also have been used by women in grave rituals. For the moment, we will consider the viewer of the vase as male, either youthful or adult, to set up the matrix in diagram 10. The lack of mature men among the spectators, but the focus of both youths and women upon a mature man as the ideal, establishes the adult warrior as the hierarchical ideal for all of the spectators. For a youth as viewer or group member, this ideal represents an aspiration for the future in terms of forming an identity. Like the youthful spectator, he would strive to assume aspects of the warrior before him. For a man as viewer or group member, the gaze of the youthful spectators toward the adult ideal is desirable as a model for the glance of the youth in the symposion toward themselves. To the degree that they can command the attention of the youth in the group, either through their physical presence or their social standing, they can see themselves in a heroic light as elite members of the community.

This dynamic of vision and identity changes when we consider the women spectators in the picture. They would appear to be korai and hence marriageable women (or already married women given the lack of age distinction), and their identification with the male ideal of the warrior must be more indirect than for a male viewer or spectator. Because they would, as maidens or wives, not be taking up arms to defend the household or city, they would have to project their husband or male guardian into the role of the male ideal and use it as a standard of measurement for their marriage or social standing.[72] Similarly, a female viewer of the vase would have to consider the male members of the household as potential embodiments of the ideal in the picture, and derive her status and identity indirectly in contemplating the picture, as we shall consider further in a moment.

The narrative nucleus here, however, is unusual among spectator vases by having a female figure as one of its components, making a woman the object of the spectators' gaze. As seen in table 12, 17 of the vases in the CVA census had a fight between an Amazon and either a male warrior or Herakles as its subject, about 2.3 percent of the total. Whereas in a picture of two anonymous and nearly identical warriors fighting, one could argue that either figure could serve as a model for the viewer or spectator, in a fight with an Amazon there is a clear dichotomy, just as there was for the fight between Herakles and Nessos in figure 14. In this case, the division is gender based, with the male representing the cultural ideal and the female its antithesis. Clearly, the Amazon is not an appropriate social model, and the contrast in dress, attributes, and action between her and the female spectators suggests that the Amazon is intended as an antithesis for the women spectators in the picture, too, with the implicit threat to them that adherence to a nonconforming social role might result in death and certainly in the loss of social identity.[73] We might label the Amazon in the picture, then, as an anti-ideal (−I, or negative I).

For each of the youthful spectators in the picture, this anti-ideal serves as the opposite of what he should strive for in a wife, who should look more like the female spectators around him. The heroic action in the nucleus models not just manly behavior and standards, but also the necessity for control over women in managing gender relationships. Youthful viewers of the amphora, then, can see their reflection in the youthful spectators in the picture and their identification with the adult warrior as the ideal. This ideal offers a model for the youthful male viewer in achieving adult status by assuming a hierarchical power over the women. For an adult male viewer, the ideal would relate less to the future than to the current management of gender relations. By introducing female spectators into the picture, the adult male would be reminded of the proper female members of his household, and of the desire for producing male offspring who would learn to take on not only the heroic ideal, but also the head of household role within the society. Thus, we can see the spectators here as reinforcing the conformity of family relationships to the heroic ideal, and the consequences of falling away from that ideal. Spectators work to model gender identity and relationships within Attic culture.

Given that this vase was a storage container, it could have been seen in a variety of domestic or funerary contexts in which women were active and would have been its viewers.[74] If one presumes that the amphora contained wine for a symposion, then it would be been seen not only in the dining room, but elsewhere in the house where its viewers would be women, or children who were not yet under their father's tutelage. However, under these circumstances the object has lost its more active functional role of providing wine for use, and instead serves here to keep its contents sealed until the proper setting and social occasion. Thus, the contents are unavailable to those members of the household who use it only as a storage container, privileging the contents for other viewers and circumstances. The vase, while closed for storage and not open for use, serves as a boundary and status marker, making the image but not the contents available.

For a female viewer under these circumstances, the heroic ideal of the warrior in the picture can only be indirectly possessed within social conventions through the male members of the household, given that women would not bear arms or even drink the wine from the container at a symposion. The options for adopting some aspect of the ideal are very limited, therefore, for the female viewer. The Amazon, by virtue of her gender, does provide a model with traits that a female viewer could adopt, but by rejecting normative female behavior for male behavior, the Amazon serves instead

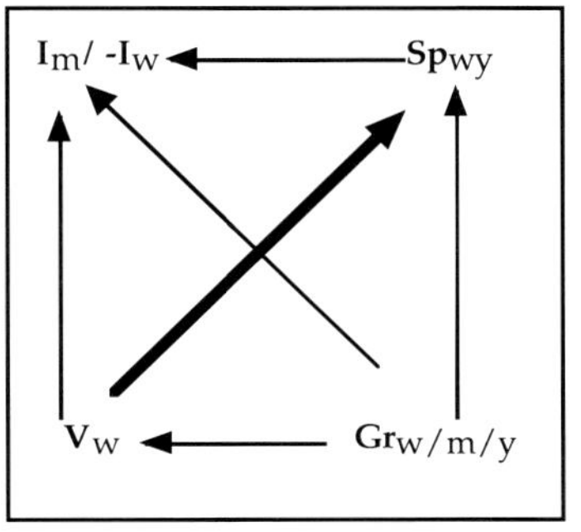

Diagram 11. Viewing Matrix of Omaha Amphora with Female Viewer (author).

as an anti-ideal by social convention, and suffers death as a result. Therefore, neither part of the nucleus forms a model from which a woman can adopt aspects of a positive identity. What is left as a functional model in the picture for a female viewer would be the female spectator, who is heavily clothed and very restrained in her behavior. This changes the dynamics of the viewing matrix considerably, as seen in diagram 11, with the bolder arrow indicating the primary glance of the female viewer in terms of social identification. In this representation, we have indicated the anti-ideal as −I, and shown the shift of glance to the female spectator by a wider line. The dynamics of transposing identity onto another figure in the matrix brings the female viewer not in line with the gaze of the group toward the nucleus of the picture, but keeps her to the side, as seen in diagram 12.

The fact that the object of transposition for a woman viewer is a spectator and not part of the narrative nucleus articulates the marginal status of women within the norms of Greek culture. The use of an element outside of the nucleus as an ideal for a specific type of viewer reflects to a real degree the spatial position of Greek women outside of the nucleus of their culture. We will explore these gender issues further in chapter 6, but for now we should note how the process of identification structured in the image works to establish a hierarchical ordering among its various types of viewers.

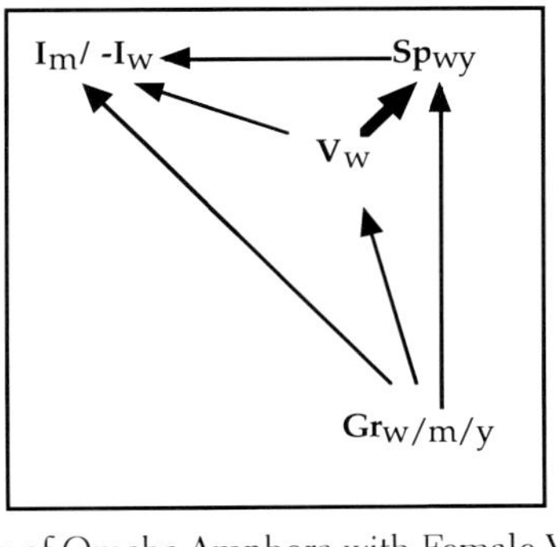

Diagram 12. Viewing Matrix of Omaha Amphora with Female Viewer Transposed (author).

So far, we have looked mostly at images featuring pure spectators who are not part of the nucleus or catalysts supporting it. We shall now turn our attention to a couple of examples in which the spectator is detached, but present at the action itself. A cup in Mainz shows a nude youth riding on horseback, accompanied by three running figures that acclaim him, and two mantled youths on the left side of the cup (figure 16).[75] The two detached spectators belong to the same time frame as the rider and runners, also making them catalysts in the picture as spectators of an actual event, but their clothing and demeanor separate them from the others. They should be understood as removed from the processional space, along the sides of the route or at its beginning or end point.

The difference in terms of the viewing matrix between a detached spectator such as these and a pure spectator such as those seen earlier is that the distance between spectator (Sp) and ideal (I) is diminished, making the potential for transposition conceptually easier. By being set in a shared time and place, the ideal is no longer so distinctly separated from the spectators and as a consequence also shares the general time and place of the viewer of the cup.[76] The spectators on this cup share many of the same physical qualities as the rider, whom we must presume from the actions of the runners is triumphant, in masterful control of his horse, and worthy of emulation. Within the civic context of the scene, it is possible or even likely that each of the spectators would, at some time, have a turn to demonstrate a similar prowess and be a participant, thereby receiving the acknowledgment of other spectators. In the meantime, they stand as idealized youths demonstrating control and poise in public while witnessing an exciting event.

If we presume that the viewer is also a youth, then we can see a reflection of the types of activities in which the youth has, himself, engaged or trained.[77] As he observes the cup, he can identify himself with both the victorious rider, placing himself at the forefront of his peers, and with the spectators watching and waiting for their turn. If we imagine the viewer as a man, then there are two lines of transposition. One, as discussed with the Bellerophon cup, is for the viewer to recall the triumphs of his own youth and the accolades received, re-imaging himself into the youthful, beautiful ideal. Additionally, we can note the potential position of the viewer as an *erastes* (lover) or mentor.[78] The ideal figure on this kylix represents an *eromenos* (beloved) or protégé, who would succeed under the adult viewer's tutelage and attention. In this sense, identification can proceed by an alternative path through the personal possession of the ideal, as was the case with having a wife in figure 14. Possessing such a youth, who rises above others, in turn elevates the status and identity of the *erastes*/viewer. Within a mixed viewing group, we can also assume that such a viewer is looking at the youths in the group, returning their gaze. By placing the spectators within the same time as the ideal and the group, this enables the adult male viewer to conflate under his glance the ideal and the spectators as he holds the cup before him, with the actual young men in the room that are also in his field of vision, as can be seen in diagram 13. Such a triple coincidence of youthful ideal, spectator, and group member would have the

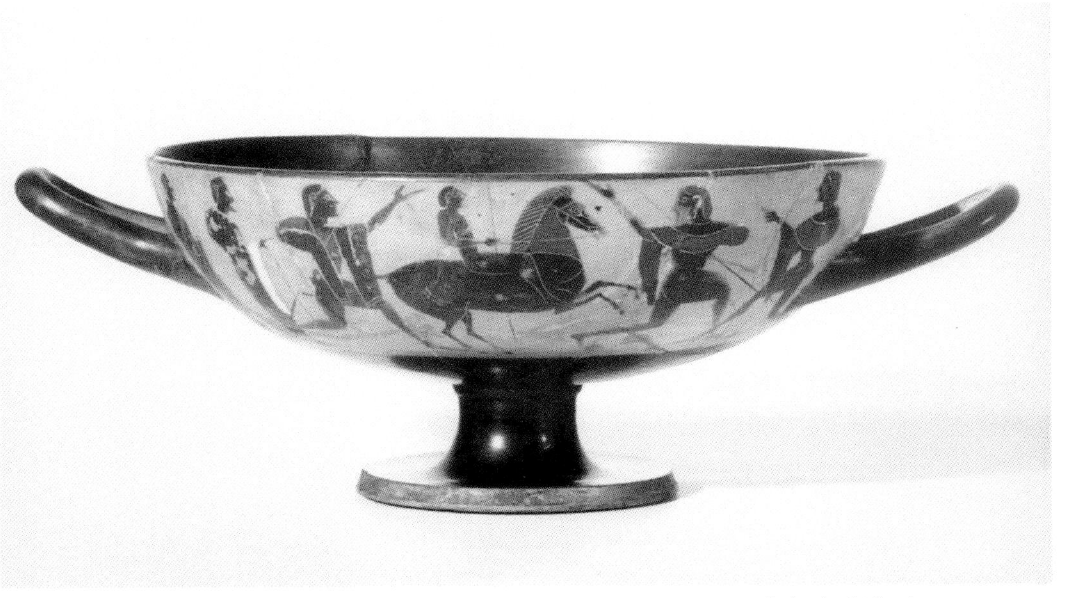

16. Attic black-figure cup attributed to the Amasis Painter, c. 540–530. Side A: Rider in procession. Mainz, Universität 88. (Photograph, Institut für Klassische Archäologie, Johannes Gutenberg-Universität Mainz)

effect of enframing and concentrating the viewer's glance. As a result, such reinforcing imagery has the potential for stirring the feelings of the viewer in the manner described earlier by Plato.[79]

So far, we have discussed the potential for the reciprocity of glance and gaze with the adult male viewer, but not with the youthful viewer. As can be seen on a kylix in Bonn, there is a decided asymmetry in the representation of the glance of adult males and youth in Greek art. In this kylix, we see a youth with a strigil on the left side, while in the center is a trainer and on the right is a cloaked and hooded adult leaning on a staff (figure 17).[80] The onlooker here is again a detached spectator, and might even be classified as interested because the potential for the figure in the nucleus to affect him emotionally would be substantial if a love interest is presumed. The separation

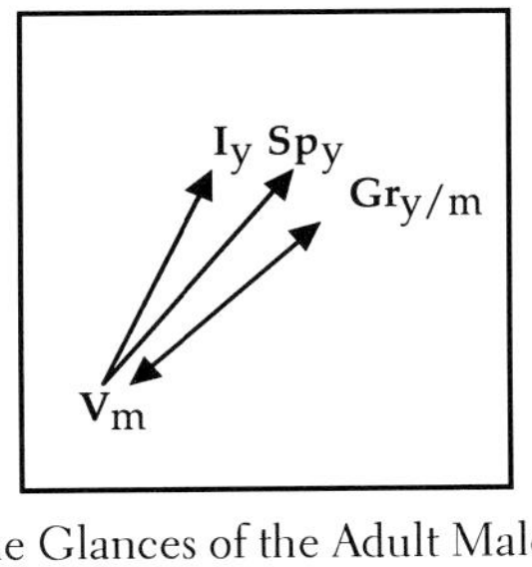

Diagram 13. Conflation of the Glances of the Adult Male in the Mainz Cup (author).

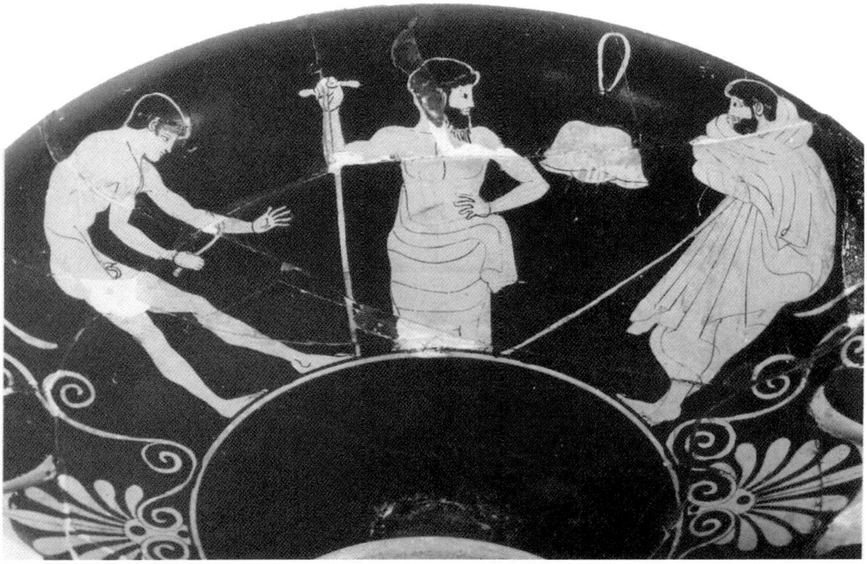

17. Attic red-figure kylix attributed to the School of Makron, c. 470. Side B: Gymnasium scene. Bonn, Akademisches Kunstmuseum 74. (Photograph, Wolfgang Lein, Akademisches Kunstmuseum – Antikensammlung der Universität Bonn)

of the spectator from the youth by the trainer, however, places him into the detached category in the absence of a defined relationship. The youth as an ideal is focused on his task, and as a nude is fully available to the glance of the spectator. While the spectator's eyes are riveted upon him, the youth exhibits *aidos* or modesty by keeping his glance turned down and focused upon his task.[81] Indeed, this is the expected code of behavior for a youth because to return the glance would be to excite the situation to an extreme degree, perhaps exceeding the bounds of decorum. In this sense, we can see the additional privilege of the adult male within the viewing matrix of ancient Greece in his ability to look back and to single out members of the group for his glance and to possess them, as well as the image.[82] The youth, for the moment, must remain more passive in his glance, aware of the gaze but not returning it. Thus, the vector for a group of older males looking at a youthful viewer, Gr→V, perfectly parallels that of the spectator and ideal in this kylix, Sp→I. To be the object of that attention, the actual youth must adopt the behavior of the ideal, turning down his glance even though he may be aware of being the object of an adoring and possessive gaze of an adult male (see diagram 13).

3.4 DISCUSSION

To summarize, Greek theories of vision considered the viewing process as both physical and psychological. To see something was to bring it into one's psyche; to see an

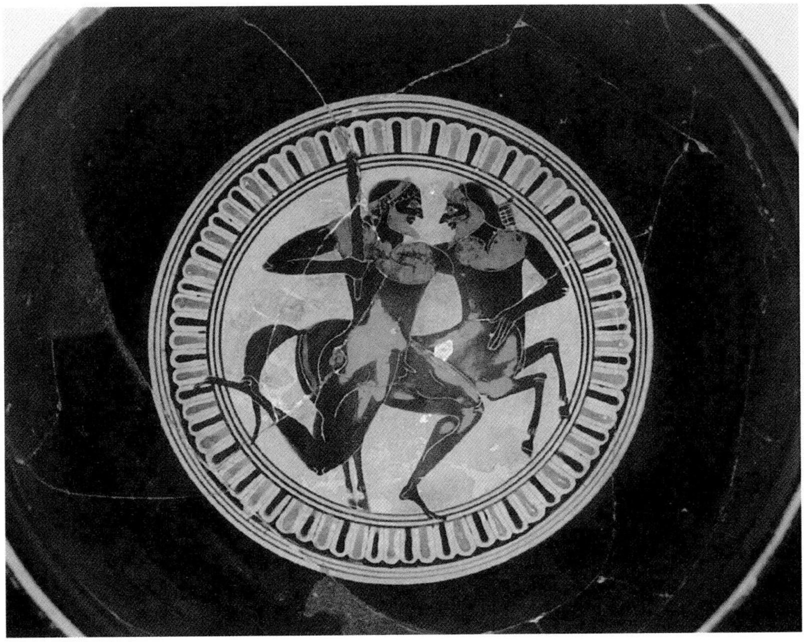

18. Attic black-figure Siana cup attributed to the Heidelberg Painter. Interior: Herakles and Nessos. Paris, Musée du Louvre, A478. (Photograph, Réunion des Musées Nationaux/Art Resource, NY)

image of something still brought one into contact with it, but at a safer remove than the real thing. The psychoanalytic approach also emphasizes the importance of the glance and the gaze in the construction of identity, and the importance of the adoption of traits of a model for the construction of that identity. Spectators provide a model for how vision and identity are intertwined in ancient Greece, and using the relationship between them and the narrative nucleus, the viewer, and the group we can describe the dynamics of the viewing process. The dynamics of vision and identity demonstrated, albeit abstractly through the diagrammatic model of the viewing matrix, can be extended more generally to images without spectators.

If we turn to the interior of the Bellerophon cup in the Louvre discussed earlier (see figure 13), we see a tondo with Herakles fighting Nessos (figure 18).[83] Structurally, the core of the nucleus is similar to that of the Munich amphora (figure 14), but Deianeira and the spectators are gone and Herakles's attributes have changed. Still, Herakles's nudity sets him apart from the normal viewer, and the ideal that he represents stands in the same relationship to the viewer as that of the Munich amphora. As a male viewer looks at the tondo, he still wishes to transpose himself into the ideal and by so doing become the focus of the group. To the degree that he can successfully emulate this ideal in the mind of the group, he can escape subservience and assure his status as a prominent member of the culture. The generic result would be something like diagram 14.

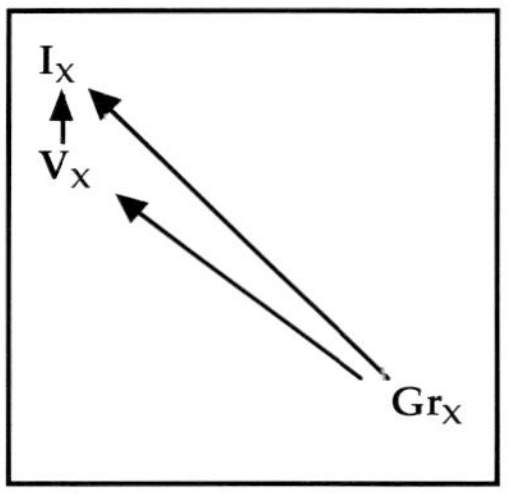

Diagram 14. Generic Viewing Matrix without Spectators (author).

Because this particular picture, however, is in a tondo, it would be unseen by the members of the group, bringing it as close as possible to a private experience as can exist within a public context. Curiously, though, when the viewer drinks, the pictures on the exterior would be better seen by the group. Pandareos and the Golden Dog (side B) would be on the bottom and upside down, whereas the picture of Bellerophon on side A would be right-side up and on top (figure 13). The act of drinking actually covers the face of the drinker like a mask, so that within the viewing matrix Bellerophon substitutes for the viewer, who assumes that heroic identity for the viewer while he drinks.[84] Thus, the drinker returns the gaze of the group as a hero and becomes that ideal, even if momentarily, in their eyes. The drinker himself has a different model before him, but now that he is a hero, too, he is looking at a peer. Given that wine should loosen and broaden one's state of mind, this transposition within the visual matrix is a illustrative demonstration of this transformation, as can be glimpsed in diagram 15, in which Bellerophon would assume the position of I_{x1} on the exterior of the cup and Herakles that of I_{x2} on the interior.[85]

To the degree that viewers imitate a quality of the ideal, then they can be associated with that ideal as part of their social identity.[86] As with the case of the pure spectators, however, there is an inevitable gap between the gods and heroes and ordinary mortals. To identify completely with the figure, to believe that one is Herakles or his equal, is to shatter the separation that spectators so carefully maintain, even when they are catalysts within the narrative picture. Such hubris, whether manifested in conversation or in other actions, breaks the visual association between the ideal and the viewer within the group gaze. When assuming a mask, the identity is transposed only for the moment, and in reverting to oneself, one must assume the appropriate identity, incorporating but not impersonating the model. A similar situation can be seen in the Amazon of figure 15, in that she as a narrative figure has not simply taken on an attribute, but has become a warrior. Within the Greek imagination this is an extreme act of hubris, crossing gender as well as personal boundaries and creating a dangerous new type, an anti-ideal.

The distinct asymmetry of vision that we have seen contributes to the hierarchical nature of identity in Greek culture. Properly modest women and youths are meant to

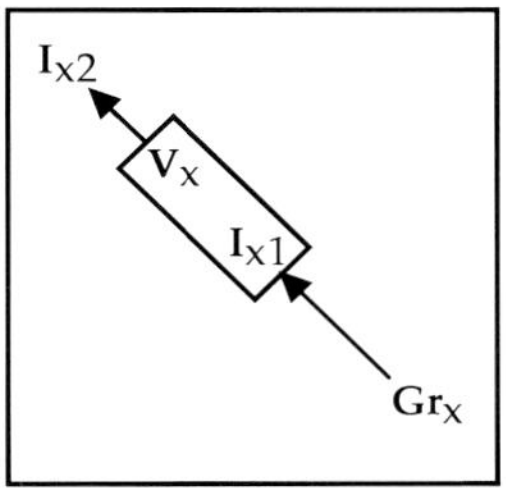

Diagram 15. Conflated Viewing Matrix of Tondo Painting (No Spectators) (author).

be passive in their behavior, turning their glance away from others, especially adult men. For women, the limited circumstances for public viewing are matched by the more limited range of models that exist in art. As spectators, they are fewer in number than males; as ideals they may even be less numerous in the nucleus of narratives than anti-ideal women such as Amazons. The lack of control over their circumstances in the picture is transposed to the lack of control that they have as viewers, and as women within society. As women, they must relate to the ideal indirectly through attachment, rather than becoming. Slaves and servants occupy a similar position, in that they cannot achieve the ideal, nor is their place even accounted among the range of spectators except when involved with the nucleus as catalysts. Their position in the visual matrix is unaccounted, and perhaps even lower than that of women because they do not have the potential for association with the ideal through marriage or family relationship.

For youthful males, there are fewer limitations and far more positive ideals are held up before them, and the value of the model as something into which they will transform in the future as they mature is a promise that their secondary status is temporary and can be resolved through their personal action. For them, it is possible to transform themselves into the ideal.

For adult men, however, the situation is somewhat different. Their glance is not only one that sees the ideal as a model to emulate, but is also one that possesses what it sees. Thus, a youthful ideal serves a double function for men, one that immortalizes their accomplishments in a beautiful and supple form and another that brings to their eye a potential *eromenos*. Their glance is not restricted, and in the visual matrix we have to recognize that alone of all the components, adult men have the greatest potential for returning the gaze back on the group. Thus, the asymmetry of vision allows an adult man not only to transpose himself upon the ideal, but to transpose spectators and members of the group into a possessive glance. By this shift in the matrix, men are ensconced at the top of the visual and social hierarchy, while youths and women occupy lesser positions according to the scope of their vision and identity.

With this general framework of the viewing experience in mind, we will turn our attention in the next chapters to more specific circumstances for civic and gender identification in archaic Athens. The relationship of viewing subject and viewed object described in this chapter becomes concrete in civic and religious ritual performances in Athens, where real spectators watch choral and other performances, and we will see that spectators not only model the viewing of a vase, but the viewing of civic ritual that embodies the performers and audience as Athenian.

FOUR

RITUAL PERFORMANCE, SPECTATORS, AND IDENTITY

Returning to the shoulder of the Minneapolis amphora (figure 19), we can see that the spectators serve to model the glance of the individual viewer and the collective gaze of a group. They affirm the status of the warriors as models of behavior, and an identity that the viewer can assume by successfully appropriating some characteristic of the warriors. This transpositioning of the viewer to the warriors links the individual and the ideal in the eyes of the group, so that the gaze of the spectators mirrors the gaze of the group, and formulates an identity for the subject/viewer. As we saw in the previous chapter, a psychoanalytic approach to viewing and identification finds some validity in Greek theories of vision, but psychoanalysis remains a nonhistorical approach and does not begin to explain the specific role that spectators have in archaic Attic vase-painting.[1] In order to ground the study of spectators historically, we must look at the Athenian social context.

To do this, we can look further at the picture and note the rather symmetrical arrangement of the spectators. Although conceptually they can be seen as one corner of a viewing matrix, the composition also meets the requirement of rhythmically filling up the surfaces of the long registers. One could look at the spectators as filling motifs that also direct the viewer's attention toward the main action, their symmetry emphasizing their formal qualities at the expense of their role as participants. In addition to their compositional arrangement, their dress and gestures are very stylized and composed, suggesting little sense of individuality and a static relationship to the action in the center of the picture. From a formal point of view, then, one can see the spectators as devices that fill up the picture surface and focus attention on the narrative.

This symmetry and formality, however, suggest an alternative approach to the spectators. Looking at the figures in terms of the picture composition and space, one can see that the spectators have two potential relationships to the figures in the nucleus. From a two-dimensional or planar point of view, the spectators form two lines of figures

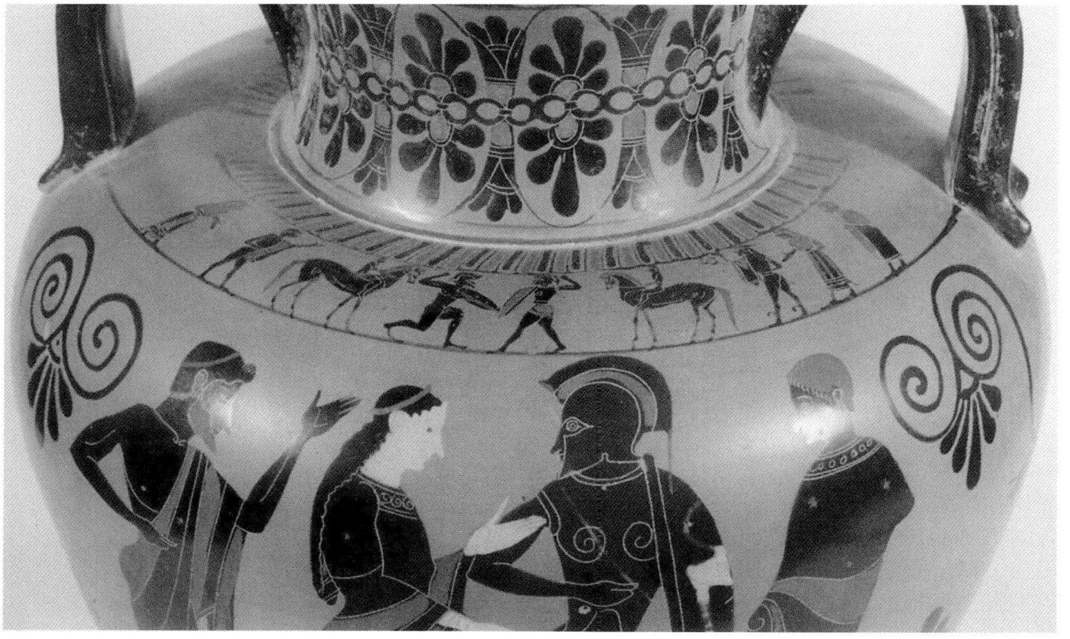

19. Attic black-figure amphora, attributed to the Painter of Vatican 359, c. 530. Side B: Detail of shoulder: warriors fighting. Minneapolis Institute of Arts, Ethel Morrison Van Derlip Fund, 57.1. (Photograph, The Minneapolis Institute of Arts)

that are converging toward the center from opposite sides. If we imagine a more three-dimensional space and a more elevated point of view, we could also see the spectators as surrounding a central space, either forming the ends of a semi-circle themselves or points on a transect of rings of figures surrounding the combat. We can see such an arrangement more clearly on the interior of a cup in Tarquinia that shows Herakles struggling with Triton in the center, and around the edge of the cup, a line of Nereids holding hands forms a circle and rotates around the central medallion (figure 20).[2] The Nereids are seen as performing a dance, perhaps accompanied by song, such as one might have seen performed during public festivals. They therefore serve as an index for the choruses of young women who would perform songs before the city's population about heroes and gods in public festivals. This is not to say that the spectators on the Minneapolis amphora are a literal snapshot or diagram or representation of a chorus, but that their visual qualities, especially their symmetry and configuration, mirror the formal patterns created by choral groups.

Whereas the previous chapter focused upon the individual viewer's identification with the spectator, here we focus more upon the context and construction of social identity. Ritual and public performance were important elements of Athenian social and political life, and played key roles in the formation of social identity. Following

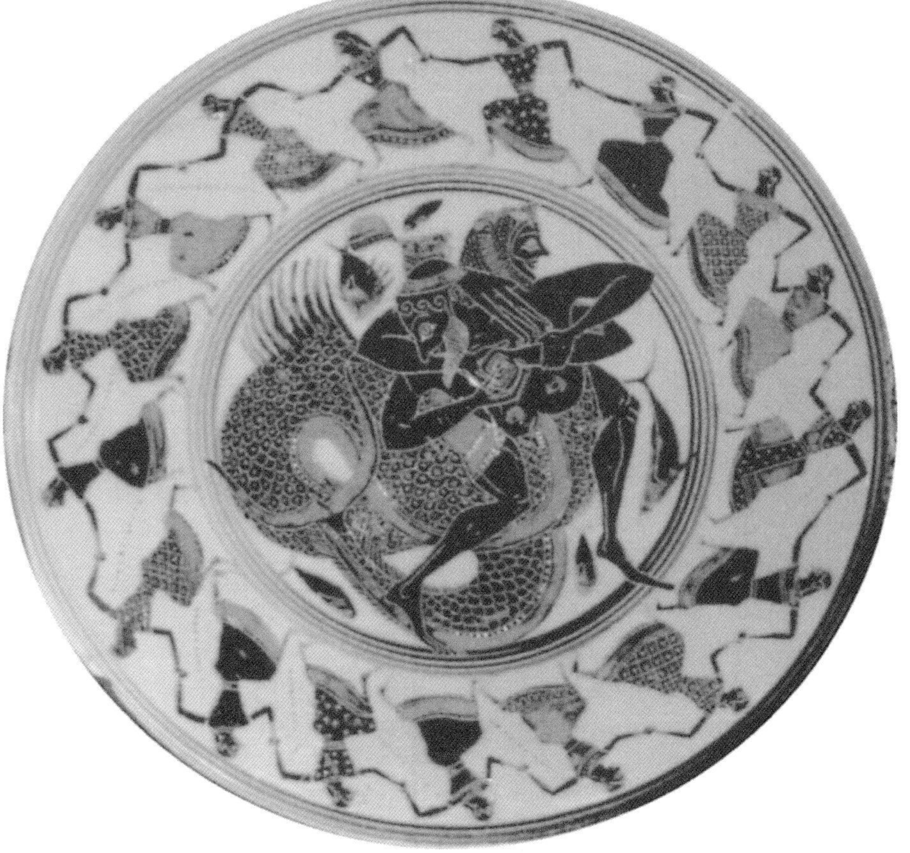

20. Attic black-figure Little Master lip cup attributed to the Xenokles Group, c. 550. Interior: Herakles and Triton. Tarquinia, Museo Nazionale Tarquiniese RC4194. (Photograph, Nimatallah/Art Resource, NY)

an overview of archaic Athenian ritual, we will then examine aspects of ritual theory that point out its dynamic social role, and some characteristics of choral poetry and performance in archaic Greece. Finally, we return to the spectators on vases and examine them as models for the ritual construction of civic identity in Athens, reflecting the relationships of viewer and spectator, of participant and observer, of ritual and citizenship, and of myth and social behavior.

4.1 RITUAL IN ARCHAIC ATHENS

We can begin by looking at a remarkable incident recorded by Herodotos about Peisistratos, who established a tyranny in Athens in 546 that lasted until the expulsion of his son and successor, Hippias, in 510, followed by the establishment of a new democratic constitution in 508/7.[3] Following his military triumph over Megara in the early 560s, Peisistratos had attempted in 561 to install himself in power on the Acropolis by a ruse, faking an attack on himself in order to obtain a guard of club-bearers or enforcers, only to be subsequently expelled by Megakles and Lycurgus.[4] Later in the 550s, having formed an alliance with his former opponent, Megakles, Peisistratos organized a different manner for installing himself in power a second time. Herodotos describes the details of the incident:[5]

> There was in the deme of Paeania a woman called Phya, and in stature she was but three fingers short of four cubits, and beautiful besides. They fitted her with full armor, put her on a chariot, arranged her pose so that she would appear at her most striking, and drove her into the city. They had sent heralds to run ahead of them, and these, when they arrived, spoke as they had been ordered: 'Men of Athens, receive with good will Pisistratus, whom Athena herself, having honored him above all mankind, is bringing back from exile to her own Acropolis.' So the heralds went about, saying these things, and the word immediately spread through the demes that Athena was bringing Pisistratus back. The people in the city believed that this woman was the goddess herself and offered prayers to her, for all that she was only human, and they welcomed Pisistratus.

Herodotos recounts this story as the silliest trick that history records and counter to the normally intelligent and critical political behavior of the Athenians, making them, for the moment, simpletons.

Indeed, the story has its incredible aspects, but rather than simply looking at it on a literal level and questioning its credibility, one should consider it contextually, as R. Sinos has done.[6] It is clear from the passage that Peisistratos was working in coordination with Megakles and others to prepare for his return to power, and it is therefore probable that support had been coordinated inside the city beforehand to achieve a bloodless coup. As Sinos argues convincingly, it is helpful to look at the story as a ritual performance rather than as a direct exercise of power. Peisistratos and his allies were suggesting that he was associated with the goddess, and was honored by her for his actions. His piety was the idea that was being promoted here, and that Athena endorsed his claim to power. The return with Phye is clearly organized like a ritual: The event is proclaimed in advance; the character of the participants is set apart from the ordinary; there was a prescribed text and set of objects used for the enactment; a large group of people is mobilized to witness; a response was solicited (and probably at least partly prepared by planted supporters) from the spectators. As Sinos points out, the use of a chariot was familiar to Athenians from wedding and other rituals, so that the structure of this performance was based upon the social and religious instincts of the Athenians. Peisistratos's success in reinstalling himself in power by these means is not so much a tribute to the gullibility of the Athenians as to their consent to an orchestrated change in power that was enacted in the ritualized return of Peisistratos.

The political use of ritual by Peisistratos points to its broader importance and appeal in sixth-century Athens. In spite of the limited evidence about archaic choral ritual in Athens itself, it is clear that the sixth century was a period of great change and developments in religious practices in the city.[7] At the beginning of the century, there was political and social turmoil along with economic enslavement that led to the appointment of Solon as archon in 594/3. He instituted a wide range of reforms concerning debts and land and created four new categories of citizens on the basis of wealth as the criterion for holding public office.[8] As P. B. Manville has described it, Solon also saw to it that "certain sacrifices, public feasts, and worship were for the first time authorized for the shared benefit of all Athenians."[9] Although the specific connection of Solon to any specific cult is tenuous, it would appear that he made some effort to reform ritual practice to be more civically inclusive than it had been earlier.[10]

There is archaeological and artistic evidence that there was a distinct growth in the number and splendor of Athenian sanctuaries during the middle quarters of the sixth century and an explosion of divine representations on Attic pottery, as H. A. Shapiro has shown in his study of art and cult in Athens.[11] The most important changes were the reorganization of the Panathenaic festival in 566/5. The details of this reorganization are few and late, but the implication is that the existing Panathenaic cult was expanded greatly in scale as well as in the variety of its activities.[12] Athletic contests were held, and the earliest Panathenaic amphorae, which held the prize oil for the victors, date to around 560, confirming the later textual tradition.[13] The institution of games at Athens follows closely in time the reorganization of the Pythian, Isthmian, and Nemean games between 586 and 573, and would seem to have been intended to rival these pan-Hellenic shrines and raise the reputation of Athens. The Panathenaic reorganization also followed the victory of Athens over Megara in their dispute over Salamis, a struggle that had continued through much of the early part of the sixth century.[14] As Shapiro concludes: "The institution of the Greater Panathenaia in 566 would have proclaimed Athens' emergence as a leading commercial and military power in Greece, under the protection (one might say 'aegis') of a city goddess whose own inclination was toward handicrafts and war."[15]

The architectural and artistic transformation of the Acropolis was a concrete visualization of Athens' emergence and an expression of Athenian civic pride and identity. Although there seems to have been a temple to Athena on the Acropolis in the later seventh century, around 560, the Athenians built a more monumental stone temple with decorated pediments.[16] Another temple, whether or not replacing the earlier building, was erected during the last quarter of the sixth century. Along with these large buildings, the entrance to and space of the Acropolis were reorganized. Small, treasury-like buildings with relief sculpture were constructed, although their location remains uncertain; Athenians dedicated large numbers of freestanding statues and other votives at the sanctuary during the last half of the sixth century. The result of this architectural and artistic transformation would have been to make the Acropolis into a far more visually impressive religious and civic center in 500 than it had been around 600.

The Panathenaic amphorae themselves are a concrete manifestation of this emerging civic identity. They were commissioned in large numbers by the city and had a relatively standardized and distinctive shape.[17] Their decoration, too, was consistent from festival to festival, showing a picture of a striding, armed Athena before a column on the obverse and a picture of an athletic competition on the reverse. It is interesting to note, for our discussion, that the vases are inscribed TON ATHENETHEN ATHLON, "from the games at Athens." This inscription, combined with the distinctive shape of the vase and its image of the city goddess, effectively brands the games as Athenian and serves to promote visually the identity, piety, and prestige of the city all at once.[18] The amphorae represent a self-conscious desire of the Athenians to demonstrate their piety in their ritual practice and the appearance of its objects, and to use their festivals to promote their identity as Athenians.

The Panathenaia was not the only festival that underwent change during the sixth century. C. Sourvinou-Inwood reconstructs a parallel, slightly later growth for the City Dionysia, the purpose of which was to recreate the initial resistance and then proper acceptance of the cult of Dionysos in Athens.[19] In its early stages, it involved the movement of the statue of the god to the *prytaneion* in the Old Agora, located somewhere on the east side of the Acropolis, preceded by ritual dining and then followed by choral hymns and a sacrifice.[20] This ritual was probably in place by the 530s, if not earlier, and by the end of the sixth century had expanded to include dithyrambic competitions among choruses of men and boys organized by the Kleisthenic tribes.[21]

In addition, the hymns were expanded to feature a narrative performed by the *hypokrites*, speaking in his own person, and the chorus, the earliest stage of proto-tragedy. According to Aristotle, tragedy had "an improvisational origin, which is true of both tragedy and comedy, the first starting from the leaders of the dithyramb" and then being enhanced by the introduction of actors and the reduction of the choral parts.[22] It would seem, then, that tragedy grew out of choral lyric as part of the ritual of the City Dionysia, and that this evolution began during the sixth century and continued into the fifth.[23] The importance of tragedy for the identity of democratic, classical Athens is beyond the scope of our interest here, and it is impossible to sort out the exact details of how this change took place given that the earliest extant tragedy comes from the fifth century.[24]

The point is that choral ritual and performance were not static in sixth-century Athens, but rather were a flexible and dynamic part of its archaic culture and were important for the formation of civic identity. Young men of 16 were introduced and registered at the festival of the Apatouria into their phrateries, the regional groupings of households sharing cults and recognizing births and marriages that existed before the Solonian reforms.[25] At 18, they were registered with the polis as ephebes and began to take on their role as warriors able to defend the city. At the City Dionysia, there was a special procession of ephebes who brought the statue of the god into the theater, a military parade or performance, and then, at least after 508 if not before, choral performances by both ephebes and adult males, making the City Dionysia an important collection of the initiation rituals that marked a partial transition to adult status.[26] It is likely that aspects of these rituals extend back into the sixth century and were adapted to meet the new political organization of the democratic city.[27]

This pattern of Athenian ritual broadly conforms to that for other Greek cities, but there were some apparent differences. The spatial configuration of ritual in Athens, for example, was concentrated in the city itself; elsewhere there was a centrifugal movement from the city to the country that F. de Polignac shows was the more typical pattern of the Greek polis.[28] As he speculates, this difference may be a result of the belief in the autochthonous origins of the citizens of Athens – that is, that the Athenians were indigenous to the land of Attica and had a common set of ancestors, unlike the traditions of migration reflected in the myths of other cities.[29] There may also be a political dimension to this proliferation of sanctuaries in the city, in that during the second half of the sixth century Peisistratos organized cults and shrines inside the city that duplicated those in the surrounding rural areas in an effort to reconcile city and countryside.[30] However, one should not overemphasize the political motivation behind Athenian cult activity at the expense of its civic motivation, because there seems to be an indication of continuous investment in cult activities throughout Attica during this period that is distinctly Attic and not just Peisistratid in its motivation, as R. Osborne has argued.[31] Whatever the causes and shape, this focus of Athenian ritual on Athens and Attica would have had the effect of making ritual performance a highly visible part of the activity of the urban environment in Athens. The splendor of the processions and performances would therefore be a reflection of the city and, as A. Kavoulaki reminds us, Athenians in the classical period, such as Plato, Aristophanes, and Xenophon, felt that they had acquired a particular reputation in the Greek world for the magnificence of their festivals.[32]

There are some other differences between Athenian ritual and that of other Greek cities. Both women and men played a role in the public rituals of Athens, but the role of women may have been smaller in scale in Athens than in Sparta or elsewhere.[33] The two partially surviving *parthenoi* songs by Alkman both name individual women before the public, but the later traditions of Athens, including the funerary oration of Perikles, suggest that such naming and attention would have been undesirable in Athens.[34] Although women were associated with the funerary lament widely in Greek culture, in Athens, their funerary role was severely limited by the legislation of Solon, as described in Plutarch's biography.[35] Women's participation was limited to the house and the graveside, and not the funerary procession, perhaps the most publicly visible part of the ritual; the number of participants and their behavior were to be as modest and orderly as possible. This regulatory spirit apparently extended to festivals as well as funerals. This restriction and emphasis on decorum was likely the custom in the City Dionysia, about which Sourvinou-Inwood speculates that women would have participated in the reception of the statue of the god and subsequent sacrifices, the "'establishment of order' nexus" of the ritual, but not in the later *komos*, a more boisterous type of singing and dancing performance that may have included masks and was associated with a symposion.[36]

There is evidence that Peisistratos and other politicians were aware of the potential for ritual and cult in furthering their agenda. As we saw earlier, Peisistratos essentially turned to ritual activity and forms to proclaim his second entry into Athens with Phye/Athena in a chariot and to obtain the consent of the Athenian polity. Following his role in securing victory over Megara for the possession of Salamis, he is given credit in one source for instituting at least the athletic competitions in the Panathenaic festival, a good five years before his first attempt to seize power in 561/0.[37] The extent of the Panathenaic reforms, however, probably meant that a number of individuals, including the archon Hippokleides, were involved in various aspects of the festival. Even earlier, Solon himself may have used a public setting to urge, through a poem, the renewal of Athens's struggle against Megara over Salamis.[38] Because, at the time, such a public advocacy was proscribed, Solon feigned madness and, according to Plutarch's sources, donned a herald's cap and rushed into the Old Agora to recite his poem. As E. Stehle argues, the poem, which starts with an individual voice, shifts to a call for civic action like other public poetry, especially choral. If the poem were indeed performed in public, although perhaps not precisely as recounted in Plutarch, it would suggest that a theatrical performance of politics á la Peisistratos was not unexpected in archaic Athens.[39]

Although Peisistratos's ambition for power was counter to Solon's efforts at civic reform, the efforts of both figures were focused on forging a conception of the city and its citizens as based, in the words of I. Morris, on the "conception of restraint and good sense."[40] Both Morris and Kurke have described this development of a "middling culture," with its notions of "equity, justice, moderation, and even misogyny," a culture that emphasized the virtues of *sophrosyne* (wisdom) and *aidos* (modesty). Ritual, with its emphasis on civic participation and acquiescence, was a primary means for achieving this transformation of Athenian culture, in contrast to the elite culture of the aristocracy.

To conclude, Athens in the sixth century saw a transformation from a small, socially distressed town into, in the words of Shapiro, "the urban center of one of the largest *poleis* in Greece. This brought with it a steady increase in population, in material wealth, and in a spiritual need for diverse cults and the kind of festivals that, though also a part of rural life, could only achieve a degree of real splendor in a pan-Hellenic sanctuary of a large city."[41] Ritual processions and performances in transformed civic spaces and sanctuaries were the embodiment of this aspiring civic identity and were an important part of the fabric of social life.

Before turning our attention to the ritualistic dimension of spectator vases, we should consider more broadly the role of ritual in shaping civic identity.

4.2 RITUAL THEORY

The study of ritual, its texts, objects, and space as a way of studying archaic culture, has become more prevalent in the past two decades. As Dougherty and Kurke recognized in their two compilations of essays, the divisions between language, literature, religion, politics, and art that we frequently find in studies of Greek civilization are artificial, particularly for the archaic period.[42] They point to the importance of cultural anthropology for the study of the archaic period, in particular, the work of C. Geertz and M. Sahlins. Using the term coined by S. Greenblatt, they look to a "cultural poetics" to signify an interdisciplinary study of text, object, and context, viewing the poem or work of art as a product of a culture as well as an individual. As Greenblatt's work attests, this approach is important in looking at works of art not merely as aesthetic objects, but rather as "the interpretive constructions the members of a society apply to their experiences."[43] His study, directed at Renaissance English literature, focuses particularly on the idea of the self-fashioning of identity, the construction of "a distinctive personality, a characteristic address to the world, a consistent mode of perceiving and behaving." Looking at individual accounts of this process provides access to the broader cultural patterns for social identification.

Cultural poetics is important as a complement to a psychoanalytic approach to identity because it looks at the group and how its members constitute a social structure and a collective identity. Politics, economics, and religion provide a framework of beliefs and institutions in which individuals situate themselves, but it is through the engagement in common activities that social identification is developed. Ritual, in particular, is one common and powerful way in which the different members of a group are bonded together. The psychoanalytic view of ritual looks at it and religion as essentially codifying the conflicts and repressions experienced by the individual as social taboos.[44] Ritual, however, is a much more fluid and dynamic activity that can meet a variety of social needs. To see the effectiveness and importance of ritual and its contribution to the formation of social identity, we need to take a more anthropological approach. In this section, we will look at the work of Geertz, Sahlins, and C. Bell to highlight aspects of their approaches to ritual, not as fixed and timeless scripts, but as organic and dynamic social practices that change with the fabric of society.[45]

Geertz advanced fundamental reasons for the relevance of ritual for the study of society in his collection of essays, *The Interpretation of Culture*. He begins by arguing in favor of G. Ryle's "thick description" of ritual – that is, one that encompasses the background and cultural context of the actions performed, rather than simply describing the winks, twitches, and nods of the participants as if these were the critical elements of ritual.[46] Geertz points out that the question to ask is what the import of the ritual is, not what is its typology or surface appearance. Analysis cannot simply be a description or classification of physical actions, for this says nothing about their meaning or importance, or how they differ depending on the context in which they are performed. The analysis of ritual must look at it as a system of signs that interact with one another within a specific context in order to understand its meaning. As Geertz elaborates:[47]

> As we are to deal with meaning, let us begin with a paradigm: vis., that sacred symbols function to synthesize a people's ethos – the tone, character,

> and quality of their life, its moral and aesthetic style and mood – and their world view – the picture they have of the way things in sheer actuality are, their most comprehensive ideas of order.

Speaking more broadly about the public nature of ritual or cultural acts, Geertz states that these are a model of reality, as well as a model for reality: "culture patterns have an intrinsic double aspect: they give meaning, that is, objective conceptual form, to social and psychological reality both by shaping themselves to it and by shaping it to themselves."[48] He goes on to define two aspects of ritual that structure this relationship: motivations and moods. Motivations are "liabilities to perform particular classes of act or have particular classes of feelings," that is, the actions that people perform. Moods are the feelings and responses brought on by the motivations. Culture, then, consists of the actions performed by the society, the motivations, which engender meaning for the members of society through the moods they create. Thus ritual provides a model for reality, articulating the actions and relationships that structure society, and become a model for reality for the individual in terms of how she or he undertakes a role in that society.

Geertz goes on to discuss the use of imagery in ritual, in the sense of actions or objects as signs that create a meaning for those who undertake or observe them: "In a ritual, the world as lived and the world as imagined, fused under the agency of a single set of symbolic forms, turn out to be the same world, producing thus that idiosyncratic transformation in one's sense of reality."[49] The forms and signs of ritual, their enactments, and their manifestation as objects or images, do not only represent what people believe, but also offer a model for how to believe and act upon their beliefs. Thus, religion helps shape the social order, particularly by means of the moral code it conveys. Symbols or signs are a particularly powerful means for encoding this process, as Geertz explains:[50]

> Such religious symbols, dramatized in rituals or related in myths, are felt somehow to sum up, for those for whom they are resonant, what is known about the way the world is, the quality of the emotional life it supports, and the way one ought to behave while in it. Sacred symbols thus relate an ontology and a cosmology to an aesthetics and a morality: their peculiar power comes from their presumed ability to identify fact with value at the most fundamental level, to give to what is otherwise merely actual, a comprehensive normative import.

By moving beyond the surface forms to the underlying context, ritual provides an opportunity to interrogate a culture and to reveal its social structure and beliefs: "belief and particularly ritual reinforce the traditional social ties between individuals; it stresses the way in which the social structure of a group is strengthened and perpetuated through the ritualistic or mythic symbolization of the underlying social values upon which it rests."[51]

Geertz argues that ritual analysis must be done within a historical framework in that the weakness of earlier studies of ritual was to treat it in a nonhistorical and timeless fashion as a means for promoting or indoctrinating a positive pattern of behavior and belief, ignoring the disruptive or disconnected aspects that ritual can sometimes acquire.[52] This need to include a historical framework in the analysis of ritual is developed further by M. Sahlins in his studies of Pacific Islands cultures, particularly Hawaii. In his work, *Historical Metaphors and Mythical Realities*, Sahlins maintains that the tendency of semiotics to analyze a sign in terms of a fixed referent and by its structural relationship to other signs ignores the changing and contemporary nature of social relationships.[53] Under the pressure of actual events, the referent of a sign can shift and be applied to a new situation, and by doing so alter the meaning of the sign. For example, when Captain Cook arrived at the Hawaiian Islands in 1778, his appearance coincided with the Makahiki festival that marked the appropriation of the island by the god Lono. Cook's actions evoked associations between him and Lono in the eyes of the Hawaiians, and, as Sahlins explains, the subsequent actions of Cook departed from the ritual norm and led to his death, itself paralleling the ritual death of Lono.[54] The point is that the appearance of Cook altered the social and cultural equation, and created a discord between the ritual structure and the contemporary situation that prompted changes.

The rituals of the Hawaiians were in one dimension a reenactment of history. The living became the gods and heroes by performing the events of that history: "Mythical incidents constitute archetypal situations. The experiences of celebrated mythical protagonists are re-experienced by the living in analogous circumstances. More, the living *become* mythical heroes."[55] The categories and relationships between individuals and groups that the ceremonies describe justified the social structure of Hawaiian society and the hierarchical relationship of the ruling elite to the commoners, and of men to women.[56] The coming of Cook altered the social dynamic by introducing the Europeans as another variable, changing the relationship between and within the social groups. The meaning of the rituals that were performed was thus transformed to reflect the changed situation; they continued to establish a hierarchical relationship between groups, but differently than before. As Sahlins summarizes, when events do not conform to system categories, the categories are revalued and redefined.[57] Thus, there is a constant interplay between the structure of the ritual and practical circumstances that changes the sense, or meaning, or the sign (the ritual or object). The source of this inflection in the sense of a sign is the actor's *interest*, and the sign's place "in an oriented scheme of means and ends." The interest of the actor in the ritual or sign can strengthen the sign when aligned with its sense, or can shift its meaning when it diverges. Ritual, then, is not a static system, but a dynamic and historical process that both shapes and responds to current situations.

More recently, C. Bell articulated an approach to ritual theory that seeks to identify the underlying structures of ritual theory and to create a new synthesis that emphasizes the immediacy of ritual within society. She argues that much of ritual theory, including the work of Geertz, is built upon a system of dichotomies.[58] The first of these divides thought from action, so that for a religious system, beliefs are separated from actions such as rituals, making rituals a discrete object of study. The second assumption of the models is that it is through ritual that thought and action are reintegrated. Geertz sets up a third dichotomy, that ritual participants act, whereas those who observe think, thus reintroducing the schism between action and thought, ritual and belief. As Bell notes,[59]

> This type of expedient logic carries another inevitable corollary, however. That is, theories of ritual that attempt to integrate thought and action in any guise simultaneously function to maintain their differentiation. This type of discourse on ritual not only constructs a model that integrates a thinking observer and an acting actor; it simultaneously functions to distinguish them clearly.

Such dichotomies also set up a hierarchy between the two components, so that ritual becomes a tool. This leads to assumptions about the purpose of ritual as a means of social control.[60] Ritual theorists differ on how ritual achieves this, but Bell identifies four main lines of thought. Ritual can control through social solidarity by promoting consensus among the participants and social values. Alternatively, ritual can channel conflicts through rites of rebellion, a catharsis that vents dissent and promotes social consensus. A third thesis is that of repression, whereby ritual controls the "chaotic and aggressive impulses" of humanity into rituals that allow for "ordered social life."[61] Finally, ritual is viewed as defining reality, a "symbolic modeling of the social order," that encodes social patterns in the participants and thereby achieves social order. The common problem with viewing ritual as a tool for social control is that it only works in closed and hierarchical societies and assumes that ritual is fixed in its form. However, as Bell explains,[62]

> studies give evidence for the ambiguity and instability of beliefs and symbols as well as the inability of ritual to control by virtue of any consensus on shared beliefs. They also suggest that ritualized activities specifically do not promote belief or conviction. On the contrary, ritualized practices afford a great diversity of interpretation in exchange for little more than consent to the form of the activities.

Thus, action and belief do not have to be integrated in ritual, and participation does not necessarily involve full belief or internalization of the values of a dominant class by all of the participants.

Bell suggests a shift in thinking about ritual, that "ritualization is first and foremost a strategy for the construction of certain types of power relationships effective within particular social organizations."[63] She distinguishes between ideology and physical force as exercises of power, noting that ideology is a strategy that expressly seeks to avoid using physical force and that does not require belief, so much as consent from its participants. This is a much looser sense of control, one that allows for individual disagreements on specific principles or policies while signaling a tacit acknowledgment of the social structure articulated by the ideology. Thus ritual becomes a process of negotiation rather than imposition.

We can begin to see how ritual works by defining it as the "differentiation or privileging of particular activities," rather than a rigid and timeless script.[64] There is no formula as to how this takes place, and elements of ritual can consist of place, timing, access, a structured mode of expression, and code of signs. Ritual, then, is a way of acting that is very formalized, but it is important for its efficacy that it must also be somewhat "instinctive" or "natural" to the participants, based on their beliefs or customs. Ritual uses its distinctiveness to articulate or constitute the relationships among the participants. This more fluid definition accommodates the responsive potential of ritual to changing historical or social circumstances.

Bell identifies two dimensions to ritualization's process of constructing these relationships. The first is the actions of the social group in a structured environment. An effective ritual draws upon the participants' socialized instincts:[65]

> Within the intricacies of this objectification and embodiment lies the ability of ritualization to create social bodies in the image of relationships of power, social bodies that are these very relationships of power. If it is at all accurate to say that ritualization controls – by modeling, defining, molding, and so on – it is this type of control that must be understood.

The second dimension of the process shows the tenuous nature of this control: "the ritual construction of power, however, involves dynamics whereby the power relations constituted by ritualization also empower those who may at first appear to be controlled by them."[66] Consent through participation is a real demonstration of the social structure and distribution of power, but the reasons for consent can be varied. Consent can mean complete belief, but it can also be based on the advantages of acquiescence through meeting material or social needs. This means that the individual participant may appropriate aspects of the ritual that provide a personal benefit, but may maintain opinions or beliefs that may not align completely with the leaders and sponsors of the ritual. For efficacy, the divergence between individual interest and social ideology should be narrow, and ritual is most effective as a social strategy in a relatively circumscribed and homogeneous setting. In a time of strong dissent, ritual can become ineffective, or can be co-opted into an instrument for change and for renegotiating the structures of a society.

The following passages summarize Bell's view of ritual:[67]

> As a strategic embodiment of schemes for power relationships – schemes that hierarchize, integrate, define, or obscure – ritualization can promote social solidarity. It can promote solidarity particularly in a fairly homogenous group with general recognition of key symbols, where a sense of unity can be achieved through consent to the forms, and where most subgroups benefit in some way from the simultaneous integration and differentiation of the social

> order. This is not a matter of simply reinforcing shared beliefs or instilling a dominant ideology . . . [but includes the] production of ritualized agents, persons who have an instinctive knowledge of these schemes embedded in their bodies, in their sense of reality, and in their understanding of how to act in ways that both maintain and qualify the complex microrelations of power. Such practical knowledge is not an inflexible set of assumptions, beliefs, or body postures; rather, it is the ability to deploy, play, and manipulate basic schemes in ways that appropriate and condition experience effectively. It is a mastery that experiences itself as relatively empowered, not as conditioned or molded.

F. G. Naerebout developed this type of model for ritual in the study of ancient Greek dance.[68] Naerebout's model, based on dance scholarship, focuses on "public events," including religious rituals. Such public events require mobilization, bringing the people into the public sphere to witness the event. Public events are also a process of communication, in which "human beings intentionally and effectively share messages and meanings."[69] Public events also contain performances, processions, songs, and dances; these are "the main venue for telling 'the story that the participants tell about themselves.'"[70]

We can see how this works by turning back to Peisistratos's second return to power, entering into Athens on a chariot with Phye dressed as Athena. The heralds had earlier proclaimed the coming event, mobilizing the citizens to gather in public to see the arrival of Peisistratos. The performance by Phye and Peisistratos embodied, through its actions, the idea that Peisistratos was favored by the goddess because of his piety. The effectiveness of this message is seen in the response of the crowd, who join in the proclamation. However, as Naerebout points out, mobilization does not imply full conversion to belief in Peisistratos or to unquestioning acceptance of Phye as Athena. For it to be effective, the performance will have to be repeated or renewed.[71] Indeed, Peisistratos was later expelled a second time from Athens and for his third, successful return to power in 546 he used a military force, rather than ritual, as his instrument of change. Still, we can see in this story the nature of ritual as a dynamic process for creating social bonding and identity, one that enhances civic prestige. Ritual is not simply a hollow script, but is an embodiment and projection of the social fabric and identity within the city.

With this in mind, we can look at the structure and performance of religious rituals as preserved in some archaic poetry and other testimony, which will, in turn, suggest parallels to the role of spectators within Attic vase painting.

4.3 CHORAL PERFORMANCE IN ARCHAIC GREECE

The dynamic model of ritual presented by Bell, Sahlins, and Geertz fits well in the circumstances of archaic Greece generally, as Naerebout's work has demonstrated.

With the emergence of the polis beginning in the late Geometric period, there was a rapid growth in sacred spaces and enclosures throughout Greece that featured larger and more impressively decorated temples and the development of subsidiary buildings.[72] By the beginning of the sixth century, stone was an increasingly common building material and would become the main building material, providing a platform for an expansion of relief sculpture decorating entablatures and pediments. Gifts to sanctuaries began to increase in number and cost in the late eighth century, and by the early sixth century, athletic contests were reorganized at the major pan-Hellenic shrines. Concurrent with this growth in religious spaces was a flourishing of choral poetry for performances at festivals and rites.[73] It is this last aspect of cultic growth that we will examine briefly as a context for viewing spectators on vase paintings.

Very little archaic choral poetry itself survives intact, but there are fragments and some later descriptions that permit us to view the broad outline of choral performance in the Greek city. It is important to emphasize that choral poetry was public and communal in its character, and was meant to be sung by groups before a large civic audience. The size of a chorus and the number of choruses varied, but could range up to 20 choirs, half men and half youths, of 50 members each, following the political reorganization of Athens under Kleisthenes in the last decade of the sixth century. Choruses were organized according to age and gender into groups of young women (parthenoi), young men (ephebes), older men, older women, and children, each of which would perform before the members of the polis.[74] As Plato notes in the *Laws*:[75]

> First, then, the right order of procedure will be for the Muses' choir of children to come forward first to sing these things with the utmost vigour and before the whole city; second will come the choir of those under thirty, invoking Apollo Paian as witness of the truth of what is said, and praying him of his grace to persuade the youth. The next singers will be the third choir, of those over thirty and under sixty . . . "

As this passage shows, the choirs perform before the entire city, requiring a large public space such as a sanctuary or agora. Further, the performance of one group is affirmed in the performance of another group, in that the second chorus of youth acknowledges the truth of the children's theme or message in the course of their song to Apollo, and it is likely that affirmations from the crowd would be an expected part of the performance.[76] The songs of the last choir, made up of fully adult members of the community, would affirm the words of both earlier choruses but, "being the best element in the State, – that which by age and judgment alike is the most influential it contains, – so that by singing its noblest songs it might do the most good."[77] Thus, through choral performance, each major age division would manifest the beliefs of the city and its share in them.

A passage from the *Heracleidae* of Euripides presents another picture of choral performance dedicated to Athena, and the gender divisions within the age groups:[78]

We honor the abundant rite
Of yours, and when the month is done,
In sequent song the young and light
Of foot can dance and chant, as one.
While night brings to the windy hill
The pulse of dance, and girls that fill
The dark with reveling.

Here, the young men sing and dance "as one." Their performance, as Calame points out, is confirmed by the *ololugmata* or ritual cry of the young women and their own dance.[79] To achieve this unity and harmony in their singing and dancing, choruses would have been well rehearsed before the festival, creating a common bond before the festival among the performers.

Many festivals would feature such multiple groups performing, and the same type of choral activity could take place at other public occasions such as funerals and weddings. In a fragmentary poem, Sappho describes the celebration in Troy of Hektor's marriage to Andromache, mixing aspects of the imagined Homeric past and contemporary Lesbos. From this, we get a picture of the movement of the groups through the city and their performances:[80]

and there rose
flute's melody sweet with the lyre
the rattle of castanets and shrill the maidens
sang the holy song and it reached bright heaven
eerie sound
and everywhere in the streets
mixing bowls and cups
myrrh and cassia and frankincense blended
and the older women with their alleluias
and all the men chanting the paeon
calling on Apollo his lyre his bright bow
praised Hector and Andromache, praised them as gods

Although describing a marriage celebration rather than a divine festival, the ritual quality is similar in that it involves processions and then performances with musical instruments and voice accompaniment by several groups, each of which represents a different constituency within the city defined by age and gender. The maidens, or *parthenoi*, sing a song to the gods, after which the older women perform a ritual cry that affirms the call of the young women.[81] The older men perform a second song to Apollo that praises the wedded couple, likening them to the gods. The praise of gods and mythological figures confirms these figures as models for identity for the singers, both within the poem and of the poem itself.[82] Indeed, the response of the groups to the wedded pair recalls the acclaim that the heralds and crowd gave to Peisistratos and Phye as they entered Athens in his second bid for power, discussed earlier.

From these testimonia, we can see that choral performance was very much a civic affair and that the performers represented the major constituencies of the polis. Stehle recently studied the context and structure of performances of choral poetry, emphasizing the communal and collective nature of choral performances and how they urged points of view on the participants and audience. Drawing on Plato's *Laws*, she notes that "the choruses represent the lawgiver's strategy for impressing on all the idea that just behavior is equated with happiness. To generalize, once the system is in operation, the chorus functions both to reflect the ideology already affirmed by the community and to model that ideology for the audience."[83] Ritual here, as Bell postulates, is a strategy for embodying the civic structure and social relationships in the polis; its forms develop out of the socialized instincts of the participants and require their consent for its effectiveness. To do this, as Stehle notes, choral poetry featured both reflection and modeling. Reflection looks back in time and draws upon myth to evoke a shared past among the participants, both the performers and the spectators.[84] Indeed, Plato advocates that the rulers of a city will urge or even compel the poet "with his fine and choice language to portray by his rhythms the gestures, and by his harmonies the tunes, of men who are temperate, courageous, and good in all respects, and thereby to compose poems aright."[85] Because the heroes of myth are the ancestors of polis and its citizens, the stories sung by the chorus also serve to confirm the social structures in the present. The behavior and proclamations of the chorus become models for the present and future; by its successful performance, the chorus presents an ideal that the city strives to achieve. Because several of the choruses consist of youth, both female and male, their performances serve to embody in themselves the ideology that they will uphold as adults, and their proclamations, as we saw in the passage from Sappho, are affirmed by the adult members of the community. Thus, past, present, and future are woven together into the choral performance.

The effectiveness of choruses in embodying the ideals and values of the polis is based not just on their performance, but also on the preparation and rehearsal that occurred beforehand. It is here that members of the chorus not only learn to sing and dance, but, according to Plato, learn discipline and harmony.[86] The delight of the chorus members felt in the songs and actions leads to the goal of education for the society, by which the chorus members:[87]

> consent thereunto though having been rightly trained in fitting practices: – this consent, viewed as a whole, is goodness, while the part of it that is rightly trained in respect of pleasures and pains, so as to hate what ought to be hated, right from the beginning up to the very end, and to love what ought to be loved.

A song charms us, holds our attention, and learning it makes us eager to sing and ~~to~~ act. By these means, virtue is instilled in the members of the chorus. It should also be noted that a proper form of action and song is necessary for this education to be effective in shaping the proper role of the chorus member. The enjoyment of "bad postures and tunes" does harm to an individual, and leads to a justification for censorship.[88] Even the rhythmic structure of the song must be appropriate, for even "the Muses would never blunder so far as to assign a feminine tune and gesture to verses composed for men, or to fit the rhythms of captives and slaves to a tune and gestures framed for free men."[89] Choral education, then, encodes social values and behavior into its members, as well as gender identification.

Calame pointed out that much of choral poetry is, in fact, for initiation rituals and:

> aims to confer on the individual, by a more or less lengthy series of rites, full-fledged membership in the community formed by the tribal society. It integrates mainly adolescents, since this type of rite is usually addressed to adolescents, male and female, into the system of institutions and norms that govern the political, social, cultural, and religious life of the adult community.[90]

Initiates are at first separated from the community, trained and instructed in their new public role, and finally reintroduced to the community. During the transitional period, they learn the myths that are important to the community and, through training in song and dance, learn to articulate and embody both the stories and ritual practices. Further, they learn the communal rules of behavior that regulate the polis. Performing the rituals reintroduces them into the society in a new role, and gradually into adult membership. The importance of rites of passage and the existence of choruses of young men and women in rituals of the city can be reflected in the strong tendency of spectators to be youthful in their appearance.

As mentioned before, very little choral poetry survives by which we can see how the performers develop and model an identity before an audience. One important exception is the *Louvre partheneion* of Alkman, a Spartan poet of the late seventh century who composed the poem for performance by a group of young Spartan women at a festival.[91] The beginning fragments of the poem mention Polydeukes and the descendants of Hippokoon. Following a maxim about inappropriate marriages, there would appear to have been a second myth recounted, perhaps also concerning a marriage. Given that the poem is written for performance by young maidens, the use of myth and genealogy would appear to provide a model for the appropriate role of marriage and to prescribe the future social role of the *parthenoi* as wives and mothers in Sparta.[92] Such mythical narrations and moralizing lessons would appear to be an important part of choral lyric generally.

Following the evocation of myth, the better-preserved portions of the text switch to the present and to the performers themselves. Here the chorus speaks in the first person, both singular and plural, and this I/we is the voice and sentiments of the chorus, not of the author, being directed to the audience.[93] The chorus sings about two women, Agido, whose connection to them is not completely clear, and the leader of the chorus, Hagesichora:[94]

> And so I sing of the brightness of Agido: I see her like the sun, which Agido summons to shine on us as our witness, but our illustrious choir-leader by no means allows me either to praise or to fault her; for she herself seems pre-eminent, just as if one were to put a horse among grazing herds, a sturdy, thunderous-hoofed prize-winner, one of those seen in rock-sheltered dreams. Why, don't you see? The race-horse is Venetic; but the hair of my cousin Hagesichora has the bloom of undefiled gold, and her silver face – why do I tell you openly? This is Hagesichora here . . .

Because there are ten members of the chorus mentioned in the poem (11 with Hagesichora), the chorus is speaking as a single individual, or "as one." The use of the first person, though, sets up a dialogue with the members of the audience in this part of the poem. In the gnome in the earlier part of the poem, the chorus uses the third person imperative when summarizing the lesson of the mythological story, "Let no man fly to heaven or attempt to marry Aphrodite," addressing the moral lesson to the community, especially the young and marriageable men among them.[95] They address the audience in a different way when singing of Hagesichora, telling them "Why do I tell you openly? This is [her] here," directing them to see for themselves, so that their own eyes and gaze confirm what the chorus sings about her. The opinions of the chorus become a model for those of the community; through their invitation they allow the audience to assume the position and viewpoint of the chorus and to adopt their opinion.[96]

The poem also provides us with a picture of the singers' appearance and performance in self-deprecating terms. In comparing themselves to the ideal embodied in Agido and Hagesichora, they say that their dress and ornament, lavish and formal as they are, do not suffice:[97]

> For abundance of purple is not sufficient for protection, nor intricate snake of solid gold, no, nor Lydian headband, pride of dark-eyed girls . . .

Although they seek the praise of the two women and the blessing of the gods for their singing, still it is inadequate:[98]

> Choir-leader, – if I may speak – I am myself only a girl screeching pointlessly, an owl from a rafter . . .

Although it is not likely that their performance was as bad as they indicate, their self-deprecation has the effect of evoking an ideal of performance that is higher than their own, however high that level may be. They acknowledge that their performance should be worthy of the Muses and uphold the standard of the community.

We should note here a gender distinction in this self-deprecation of the Spartan *parthenoi*. As Stehle concludes, women must speak without a distinctive, affirmative voice, and when they do refer to themselves, it is through negatives about themselves.[99] Boys, on the other hand, assert that their strength will surpass that of present-day men, and come closer to the ideal of the mythic past. The projection of men's strength and agility was an important part of their public display, whereas women were to be desirable but modest.

One additional aspect of general choral performance that needs to be considered is its spatial organization. Typically, the dancers and singers were arranged and moved in a circle as they performed at an altar or shrine, like the Nereids on the Taranto cup seen earlier (figure 20).[100] As the *Homeric Hymn to Aphrodite* recounts, the performers, in this case young women, were surrounded on all sides by the audience:[101]

> Many of us nymphs and much-courted maidens were dancing, and an immense throng encircled us around.

The women themselves would most likely be arranged in a circle within the crowd, and in the center of these concentric circles of audience/viewers and choral performers could also be an object like an altar or other cultic object, or the chorus leader.[102]

There is a second type of spatial configuration for ritual, the procession or *pompe*, which was also used by the chorus and other performers.[103] Many of the songs and dances were performed in open areas of the city, but the performers would arrive at and exit from the performance place in a linear procession and would sing while moving. In many Greek cities, these ritual processions began in the city and moved outward to extra-urban sanctuaries, but the pattern in Athens was to move from the outskirts of the city to the sanctuary within it.[104] For example, as Sourvinou-Inwood reconstructs the early phases of the City Dionysia in Athens from inscriptions and later testimonia, the movement of the statue of Dionysos from the Academy to the *pyrtaneion* in the Old Agora was accompanied with hymns sung both during the procession and at the destination.[105] The movement through the streets of the chorus, arrayed in their best clothing and adornment, distinguished the performers from the normal flow of city traffic, and drew attention to them. This movement is important conceptually, because it made the ritual part of the civic order, tying the areas outside of the sanctuary or agora to the activity within it. In drawing the spectators from their homes to the public areas of the city to witness the performance, the processions connected the activity of the central sites to the more private spaces of the city.[106]

Witnessing a procession or set performance was more than simply a passive act of watching. By participating through their own movement, the processions of both performers and spectators signaled their consent to the ideology of the city and affirmed their identity as members of the polis.[107] The term *theoria*, signifying viewing or being a spectator at a public performance, also implies an act of judgment and membership.[108] The importance of this civic act of witnessing is summarized by Kavoulaki: "The term and practice of *theoria* aligns most closely the aspect of viewing with participation: watching the *heorte* [festival], seeing what was taking place, meant actually participating in the *heorte*."[109] The same terminology also applies to delegations and pilgrimages sent by the city to perform at religious festivities outside of Athens; by sending witnesses, the city asserts its identity.[110] Thus, ritual performance in Athens should be seen as a model for how performing and viewing are intertwined and work collectively to build a collective civic identity. We can use this model of choral performance to look again at the spectators on vases to see how they, too, can embody Athenian identity.

4.4 REFLECTIONS OF RITUAL IN SPECTATORS

The purpose of this discussion of ritual theory and of choral and ritual performance in archaic Greece and Athens has been to establish a contextual background for the appearance of spectators in Attic vase painting. It is significant that spectators do not become a common phenomenon in Attic vase painting until the second quarter of the sixth century, and that the phenomenon continues to develop through the rest of the century. This flourishing of spectator vases corresponds to the period during which we see the reorganization of the Panathenaic festival, the development of the City Dionysia, and, in general, an expansion of both ritual activity and building. It is not possible to link this activity solely to the efforts of Peisistratos and his sons, but their activities show the potential for ritual activity to convey political and social legitimacy.

In turning our attention to spectator vases, we must keep in mind that many of the vessels would have been used in a formal and defined way. Sympotic vessels would be used by members of a small group, cohesive and homogeneous by gender and by social class and ideology, either in a public setting as part of a festival or in a more domestic setting such as a symposion. Such male users would have been part of the social body that either performed or witnessed the public rituals. In either case, the vase needs to be considered as being used at an occasion where the male user's social and public identity would be affirmed in the more intimate activity of the symposion or the *syssiton*, its public counterpart.[111]

Similarly, sympotic vessels could be used for a graveside ritual or as grave goods.[112] Heroization of the dead, either linking them to the mythic past or to models of current excellence such as athletes, would have been an appropriate activity, either visually, in the form of funerary vessels, or verbally, through the threnody, lamentations, and elegies. Here, too, the vessels would have been used by a group collectively, defining social relationships and standing both for the dead and the living. These same factors apply to other vases associated with funerary ritual, such as lekythoi and hydriai.

If we consider that these rituals helped those present to define, through their participation, membership in the polis and their role and position within its social and political structure, then the imagery affirms an ideology. A more private or semi-public ritual such as the symposion or funeral would cement social and family ties, but within a larger public context. In such a setting, one might find not complete agreement over the public ideology, but it would be a place to expect at least a level of consent to its operation and perhaps even a co-opting by the small group of the ideas and values for their own purposes.[113]

Let us begin looking at the spectators as potential reflections of ritualistic practice by examining a Siana cup in New York (figure 21).[114] The nucleus of the image is a duel between two warriors. The six figures to either side are heavily draped in chitons and mantles and stand quietly. The figures are symmetrically arranged, with the outward members of each trio having a mantle with a heavy stripe of red and two dots, and the inner figure a mantle with four dots. The only major discrepancy in the symmetry is that the middle figure on the left has a beard, whereas the other five spectators are beardless youths.

The spectators are arrayed such that we could view them as a chorus singing about a battle. Because the figures face each other across a space, they mimic the arrangement of a chorus in a circle facing inward during performance around a central space.[115] Because their mouths are closed, the spectators are not shown as actually singing a song; even in representations of choruses and speaking figures proper, artists usually chose not to show figures who are speaking or singing with open mouths (and even the vigorous dancers in figure 26 have their mouths closed, even though their level of activity would require an open mouth).[116] We should not look for a literal representation of a chorus singing, but rather for a signification of a chorus and the theme of its song. In this light, the narrative nucleus serves as the subject of the song; rather than words of speech inscribed on the vase's surface, we see the heroic subjects themselves, but as separate from the spectators in the picture and, so, like the chorus singing a song about the mythological past. The bearded man on the left side of the cup, placed in the middle among the singing youths, would seem to be in the position of the choral leader, playing the role that Hagesichora had in Alkman's *Partheneion*.[117]

This chorus's "song" evokes an image of two warriors fighting in the mind's eye of the audience and in the real eye of the viewer. By singing about the warriors, the youths of a chorus would use the narrative as a moral model and express verbally their desire to identify with that civic ideal. Visually, by looking at the warriors, the youths on the cup acknowledge their aspiration and identity with their gaze by looking toward the image of the warriors in the center, where altar or cult object would normally appear in an actual choral performance. Thus, the mythic past or heroic ideal of the choral song correlates with the narrative nucleus of the picture, whereas the present of the choral performers is seen in the contemporary dress, arrangement, and formal behavior of the spectators. The appropriation of the ideal by the members of the chorus should then affirm their present and future identity with the heroic model and the well being of the city. Thus, we could view the image on the cup as being a model recreating a ritualized choral performance, with the spectators as the chorus and the nucleus as the subject of their song.

If we consider on one level that the spectators are the chorus and the narrative nucleus their song, then we must also consider that the audience for a choral performance was assembled in an array surrounding the performers, and therefore were in a circular or semi-circular arrangement themselves [118] On a second level, then, we could look at the narrative nucleus on the Sandal Painter's cup as being an index for the chorus, who, through their ritual performance, evoke and become identified directly with the fighting warriors, in a transposition like that described in chapter 3.3. If the duel is an index for the chorus and its song, then the spectators become the audience, the

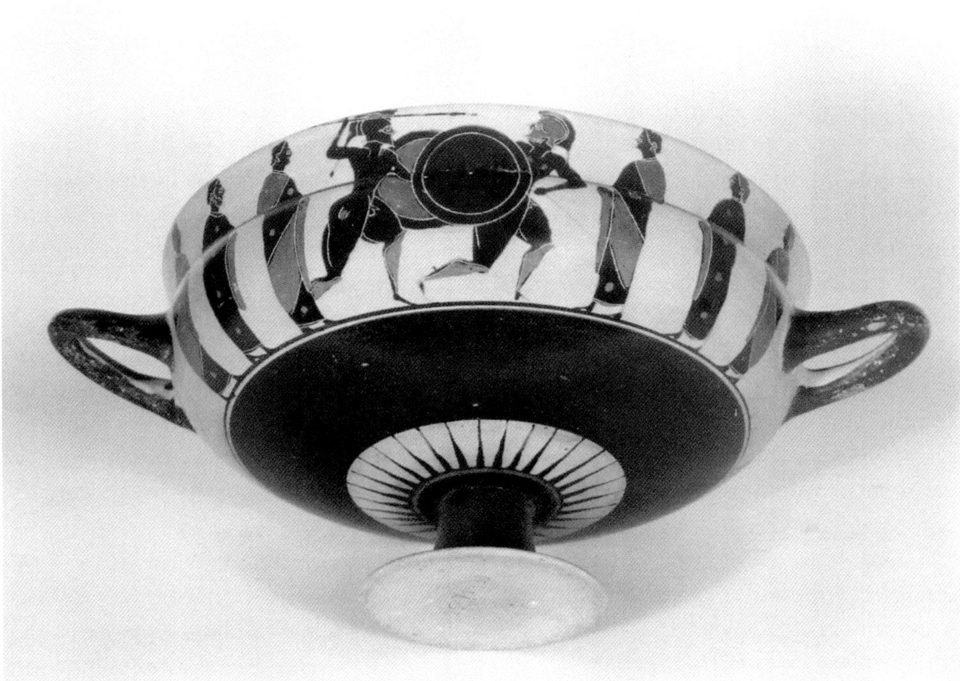

21. Attic black-figure cup attributed to the Sandal Painter, c. 560. Side A: Warriors fighting. New York, The Metropolitan Museum of Art, Fletcher Fund, 1925 (25.78.33). (Photograph, all rights reserved, The Metropolitan Museum of Art)

members of the polis who listened to the chorus singing, watched their processions and dances, and affirmed, through their response and witnessing gaze, consent to the ideal expressed in the performance. Although it is unlikely that the archaic audience was arranged as carefully and symmetrically in practice as the spectators on the cup, the formal wear and behavior of the spectators would be appropriate models for the behavior and appearance of the civic audience for the choral performance.

If we consider that the cup was intended for drinking, whether in a sympotic or funerary setting, then we find a third level of ritual reflection. For a funerary ritual, it is likely that participants would be standing, so that the spectators here mirror more directly their appearance at the graveside. Their commemoration of the deceased raises him to the level of the heroic. The symposion, too, was itself a ritualized occasion, with its own lyric songs that could evoke the mythic past or the excellence of present events. Because the figures on the cup are standing, we cannot see them directly as symposiasts. Rather, we should see the spectators as the public image of the symposiasts earlier in the day. The viewers of the cup are reminded of their public and civic identity by this reflection of their earlier ritualized behavior. The spectator thus becomes the public image of the symposiast and viewer, and the nucleus, an affirmation of the civic ideal and ideology.

The spectators acknowledge the heroic ideal of the narrative nucleus on several different levels. However, to the degree that an individual viewer's conception of the ideal differed from the program of a ruling faction, the ritualized image here could be appropriated in a personal way, as we saw in the viewing matrix of the previous chapter. The anonymous quality of the warriors in this cup, and on so many archaic vase-paintings, is important in this regard. The actions of the figures in the nucleus are such that they evoke a universal level of consent from the viewer, whether or not elite. In its anonymity, the image of the warrior can more readily become associated with the mortal viewer who aspires to the ideal. However, if the viewer were to place a more specific identity on the figure, such as a particular mythological figure, the ideal can be shaped by the viewer to reflect a more individual point of view. By labeling the warrior in the mind's eye as a mythological figure from whom one claims descent, for example, this picture could sustain an aristocratic identity for a viewer that would not be available for someone else. By identifying mentally the warrior as someone who would be set in opposition to the ideal of a particular faction, then the image can be appropriated to another purpose of subtle resistance.

This potential for a subversive sub-reading of the ritualized image provides at least theoretical support for an indirect political reading of archaic paintings. J. Boardman, for example, has proposed that images of Herakles being taken by chariot with Athena, a theme that appears in vase-painting in the latter sixth century, is a metaphor for the triumphant procession of Phye and Peisistratos in the his second bid for power.[119] Boardman also proposed that Exekias's image of Aias and Achilles gaming was a critique of Athenian lack of vigilance during Peisistratos's third and ultimately successful bid for power.[120] Here, the nonheroic action of the figures becomes a critique of the hierarchy and power relationships. Alternatively, D. Williams has proposed that the popularity of Aias on Exekian vases is attributable to Athens' control of his homeland Salamis, so that the hero becomes a symbol of the appropriation of the land.[121] Ultimately, either reading of the gaming scene would depend upon the political sentiments of the viewer, and the broad quality of ritualistic imagery conceptually permits such a fluidity of interpretation. Without knowing the specific circumstances of a particular vase's ownership and use, however, deciding whether a specific image is intended to be subversive in its reading is difficult, if not impossible, to determine, and it is entirely possible that an image painted with one intention can be reinterpreted in an opposite way by a viewer. Given this, it is easier to see these images not as specifically political, but open to a range of expression in much the same vein as ritual.[122]

Another vase shows a different dimension of the ritual aspect of spectators. A Tyrrhenian amphora in Karlsruhe shows two warriors fighting, while two other warriors pull at different ends of a corpse lying on the ground (figure 22).[123] The scene clearly recalls episodes of the fights over fallen warriors in epics such as the *Iliad*, except for the spectators that stand to either side of the composition. On the left side stand two bearded men and a woman, who raise up their left forearms and extend their fingers and thumb fully outward. To the right is a pair of women close together and two more

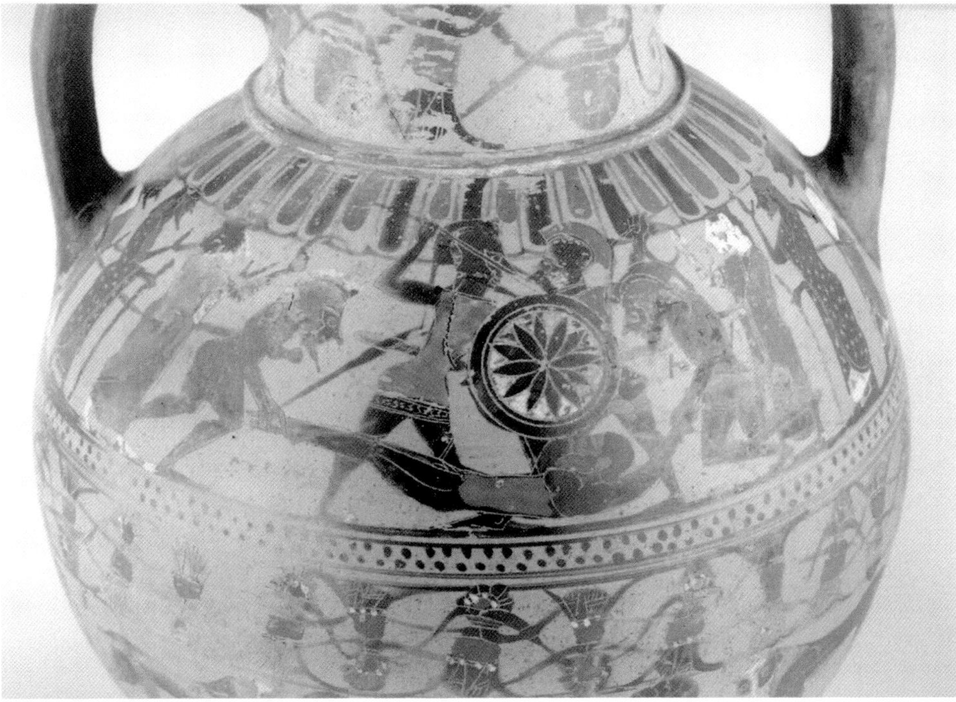

22. Attic black-figure Tyrrhenian amphora attributed to the Castellani Painter, c. 555–550. Side A: Warriors fighting. Badisches Landesmuseum Karlsruhe Inv. B2423. (Photograph, Badisches Landesmuseum Karlsruhe)

bearded men making similar gestures with their right arms. All of the figures hold their one arm horizontally close to the body, with the men holding walking sticks. The upraised hand and arm would be a gesture of acclamation, and the synchronization of the movement among the seven figures would suggest a choral choreography, perhaps to coincide with a particular moment of the song.[124] The gesture suggests verbal expression, and is particularly linked to the idea of farewell or salute, both of which would fit a mood of reminiscence or praise in a choral narrative.

Of particular interest in the Karlsruhe amphora is the inclusion of both men and women as spectators. Although choruses were usually segregated by gender, the passage from the *Herakleidae* of Euripides mentioned earlier suggests that the choirs of men and women would perform, at some festivals, with and in response to each other. There is evidence for mixed-gender choirs in Sparta, and the Crane Dance performed on Delos, celebrating the safe escape from the Minotaur by Theseus with the maidens and youths of Athens, was for a mixed group of men and women.[125] However, the representation of that arrival on the François Vase is the only explicit example of a mixed chorus in Attic black-figure vase-painting, according to Crowhurst, and it is more likely that on the Karlsruhe amphora we are looking at separate but adjacent groups of men and women. The arrangement of the male and female figures in the

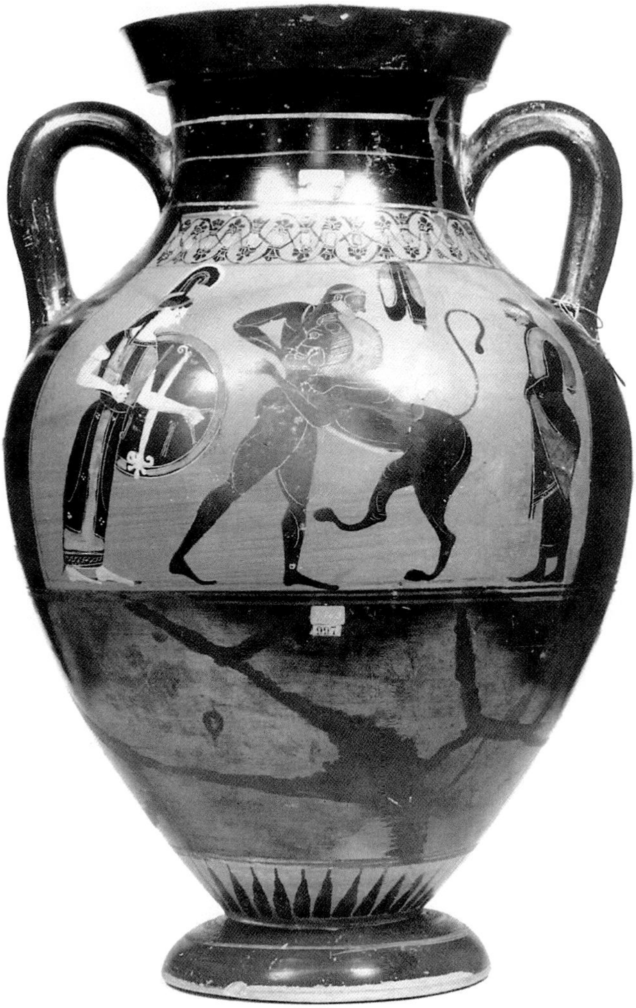

23. Attic black-figure amphora attributed to the Swing Painter, c. 550–30. Side A: Herakles and lion. Naples, Museo Archeologico Nazionale 81186. (Photographer: Rossa. Photo courtesy Deutsches Archäologisches Institut, Rome, neg. #74.1410)

picture would suggest that the women were in an inner ring or circle arranged around a central space, or perhaps in the lead of two processional lines leading through the city. The men followed behind, or formed an outer ring around the women's chorus. It is possible that one danced while the other sang, or that they sang antiphonally and danced simultaneously, but in the picture there is an emphasis upon their unified action and common subject, the heroized dead and heroic warriors. Indeed, it is only within a ritual context that the mixture of men and women around a battle scene would be plausible and a reflection of the activities and ideology of the polis.

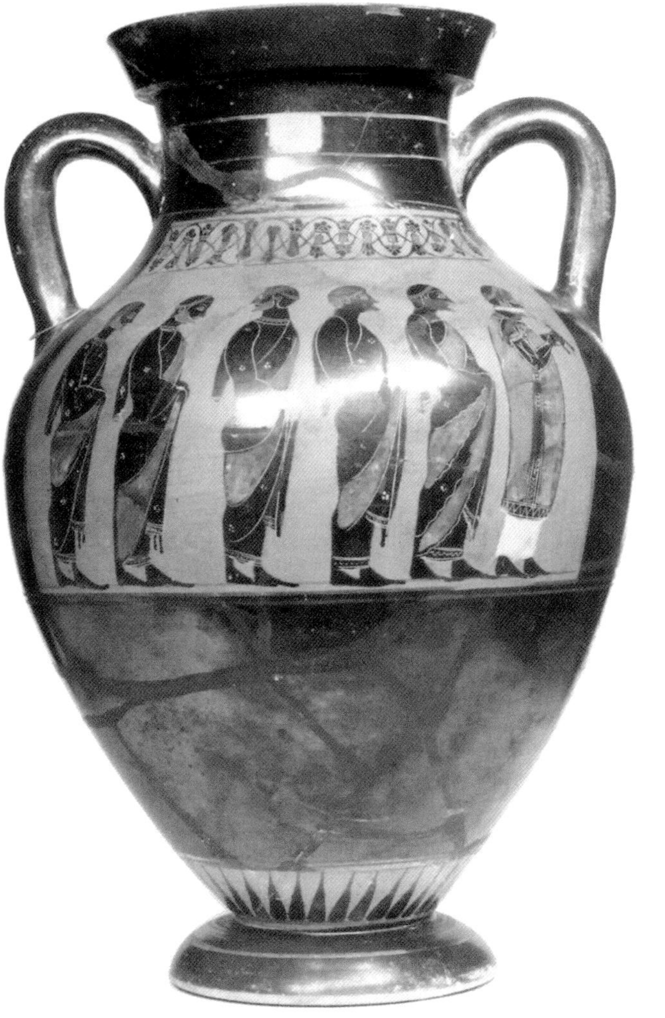

24. Attic black-figure amphora attributed to the Swing Painter, c. 550–30. Side B: Procession. Naples, Museo Archeologico Nazionale 81186. (Photographer: Rossa. Photo courtesy Deutsches Archäologisches Institut, Rome, neg. #74.1411)

That we can understand pictures of spectators within a ritualized context is confirmed by the subject on the other side of the Karlsruhe amphora, a horse race, such as one might expect at the funeral of a warrior or in games associated with a festival. A more immediate evocation of a ritualized context can be seen on several other vases that feature spectators watching a narrative on one side and a ritual procession or performance on the other side of the vase. For example, an amphora in Naples attributed to the Swing Painter shows Herakles fighting the Nemean lion (figure 23).[126] Athena stands behind Herakles, and to the right in the picture is a beardless man. In many pictures of the scene this youth would be Iolaos, but here the figure holds no object

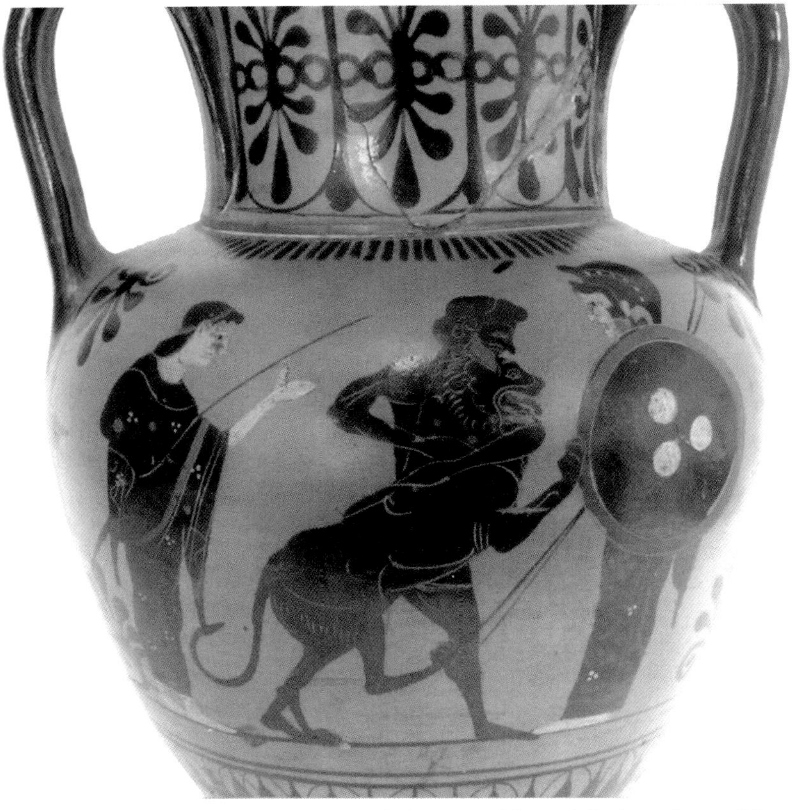

25. Attic black-figure neck amphora, c. 520–510. Side A: Herakles and the lion. Como, Museo Civico D3359. (Photograph, Dr. Isabella Nobile, Curator, Museo Civico di Como)

for Herakles, nor is he dressed in a similarly heroic manner. Instead, he wears a chiton and heavy mantle, the end of which falls over his shoulder and hangs down his back. His quiet posture is distinctly unreactive to the action, and we have to conclude that structurally he is a spectator and not Iolaos, and so not present at the narrative event.

That this single figure serves an index for an entire choral group can be seen on the other side of the vase (figure 24). Here, six figures stand in a line; foremost is a flute player whose instrument and white chiton distinguish him from the other five. The presence of a musician confirms the idea that this is a ritual procession and performance. It is important, then, to note that the men behind the flutist are dressed identically to the spectator on side A of the vase. The dress is an index that links the two sides of the vase as a single concept. The numbers of men and boys on the vase confirm this. On side B, there are three men and two youths behind the flutist, but the youth on side A would make the numbers balance, suggesting that there are two choruses, one older and one younger, being shown on the vase. Indeed, the lead man in the middle of side B looks back to his two colleagues, as if he were directing them in the role of chorus leader, and we could similarly consider the spectator on side A as

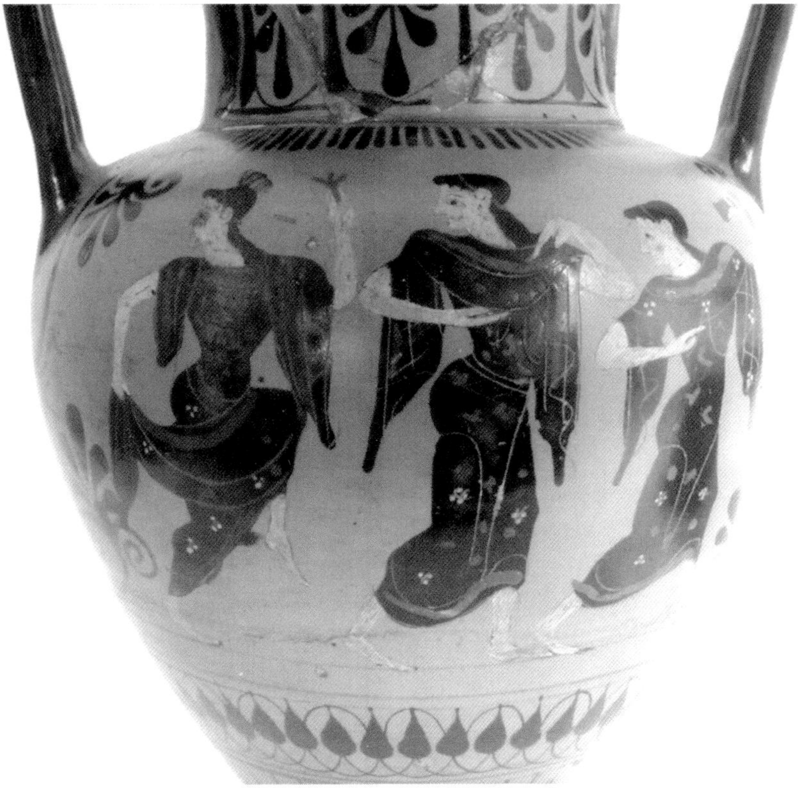

26. Attic black-figure neck amphora, c. 520–510. Side B: Women dancing. Como, Museo Civico D3359. (Photograph, Dr. Isabella Nobile, Curator, Museo Civico di Como)

a lead figure for the other two youths given that his back is turned toward the moving procession, placing him at its head if the two pictures were to be combined.

Considering the two sides of the vase as a single entity, we have to consider that it represents a ritual procession and performance by two choirs, one of men and one of youths, in honor of Herakles and Athena as his patron, and perhaps a song that told the story of the Nemean lion as the emblematic deed of that hero. Athena appears very stiff, like a statue, so perhaps we should consider this performance to be set in a sanctuary of Athena, honoring her patronage of a hero and a city.[127]

A slightly later neck amphora in Como again shows Herakles fighting the lion with an armed Athena looking on (figure 25).[128] To the left is a second female figure in chiton and mantle, holding a spear with her right hand and raising her left hand with palm up and fingers extended. Her dress is very similar to that of Athena, except for the goddess's armor. Her dress and hairstyle are identical to the three women who appear on the other side of the vase; like the Naples amphora, we should understand the female spectator as part of this group on the reverse (figure 26).[129] These figures would appear to be performing a dance, and the different placement of arms and legs in each figure seems to be a synchronous picture of the different steps of the dance, arranged as a progression as the line moves through space.[130] As we have seen, dance and song were inextricably linked in choral performances, and here on side B the emphasis would appear to be on dance rather than song. The female spectator does not dance, and she also seems to stand apart from the dancers in a way suggested by Alkman's chorus and their leader, Hagesichora. The woman's spear would also link her to Athena rather than to the dancers, giving her an index of authority that would accord with a choral leader or perhaps a priestess overseeing the ritual.

The connection between ritual and spectators can be seen in another category of vases that were not counted as examples of spectators in the CVA census: Theseus slaying the Minotaur. On a Tyrrhenian amphora in the Louvre, for example, we see Theseus attacking the Minotaur in the center of the shoulder, and to either side stand three spectators (figure 27).[131] These include three women on the left, and an adult and two young men to the right. The presence of the young men and women can be explained within the context of the narrative, in that they can be identified as some of the seven young men and women of Athens who were to be sacrificed to the Minotaur, and whom Theseus rescued by his actions. They are spectators to the nucleus, but because the result of that action has a direct impact on their life and death, they are in the time and place of the action and therefore do not have the boundary that would make them detached or inert spectators. Despite their structural integration with the nucleus, however, they manifest the comportment and behavior of the spectators that we have seen. The presence of the adult man, however, resembles that of the mixture of male figures found on the Siana cup in figure 21 and on the Naples amphora in figures 23–24. This suggests that the spectators on this vase can also represent a choir singing about Theseus, with the choral members being more directly associated with the original young men and women sent to Crete.

This vase shows a distinctly Athenian version of the Minotaur story in archaic iconography.[132] The presence of the men and women may refer to the Crane Dance that they performed on Delos following their rescue, and their inclusion in the form of spectators in the picture also situates the story firmly within a ritual setting that recognized the sacrifice that the victims were making on behalf of their city. As mythological figures, the companions of Theseus would be appropriate models for the choruses of young men and women in archaic Athens, and their arrangement in the picture makes them double as images of the choruses as they would perform a song about Theseus, who figured prominently as a figure in the myths surrounding many Attic festivals. The importance of Theseus as a model for civic identity during the sixth century can be seen in the actions of Peisistratos on Delos.[133] According to Plutarch, Delos is where Theseus and his companions stopped after escaping from Crete and performed the Crane Dance. During Peisistratos's rule, probably in the 540s, the Athenians saw to the purification of Delos by digging up and relocating the graves around the Temple of Apollo. Following this there was a revival of the Delia festival, which included music and choral competitions by groups from Athens and other Ionian cities. The backside

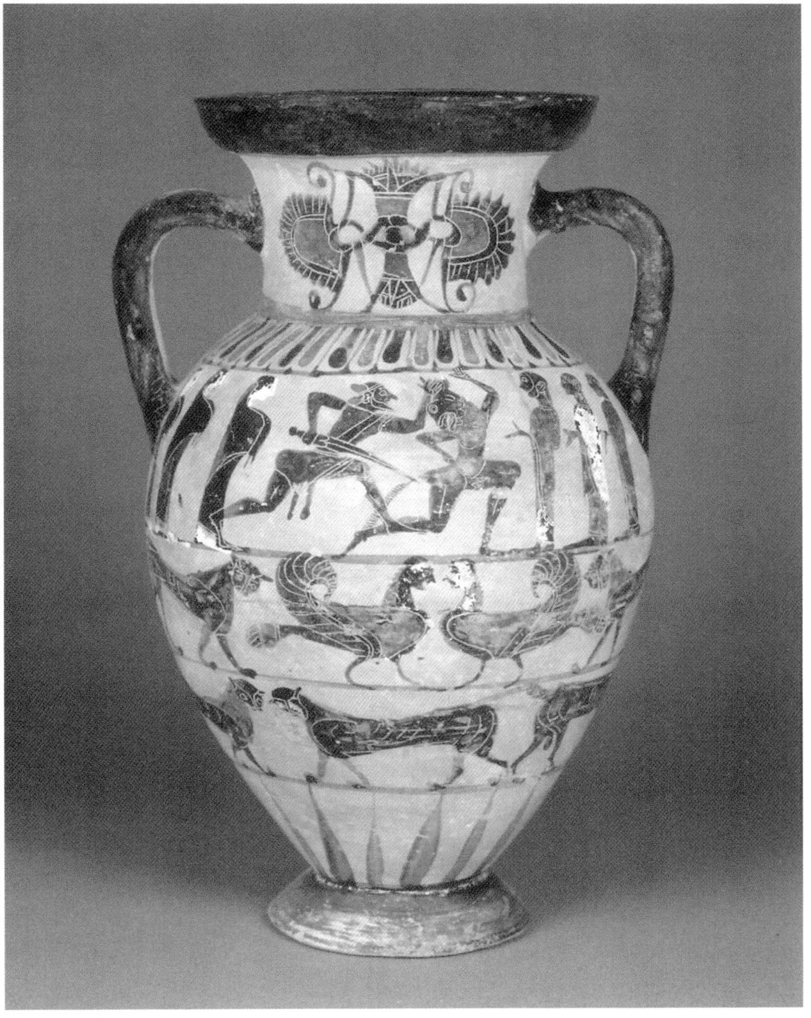

27. Attic black-figure Tyrrhenian amphora attributed to the Castellani Painter, c. 560–555. Side A: Theseus and the Minotaur. Paris, Musée du Louvre E850. (Photograph, Réunion des Musées Nationaux/Art Resource, NY)

of the Louvre vase features komos dancers, further grounding the ritualistic context of the spectators on the front side.[134]

The parallels between ritual performance and spectators in vase-painting can also be seen on vases with processional imagery. As we saw earlier, in figure 9, the mantled spectators on the left watch what is likely a procession of riders accompanied by mostly nude youths. Dress and lack of action distinguish the spectators from the performing figures. The regular but unsymmetrical arrangement of the spectators in the composition suggests that they are not arranged in a circle around the central figures, but rather line the processional way in an arranged order. Here, the spectators could be understood simultaneously as groups who would sing or chant in praise of the youth, like a chorus, but even more as members of the polis who would show their assent to the acclamations. A similar arrangement can be seen in figure 76, in which a man and two women confront a rider and nude youth. The women pull their mantle before them, a gesture that reminds the viewer of the *anakalypsis* or wedding gesture, as will be discussed further in chapter 6.1.

Other events associated with spectators are athletic and music contests, all of which were included in the Panathenaic festival.[135] On an amphora by Group E in Munich, for example, we see a foot race of two nude men and a nude youth, who is running last (figure 28).[136] Before them, a clothed man converses with another nude youth; their pairing would suggest a side conversation about the event, perhaps between a mentor or trainer and a youth who will be competing in future games. This pair constitutes a subsidiary nucleus in the picture, and suggests that the action of the race is a topic for discussion and consideration, but with the man's back to the scene and their gaze directed at each other, they are not really spectators of the race. Spectators are at either end of the composition: to the left, before a prize tripod, is a mantled youth; to the right is another mantled youth whose hand projects from his mantle.

Most pictures of athletic contests with spectators feature youths and sometimes men standing quietly while watching the contests. There are only a few examples that show spectators in stands or on steps, gesturing in a more animated manner, such as the pseudo-Panathenaic amphora seen earlier in figure 7.[137] In these cases, the presence of stands would seem to have provided more latitude in showing spectator reaction, perhaps because the stands were a significant indicator of the separation of performer and observer within the picture. In the more typical picture, spectators are distinguished by their dress and their more restrained actions compared with the performers (see also figure 8). We should consider that these pictures of athletes with spectators convey the ritualistic nature of the competitions by the formal arrangement, dress, and behavior of the spectators. Indeed, the shoulder of the Munich amphora features Herakles and the lion, with both inert and mimetic spectators to either side. The heroic ideal and the athletic ideal, then, align on the central axis, each surrounded by spectators who, through ritual participation and observation, bring both ideals to the attention of the polis.

The gaze of the spectators in the picture links them with the idealized figures in the center, and reminds us of the admiration that Greek cities gave to victorious athletes. As D. Steiner has discussed, this visual contact between the viewer and athlete was intense, and the viewing experience of a statue of a victor was meant to evoke the same feelings as the original.[138] The ritualized context of the spectator in the picture makes this visual link between viewer and ideal operate not only as a matter of personal identification, as we saw in the previous chapter, but one of social identification as well.

The presence of spectators at a civic scene demonstrates that spectators are signs of ritualized occasions and behavior. This is also true of the more occasional events

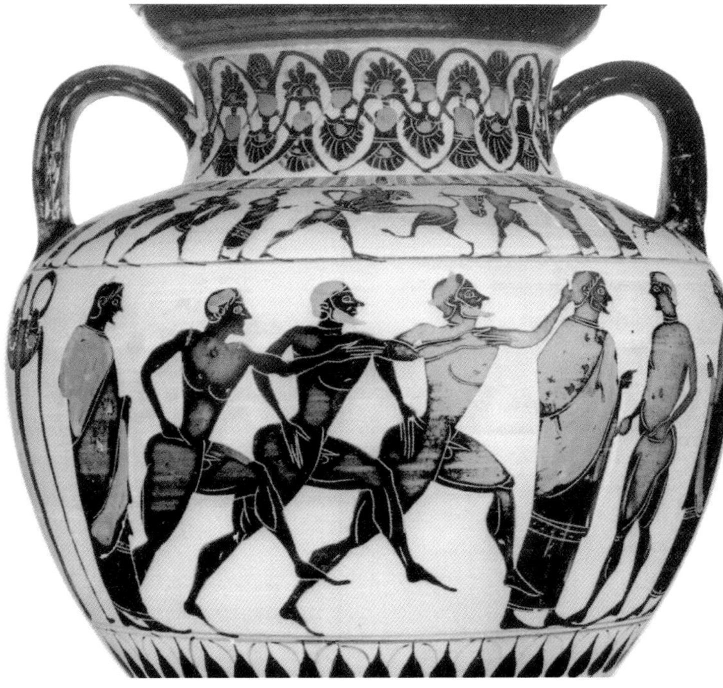

28. Attic black-figure neck amphora attributed to Group E, c. 540. Side A: Racing men. Munich, Antikensammlung 1471. (Photograph, Staatliche Antikensammlungen und Glyptothek München)

that brought members of a specific family to the public attention, such as a funeral. Although such occasions might be less grand in scale than festivals, they still involved the acclamation of a subject, an evocation of an ideal, and the participation and assent of members of the community as a ritual performance. Attic vases show in great detail some aspects of archaic funerary ritual, such as the prothesis of laying out of the body and the differentiated mourning behavior of women and men.[139] Because such figures are participants, they do not fall into the class of detached spectators discussed here. There are, however, a number of vases with spectators that need to be viewed within this context of funerary ritual. One example is a band cup in the Sackler Museum, which shows a sphinx in the center of the frieze flanked by two nude youths striding from left to right (figure 29).[140] The youth on the right turns his head back toward the sphinx, and both youths raise their left arms in a gesture of acclamation, or perhaps proclamation. To either side are mantled youths holding one hand forward and looking at the central scene.

The presence of the sphinx in the nucleus of the picture signals a funerary theme, serving as an index for the deceased. The cup is said to be from Vari and may well be, as are so many excavated band cups with spectators, from a grave. The nude youths serve as idealized images for the deceased, but given that their actions are identical to those found on processional pictures such as figure 10, they should also be understood

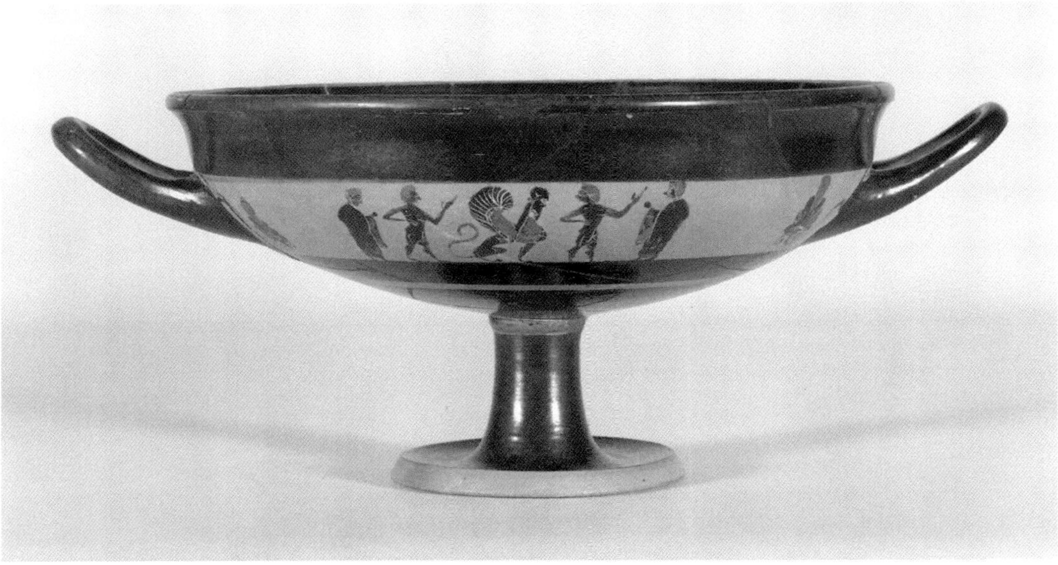

29. Attic black-figure 'Little Master' cup, mid-sixth century. Side A: Sphinx. Courtesy of the Arthur M. Sackler Museum, Harvard University Art Museums, Bequest of David M. Robinson, 60.320. (Photograph, Photographic Services)

as performers within a funerary ritual proclaiming the excellence of the deceased. The mantled spectators signal their assent through gaze and gesture, and evoke the formal and solemn occasion. In their very contained form, the spectators resemble statues, and one should view them in a funerary context as permanent witnesses to the deceased and his value to the community. In this sense, the spectator creates a parallel to the viewer of a funerary statue and inscription, who, by reading aloud the inscription, proclaims the excellence of the deceased and maintains an active civic memory of his or her existence.[141] That the vase's shape can also be sympotic in function reminds us that the remembrance of the dead also took place at the symposion, where elegies would be performed that recalled the deeds and men as models for the behavior of those present.[142]

Recent studies have highlighted the different roles men and women played in funerary ritual. Women lamented the deceased, and their performance is characterized as shrill and piercing in its tone.[143] Men, by comparison, groaned and responded in a more muted fashion. In funerary iconography, women are shown pulling their hair and scratching their skin around the deceased, whereas men are shown to the side and acting more formally, in more ordered ranks and with more studied gestures, such as the acclamations of the youths on the Sackler cup.[144] Within a sympotic setting, remembrance of the dead would follow a more restrained style, like the formal language of funerary inscriptions. It is noteworthy, in light of the distinct tones of male and female responses in funerary ritual and commemoration, that the spectators on the Sackler cup are male and restrained in their comportment and gesture. In the

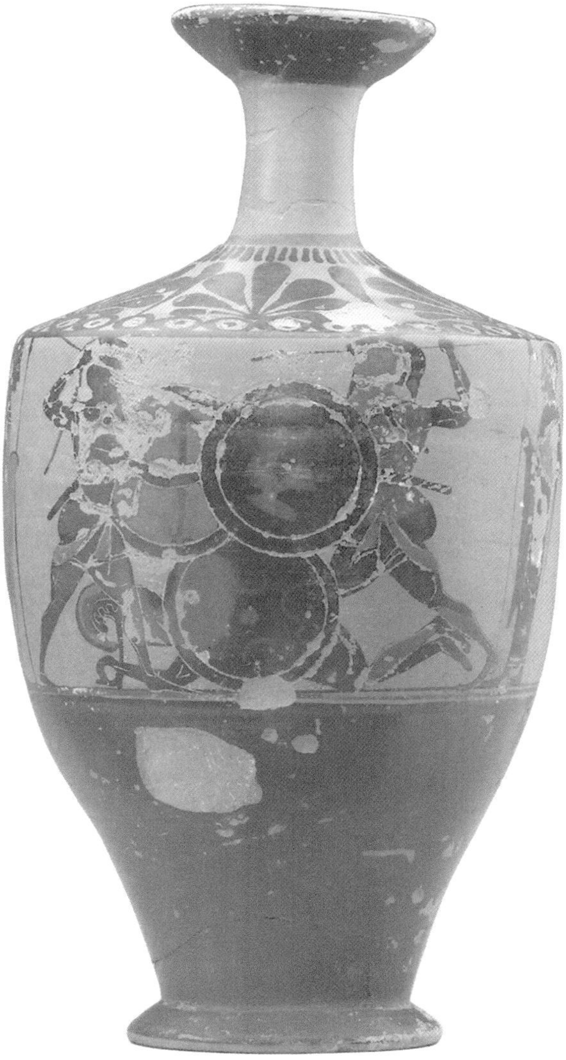

30. Attic black-figure lekythos, c. 530–500. Warriors fighting. New Haven, Yale University Art Gallery, 1993.46.16. Gift of Ambassador and Mrs. William Witman II, B. A. 1935. (Photograph, Yale University Art Gallery)

CVA census, there are 14 examples of the sphinx flanked by spectators; in all cases, there are inert youths as spectators, with the inclusion of a woman in only a single example.[145] Rather than lamentation, which is associated with women's function in the prothesis and entombment, the funerary aspect of spectators should be seen as taking place within the context of commemoration, either in the symposion or in the memorial and offerings at the tomb.

This discussion of funerary ritual brings us to consider spectators on lekythoi, one of the three most common types of vases featuring onlookers. Almost one-fourth of the vases in the CVA census are lekythoi.[146] Most of these date to the last third of the sixth century and beginning of the fifth century, signaling a change in the deployment of spectators, as we saw in chapter 2.3. The composition and structural elements of the spectator lekythoi, however, continue the same themes found with spectators on earlier vases, as can be seen on an example in the Yale University Art Gallery (figure 30).[147] On the front of the body of the vase, we see two warriors fighting over a fallen warrior. On either side is a mantled youth who holds a spear in the back, draped hand. Within a funerary context, these spectators can be seen on a couple of different levels. If we consider that the warriors are an ideal that serves as an index for the deceased, then the spectators become the members of family and society who observe and recall the excellence of the deceased. The warriors embody the same ideal as the nude and warrior figures on relief stelai from this period, so that their commemoration on one level can be seen as taking place at the tomb of the deceased, where the lekythos could be deposited.[148] Thus, the lekythos becomes a surrogate picture of the visitation of the dead by family and others. We can also see the spectators like a chorus, singing in elegiac fashion about the deceased at a symposion or in a nonfunerary setting. The nucleus of the composition becomes a link from the contemporary world of the user and spectator to the past. In both cases, the spectator lekythos conveys the idea that formal recognition and proclamation of the deceased are important civic functions, and links the living to the dead.

This ritualistic dimension to spectators on funerary lekythoi finds confirmation on a lekythos in Heidelberg.[149] The shoulder shows a nude runner, flanked by a mantled spectator on either side. On the body is a group of five men wearing chitons and mantles. Four stand in line facing to the right; the fifth man faces the other four and raises his hand up slightly. The figures are very much like those on the Naples amphora discussed previously (figure 24), and clearly resemble a chorus or procession with a leader. The subject of their performance must be signified by the nude runner mentioned earlier, and the implication of a ritualized form of commemoration for the deceased seems implicit in the alignment of the pictures on the lekythos. Images of men performing at the prothesis, however, often show their arms projecting fully and raised above their shoulder or head.[150] The difference in deportment suggests a post-funerary commemoration, such as an elegy.

A look at the types of spectators appearing on funerary lekythoi suggests that their target audience is youth, either as idealized representations of the deceased or as future members of the polis. Of the 173 lekythoi in the CVA census, 150 (86.7 percent) feature standing youths as spectators. Thirty vases (17.3 percent) have adult male spectators, and only nine (5.2 percent) have women (see table 10 in chapter 2). Commemoration of the deceased, and future remembrance of their own deeds, helps to convey a sense of civic identity for youth who are beginning their training and enculturation as members of the polis. The fact that these lekythoi were widely distributed clearly shows the broad appeal of the theme and its fit with funerary and commemorative rituals throughout the Greek world.

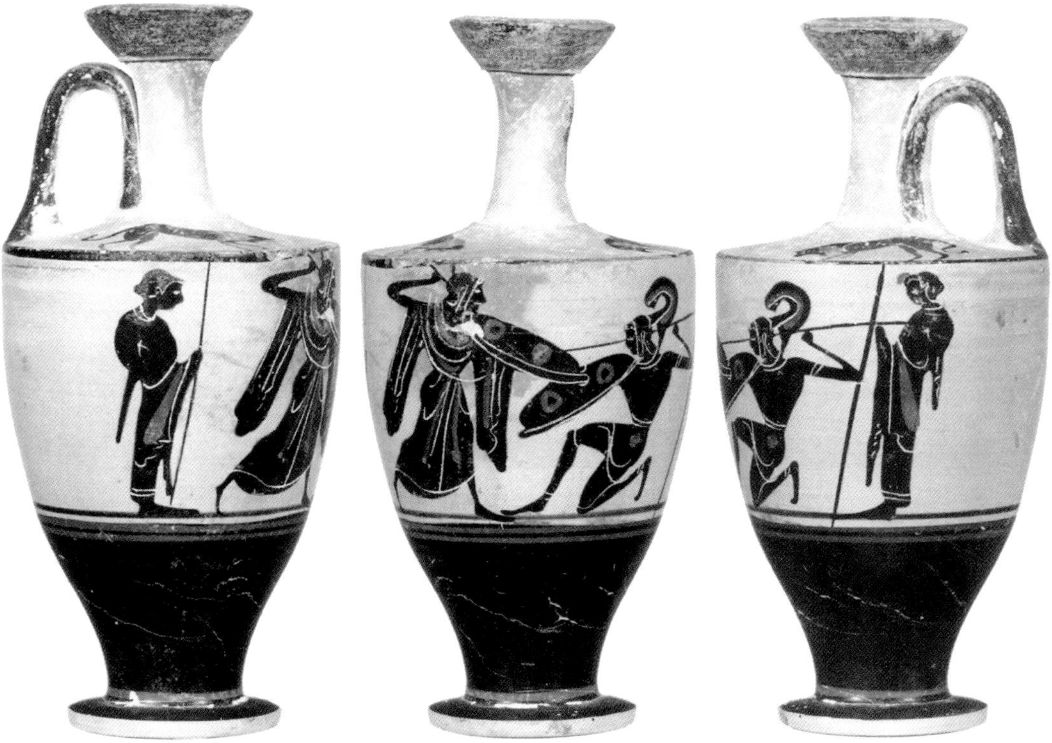

31. Attic black-figure lekythos attributed to the Little Lion Class, Krotala Group, c. 500–490. Gigantomachy with Athena. Malibu, California, The J. Paul Getty Museum, 86.AE.135. (Photograph © The J. Paul Getty Museum)

Some of the spectator lekythoi feature mythological narratives as their nucleus, rather than more generic and ambiguous figures such as warriors or athletes. An example in the Getty Museum shows Athena battling a giant (figure 31).[151] To either side are once again mantled youths, but here they hold spears or staves while observing the action. The spear-bearing youth is a common type of spectator on lekythoi, being found on 76 of the 173 lekythoi in the CVA catalog, and on five of the seven examples of lekythoi showing Athena battling a giant. In form, the spectators very closely resemble the spear-bearing warrior who is a frequent theme on surviving funerary reliefs, and their popularity as a motif for contemporary funerary lekythoi is understandable.[152] The depiction of armed youth as spectators also reminds the viewer of the importance of the youth for the future defense of the city, and the model of Athena defending the realm of the gods is an appropriate ideal for Athenian youth to follow and would parallel the monumental pedimental composition of that theme that stood on the Acropolis at this time.[153] In terms of ritual, one should see the youth as they might have appeared in public festivals during their training.[154] Indeed, the lines sung successively by the three Spartan groups in a triple choral performance – old men, youths, and boys – is appropriate for this context:[155]

> We once were vigorous young men.
> And we now are, in truth; if you will, look!
> And we indeed will be stronger by far.

The middle lines, uttered by the young men, proclaim their vigor and ask the audience to bear witness to the fact with their gaze. On the Getty lekythos, the spectators draw attention to the mythical subject of their song and to their readiness to act in a similar fashion. The similarity of their outfits to that of Athena is visual testimony to their readiness. Such is the ideal that would be evoked for the deceased as well as for those who continue to live as citizens.

4.5 DISCUSSION

In this chapter we have looked at spectators in terms of civic and social identification. The spectators function like a chorus performing at a festival, singing about mythological figures belonging to the city's past or idealized figures of the present, and articulating their own role as current or future members of the polis.[156] Their gaze, like the words of an actual chorus, directs the viewer's attention to the narrative example. Their formal arrangement, dress, and behavior belong to the realm of a ritualistic occasion, rather than the casual or everyday, and serve as models not only for the behavior of members of a chorus, but also for the behavior of the audience for a choral performance. Because the user/viewer of the vase is also a member of the polis and had either performed or observed such rituals, the spectators become models for the viewer of the vase in terms of social behavior and identification.

In this sense, we can see the importance of ritual and its themes for the construction of what it means to be a citizen of Athens during the sixth century. The reforms of Solon at the beginning of the century articulated four classes, divided according to productive wealth, defining rights and responsibilities of each and giving all citizens a stake in the city.[157] Citizenship was conceived not so much in legalistic terms, but rather as the investment of the individual in the polis. As P. Manville has argued, embracing the Solonian reforms meant that a new civic spirit developed in Athens, and Athenians moved from being defined as members of neighborhoods, regions, and clans to being citizens of the polis.[158] This civic spirit oversaw the reform and expansion of the religious festivals, and stimulated the construction of more splendid sanctuaries and public spaces, so that Athens at the end of the sixth century was a far more splendid and vibrant environment than it had been at the beginning.

As Frost has pointed out, there were no real political gains between 561 and 510, as least in terms of the constitutional powers of the citizens to select a government.[159] However, a Panathenaic ideal was promoted and served to create a common bond among the citizens. The primary means for this were the festivals and rituals that were, as Manville states, "for the shared benefit of all Athenians."[160] Citizenship during this period was developed not legally so much as ideologically, socially, and religiously, and when Hippias was expelled in 510, a new political ordering developed this concept of Athenian identity further. In the absence of political enfranchisement, we can see participation in ritual behavior as both a momentary consent to the status quo, and as a statement potentially subversive to the Peisistratids by emphasizing a civic identity over the political.

It is, quite possibly, not coincidental that spectators begin to appear in large numbers on vases concurrently with the reform and growth of the Panathenaic festival. Indeed, Brijder has already pointed to such potential changes in the main themes of the Siana cup painters following 565.[161] The spectators on vases, then, take on a level of meaning from the socio-political context during their production. Athenians during the last two-thirds of the century performed and participated in an expanding array of rituals. Through this, they learned, as Plutarch states, "as members of one body, to feel and sympathize with one another's wrongs."[162]

FIVE

MEN AND YOUTHS

Gender and Social Identity

In the previous two chapters, we explored the ways in which spectators generally reflect the individual and social identity of the viewer, particularly sixth-century Athenians. Looking back once more at the shoulder of the Minneapolis amphora, we can see that the reactions of the spectators are not the same (figure 32). The youth next to the end on the left strides forward and raises his left arm, with palm facing out and fingers and thumb extended; the mantled youth on the far right lifts his left hand up within his mantle, but essentially stands quietly, not reacting to the scene. In chapter 2, these figures were defined as reactive and inert respectively, but a quick look at other spectators shows that each of these categories contains a variety of different poses, gestures, and actions, and that the responses of spectators within a picture are by no means uniform. The variety of responses offers an opportunity to consider just what kind of reactions were prescribed for spectators to different kinds of actions in the nucleus, whether mythological, heroic, or more contemporary. By defining, quantifying, and analyzing spectator reactions, we can think about the expectations that Athenian society placed on its members, both as viewers and as participants. Because spectators fall into three main categories based on gender and age – men, youth, and women – we shall examine the reactions of men and youth in this chapter, and focus upon women spectators in the next. Following a discussion of previous work on gestures and the classification scheme to be used here, we will look first at types and frequencies of men as spectators, and then at youths. After this, we will look at both types within the context of a series of narrative scenes to distinguish the reactions of men and youths to different kinds of narrative nuclei.

5.1 GESTURES AND CATEGORIZATION

The reactions of spectators, as well as participants in scenes, are defined by gestures using the arms and hands, movement of the head, and movement of the legs. In

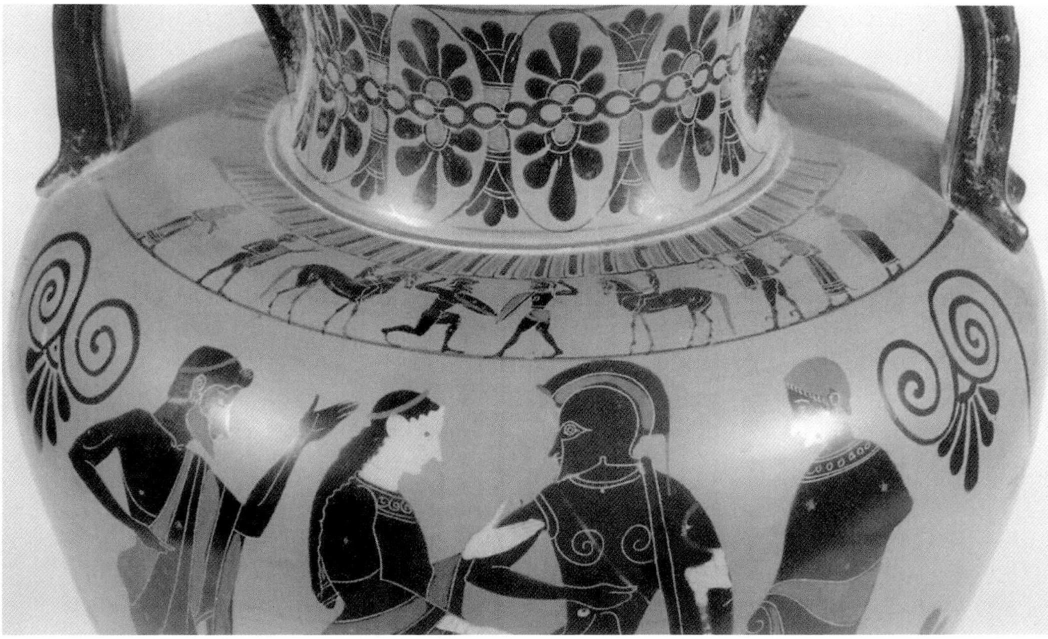

32. Attic black-figure amphora, attributed to the Painter of Vatican 359, c. 530. Side B: Detail of shoulder: warriors fighting. Minneapolis Institute of Arts, Ethel Morrison Van Derlip Fund, 57.1. (Photograph, The Minneapolis Institute of Arts)

addition, spectators can also carry objects in their hands such as staffs, spears, or wreaths. The number of different reactions, however, is limited and subject to classification and interpretation, as several scholars have sought to do in studies of communication and expressions of figures in Greek art.

G. Neumann produced a comprehensive study of gestures in 1965, placing them into broad categories of everyday gestures, ritualistic gestures, divine gestures used for communication or interaction between figures, and expressions of the moment or of the general condition of the psyche.[1] Within each category, he illustrated different types of gestures, linking them to literary references and terminology and considering their historical development or change. There are, however, a number of gestures that do not appear in his work, particularly those that do not involve strong movement of the arms or hands; nor is there a classification scheme that would allow one to study the prevalence and pattern of different types of gestures.

A. Boegehold has very recently argued strongly for the consideration of gesture as part of poetic expression, and reviewed a range of gestures that fit into the general categories of dialogue or recitation, drawing upon vase paintings for illustrations.[2] He places these into several types, such as control, connecting, summoning, modesty, reaction, etc., and reexamines a number of literary texts with an eye toward imagining their physical as well as verbal performance based upon internal references within the text. Like Neumann, there is no classification scheme, and the work is not intended to be a comprehensive review of gesture.

T. McNiven did develop such a classification scheme in his 1982 dissertation, devising a detailed coding scheme that encompassed almost all movements of the head, hands, arms, and legs.[3] Using this scheme, he was able to show that some gestures were favored by certain artists and was able to trace more precisely developments in the use of gesture during the archaic and early classical periods. This provided another tool for the attribution of vase painters, but the classification scheme itself is a little complicated for adaptation to other purposes. His study also showed that gestures were often not precise in their meaning as individual signs, and their meaning could vary greatly according to context. His recent article on how certain kinds of gestures can express a figure's status as an outsider or "other" to the Greek male norm offers a model for the study and interpretation of gesture within a social context.[4]

These studies demonstrate the rich material that gesture in vase-painting can offer for understanding the intention or the emotional state of the figure using them, and also the need for being able to classify gestures. For the study of spectators, which include a very large number of figures who do not actively gesture like the standing, mantled youth in figure 32, we will have to develop a special classification scheme based on the degree of movement and action. Figures and their gestures will be classified first according to the gender of the figure: man, youth, or woman, and so are coded "M," "Y," or "W" respectively. Within each gender, spectators are placed into one of six *categories*, according to the degree to which the hands, arms, and legs project from the torso of the body or the silhouette of the figure and whether they use specific props such as spears, long staffs, or walking sticks. The figure with the least movement is assigned to category 1 for each gender (M.1, Y.1, W.1). Figures with spears or spear-length staffs, whether standing still or striding, are assigned to category 2 (M.2, Y.2, W.2). Figures whose arms project in front of the body up to the elbow and whose feet may be slightly spread are assigned to category 3 (M.3, Y.3, W.3), whereas those whose arms project more fully and who stride strongly are placed in category 4 (M.4, Y.4, W.4). Figures who lean on long sticks are placed in category 5 (M.5, Y.5, W.5), and figures who sit are placed in category 6 (M.6, Y.6, W.6). Different *types* of gestures within each category are assigned a lower case letter after the number to distinguish them (hence M.1a, M.1b, etc.). The general coding scheme is as seen in table 17.

Each of the individual types can, in turn, be placed into one of the three behavioral *moods* for spectators defined in chapter 2: inert, reactive, and mimetic. Generally, the assumption is made that the more vigorous the movement of the figure, the more expressive it is intended to be, and the more reactive to the action of the narrative nucleus. Hence the figures falling into categories 3 and 4 are considered either reactive or mimetic; figures in category 1, inert. Types in categories 2, 5, and 6 include all three behavioral moods, depending upon the action.

Table 17. *General Coding Scheme for Spectator Gesture Categories*

	Man (adult male)	Youth (male)	Woman
Standing, still	M.1	Y.1	W.1
Standing or striding, spear-bearing	M.2	Y.2	W.2
Standing, forearm and hand extended	M.3	Y.3	W.3
Arm/elbow extended, longer stride	M.4	Y.4	W.4
Leaning on stick	M.5	Y.5	W.5
Sitting	M.6	Y.6	W.6

To demonstrate the scheme, we will first look at adult male spectators, as recognized by their beard and generally shorter hair, and define individual spectator types within each main category. For each type, we will look at its frequency, first in terms of the number of vases on which the type appears, and second in terms of its relative frequency among all vases in the CVA census with spectators of that gender. After this, we will develop the same definitions and data for youth, and compare the distribution of specific categories and types within the two gender classes.

For the purposes of quantification and of establishing relative frequency, I have chosen to use the total number of vases on which a type occurs and not the total number of figures of that type, and to look at the percentage of vases that this represents within the gender class, that is, the 223 vases with men and 527 vases with youths in the CVA census. Because many vases feature more than one type of spectator, this means that percentages will add up to considerably more than 100. Although not perfect, maintaining this method of determining relative frequency within each gender group offers a consistent manner for comparing spectator types across gender and other categories such as different types of narrative subjects, as we will consider in the last section of this chapter.

5.2 GESTURES AMONG ADULT MALE SPECTATORS

M.1: Inert/Inactive Spectators

The first category of adult male spectators consists of figures that maintain a closed form, with only a hand, at most, projecting from the silhouette of the figure; this type is labeled M.1 (see the chart of all male spectators in figure 33). This category includes the traditional mantled figures that appear frequently in pictures of spectators and can be seen on an amphora in Boston showing a nude youth riding a horse, followed by a mostly nude warrior with spear, shield, and helmet (figure 34).[5] On the right side stands a man wearing a mantle that extends down to his ankles, creating a heavy silhouette; his feet are pointed in the same direction as the rider and warrior, but his head is turned back toward those figures. His feet are close together, and when compared to

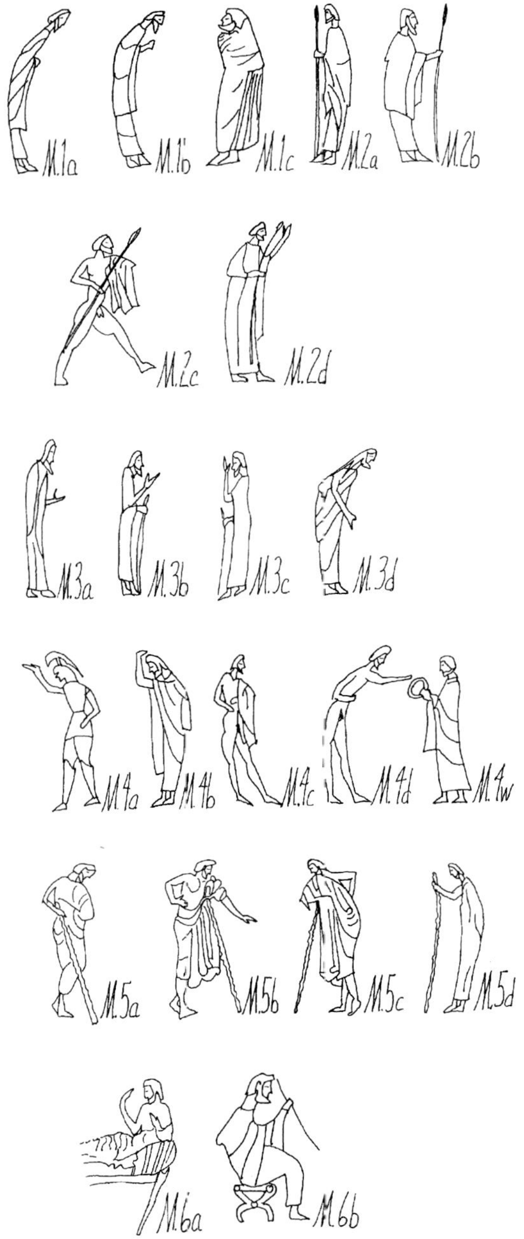

33. Chart of adult male spectator types. (Drawing, author)

the stride of the warrior, the spectator must be understood as either stationary or as advancing very slowly. Both hands are within the mantle, but the left projects forward slightly to create a bulge in the silhouette. This type of figure, the most common of the category, is coded as type M.1a, which more typically has the head facing in the same

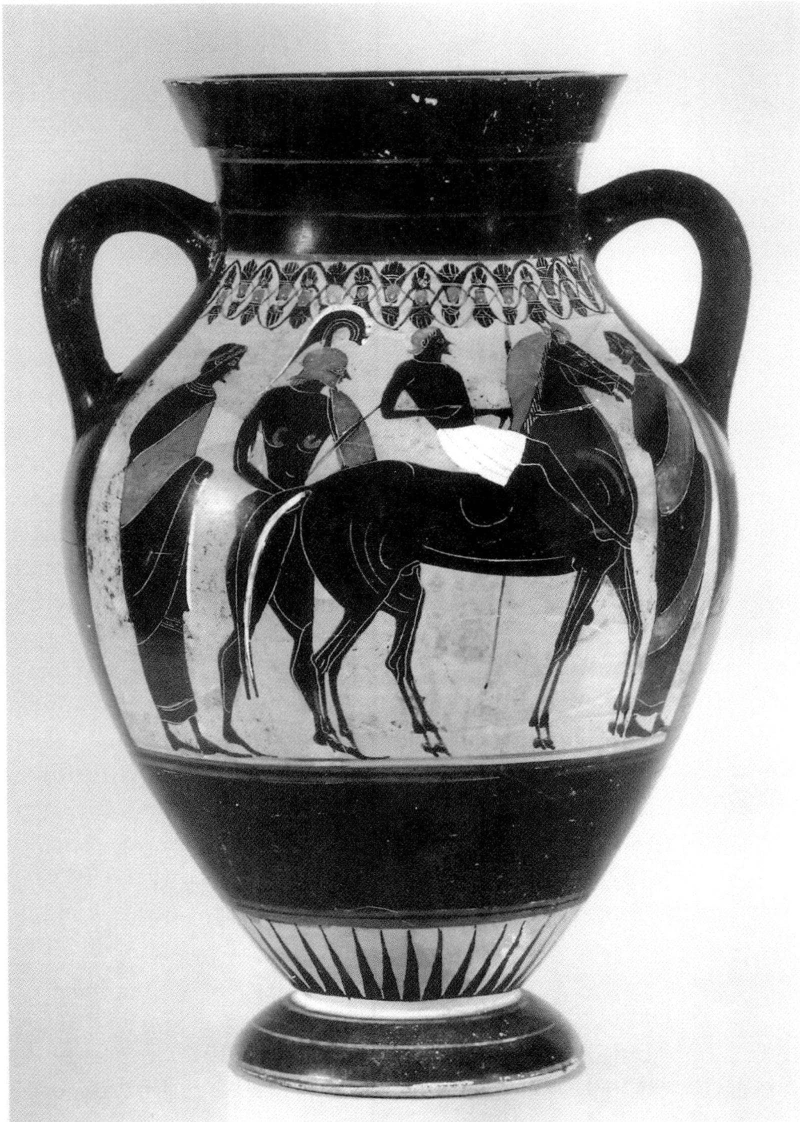

34. Attic black-figure amphora attributed to the Painter of the Vatican Mourner, c. 530. Side B: Rider. Museum of Fine Arts, Boston. William E. Nickerson Fund, 1970.8. (Photograph © 2004 Museum of Fine Arts, Boston)

direction of the feet, like the mantled youth on the left side of the vase.[6] The turn of the head, however, as long as it directs the spectator's attention toward the nucleus, does not signify a different reaction on the part of the spectator. Another variation on the type can have the hand or fist emerge from the mantle, but maintains the same closed silhouette. A second, but closely related type to this shows the hand projecting

Table 18. *Frequency of Types in Spectator Category M.1*

Type	Description	Number of Vases with Type	Frequency, Total Vases with M (223)
M.1a	Standing still, closed form	64	28.7%
M.1b	Standing still, hand projects beyond edge of body	6	2.7%
M.1c	Standing still, encased in mantle	1	0.4%
		Total = 71	31.8%

more fully from the mantle, sometimes up to the wrist (see figure 33 and leftmost man in figure 47). This type is coded M.1b, but in terms of behavior it is virtually the same as M.1a; both fall into the behavioral mood of inert spectators. This type of spectator should be understood as offering a calm, focused attention on the nucleus, observing the action and signifying its importance by the gaze and the bulge or slight projection created by the hand. Basically, both types of figures function to proclaim the worthiness of the nucleus for the viewer's attention, and model a decorous, controlled reaction for the viewer toward such a scene, whether on the vase or in actual public events.

The frequency of this type of spectator signals its importance as a model for viewing (see table 18). Of the 223 vases with men as spectators, 71 have spectators of the category M.1. Sixty-four are of the type found on the Boston vase (M.1a), and six are of the variation M.1b. There is one other spectator type that belongs in the category M.1, in which the figure is completely enveloped by the mantle, which is pulled up to cover part or all of the head (M.1c, see chart in figure 33). There is only one occurrence of this type among male spectators, but the type is more common for youths, as we shall see subsequently.[7] With a relative frequency of 28.7 percent of all vases with men as spectators, the mantled man (M.1a) is the single most common type for its gender group.

M.2: Spear-Bearing Spectators

The standing still, attentive pose of M.1a is replicated in a second category of figures that carry spears or very long staffs that reach the level of the head. These figures with spears have been categorized as M.2 because the majority of the figures follow closely the inert deportment of figures in category M.1, as can be seen on a Siana cup at Washington University in St. Louis (figure 35).[8] In the central scene are two warriors fighting, flanked by semi-nude youths with spears, holding horses. The spectators are two men at the sides of the picture wearing chitons and mantles. Each stands with feet slightly separated and holds a spear upright before and close to his body. Basically, the scheme is the same as the mantled male spectator of M.1a, and is coded as type M.2a. There also exists a variation with the hand projecting more clearly from the body while holding the spear (M.2b, see chart in figure 33 and example in figure 13).

Table 19. *Frequency of Types in Spectator Category M.2*

Type	Description	Number of Vases with Type	Frequency, Total Vases with M (223)
M.2a	Spear-bearing, standing still, closed form	59	26.5%
M.2b	Spear-bearing, standing still, hand projects	14	6.3%
M.2c	Spear-bearing, striding, arms and elbows out	5	2.3%
M.2d	Spear-bearing, small stride, one arm up straight	2	1.3%
		Total = 76	34.1%
M.2a–b	Inert, spear-bearing spectator (M.2a & M.2b)	70	31.4%
M.2c–d	Mimetic, spear-bearing spectator (M.2c & M.2d)	8	3.6%

Together, these two types, M.2a and M.2b, belong to the group of inert spectators, like those in category M.1. Again, the spectator signals the importance of the scene that he witnesses, but the addition of the spear serves as an index to recall that the spectator also stands equipped to function like the warriors in the center of the picture, fulfilling an important role as citizen.

Spear-bearing spectators are quite popular on vases, occurring on 76 out of 223 vases with men as spectators (see table 19). Fifty-nine are of the more closed form, M.2a, and an additional 14 belong to the variation M.2b; M.2a is the second most common type of man as spectator after M.1a.

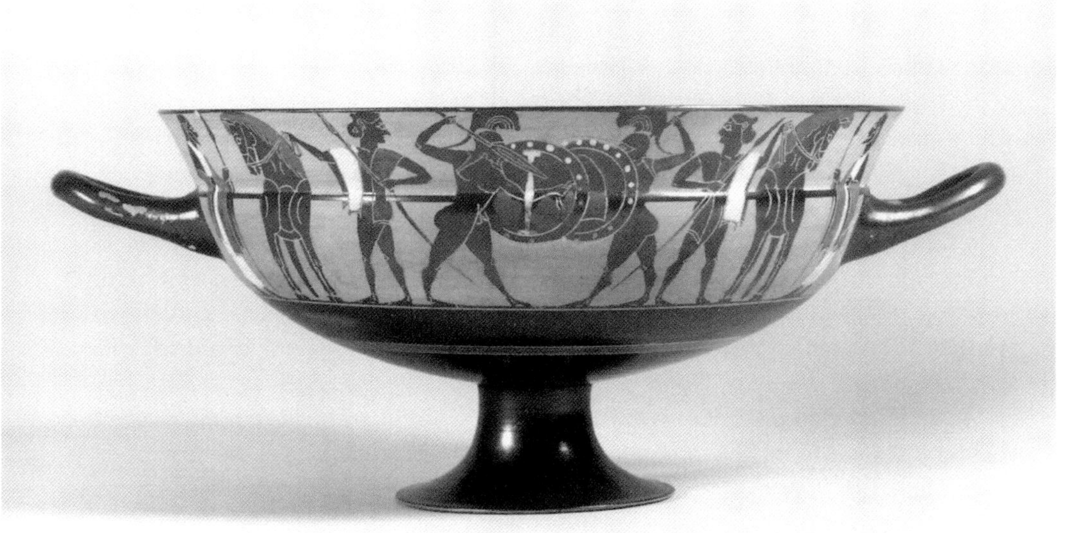

35. Attic black-figure Siana cup attributed to the C Painter, c. 560–550. 5-3/16″ × 12-3/4″ diam. Side A: Warriors fighting. Washington University Gallery of Art, St. Louis, Gift of Robert Brookings and Charles Parson, 1904, WU 3272. (Photograph, Collection, Washington University, St. Louis)

Altogether, inert spectators (M.1 and M.2a/b) are found on 125 vases, accounting for a majority (56.1 percent) of vases with men as spectators (see table 11 in chapter 2). Basically, the inert adult male spectator mirrors the conception of the idealized male form expressed in the kouros statue or in funerary reliefs from the archaic period: arms held close to the body, feet close together, head level with the gaze directed forward, and a tranquil countenance. It also reflects Aristotle's description of the ideal young man: "good in bodily excellences, such as stature, beauty, strength, fitness for athletic contests; the moral excellences of a young man are self-control (*sophrosyne*) and courage (*andreia*)."[9] Adult citizens will display and use these qualities as they lead the city. The self-control demonstrated by the spectator in the face of the spectacle in the narrative nucleus embodies the courage and resolve that mature citizens will have demonstrated in their public life and actions, making them worthy of public respect. Being thus the privileged members of the polis, adult male citizens would demonstrate their position publicly through such formal and restrained behavior. The focused gaze of these "manly" spectators, on the nucleus rather than on the other spectators, is not unlike the downturned gaze expected of athletes, who display modesty or *aidos* by avoiding the gaze of the crowd.[10] Like the kouros, the manly spectator does not meet the gaze of those who can see him, whether other spectator or the viewer of the vase, but looks off to a more timeless situation that exists beyond the time and place of viewing. This also embodies a quality of the thoughtfulness and intentionality in adult men that is also part of the virtues of the ideal citizen. As G. Ferrari has summarized, "*andreia* carries within also the attainment of virtue, and even more, the acquisition of the ability to think."[11]

By their behavior, these inert spectators represent the ideal of the adult male citizen of the polis and provide a model for the viewer of the vase on several levels. As viewers of the vase, they suggest that the proper reaction to a narrative scene should be calm, steady, and reflective, even while consuming the inebriating contents of many of the vases. The heroic qualities of the nucleus thus become embodied in the viewer of the vase by following the behavior of the spectator. On another level, the inert spectator also represents the idealized public behavior of the citizen who is at the apex of the polis. Whether leaving to fight in the army or participating either as audience or performer in public ritual, the inert spectator is how the citizen should appear, reflecting the dignity and strength of the city. A city filled with such citizens would be orderly, grand, and prosperous.

Although the inert spectators account for the majority of all adult male spectators, there are several types of more active, spear-bearing spectators that we also need to examine. In the nucleus of a Siana cup in Copenhagen, we see three armored warriors fighting (figure 36).[12] On either side are youths in mantles, but the next figures out from the center are figures bearing helmets, spears, and shields. They lack the body armor or skirts of the figures in the center, and being separated from the nucleus by the mantled youths, they must be understood as spectators rather than participants in the nucleus. The legs are separated, indicating a strong stride, although their stride is not as

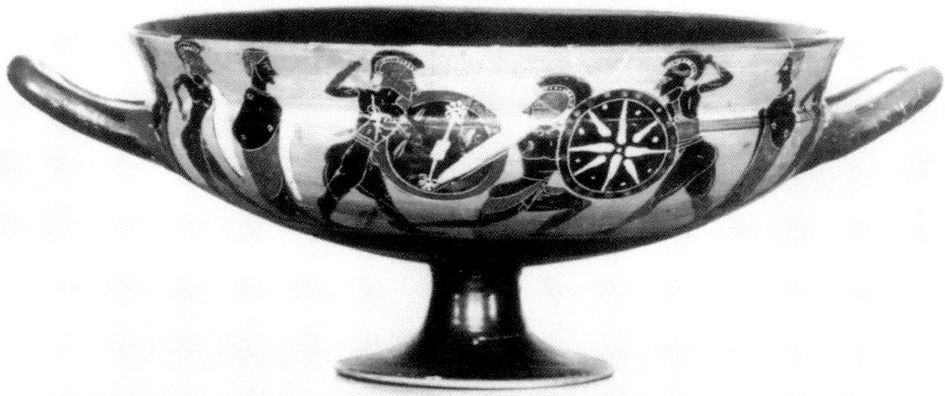

36. Attic black-figure Siana cup attributed to the manner of Lydos, mid-sixth century. Side A: Warriors fighting. Copenhagen, Department of Classical and Near Eastern Antiquities, National Museum of Denmark 6585. (Photo, Museum)

long as those of the central warriors and is more contained. The arms are held out from the body, with the elbows projecting and bent at a right angle. In form, this mimics the arm placement of the central warriors. Generally, the action of this spectator mimics that of the fighting warrior, but is scaled back to the point where the lethal potential of the figure's action is only suggested rather than demonstrated. This figure is coded as type M.2c.[13] The action, indeed, looks more like a parade ground demonstration than a fighting action. Such a marching warrior would have been a part of public display in archaic Athens, and the position of the spectator's arm conveys the sense of marching rather than killing. Like later day military parades, this figure demonstrates strength and skill in wielding spear and shield, and shows a more mimetic behavior than the inert spectator types M.2a and M.2b. His action demonstrates his skill, and that he has earned his position as a citizen of the polis.

While seemingly important as a spectator type because of its activity, the frequency of this figure (M.2c) is actually quite small, being found on five vases. The other active version of the spear-bearing spectator is even less frequent than this, being found on only three vases, two of them works of the Affecter.[14] In this spectator type, the free arm is held out from the body, with the elbow bent at 90°, forearm and hand raised vertically, and the fingers extended (coded M.2d, see figure 33; a parallel can be seen in the youths in figure 44). Both of these types equate the spectator and heroic figure visually, but this is apparently not an important point given their relatively low frequency. Together, the mimetic types of spear-bearing men, M.2c and M.2d, account for only eight vases, 3.5 percent of vases with men as spectators. These types, however, are more important among youthful spectators, as we shall see in the next section.

Table 20. *Frequency of Types in Spectator Category M.3*

Type	Description	Number of Vases with Type	Frequency, Total Vases with M (223)
M.3a	Arm extended, hand and forearm level with waist	17	7.6%
M.3b	Arm extended, hand and forearm lifted up 45°	10	4.5%
M.3c	Arm extended, hand and forearm held vertical	4	1.8%
M.3d	Arm extended, hand and forearm held downward	2	0.9%
		Total = 27	12.1%

M.3: Active Spectators

A third category of adult male spectators consists of figures whose limbs extend further from the body. The hand and usually the entire forearm are clearly extended beyond the silhouette of the torso, and the hand is usually fully extended and often raised to the level of the shoulders or head. The legs are sometimes more spread than with the quieter figures, although there is not a strong indication of motion with these figures. Three different types of this category of active spectators can be seen on the Tyrrhenian type amphora in Karlsruhe that we saw in the previous chapter (figure 22).[15] On the far left is a man holding a walking stick in his right hand, while his left forearm and hand project beyond his torso, level at the waist (coded M.3a). Before him is another man whose right arm also holds a stick, but his left forearm lifts upward at a 45° angle, level with the shoulders (M.3b). The fingers are extended and flat, and the thumb is also held out. Finally, on the right side of the vase, the first male spectator behind the woman lifts his upper arm forward and holds his left forearm straight up with the hand fully extended (M.3c).[16] The gestures have the same general meaning indicating encouragement, attention and watching, and address, either as a farewell or as a greeting. One other gesture type (M.3d) belongs in this category, in which the arm is extended downward at a 45° angle (see figure 33). However, there are only two examples of this gesture and its meaning is basically the same as the others seen here (see table 20).[17]

The figures in this category of active male spectators (M.3) acknowledge the actions of the nucleus not only by their gaze, as do the inert spectators, but they also signal the importance of the event by their arm gestures. These more active gestures would be consistent with a ritualistic context and performance, as we saw in the previous chapter, with the spectators as members of a chorus singing about the deeds that are visualized in the nucleus. As Boegehold has pointed out, Aristotle encourages the inclusion of gestures in the composition of poetry, in order to enter into the emotional state of the action.[18] The use of a single arm for the gesture, with the other arm held tight against the body, signifies a degree of control that would be consistent with a ritualistic context. These gestures, although demonstrative, would not break the decorum and discipline that one would expect from a choral performance.

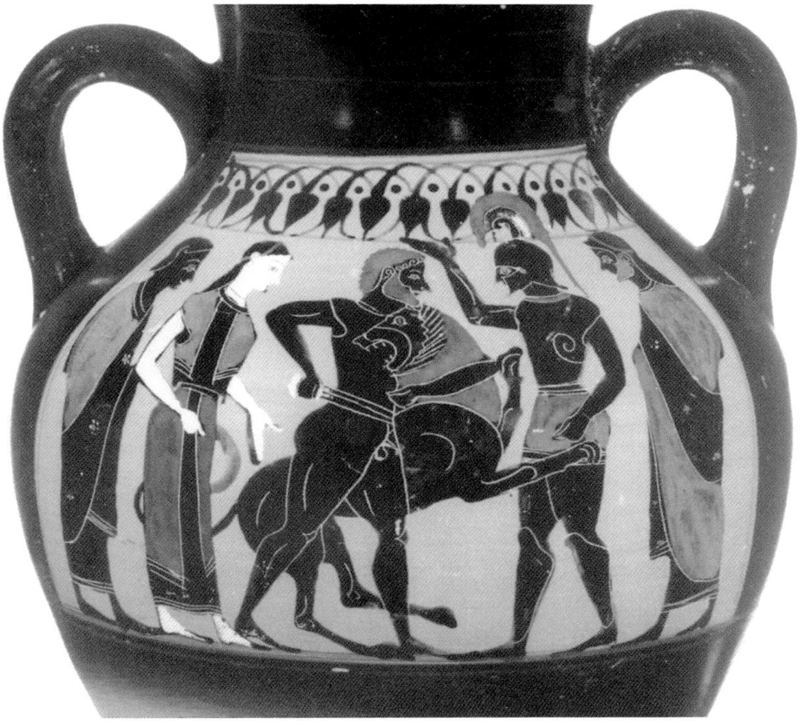

37. Attic black-figure amphora attributed to the Swing Painter, c. 530. Side A: Herakles and the lion. Munich, Antikensammlung 1385. (Photograph, Staatliche Antikensammlungen und Glyptothek München)

The frequency of this category of gesture, however, is much less than either of the previous two categories, M.1 or M.2. There are only 27 total vases, about one in eight vases with men as spectators. The majority (17 of 27) of this category of active spectator is of the first type, M.3a, the one that most closely resembles M.1a and M.2a by having the projecting hand at the level of the waist. This suggests that a more restrained reaction is preferred, even among those spectators who are intended to be more demonstrative in proclaiming the action of the nucleus.

M.4: Very Active Spectators

A fourth category of spectators involves much more dramatic action on the part of the spectator: elbows and arms extending more fully from the body, both arms or hands being used, the feet wider apart and usually conveying a sense of motion, and, frequently, the head turned in the opposite direction from the body. The most common type of these can be seen on an amphora in Munich (figure 37).[19] The nucleus consists of Herakles wrestling the lion, while four figures – a youth, a woman, and two men, look on. The end figures belong to the quiet category of mantled spectators (Y.1a and M.1a),

Table 21. *Frequency of Types in Spectator Category M.4*

Type	Description	Number of Vases with Type	Frequency, Total Vases with M (223)
M.4a	Arm fully extended, held up and out at angle	19	8.5%
M.4b	Arm fully extended, forearm and hand straight up with elbow at 90°	1	0.4%
M.4c	Both arms extended with elbows bent and projecting from body (see also M.2c)	8	3.6%
M.4d	Arm fully extended, held horizontally from shoulder	2	0.9%
M.4w	Arm projects and hand holds up a wreath	6	2.7%
		Total = 33	14.8%

but the figure in front of the lion stretches out his right arm fully and extends his hand to the level of his head (coded M.4a).[20] His left arm is crooked and the elbow projects back, breaking the silhouette on the other side of the torso. The gesture of the extended arm and hand is stronger than the more restrained spectators on either side and indicates a strong response on the part of the spectator. The gesture and position of the arm are the same as those found on men who sing in honor of the dead in prothesis scenes, suggesting a meaning of acclamation, although in funerary scenes both arms are raised, rather than only one arm in the case of this spectator.[21] This use of one arm implies a more restrained action than that associated with mourning, and would indicate that the action is intended to be one of greeting, encouragement, or acclaim.[22] Interestingly, this type of figure, which is found on 19 vases in the CVA census (see table 21), occurs in 10 cases with other spectators who respond in a more restrained manner, such as M.1-3, Y.1-3, or W.1-3. Within the context of a group of spectators, this particular type might well be seen as a "leader" type, actively directing the attention of other spectators or the viewer of the vase to the focal point and perhaps prompting a response or affirmation of his acclaim. Indeed, the inscription on the pseudo-Panathenaic amphora in the Cabinet des Médailles (see figure 7) includes an inscription with the words of praise from the spectators: "good for the tumbler." This gesture, then, suggests a strong link between the action of the nucleus and the spectator and is meant to be a directive for other spectators, including the viewer of the vase.

A rare variation of the acclamation gesture has the arm bent 90° at the elbow, with the forearm straight up and the hand extended with the palm facing sideways or back toward the face of the spectator (type M.4b, see figure 33).[23] The arm position is similar to gesture type M.3c, but the arm projects more from the body. Like M.4a, this is likely a gesture of greeting, encouragement, or acclamation, but it is only found on one vase in the CVA census.

A different type of gesture is found on side B of the amphora Munich 1471, where we see a nude spectator with a chlamys draped over his left arm holding both of his arms

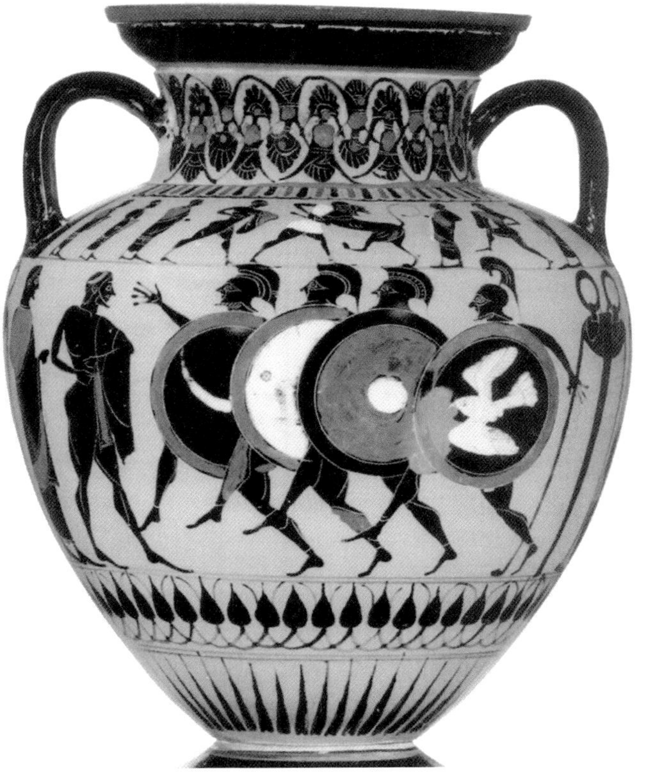

38. Attic black-figure amphora attributed to Group E, c. 540. Side B: Hoplites running. Munich, Antikensammlung 1471. (Photograph, Staatliche Antikensammlungen und Glyptothek München)

out from his body, with the elbows bent sharply at 90° and the hands brought back in front of the chest or abdomen (type M.4c, figure 38).[24] This figure is generally the same in the pose and arm position as the spear-bearing spectator, M.2c, and the use of both arms indicates a strong response to the action, in this case a race of hoplites. Generally, the pose of the figure mimics the extension or position of the arms of the hero in the nucleus of the picture, which, in four of the eight examples of this type, is Herakles. In figure 38, the position of the spectator's upper arms and his lifting of the heels reflect, in a slightly restrained form, the upper arms and feet of the runners. The mimetic quality of this spectator indicates not only an acknowledgment of the figures in the nucleus of the picture, but identification through imitation of the spectator with those figures. Such a pose would be extremely unlikely for a viewer holding the vase, who would appear more like the youth behind the man, but it would evoke memories on the part of the viewer of his own or others' participation and the excitement and response that it can generate within the body. Interestingly, in five of the eight examples, there is a quiet, standing youth (Y.1a or Y.2a) in the picture, and it is possible to think of the adult spectator as well as the hero as being the secondary object of the youth's gaze, as we saw in figure 14. Still, this type of spectator is found in only 3.6 percent of all vases with adult male spectators, suggesting that although not rare, it is not a common type.

Two other types need to be mentioned in the category of very active spectators. The first, type M.4d, consists of a striding figure whose arm reaches straight out as in type M.4a, but with the arm kept level at the shoulders (see figure 33). There are only two examples of this gesture type, but its function as one of speaking and acclamation is similar to M.4a.[25] Finally, there is the adult male spectator who holds a wreath while observing the central scene in the nucleus (figure 33).[26] Although the arms do not extend from the body as much as the other M.4 gestures, the act of offering an object signifying triumph toward the nucleus establishes a strong structural connection between the spectator and the nucleus. There are six examples of this type, which is also found among youth and women spectators.

As a category, very active men are slightly more frequent as spectators than the more restrained figures of category M.3. There is, however, a particular interest in the acclamation/leader type of M.4a and its variant M.4d, together accounting for about one in 10 vases with men as spectators.

M.5: Spectators Leaning on Sticks; M.6: Spectators Sitting

The last two categories of adult male spectators are those leaning on sticks and those who are seated. An example of the former can be found on an amphora in London that features an aulos player and singer on a bema (figure 39).[27] To the left is an adult male wearing a mantle loosely wrapped over one shoulder and his torso and a wreath on his head. He bows his head and brings his bent arms across the front of his body to rest on his stick. This type, M.5a, constitutes half of the 18 examples of spectators leaning on sticks (see table 22). Less common versions have the spectator stretch one arm out and down toward the central scene (M.5b, two examples), lift his back arm to place his hand on his hip (M.5c, three examples), or to stand up straight and hold the stick out straight, not unlike the quietly standing, spear-bearing spectators (M.5d, five examples, see figure 33 for all types).[28] Only two of the examples occur with mythological scenes; most are placed in music, palaistra, or athletic contexts. The category only begins to appear in the last quarter of the sixth century, and is more popular on red-figure work of the fifth century. The appearance of this category of spectators on scenes closely associated with public musical performances suggests a strong link between the elaborations or refinements of the festival in the late sixth century and the development of a new type of spectator modeled on behavior at the festivals. Certainly the tilt of the head on many of the figures, especially in recitals, suggests an emphasis on attentiveness, whereas the stick becomes a sign of the privileged citizen about town.[29]

The seated spectator appears more frequently as a category than the spectator leaning on a stick. The category has been divided into two main types based on posture, without subdivision by gesture: spectators reclining on a kline or couch (M.6a), and

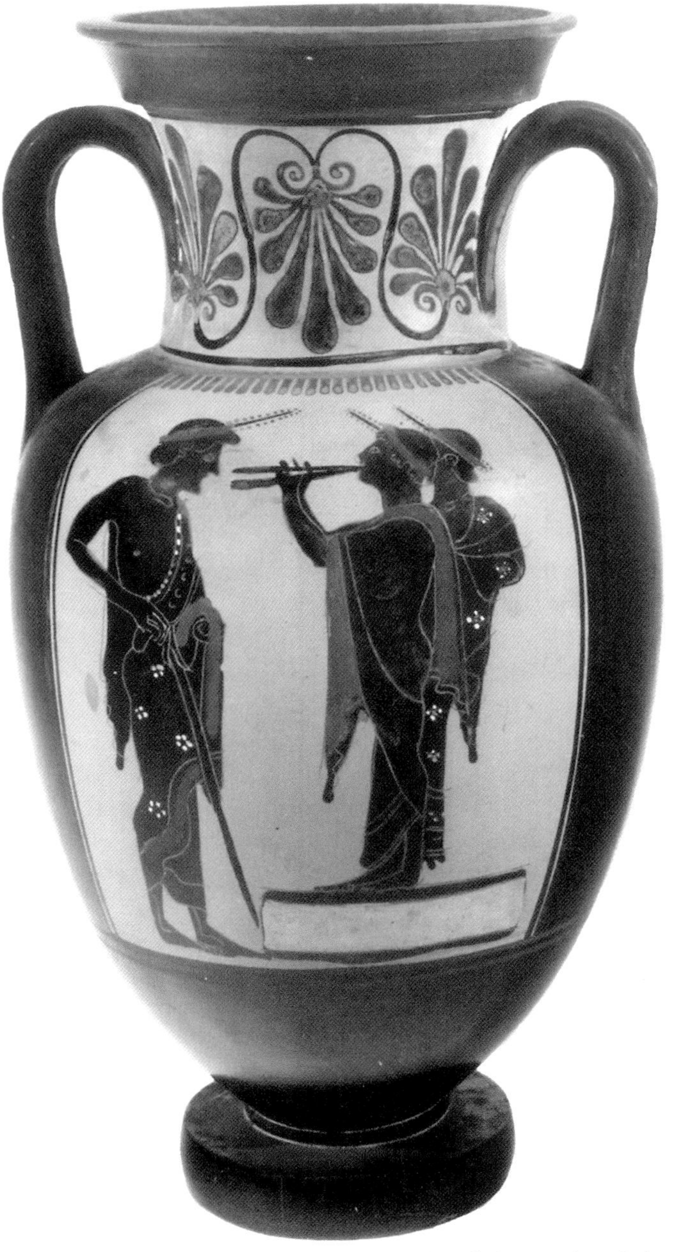

39. Attic black-figure neck amphora attributed to the Edinburgh Painter, late sixth century. Side A: Flute player. London, British Museum B188. (Photograph © Copyright The Trustees of The British Museum)

Table 22. *Frequency of Types in Spectator Categories M.5 and M.6*

Type	Description	Number of Vases with Type	Frequency, Total Vases with M (223)
M.5a	Leaning on stick, arms drawn in front of body	9	4.0%
M.5b	Leaning on stick, one arm extended down & out	2	0.9%
M.5c	Leaning on stick, one hand back on hip	3	1.3%
M.5d	Standing and holding stick upright at arm's length	6	2.7%
		Total = 18	8.1%
M.6a	Reclining on a couch, usually listening intently	12	5.4%
M.6b	Sitting upright, on chair, stool, or ground	16	7.2%
		Total = 28	12.6%

those sitting upright on a chair, stool, bench, or the ground (M.6b). There are 12 examples of the reclining spectator (see figure 54); all belong, not surprisingly, to a symposion setting, and two-thirds are from the fifth century. There are, of course, many such scenes with symposiasts observing servers or entertainers, but most of these have been excluded from the CVA census because a boundary between the onlooker and the performer, in terms of dress, behavior, or intention, is not clearly demarcated. The examples included in the CVA census feature musicians as the nucleus of the composition, a distinction in the dress or attributes of the musician and the listener, and a lack of movement on the part of the spectator to show anything more than an intention to listen to the music. That most of these situations would fall in the fifth century, at a time when spectators were no longer an active part of the visual repertory, suggests a shift in the role of the spectator and a concept closer to our idea of a concert being at work in the representation of these spectators.

There are 16 examples of the seated upright spectator, all but one coming from the sixth century or first decade of the fifth. Typical are the figures found on the shoulder of an amphora in Kansas City (figure 40).[30] In the central nucleus are two boxers; two men sit on either side, holding a staff upright at a slight angle with one hand. The spectators here may be judges rather than simple observers, but they make no movement toward the scene and do not convey a sense of any decision-making role in the picture.[31] Indeed, seated spectators would be expected as part of an athletic contest (see figure 7), so one could think of these figures as elite observers. Their seated position does emphasize the formal as well as public nature of the contest, as would be appropriate at the Panathenaia. In addition to athletic contests, seated spectators are found with musical performances, mythological scenes, and anonymous warriors fighting. The range of subject matter indicates that these figures have the same flexibility of use as that of the other types of spectators, unlike the reclining spectators. Their presence at mythological and fighting scenes, which might be the subject of choral poem and performance, suggests that seated figures would have been familiar at ritualistic ceremonies as well as contests. Certainly the seated figure seems to imply

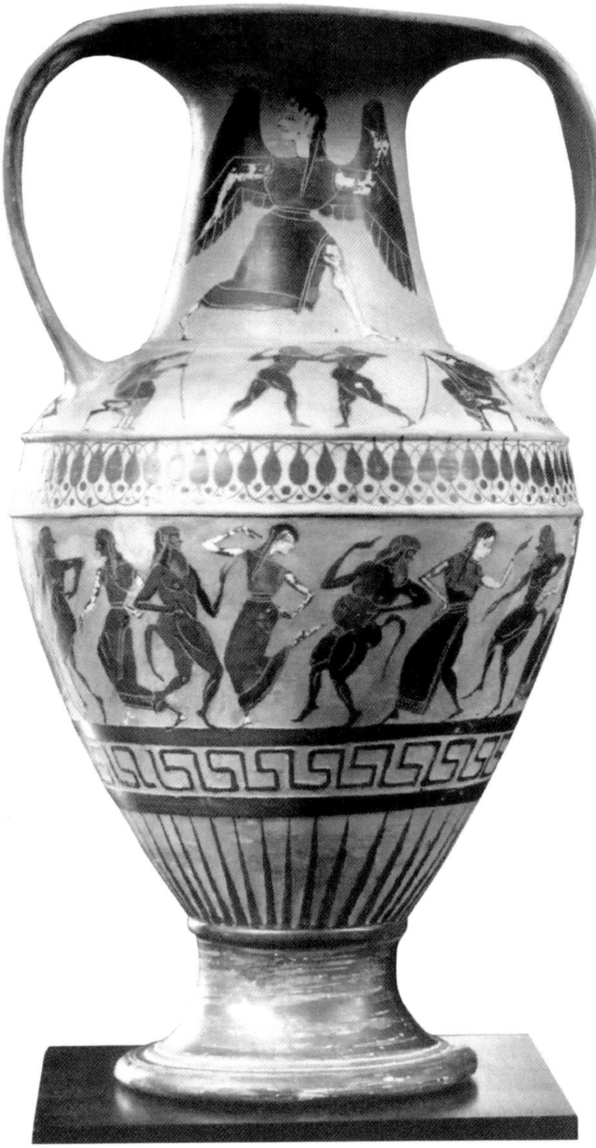

40. Attic black-figure Nikosthenic amphora attributed to the N Painter, c. 535–520. Side A, Shoulder: Boxers. The Nelson-Atkins Museum of Art, Kansas City, Missouri, (Purchase: Nelson Trust) 52–22. (Photograph, Nelson-Atkins Museum)

the sense of a public occasion, whereas the reclining spectator is a sign of a more private or domestic setting.

To review, we can look once more at the behavioral moods of inert, reactive, and mimetic men as spectators to see the broader patterns of behavior (table 23). A small majority has figures that belong to the inert behavioral mood of spectator. Within this

Table 23. *Men as Spectators by Mood*

Mood	Types	Number	Frequency, Total Vases with M (223)
Inert	M.1; M.2a–b	125	56.1%
Reactive	M.2d; M.3; M.4a–b, w; M.5; M.6	93	41.7%
Mimetic	M.2c; M.4c–d	15	6.7%

group, the fact that the spear-bearing types are about equal in number to the simple, mantled figures points to the adult male's status and importance within the polis. A little more than four out of 10 vases with men have reactive spectators, whereas only one in 15 has a mimetic spectator. The difference in frequency between inert and reactive spectators is less than with youths or women, suggesting that some kind of action was expected of these figures, albeit within the model of the controlled behavior of the inert spectator. Among the reactive types, the most common are those using gestures that would be appropriate for a choral performance (M.3a), the "leader" type making an acclamation (M.4a), and the seated upright figure that would indicate an elite status as observer (M.6b). Each of these individually is higher in frequency than the mimetic types, suggesting that when showing a spectator responding to the scene in front of him, it was more important to convey a sense of his position within the community: upright, steady, focused. Perhaps, having achieved the status of full membership in the polis and having some deeds already to his credit, there was no need for these figures to acclaim themselves in public except to show their authority. Rather, they stand ready to receive the gaze of the viewer as worthy of attention, like the nucleus of the picture.

5.3 GESTURES AMONG YOUTHFUL MALE SPECTATORS

Y.1: Inert/Inactive Spectators

The types of youthful spectators follow generally those of the adult men, but there are some important differences in the frequency of some types and in the greater variety of poses and gestures for active youths than for men. Where possible, this correspondence is indicated by using the same small letter designation, hence type Y.1a is like type M.1a. Where such comparisons exist, the adult type will be referenced under the descriptions of youthful types in tables 24 to 28.

The most common single type of adult man, the mantled figure with the hand projecting slightly (M.1a), has an exact parallel among youthful spectators. As can be seen on an amphora in Munich (figure 41), the youthful figures are completely encased in their mantle, and the hands project under the fold or edge of the mantle falling in front of the body.[32] The two figures watch a warrior with shield and spear

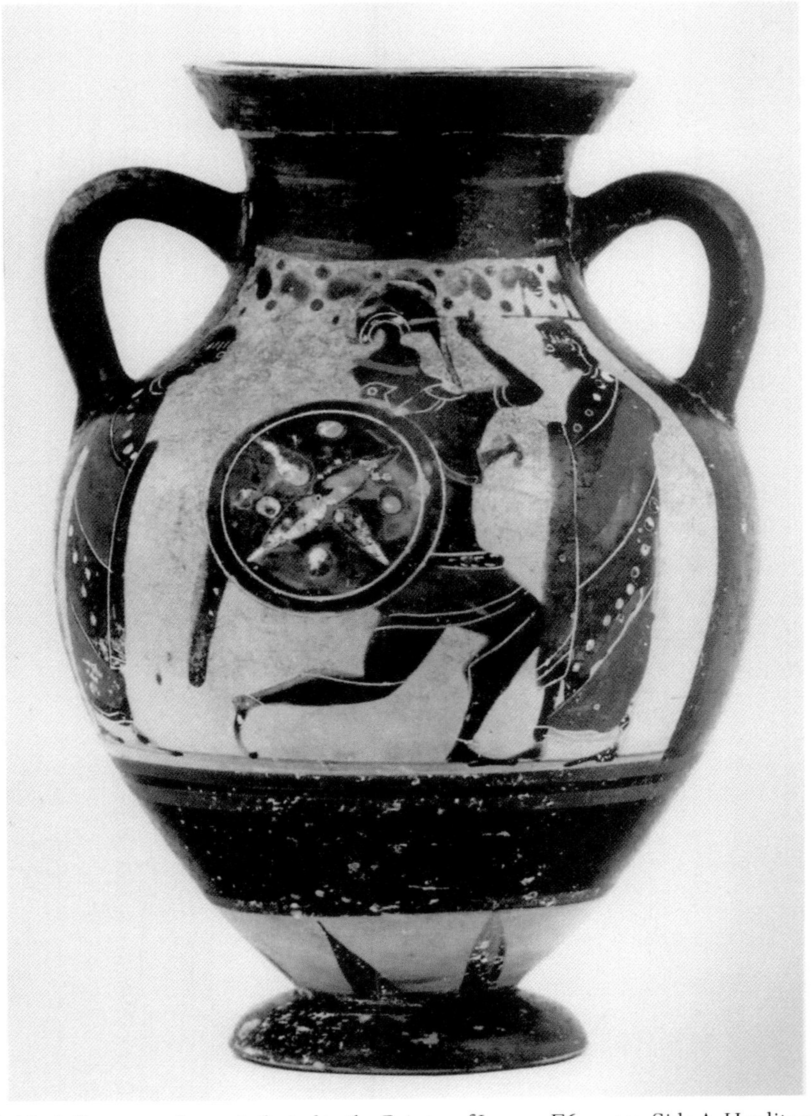

41. Attic black-figure amphora attributed to the Painter of Louvre F6, c. 550. Side A: Hoplite performing. Munich, Antikensammlung 1369. (Photograph, Staatliche Antikensammlungen und Glyptothek München)

who turns 180° in a reverse pivot. The scene is probably intended to show a demonstration of the warrior's agility and prowess as part of a civic display, or may be part of a competition involving hoplites or a pyrrhic dance.[33] The youths show virtually no movement or reaction, and their gaze is focused intently on the nucleus of the composition. A variation, with the hand extended from the torso (Y.1b), conforms to the same basic concept of the mantled youth (see the chart of youthful spectators in

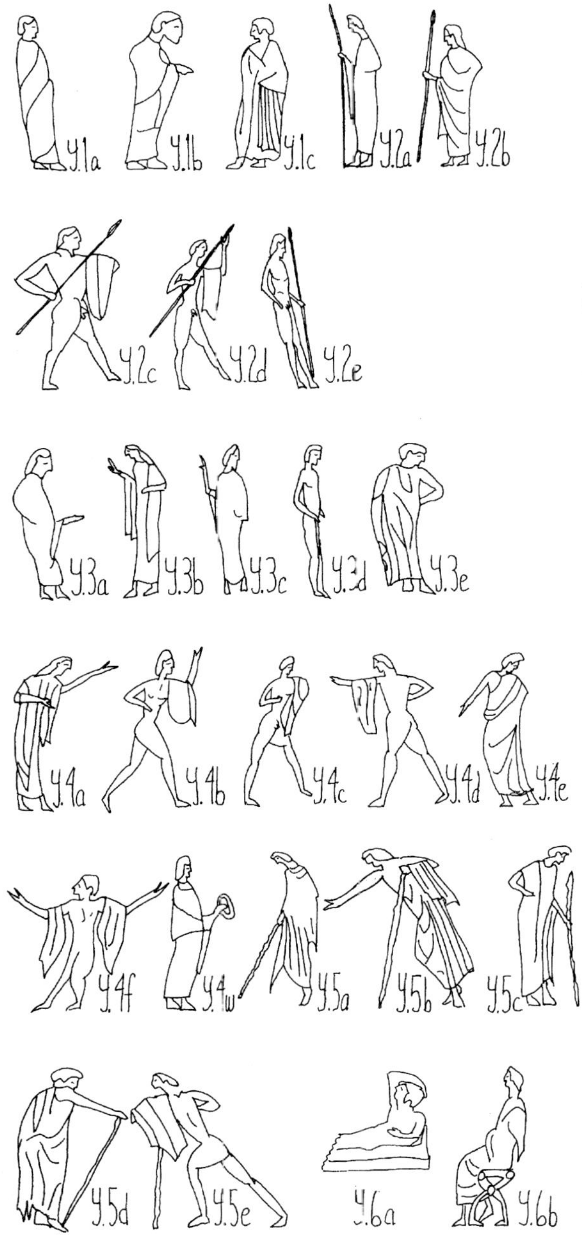

42. Chart of youth spectator types. (Drawings, author)

figure 42). Like adult men, there is also a variation of the youth completely encased in his mantle (Y.1c), but this is found only on 13 red-figure vases of the fifth century.[34]

Although the formal parallel between the standing, mantled spectator for men and youths is clear, their frequency is strikingly different. There are 259 vases with

Table 24. *Frequency of Types in Spectator Category Y.1*

Type	Description	Number of Vases with Type	Frequency, Total Vases with Y (527)
Y.1a	Standing still, closed form (compare M.1a)	219	41.6%
Y.1b	Standing still, hand projects beyond body (cf. M.1b)	34	6.5%
Y.1c	Standing still, encased in mantle (cf. M.1c)	13	2.5%
		Total = 259	49.1%

examples of Y.1, out of 527 vases featuring youths, almost one-half the entire corpus (see table 24). This frequency, 49.1 percent, compares with 31.8 percent for adult males, strongly suggesting that the mantled youth was a much more important prototype for the youthful citizen and viewer of a vase. Indeed, the mantle and the level or downturned gaze emphasize the modesty or *aidos* that was a primary virtue for youth, as well as the nonreactive demeanor when confronting a scene.[35] This behavior is in the same vein as the response expected of the *eromenos* that we saw in chapter 3, in which the youthful object of love, even while surrounded or pressed with the attentions of an admiring adult male, was to show little reaction or pleasure to the caresses or

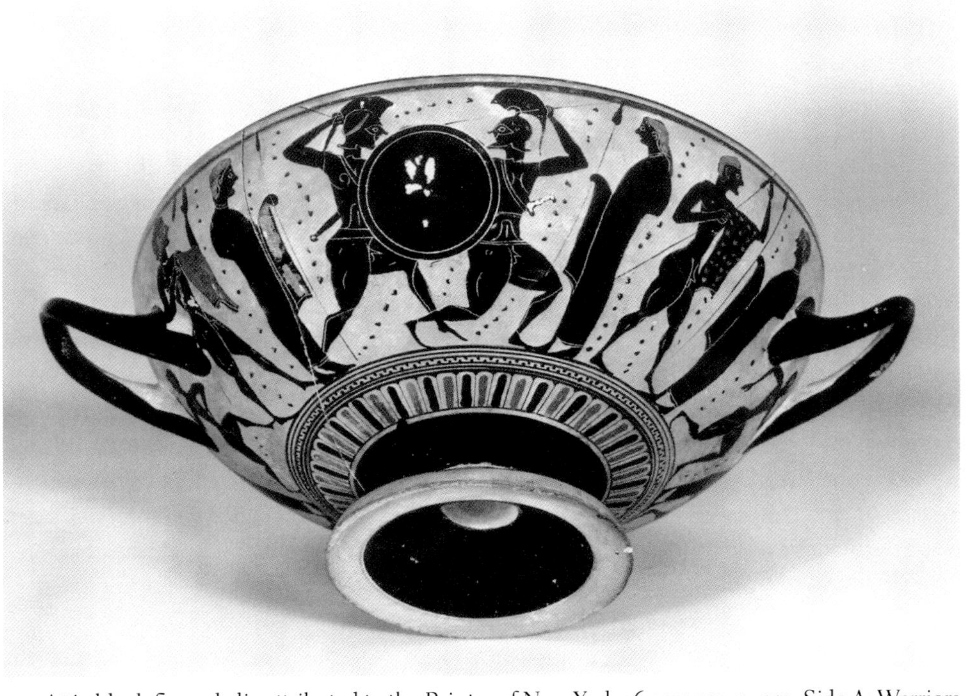

43. Attic black-figure kylix attributed to the Painter of New York 06.1021.159, c. 550. Side A: Warriors fighting. New York, The Metropolitan Museum of Art, Rogers Fund (06.1021.159). (Photograph, all rights reserved, The Metropolitan Museum of Art)

entreaties of the *erastes*. The strong prevalence of this kind of spectator indicates that the behavior expected in a personal relationship extended more broadly to public behavior at festivals and other civic occasions.

Y.2: Spear-Bearing Spectators

Spear-bearing youths occur in the same types and with the same overall percentage frequency as adult men, but there is one additional active type that we shall see in a moment. The quietly standing, spear-bearing youth (Y.2a) can be seen on a kylix in New York on which two warriors are fighting (figure 43).[36] The spectators at either end of the composition are mantled youths who quietly hold a spear in front of them and have their mantle completely covering their wrist. Other than their age distinction, these figures are the same as the most common type of male spear-bearing spectator (M.2a). A variation with the hand extended further from the mantle (Y.2b) can be seen on the shoulder of a hydria in London, in which two mantled youths watch two warriors fighting over a corpse (figure 44).[37]

Both of these vases also depict active spear-bearing youths as spectators alongside the inert types. The London hydria has two mostly nude youths, with only a chlamys draped over the arm, striding vigorously from the ends of the panel toward the central action (type Y.2c).[38] Their spears are held at an angle and their arms and elbows are extended sharply with their hands brought together in front of their body. The arm position and angled spear are indexes that mimic the action and weapon of the warriors in the center, making these mimetic spectators. The New York kylix (figure 43) also shows a mostly nude, striding youth with a chlamys over the arm, holding out the left arm with the elbow bent at 90° and the hand extended fully in a gesture that suggests more acclaim than mimesis (type Y.2d).[39] Both of these types of active spear-bearing youths recall elements of the performing warrior seen in figure 41. Although it is clear that none of these youths has any of the visual elements that belong to the pyrrhic dance – aulist, close synchronized formation, shield, helmet – their movement and arm positions do imitate those of weapons dancers or publicly performing warrriors. These figures are thus metonymic in character, borrowing an aspect of a more defined type of figure and action and thereby adopting elements of its virtues and identity. It might be best to consider such spectators as analogous to those 16-year old boys who are introduced to the phrateries and begin to participate and train for public performances and duties, rather than as trained and accomplished dancers.[40] The character of these figures provides an active model for the viewer of the cup in terms of the proper active response of a youth to an event or narrative and the connection between the actions of youths and their future role in the polis.

There is one additional type of spear-bearing spectator found for youths that does not occur among men – a standing, fully nude type seen on a skyphos in Mainz (figure 45).[41] Again, a combat forms the nucleus of the composition, with Herakles

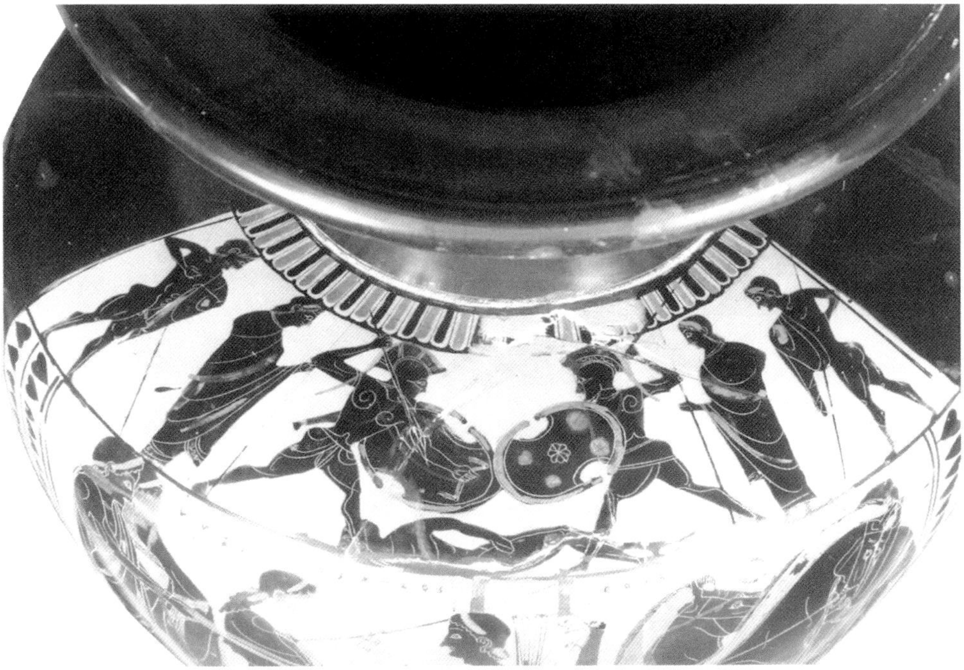

44. Attic black-figure hydria akin to the Lysippides Painter, c. 525–510. Shoulder: Warriors fighting. London, British Museum B339. (Photograph © Copyright The Trustees of The British Museum)

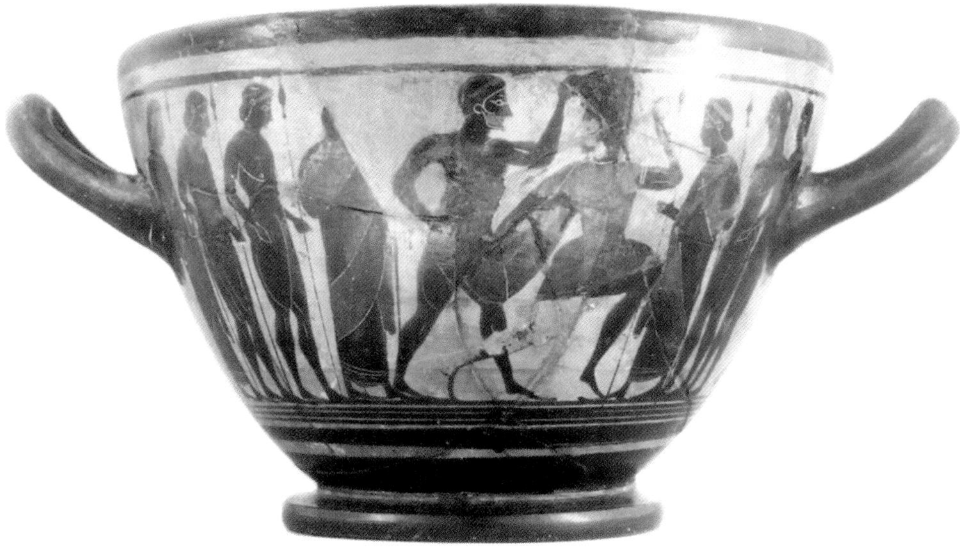

45. Attic black-figure skyphos attributed to Ure's Class of Skyphoi, c. 530. Side A: Herakles fighting an Amazon. Mainz, Universität 75. (Photograph, Institut für Klassische Archäologie, Johannes Gutenberg-Universität Mainz)

Table 25. *Frequency of Types in Spectator Category Y.2*

Type	Description	Number of Vases with Type	Frequency, Total Vases with Y (527)
Y.2a	Spear-bearing, standing still, closed form (cf. M.2a)	133	25.2%
Y.2b	Spear-bearing, standing still, hand projects (cf. M.2b)	33	6.3%
Y.2c	Spear-bearing, striding, arms and elbows out (cf. M.2c)	14	2.7%
Y.2d	Spear-bearing, small stride, one arm up straight (cf. M.2d)	15	2.8%
Y.2e	Spear-bearing, nude, small stride, arms bent, "kouros" type (cf. Y.3d)	9	1.7%
		Total = 177	33.6%
Y.2a–b	Inert, spear-bearing spectators	162	30.7%
Y.2c–e	Active, spear-bearing spectators (reactive and mimetic)	32	6.1%

attacking an Amazon, while youths watch from both sides. Half are of the type Y.2a, but half are nude with the front arm drawn back and their back, spear-holding hand projecting forward (type Y.2e). The pose is similar to that of the mantled youth, but without the clothing there is more disruption in the silhouette and a slightly more active pose results. The figure most closely resembles a kouros statue, although the arm position is more bent and the arms are more extended. Undoubtedly the kouros statue is the model for this type of figure and serves as an ideal model for the youthful male, and we will refer to this pose as the kouros-type, whether with or without a spear (see type Y.3d, discussed later).

The overall frequency of vases with spear-bearing youths is comparable to that for adult men, but there are some differences among specific types. About one-third of vases with youths have spear-bearing spectators (see table 25), almost exactly the same proportion as in vases with men. Whereas types M.1 and M.2 were nearly equal in number, spear-bearing youths are notably less frequent than their mantled counterparts. However, the proportion of active spear-bearing youths (Y.2c-e), 6.1 percent, is nearly double that for men, suggesting that the active spear-bearing spectator is more important as a model for youth. As on the London and New York vases, these active types are usually found paired with inert types in the same composition, so that we frequently find two types of responses for youthful spectators shown on the same work: one restrained and impassive, the other mimicking or acclaiming the behavior of the model in the nucleus of the picture.

Y.3: Active Spectators

Like adult men, the more active types of youthful spectators (Y.3 and Y.4) are fewer than the inert mood of spectators, and are about equally divided between active and very active types. There are 60 vases with the active category of spectator (Y.3), or 11.4 percent of the total vases with youths, compared with 12.1 percent of vases with

Table 26. *Frequency of Types in Spectator Category Y.3*

Type	Description	Number of Vases with Type	Frequency, Total Vases with Y (527)
Y.3a	Arm extended, hand and forearm level with waist (compare M.3a)	32	6.1%
Y.3b	Arm extended, hand and forearm lifted up 45° (compare M.4b)	9	1.7%
Y.3c	Arm extended, hand and forearm held vertical (compare M.4c)	5	0.9%
Y.3d	Standing still, arms bent and hands forward from body ("kouros" type)	18	3.4%
Y.3e	Standing with one hand on hip, elbow bent	1	0.2%
		Total = 60	11.4%

men (see table 26). The first three types are like those defined for M.3, with the figure standing and extending one forearm straight out (Y.3a, see chart at figure 42), up at a 45° angle (Y.3b), or vertically with the elbow bent 90° (Y.3c). A band cup in Tübingen with Herakles and the lion as the nucleus shows two standing spectators flanking the hero with their back arms extended from their body and their front arms and elbows held back slightly (figure 46).[42] A Nikosthenic amphora in the Louvre shows a mantled youth to the right of the rider raising his arm at a 45° angle, type Y.3b (figure 47).[43] The type with horizontal arm (Y.3a), however, is found more than twice as frequently as the other two types combined, a more lopsided distribution than was found for the types M.3a–c (compare Table 20).

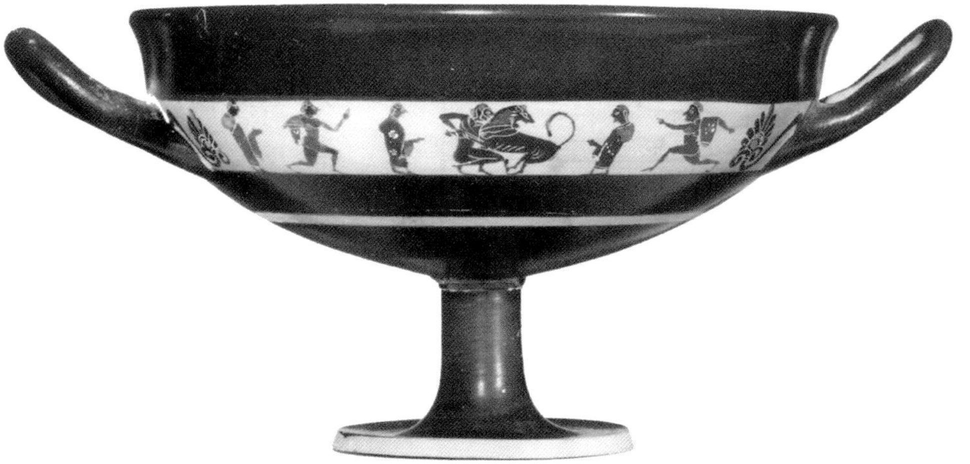

46. Attic black-figure band cup, c. 530. Side A: Herakles and the lion. Institut für Klassische Archäologie, Eberhard-Karls-Universität Tübingen, S./705. (Photograph, Institut für Klassische Archäologie)

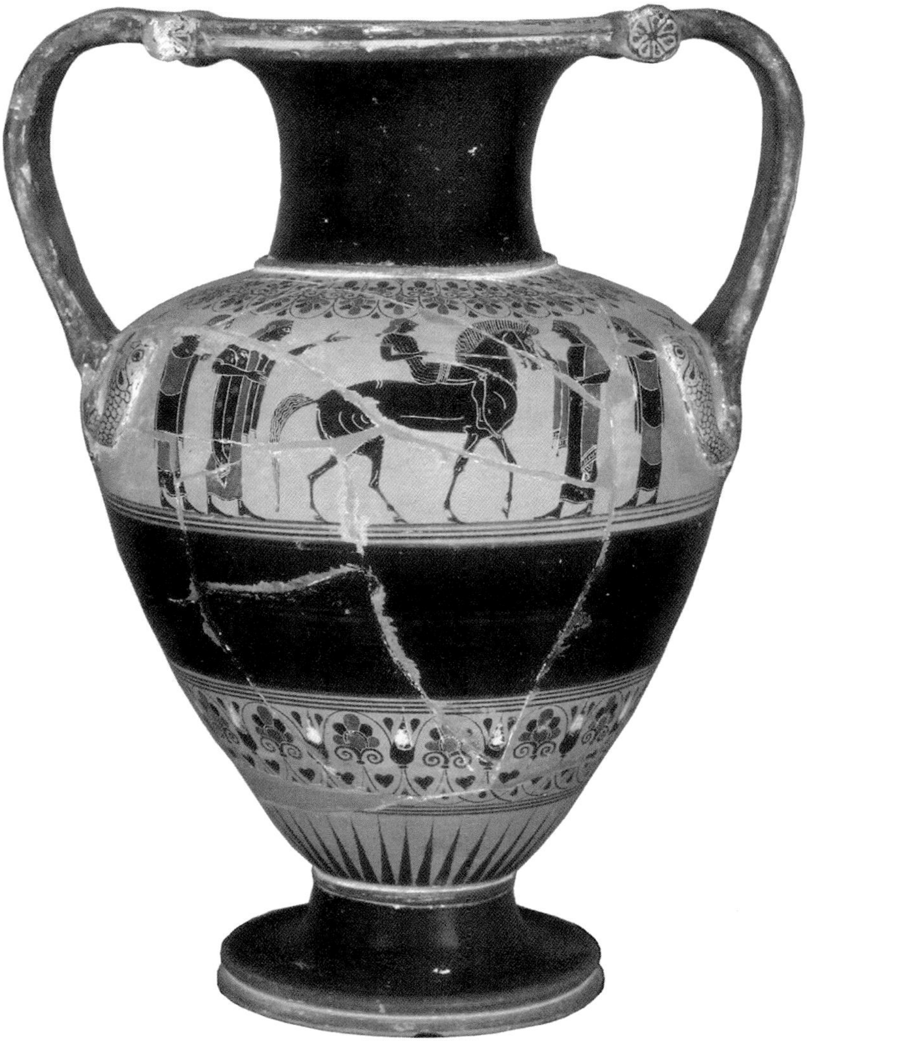

47. Attic black-figure Nikosthenic amphora attributed to the BMN Painter, c. 525. Side B: Rider. Paris, Musée du Louvre F99. (Photograph, Réunion des Musées Nationaux/Art Resource, NY)

In addition to these three types that are common to both men and youths, there is a type of spectator in this category exclusive to youths – the standing nude youth or kouros type that we saw among the active spear-bearing types (Y.2e). The type without the spear (Y.3d) can be found on a skyphos in Karlsruhe, where there are four of the nude youths at the ends of the composition watching Herakles and the lion (figure 48).[44] There are 18 vases with this type of spectator, and combined with the nine examples of the spear-bearing kouros type (Y.2e), there are 26 vases with kouros-type figures, 5.1 percent of all vases with youthful spectators. Although not a huge group, it is a significant type that is exclusive to youths and emphasizes the appeal of the nude ideal for that group.

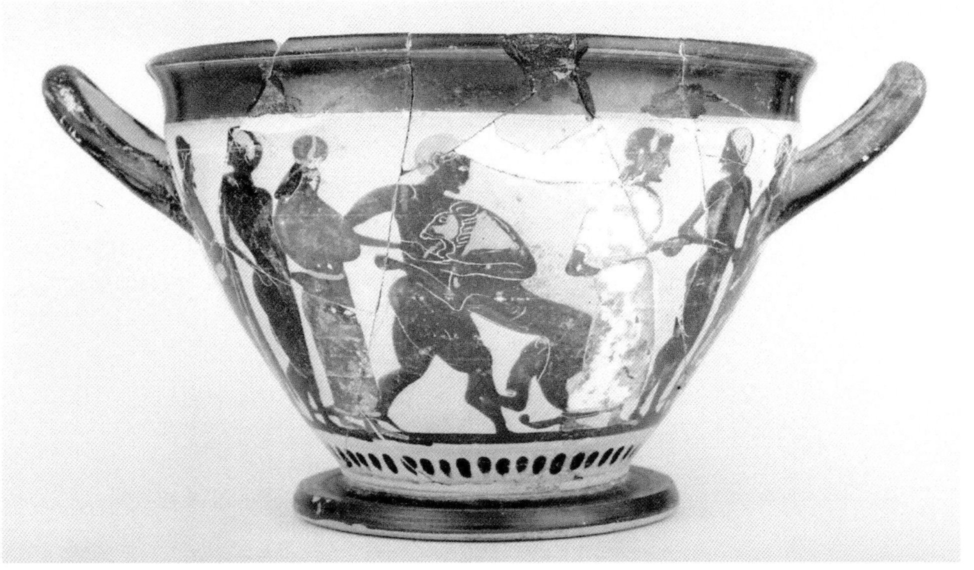

48. Attic black-figure skyphos attributed to the Painter of the Karlsruhe Skyphos, beginning fifth century. Side B: Herakles and the lion. Badisches Landesmuseum Karlsruhe Inv. B 3048. (Photograph, Badisches Landesmuseum Karlsruhe)

There is one additional example of this category, a standing youth with one hand on his hip, for which there is one red-figure example (type Y.3e, see chart at figure 42).[45] The type appears with and is more related to the stick-bearing figures (Y.5) found in the fifth century that will be discussed subsequently.

Y.4: Very Active Spectators

The category of very active, youthful spectators, Y.4, has a slightly lower frequency on vases than the same category of adult males – 12.9 percent compared with 14.8 percent respectively. There are some distinctions in types as well (see table 27). The first type of adult male spectator, which was likened to the role of a chorus leader (M.4a), does find a counterpart among youths (Y.4a, see diagram in figure 42), but the frequency of the type is vastly different. Whereas this type was by far the largest for very active adult males (see table 21), there are only six vases with examples for youth. One of these examples can be seen in the shoulder scene on the Minneapolis amphora that we saw at the beginning of this chapter (figure 32), and another on the Nikosthenic amphora in the Louvre (figure 47). In both cases, the youth raises his arm out and upward toward the nucleus. The appearance of this figure in the midst of inert spectators confirms the idea of the figure as a leader type, and the gesture as proclaiming the importance of the action in the center and firmly directing the attention of the other spectators and the viewer. Its relatively lower frequency on vases with youths, however, points out that this type is primarily the prerogative of the adult male citizen.

Table 27. *Frequency of Types in Spectator Category Y.4*

Type	Description	Number of Vases with Type	Frequency, Total Vases with Y (527)
Y.4a	Arm fully extended, held up and out at angle (cf. M.4a)	6	1.1%
Y.4b	Arm fully extended, forearm and hand straight up and elbow at 90° (cf. M.4b)	22	4.2%
Y.4c	Both elbows bent and projecting from body (see also Y.2c, cf. M.4c)	29	5.5%
Y.4d	One arm extended straight out from body, other arm bent back, large stride	15	2.8%
Y.4e	Both arms held forward at 45° from horizontal	2	0.4%
Y.4f	Both arms held straight out on either side of body	2	0.4%
Y.4w	Arm projects and hand holds up a wreath (cf. M.4w)	4	0.8%
		Total = 66	12.9%

A variation on this type is more common among youths, in which the arm is bent 90° at the elbow and the arm is held straight up, as can be seen on the shoulder of a hydria in Berlin (type Y.4b, figure 49).[46] Only one example of the similar type for men (M.4b) is found in the CVA census, whereas 22 vases have type Y.4b. The significance of the bent elbow compared with the straightened arm is not clear because both of these gestures are used for greetings, farewells, and encouragement, although McNiven sees a significant number of the bent-elbow gestures in use for conversation, and none for the straight-arm gesture.[47] Perhaps the gesture should be seen as one of response and affirmation, rather than of direction and proclamation, and therefore considered more appropriate for a youth than a man.

A third type of very active spectator is similar to the spear-bearing type Y.2c, a striding youth with both elbows sharply bent and extended, and the hands brought back in front of the body (Y.4c), as can be seen on the shoulder of Munich 1471 (figure 50).[48] To the left of Herakles and the lion are two mostly nude youths, each with a chlamys over his arm, striding toward the center scene. The pose here is mimetic of the action in the center, and this is typically the function of this type, to have the youth imitate the action of the hero in the center of the picture field. Flanked by two different types of mantled spectators, Y.1a and Y.3a, we have a picture here that resembles a chorus that sings and a second group that might be thought to be as dancing, each acknowledging in a different manner the deeds of the hero Herakles. This mimetic type is the most common type of very active youthful spectator, with examples on 29 vases.

The picture on the shoulder of the Munich amphora also has another type of active spectator, a striding youth with his arm held straight out and level with the shoulder (Y.4d).[49] Again, the difference between this gesture and that of the arm held up at an angle (Y.4a) is perhaps subtle, but it is worth noting that the same type with chlamys over the arm is not found among adult male spectators. The gesture is sometimes

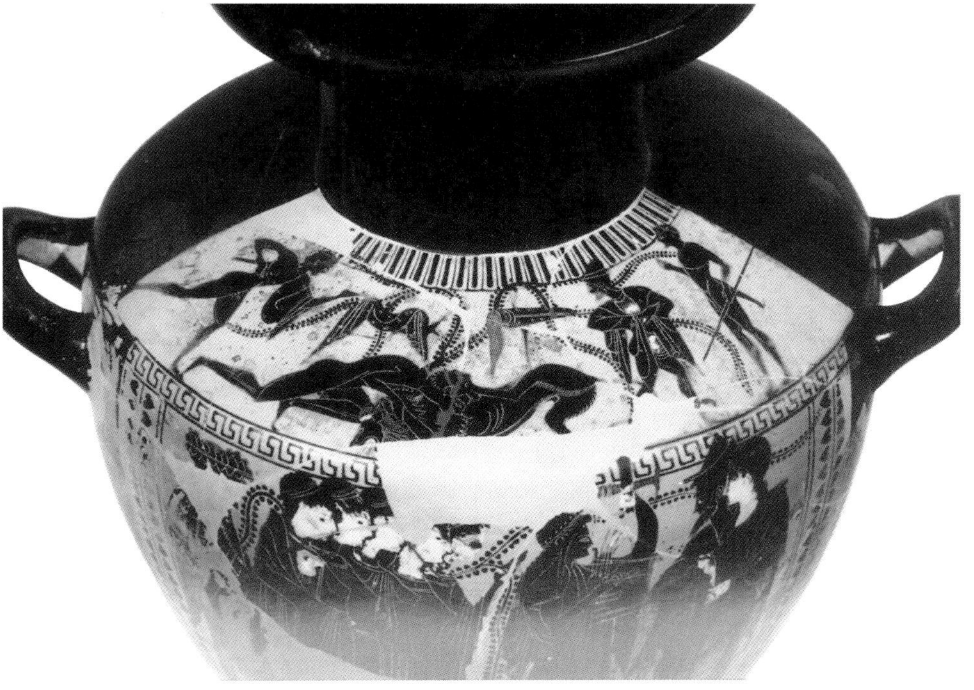

49. Attic black-figure hydria attributed to the Priam Painter, c. 525–500. Shoulder: Herakles and the lion. Berlin, Staatliche Museen zu Berlin – Preussischer Kulturbesitz Antikensammlung F1905. (Photograph, Bildarchiv Preussischer Kulturbesitz/Art Resource, NY)

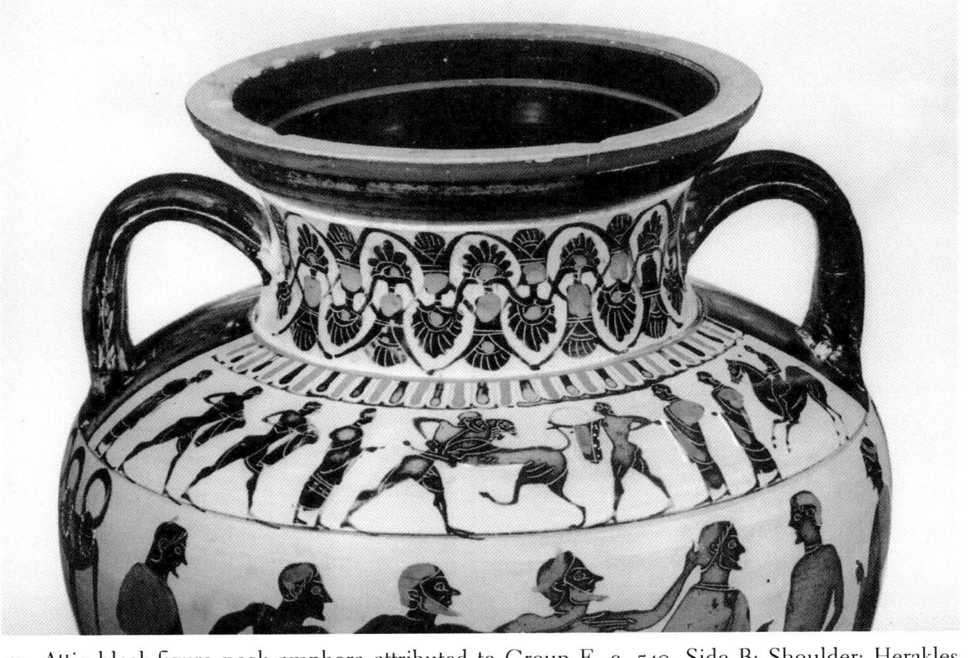

50. Attic black-figure neck amphora attributed to Group E, c. 540. Side B: Shoulder: Herakles and lion. Munich, Antikensammlung 1471. (Photograph, Staatliche Antikensammlungen und Glyptothek München)

linked to the idea of supplication, but most of the examples that McNiven found could be classified as threat or attack. Its frequency in hunting scenes is notable, and so should probably fall into the category of mimetic, such as Y.2c, although with an overtone of pointing and acclamation.[50] There are 15 examples of this type, making it third most common in this category. Its role as a mimetic, rather than reactive, gesture makes it similar to Y.4c.

There are a few additional types that are not frequently represented in the very active category. As with men, there is a wreath-bearing youth (Y.4w, see chart in figure 42), but it is found at a lower frequency (0.8 percent) than for men (2.7 percent).[51] There are also two gestures unique to youths, but with only a couple of examples of each. One has one arm held forward from the body at a 45° angle (Y.4e, see figure 43).[52] The other is found on a band cup in Boston, on which we see a youth with both arms extended straight out on opposite sides of the body (type Y.4f, figure 51).[53] The nucleus of the picture consists of an armed warrior somersaulting. Although the spectator's gesture usually conveys alarm, within the context it can also represent surprise at the feat of the upside-down warrior in the center.

The reaction of the spectator to the nucleus of the scene reminds us of the importance of warriors performing within civic and religious rituals in Athens. Although most of our written sources regarding the pyrrhic dance in Athens are from the fourth century, it is certain that the practice of dancing with weapons is attested in Homeric and early Archaic times and that some type of pyrrhic dance or performance with weapons may have been part of cult ritual in Athens during the sixth century.[54] Indeed, vase paintings such as figure 41 show figures armed with shield and spear moving vigorously among spectators, and in crouching, twisting, or leaping poses that are typical of the maneuvers of the pyrrhic dance.[55] Whereas the spectators in figure 41 show a calm restraint in witnessing the dance, the youth on the Boston cup exhibits a much stronger emotional reaction. That the latter style is extremely low in its frequency, however, shows that it was not an ideal type of reaction for a spectator.

The presence of spectators at performances by armed dancers, however, provides a context for understanding some of the actions of youths like those of type Y.4c and Y.4d, and especially of the same movement with a spear in type Y.2c (see figure 44). The youth with both elbows thrown out has an arm configuration that is parallel to that of the performer. The left arm, holding the shield, is by necessity, bent sharply at the elbow in order to hold the shield before the body. Moving with an offensive weapon also requires a bent arm, with the hand held down to carry the weapon (see warrior in figure 34) or up to throw it (see figure 35). The elbows-out pose of these types of spectators not only mimics the actions of heroes and warriors, but recalls the movement of warriors or spear-bearing performers at the festivals. On one level, the spectators imitate the actions that dance and song mime narratively, but one might also understand these youths as the performers, too, therefore standing for both audience and performer, as we saw in the previous chapter (see discussion of figure 21). Pyrrhic dancers were also said to have danced nude and to have imitated the movements

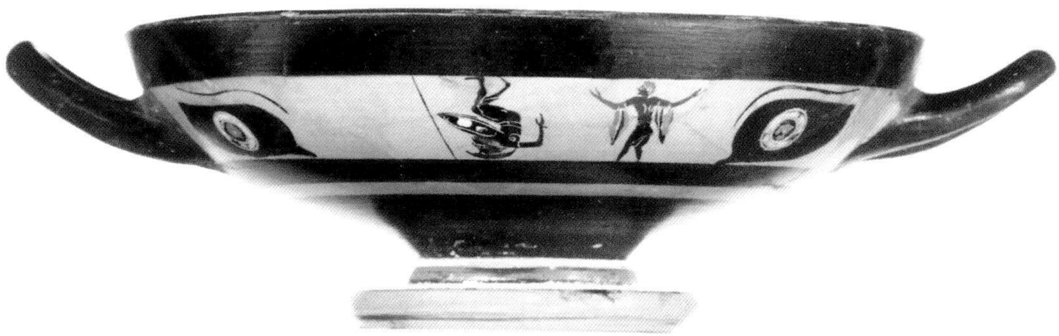

51. Attic black-figure band cup, c. 530. Side A: Warrior-acrobat. Museum of Fine Arts, Boston. Gift of Charles S. Lipson, 67.861. (Photograph © 2004 Museum of Fine Arts, Boston)

required of offensive weapons, even when performing unarmed, and this suggests that the spectators without spears should be seen in the same light as those with spears and in the same pose, and with the same lack of clothing.[56]

Based on this discussion, we can therefore divide this category of very active youthful spectators into two types – reactive (Y.4a, Y.4b, Y.4e, Y.4f, Y.4w: 34 total vases) and mimetic (Y.4c and Y.4d: 41 total vases).[57] The number of vases with mimetic spectators is higher than that of those with the reactive type; in contrast, the numbers of reactive and mimetic men are reversed in order, with more than double the number of reactive types (24 vases) compared with the mimetic type (9 vases). This difference makes sense if we consider the relative status and role of the two ages of male spectators – one that has already achieved privileged status in the polis, and one that is learning its place and aspires to that role for itself. The latter, youths, must still prove themselves through their actions before the city, and so their behavior as spectators is more frequently mimetic than that of men as spectators.

Y.5: Spectators Leaning on Sticks; Y.6: Spectators Sitting

The next category of youthful spectators, those leaning on sticks (Y.5), is found on 28 vases. The types are similar to those of men, as can be seen in table 28. There are six examples of figures leaning on a stick with the arms close to the body, as can be seen on the amphora in Berlin, F1873 (figure 52).[58] While a kitharode performs on a podium in the center, the youth listens attentively on the right side. There are three examples of the youth extending one arm (Y.5b, see figure 43), but a more common type is with one hand on the hip and the other arm extended (Y.5c), a more expansive pose seen on an amphora in the British Museum (figure 53).[59] Indeed, this figure would seem to be reacting or commenting directly on what he experiences, although he seems to be in the role of observer rather than trainer, judge, or fellow competitor. Two additional types with sticks are found, one with one arm fully extended downward (Y.5d) and

Table 28. *Frequency of Types in Spectator Categories Y.5 and Y.6*

Type	Description	Number of Vases with Type	Frequency, Total Vases with Y (527)
Y.5a	Leans on stick, arms close to body (cf. M.5a)	6	1.1%
Y.5b	Leans on stick, extends one arm (cf. M.5b)	4	0.8%
Y.5c	Leans on stick, hand on hip (cf. M.5c)	16	3.0%
Y.5d	Arm extended out holding onto stick (cf. M.5d)	5	0.9%
Y.5e	Leans on stick, both elbows out (like Y.4c)	2	0.4%
		Total = 28	5.3%
Y.6a	Reclines on couch (cf. M.6a)	13	2.5%
Y.6b	Sits on chair, ground, or crouches (M.6b)	20	3.8%
		Total = 33	6.3%

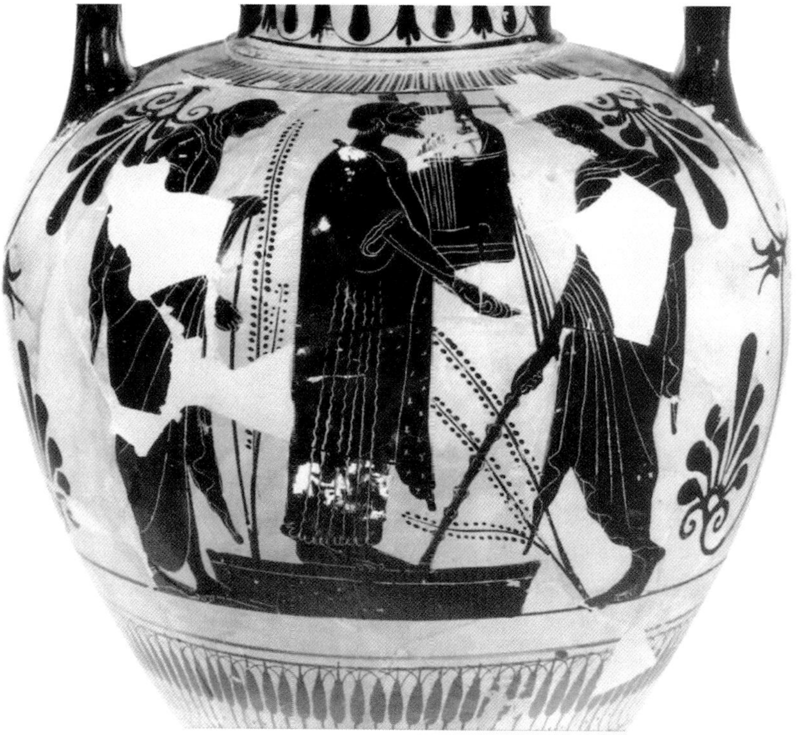

52. Attic black-figure neck amphora attributed to Group of Vatican G.23, c. 500–475. Side B: Kitharode. Berlin, Staatliche Museen zu Berlin – Preussischer Kulturbesitz Antikensammlung F1873. (Photograph, Bildarchiv Preussischer Kulturbesitz/Art Resource, NY)

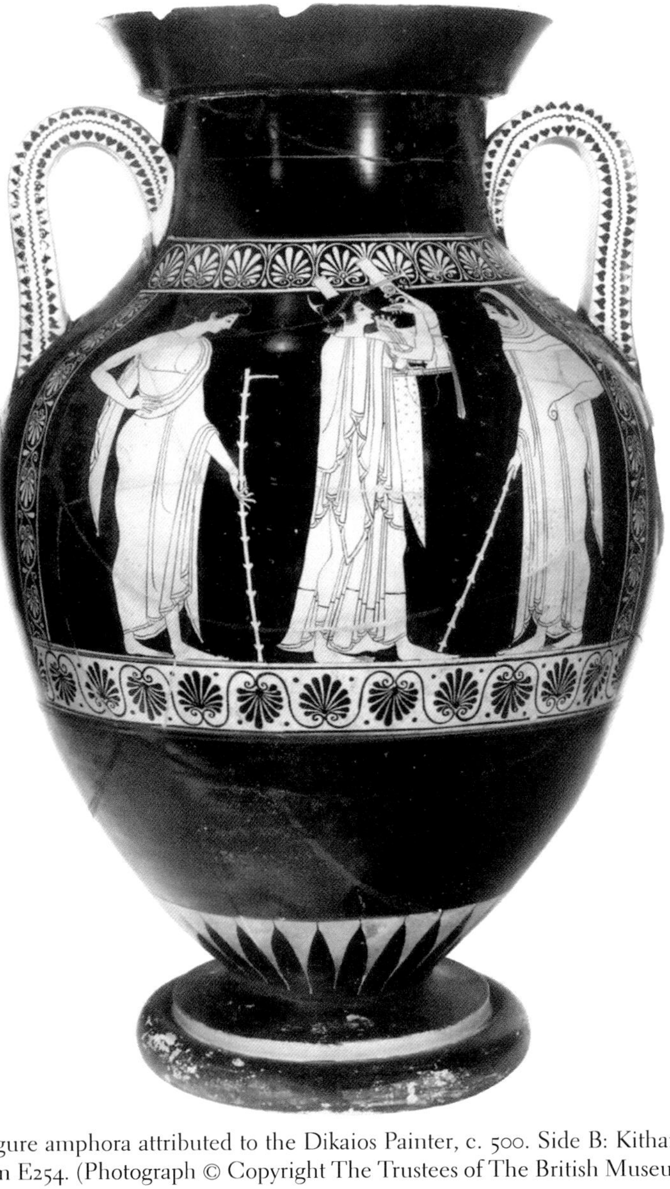

53. Attic red-figure amphora attributed to the Dikaios Painter, c. 500. Side B: Kitharode. London, British Museum E254. (Photograph © Copyright The Trustees of The British Museum)

one example with both elbows out (Y.5e, see figure 42) that recalls types Y.4c and Y.2c, discussed earlier.[60]

Of the 28 vases in this category, only two are black-figure. Twenty-one are from the fifth century, so this spectator type clearly belongs to a late phase of the spectators. Indeed, figures leaning on sticks proliferate from the late sixth century onward, and usually in scenes in which they are more active participants or have a role in the narrative, leaving them out of the classes of spectators considered in this study. In

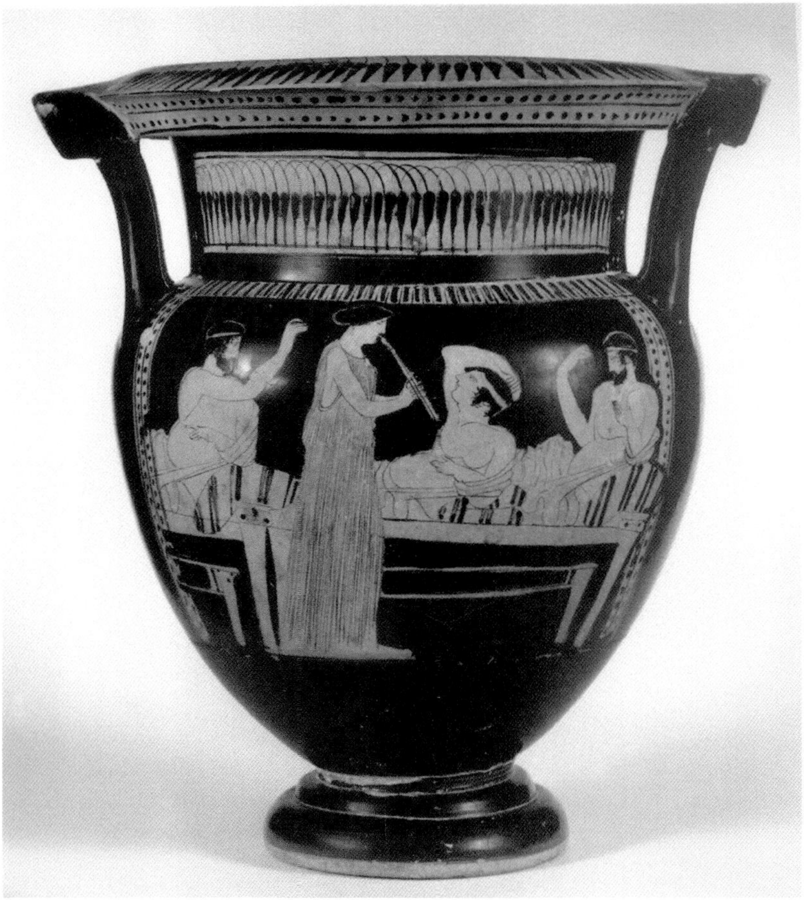

54. Attic red-figure column krater attributed to the Naples Painter, c. 440. Side A: Symposion. Baltimore, The Walters Art Museum 48.67. (Photograph, The Walters Art Museum, Baltimore)

general, the presence of the stick implies a prolonged observation and enhances the importance of the gaze as the medium of engagement by the spectator or viewer.

The last category (Y.6), sitting spectators, has two main types, as is the case for men. In terms of frequency, seated men are about twice as common as seated youths (compare tables 22 and 28). Because sitting can be associated with a position of prominence, it is not surprising that seated men would be found relatively more frequently than youths. The first type of seated spectator consists of youths reclining on couches, for which there are 13 examples (Y.6a, see table 28). As can be see in figure 54, a youth reclines on a kline and holds his right arm over his tilted head while listening to an aulist.[61] As in figure 52, the boundary between spectator and performer is thin, but at least in this scene, there seems to be an intention for the youth only to listen and not to molest the performer, as happens frequently in symposion scenes. This lack of a boundary excludes many other similar vases from this discussion, as it did with

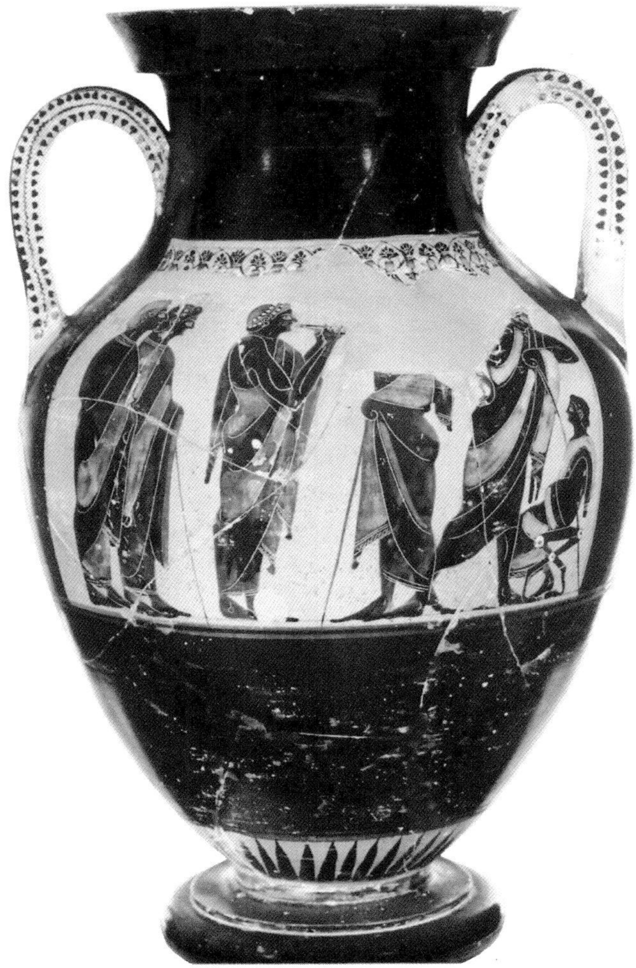

55. Attic black-figure amphora attributed to the Painter of Munich 1410, c. 520. Side B: Flute player. Munich, Antikensammlung 1411. (Photograph, Staatliche Antikensammlungen und Glyptothek München)

category Y.5. Like the stick-leaning spectators, too, the reclining spectator is primarily a fifth-century phenomenon (12 of 13 examples) and found almost exclusively in red-figure (12 of 13 examples) vessels. Finally, 10 of the 13 examples also feature reclining male spectators, as in figure 54, suggesting that this type of youthful spectator must be understood within the context of the men's world of the symposion.

The upright, seated spectator (Y.6b) is slightly more common than the reclining spectator; it is, in contrast, primarily a black-figure type (16 of 20 vases). Only five vases also feature men in the same picture, so that this type of youthful spectator exists independently of men. One such example is an amphora in Munich that shows an aulist playing between standing youths, several holding knobbed sticks (figure 55).[62]

Table 29. *Youths as Spectators by Mood*

Mood	Types	Number	Frequency, Total Vases with Y (527)
Inert	Y.1; Y.2a–b	411	78.0%
Reactive	Y.2d–e; Y.3; Y.4a–b, e–f, w; Y.5; Y.6	158	30.0%
Mimetic	Y.2c; Y.4c–d	55	10.4%

On the far right is a seated, mantled youth, smaller in scale than the others to suggest that he is yet a boy. The figure sits in a reserved manner, showing no reaction to the music but focusing intently on it and the performer. At least for the classical period, we know that war orphans who had been educated by the state were given a place of honor and their armor upon reaching the ephebe stage, and perhaps a similar type of practice existed earlier in the sixth century and is reflected in these spectators.[63] Perhaps one should consider these figures as part of a group of youths honored at a festival.

To conclude, although there are many similarities in the types of youthful and adult male spectators, there are some significant differences that reflect on their different role and position within the city. The standing, mantled figure (M.1 and Y.1), is far more frequent on vases with youth than on those with men, suggesting its special importance as a model for youth. Indeed, inert spectators occur on more than three-fourths of all CVA census vases with youths, more than 20 percentage points greater than inert men (table 29). Reactive youths are lower in frequency, whereas mimetic youths are higher, and these differences may be seen in light of the different social positions and expectations of the two groups. The kouros type of spectator (Y.2e and Y.3d) is exclusive to youths, and suggests a more heroic ideal than the mantled spectator. The mimetic type of spectator seen in Y.2c, Y.4c, and Y.4d is found more frequently on vases with youths than on those with men, whereas the reactive type is more frequent on vases with men than on those with youths. Leading gestures, such as Y.4a, are far less common for youths than men, as are spectators in seated poses, both types being associated with control and status. In general, one might say that youths are meant to be both less reactive than men and more mimetic. In different ways, both inert and mimetic youths reflect the ideal that they strive to attain as well as the training and performance that will enable them to reach it and a position of privilege within the polis.

5.4 REACTIONS OF MALE SPECTATORS TO EVENTS

Having looked at the range and relative frequency of spectator types among men and youths, we should consider whether specific reactions are more prevalent for one narrative action than another. For example, do the spectators of a certain narrative scene, such as Herakles wrestling the lion, conform to the broad range and distribution of spectator types that we have seen in tables 18 to 29, or is a narrower range of types selected and employed, and are these types the same in adult men as in youths? Are the spectator reactions to one mythological scene similar to those of other myths, such as Herakles and Nessos or Greeks fighting Amazons? Does a more generic type of scene that has potential mythological overtones, such as two warriors fighting, follow a different pattern than the recognizably mythological scenes? Further, what patterns can be found in the selection of spectators for more contemporary, civic scenes such as a parade featuring a youthful rider, or athletic or music contests? If one assumes that the meaning of a narrative changes with the story that is being represented, then should one expect the spectators to change as well?

If some such differences consistently exist, then one can presume an intentionality in the choice of spectator type. To answer these questions, we will look at a series of scenes for which there are multiple examples, drawing nine categories from the list of scenes with spectators in table 12 in chapter 2. In each case, we will look at the distribution of types for both adult male and youthful spectators, concentrating on the broader categories (M.1, M.2, etc.) first, and then looking at specific types when significant. We will begin with mythological scenes first, in which we find predominantly "pure" spectators, and then turn our attention to civic scenes featuring detached spectators who are more connected to the narrative nucleus as catalysts.

In order to determine whether the pattern of spectator types for a specific scene is particular to it, we will compare the relative frequency of spectator distribution for vases with each scene to the relative frequency of the same categories and types within the CVA census generally. Thus, for the scene of Herakles and the lion, we will compare the distribution of spectator types on the 20 vases with men as spectators, and the 223 vases with men in the CVA census. Similarly, we will compare the 51 Herakles and lion vases with youths to the 527 vases with youths in the CVA census. With the CVA census acting as a baseline distribution for spectator categories, we can then note situations in which specific scenes do not follow that pattern, paying particular attention to categories in which the difference in relative frequency between the scene and the CVA census is more than 10 percentage points.

Herakles and the Lion

To begin, we can look at one of the most common narrative scenes with spectators, Herakles wrestling the lion. This is, indeed, one of the most popular scenes in Attic vase-painting generally and, from the beginning, the scene frequently included catalysts such as Athena and Iolaos.[64] The goddess is consistently identified by her armor or aegis, and as a spectator, belongs to the class of interested spectator, having a vested interest in the result of the action. Iolaos is identified by what he holds for Herakles while the hero fights, usually a club or other weapon. As Herakles's helper, he is not a true spectator because he is involved in the action. Whereas both of these figures have a standard place within the story, there are frequently other figures, both adult

Table 30. *Frequency of Spectator Categories in Herakles and the Lion Vases*

Category	Herakles/Lion Vases with Men	CVA Vases with Men (223)	Category	Herakles/lion Vases with Youths	CVA Vases with Youths (527)
M.1	20.0% (4/20)	31.8%	Y.1	39.2% (20/51)	49.1%
M.2a–b	20.0% (4/20)	31.4%	Y.2a–b	21.6% (11/51)	30.7%
M.inert	40.0% (8/20)	56.1%	Y.inert	60.7% (31/51)	78.0%
M.2c–d	5.0% (1/20)	3.6%	Y.2c–e	11.7% (6/51)	6.1%
M.3	5.0% (1/20)	12.1%	Y.3	23.5% (12/51)	11.4%
M.4	50.0% (10/20)	14.8%	Y.4	39.2% (20/51)	12.9%
M.5	0	8.1%	Y.5	0	5.3%
M.6	5.0% (1/20)	12.6%	Y.6	9.8% (5/51)	6.3%

males and youths, who appear in pictures of Herakles and the lion. Sometimes these appear in addition to Iolaos and Athena, but in many cases they appear when the mythological figures are absent. In either case, the figures are distinguished by the lack of an attribute that would be appropriate for the scene, and therefore should be seen as being removed from the immediate time and place of the action.[65] For example, the band cup in Tübingen that we saw earlier (figure 46) shows three mantled youths and two running youths, each with chlamys over his arm. Although the youths might be seen as being derived from Iolaos's place in the iconography of the scene, none holds a weapon or assists Herakles in any way, nor is any one figure sufficiently marked as to be identified as Iolaos. All of the figures here are pure spectators, removed from the action.

There are 75 vases in the CVA census that show Herakles and the lion, about one-tenth of the total, making it second only to the scene of generic warriors fighting in overall frequency (see figures 4, 23, 25, 37, 46, 48–50 for examples). Twenty of these vases have adult male spectators and 51 feature youths (36 have women spectators, which we will examine in the next chapter). The proportions that these numbers represent are similar to the frequency of men and youths in the CVA census, but when we look at specific categories of spectators we see differences emerging. For example, both category 1 and 2 spectators are lower in frequency for men and youths than in the broader CVA census, about 10 percentage points in each case (see table 30). Thus, for both men and youths, the most common behavioral mood of spectator, the inert, is notably lower in frequency than in the broader CVA census.

The opposite is generally true for the more active categories of youthful spectators. For example, Y.3 is more than double in frequency on the Herakles/lion vases compared with the CVA census. Category Y.4 shows even more disparity, constituting almost two-fifths of the entire group of lion vases with youths, compared with one-eighth for the CVA census. When we add the active spear-bearing types (Y.2c–e) to this group of the most active spectators, the frequency increases to more than half of all Herakles/lion vases with youths. Turning to active adult male spectators, however, we see a slightly different pattern. There is only one example of category M.3, but the number for M.4 is extremely high, half of the Herakles/lion vases with men. In particular, the "leader" type, M.4a, is found on 30 percent of the vases with men, much higher than the 8.5 percent frequency in the CVA census. In figure 37, for example, the figure in front of Herakles wears armor and raises his right arm with the hand and palm facing up, directing the attention of the others toward the narrative nucleus. That he wears armor and Herakles uses a sword links him as closest to the hero, and the armor also elevates his status among the spectators.

What these numbers reveal is that, for the story of Herakles and the lion, an active spectator, either reactive or mimetic in mood, is the most frequent type of male spectator, even though it is less common in the CVA census. Among the active youths, most of the figures can be seen as mimetic in their behavior, their strides and the positions of their arms imitating those of the hero. For example, the two youths on the left side of Munich 1471 (see figure 50) hold their arms in the exact position of Herakles as he holds up the lion, and their strides are only slightly less wide than his. The right arm of the spectator on the other side similarly mimics Herakles, and the left arm also points to the hero, drawing the viewer's eye from the youth back to the nucleus of the composition. On the band cup in Tübingen (see figure 46), the crouch-like pose of the legs in the running youths reflects the position of Herakles, and the extended upper arms model a readiness for action. These active figures frequently occur in combination with the inert mantled spectator, as on both of these vases, so that there are clearly two modes of response that this narrative elicits. The calm and composed contemplation of the mythological hero and his deed is clearly an appropriate response, but the high frequency of active, mimetic types of spectators signals that a male viewer should consider himself to be like Herakles by acting as the spectators do, vigorously and athletically.

One final point to note is the frequency of seated spectators, 5 percent for men and 9.8 percent for youths. As we shall see in many of the following scenes, seated spectators are quite unusual for mythological and fighting scenes, and are found largely in connection with music scenes. The fact that one-fourth of all youthful seated spectators are found in scenes with Herakles and the lion is worthy of comment, but the precise reason for this coincidence is not clear. As we shall see with music, the seated pose suggests not only a position of honor, but also a position that allows focused concentration. Certainly Herakles is worthy of attention as a role model, and we shall return to this unusual concentration of seated spectators with him in the next chapter when we look at women spectators for the same scene.

Herakles and Nessos

Another popular scene with Herakles is his confrontation with the centaur Nessos.[66] There are 35 examples of the narrative in the CVA census, making it about half as common as the hero's struggle with the lion. The distribution of spectators for the

Table 31. *Frequency of Spectator Categories in Herakles and Nessos Vases*

Category	Herakles/Nessos Vases with Men	CVA Vases with Men (223)	Category	Herakles/Nessos Vases with Youths	CVA Vases with Youths (527)
M.1	50.0% (9/18)	31.8%	Y.1	52.3% (11/21)	49.1%
M.2a–b	33.3% (6/18)	31.4%	Y.2a–b	33.3% (7/21)	30.7%
M.2c–d	0	3.6%	Y.2c–e	0	6.1%
M.3	5.6% (1/18)	12.1%	Y.3	19.0% (4/21)	11.4%
M.4	22.2% (4/18)	14.8%	Y.4	9.5% (3/21)	12.9%
M.5	0	8.1%	Y.5	0	5.3%
M.6	0	12.6%	Y.6	4.8% (1/21)	6.3%

Nessos scene, however, is strikingly different from the Herakles/lion scene and from the CVA census, as well. Most notably, just over half of the vases (18/35) feature adult male spectators, much greater than the 30.1 percent frequency of adult men on vases within the CVA census (see table 31). In contrast, the number of vases with youthful spectators is lower than for the CVA census (60% versus 71.0%). This suggests that the scene has particular meaning for men and that it is directed as much at them as at youths.

Category M.1 is the most frequent for men, appearing on half of all vases with men. An example can be seen on a Siana cup in Copenhagen (figure 56), on which we see three men wearing mantles on both sides, with a woman and youth closer to the action on the left.[67]

The frequency of spear-bearing (M.2), active (M.3), and very active (M.4) spectators is closer to that in the CVA census. It should be noted, however, that there are three examples of the "leader" type, M.4a (see figure 14), making it almost double in frequency for Nessos scenes compared with the CVA census, a pattern we also saw in the Herakles and lion scenes. This suggests a particular link between the leader type of spectator for men and the hero Herakles; indeed, three-fifths of all the leader type (M.4a) are found on scenes with Herakles.

As can be seen in Table 31, the distribution of youthful spectators is similar to the overall pattern of the CVA census, with only Y.3 noticeably greater than the CVA census overall. This conformity would strengthen the suggestion that this was a scene that had particular resonance for adult male spectators, given there is no similar discernible selectivity in the pattern of youthful spectators as there is for men.

The pattern of spectator choice for the scene of Herakles and Nessos suggests that it has a different social meaning than the story of the same hero confronting the lion. Whereas the latter narrative represents the hero's elimination of a scourge that threatened the well-being of human society, the actions of Nessos represent a threat to the domestic social order given that he attempts to abduct the wife of Herakles. Thus, the threat is personal to Herakles and to the well-being of his household, and his actions restore order to the *oikos* and, more indirectly, to the social fabric of the

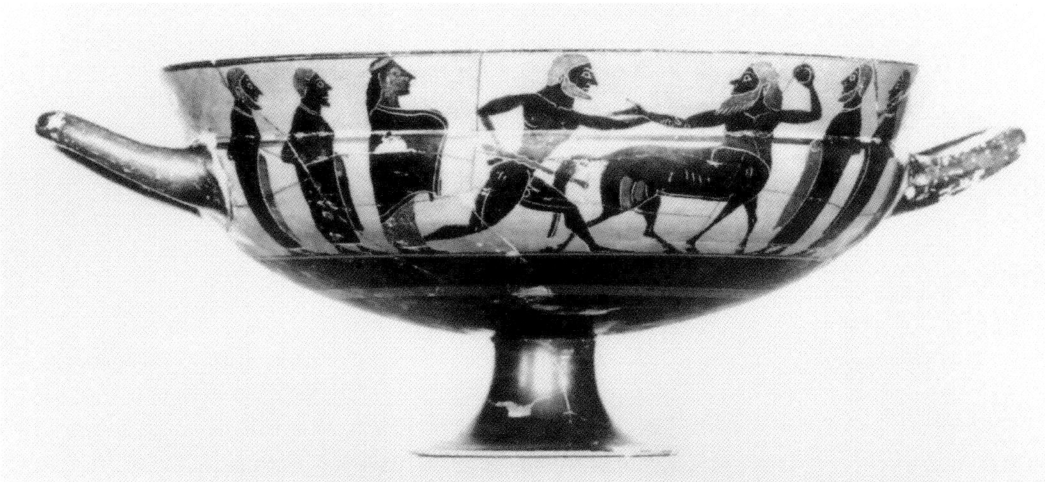

56. Attic black-figure Siana cup attributed to the Painter of Boston CA, c. 575–550. Side A: Herakles and Nessos. Copenhagen, Department of Classical and Near Eastern Antiquities, National Museum of Denmark 5180. (Photo, Museum)

city. The actions of the hero and the nature of the threat in the story, therefore, have a greater resonance with the adult male viewer, who, himself, would be a householder with the common worries for the prosperity, stability, and longevity of his *oikos*. It is not surprising, then, that adult male spectators are found in greater relative frequency than in the CVA census. The emphasis upon a calm, guardian-like demeanor presents a dignified image of the citizen's response to a threat.

The high incidence of the leader type (M.4a) among the Nessos scenes also shows the importance of the example that Herakles sets as a symbol of social order. Indeed, the coincidence of this particular type of spectator in scenes with Herakles, three-fifths (12/19) of the examples of type M.4a, suggests a particularly strong link between the concept of the hero and the image of the adult male citizen who directs the attention of the community to this ideal, and its reflection onto himself.

Warriors Fighting

The most popular scene for spectators to watch is not an action of Herakles, but rather the confrontation between two warriors who are not identifiable. Such pictures can include a supporting warrior who is part of the nucleus and not a spectator, and a dead warrior frequently lies on the ground between the fighting warriors. Such scenes are neither mythological nor real, and should be seen as representing the idea of fighting more broadly, whether in the heroic imagination or in the army of a polis.[68] There are 168 vases with such scenes in the CVA census, 35 of which (20.8 percent) have adult male spectators and 98 (58.3 percent), youths (for examples in this chapter see figures 32, 35, 36, 43, 44). The incidence of both men and youths as spectators

Table 32. *Frequency of Spectator Categories in Vases with Warriors Fighting*

Category	Warriors Fighting Vases with Men	CVA Vases with Men (223)	Category	Warriors Fighting Vases with Youths	CVA Vases with Youths (527)
M.1	42.9% (15/35)	31.8%	Y.1	44.9% (44/98)	49.1%
M.2a–b	45.7% (16/35)	31.4%	Y.2a–b	49.0% (48/98)	30.7%
M.2c–e	17.1% (6/35)	3.6%	Y.2c–e	8.2% (8/98)	6.1%
M.3	8.6% (3/35)	12.1%	Y.3	8.2% (8/98)	11.4%
M.4	0	14.8%	Y.4	8.2% (8/98)	12.9%
M.5	0	8.1%	Y.5	0	5.3%
M.6	2.9% (1/35)	12.6%	Y.6	0	6.3%

is about 10 percentage points lower compared with the CVA census we shall see in the next chapter that this is a scene with a significantly higher frequency for women spectators (see table 52 in chapter 6).

Looking at the various categories of men and youths, we find that the frequency of the mantled figures, M.1 and Y.1, is almost the same for both groups, which represents an increase in frequency for men (table 32). The virtual equivalence in the frequency of this category for both men and youth suggests that inert and attentive behavior is equally appropriate for both groups as a reaction. The frequency of inert, spear-bearing spectators is almost half of all vases for both men and youths; this is a significantly higher frequency than in the CVA census, as might be expected for a war scene. This increase is also true for active, spear-bearing spectators (M.2c–d and Y.2c–e), especially among men. In contrast, the remaining categories of active, very active, seated, and stick-bearing figures is consistently smaller than in the CVA census. From the numbers in table 32, we can see that there is a clear selectivity of spectators for this particular type of narrative scene, with an emphasis on spear-bearing spectators of all kinds, especially for adult men, and an expectation of a similar response from both men and youth to the central scene.

The spear for the spectators in categories M.2 and Y.2 should be seen as a metonym for the warrior. Its presence in the hands of the otherwise not warrior-like spectator allows him to identify with the fighting warrior as ready and willing to follow his example. For the male viewers of the vase as well, the spectator provides a model for their behavior within the polis, particularly training or performing with a weapon, that equates their actions with heroic figures like those in the narrative. The actions of the mimetic types of spear-bearers mirror such actions by the viewer, whereas the inert, spear-bearing spectators embody the calm and discipline that will also be needed for courage in the face of fighting. Because the patterns of behavior are virtually the same for men as for youths, this suggests that this behavior is equally important to both, and embodies the fact that a call to arms is something that may lie in the future for both groups, and is not simply an achievement that lies in the past for one group and in the future for another.

Table 33. *Frequency of Spectator Categories in Amazon Vases*

Category	Amazon Vases with Men	CVA Vases with Men (223)	Category	Amazon Vases with Youths	CVA Vases with Youths (527)
M.1	30.0% (3/10)	31.8%	Y.1	22.5% (9/40)	49.1%
M.2	80.0% (8/10)	34.1%	Y.2	77.5% (31/40)	33.6%
M.3	0	12.1%	Y.3	7.5% (3/40)	11.4%
M.4	0	14.8%	Y.4	2.5% (1/40)	12.9%
M.5	0	8.1%	Y.5	0	5.3%
M.6	0	12.6%	Y.6	2.5% (1/40)	6.3%

Amazons

A variation on the warriors fighting scene is that of a warrior confronting an Amazon. Such scenes include Herakles confronting one or more Amazons, as well as pictures with other heroes or unidentified warriors. To study in more detail spectator reactions to scenes of Amazon combats, a larger, supplemental database of 49 Amazonomachy vases with spectators was compiled, drawing upon the iconographic study of D. von Bothmer and supplemented by the CVA, LIMC, and the Beazley Archive.[69] Additional examples exist, but the database has been limited to those examples for which there are sufficiently detailed illustrations to allow the classification of the spectators. Seventeen of the vases also appear in the CVA census. Ten of the 49 vases feature men as spectators and 40 have youths (see table 33).

A very different pattern of distribution is found in Amazon vases compared with scenes of warriors fighting or the CVA census. By far the most frequent category of adult male spectator is M.2, being found on 80 percent of Amazon vases with men, including a pyxis in Berlin (see figure 60). There are three vases in category M.1 (30 percent), but no example of categories M.3 to M.6. The frequency of type M.1 is close to the CVA census, but that of type M.2 is two and one-half times, and almost 30 percentage points, higher than in scenes with warriors fighting. Thus, the distribution of male spectators in Amazon scenes is strikingly focused on inert, spear-bearing figures. This suggests that in the face of an Amazon scene, there is a particular response that is thought most appropriate for an adult male spectator. Adult men, as the vested members of the community who would stand to lose the most from such a hypothetical, double-barrel threat like the Amazons, stand attentive and on guard with their spears. Their quiet pose shows a counterbalancing restraint in the face of provocative action.

A similar pattern can be seen among youths, although there is more variety than among adult male spectators. The prototypical mantled youth is found on just over 20 percent of Amazon vases with youths, less than half the frequency in the CVA census. On the other hand, the spear-bearing youth, in both the mantled and the nude, kouros-like forms (Y.2a and Y.2e) seen together on the skyphos in Mainz (figure 45), accounts for almost four-fifths of vases with youths, much more than double their frequency in the CVA census. Their frequency is also substantially higher than that of spear-bearing youths for scenes of warriors fighting.

A few of the spear-bearing youths are mimetic in mood.[70] The twisting movement of these figures recalls processions and performances of youths in festivals, and one might consider the action of the spectator in light of the pyrrhic dance and ritual performances discussed in chapter 4. In either case, the spectator in this case creates a more active link between his action and that of the viewer, and models an animated, perhaps ceremonial response to the scene in the center. Other than mimetic, spear-bearing youths, the overall frequency of spearless, active youths is lower than that for the CVA census, suggesting that a reactive response to an Amazon scene is not generally desirable.

In conclusion, for men and youths, the attentive, guarding figure with a spear is by far the predominant spectator type in Amazon scenes, indexing a preparedness to act like the hero against a threat to the values of the city. That most of the vases feature youths as spectators suggests that they were a target audience for the imagery, either as models for their own behavior as they become men, or as proper objects of attention for adult male viewers who will instill in youths their own values.

Nike and Sphinx

A number of vases feature as the nucleus either a sphinx or a moving, winged female figure whose exact identity is ambiguous, but is most similar to Nike or Iris (figure 57).[71] These mythological figures are signs referring to death and to a funerary context generally, and the figures have been found in archaic cemeteries as both guardians and commemorative markers.[72] The distribution of spectators with these figures is weighted heavily toward youths rather than men. For example, youths are the only type of spectator in all 14 examples with the sphinx (see figure 29 and table 34). For the Nike figure, three of 18 vases have men as spectators (16.7 percent), whereas 16 (88.9 percent) have youths. For both types of subjects, then, men are virtually absent as spectators, who are almost exclusively youths, suggesting that this subject is focused upon youth in its meaning.

The very low number of vases with men as spectators makes it difficult to draw conclusions about the distribution of spectator categories. Among the runners youths, there is an emphasis on the inert spectators, with or without spears, whereas the proportion of active and very active spectators is closer to the frequencies in the CVA census. However, there is a distinction between the Nike and sphinx groups, in that the Nike vases emphasize spear-bearing spectators (56.3 percent of vases), whereas the sphinx vases have the more prototypical mantled youth (71.4 percent of vases), as can be seen in table 34.

Both the Nike and sphinx vases are focused upon youth and may well have served a funerary context, either as grave goods or as offering vessels. The sphinx is found

Table 34. *Frequency of Spectator Categories in Nike and Sphinx Vases*

Category	Nike Vases with Men	Sphinx Vases with Men (0)	CVA Vases with Men (223)	Category	Nike Vases with Youths	Sphinx Vases with Youths	CVA Vases with Youths (527)
M.1	66.7% (2/3)	0	31.8%	Y.1	37.5% (6/16)	71.4% (10/14)	49.1%
M.2	33.3% (1/3)	0	34.1%	Y.2	56.3% (9/16)	21.4% (3/14)	33.6%
M.3	0	0	12.1%	Y.3	6.3% (1/16)	7.1% (1/14)	11.4%
M.4	66.7% (2/3)	0	14.8%	Y.4	18.8% (3/16)	21.4% (3/14)	12.9%
M.5	0	0	8.1%	Y.5	0	0	5.3%
M.6	0	0	12.6%	Y.6	0	0	6.3%

equally on lekythoi and band cups (five each), whereas Nike appears twice as frequently on band cups compared with lekythoi (six to three). Either shape is found as a grave good, and we should consider the appearance of both subjects on spectator vases in light of the elegiac commemoration of individuals that we saw in the previous chapter.

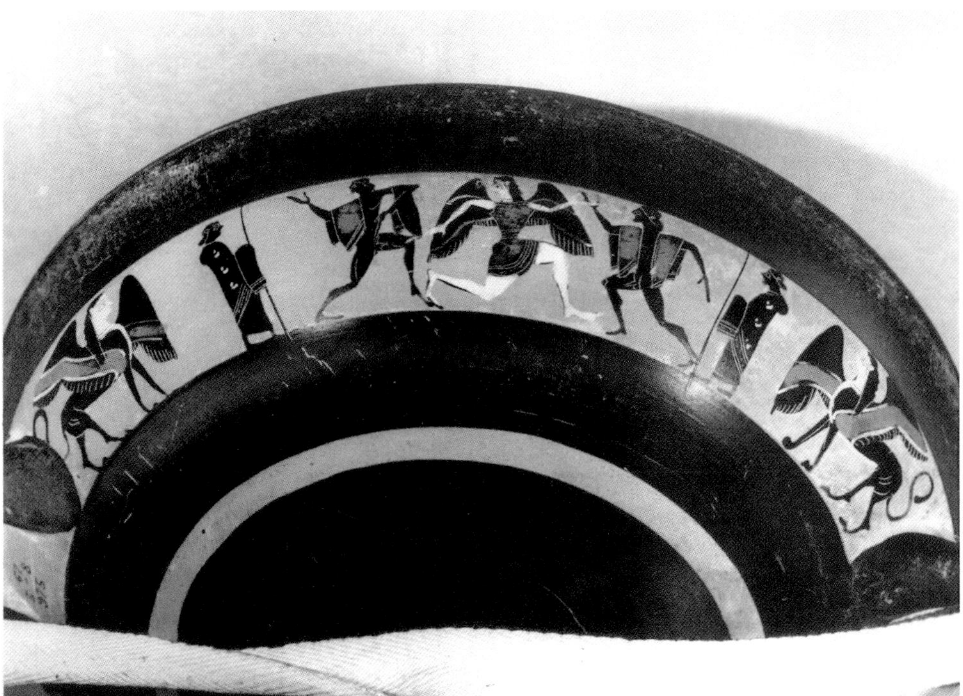

57. Attic black-figure band cup, c. 550–525. Side A: Nike (winged woman) between youths and sphinxes. London, British Museum B387. (Photograph © Copyright The Trustees of The British Museum)

Table 35. *Frequency of Spectator Categories in Rider Vases*

Category	Rider Vases with Men	CVA Vases with Men (223)	Category	Rider vases with youths	CVA Vases with Youths (527)
M.1	54.2% (13/24)	31.8%	Y.1	62.9% (39/62)	49.1%
M.2	20.8% (5/24)	34.1%	Y.2	29.0% (18/62)	33.6%
M.3	20.8% (5/24)	12.1%	Y.3	17.7% (11/62)	11.4%
M.4	12.5% (3/24)	14.8%	Y.4	17.7% (11/62)	12.9%
M.5	0	8.1%	Y.5	0	5.3%
M.6	4.2% (1/24)	12.6%	Y.6	0	6.3%

Rider

We can turn our attention from mythological and quasi-mythological scenes such as warriors fighting to narrative nuclei that are similar to scenes that would have been witnessed in contemporary Athens, such as pompe or parades, athletes competing, and musical performances. It should be emphasized that these scenes are not snapshots of real life, but that they epitomize some of the notable activities that took place within the city. Most of these spectators in such scenes are detached in their classification, so there is less separation structurally between the spectator and the performer/actor than in more mythological or heroic scenes like those we have already examined. In these scenes, we can assume that the spectators actually see the figures who constitute the nucleus, and that their reactions could, in turn, be seen by the figures. Nevertheless, qualities of dress and arrangement in space separate the spectators from the actors/performers.

This can be seen, for example, in the numerous vases featuring riders on horses, such as we saw in figures 34 and 47.[73] The riders are youths, either nude or, more often, wearing a short chiton, frequently painted with added white; the spectators wear heavy mantles, sometimes with added red, as in figure 34. The rider is usually single, but in many of the vases is accompanied by striding figures such as the nude warrior in figure 34, making a procession or pompe the nucleus of the composition. In such cases, the walking figures are catalysts who magnify the splendor and importance of the rider before the eyes of the spectators and the viewer. It is possible that these particular scenes reflect the origins of the theme in the warrior leaving home, but in most cases we need to consider them in terms of civic rather than military events because armored figures appear rarely in rider scenes.[74] As U. Vedder has noted, these youths are likely to be aristocratic ephebes, and hence models for the spectators watching them, making the figure something of a self-portrait for an aristocratic viewer.[75]

Of the 76 vases featuring riders with spectators, 24 have men as spectators and 62 have youths; the latter number is more than 10 percentage points higher as a relative frequency than in the CVA census (see table 35). Because the narrative nucleus consists of a youth, the increase in the number of youthful spectators makes sense because the rider serves as an immediate ideal for these observers. Among vases with men as spectators, there is a distinct preference for the standing, mantled spectator, who appears on more than half the vases. Altogether with inert, spear-bearing men, the inert spectator is found on three-fourths of all rider vases with men as spectators, showing a distinct preference for this type of figure compared with the CVA census. The active type of spectator, M.3, is also found at a greater frequency than in the CVA census; all of these examples are either types M.3a or M.3b, whose gestures might be associated with choral responses. Of the vases with very active spectators (M.4), all are either the leader type (M.4a) or the wreath-bearing type (M.4w), so the spectator should be seen as actively signaling the excellence of the rider for the other spectators. For youths, in comparison, the distribution of spectator types is very close to the overall distribution in the CVA group of vases, except for a lack of stick-bearing or seated figures (Y.5 and Y.6) and a corresponding increase in the standing, mantled figure Y.1.

All in all, the distribution of spectator types for scenes of riders comes closer to the overall proportions found in the CVA census, apart from a general lack of seated and stick-leaning spectators. Frequently, both inert and reactive spectators are included in the same picture, so that overall we see less significant selectivity among spectator types than we saw in scenes such as warriors fighting or an Amazonomachy. One might speculate that this is a result of the shift from a mythological or fighting subject in the narrative nucleus to a scene that signifies the activities of the polis, so that the reactions of spectators are keyed to the expected behavior of the community to such events. The continuing importance of spear-bearing spectators, even though at a lower frequency than in the CVA census, may be a reflection of the original connection of rider to the theme of the warrior departing. If so, then one should expect that spear-bearing spectators would be less frequent in scenes that do not have warrior overtones, such as athletic events, as we shall examine next.

Runners

Unlike riders, there is a much greater departure from the CVA census among spectators on vases featuring one or more, usually nude, runners as the narrative nucleus.[76] Sixteen of the 59 vases with this subject in the CVA census have two or more runners with spectators (see figure 28), with the implication that they are racing in a competition. Although the vast majority of vases feature only one nude runner, these should still be seen within the context of a race, either as a figure in training or as a victor in competition, evoking his excellence as a model for the viewer. Of the 59 vases with runners, only six have men as spectators, about one-third the general frequency of vases with men in the CVA census (10.2 percent versus 30.1 percent). It would seem, then, that the race was not of particular importance as a subject for vases with men as spectators. Among this small group of vases, half are of category M.1 (table 36), an increase over the frequency in the CVA census, but the small number makes it difficult to discern a broad pattern in the selection of spectator types.

Table 36. *Frequency of Spectator Categories in Runner Vases*

Category	Runner Vases with Men	CVA Vases with Men (223)	Category	Runner Vases with Youths	CVA Vases with Youths (527)
M.1	50.0% (3/6)	31.8%	Y.1	83.3% (45/54)	49.1%
M.2	16.7% (1/6)	34.1%	Y.2	7.4% (4/54)	33.6%
M.3	33.3% (2/6)	12.1%	Y.3	7.4% (4/54)	11.4%
M.4	0	14.8%	Y.4	1.9% (1/54)	12.9%
M.5	0	8.1%	Y.5	0	5.3%
M.6	16.7% (1/6)	12.6%	Y.6	1.9% (1/54)	6.3%

Whereas men are missing as spectators for runners, youths appear at a much higher frequency. More than 90 percent of runner vases have youths as spectators, more than 20 percentage points higher than the CVA census (91.5 percent versus 71.0 percent), suggesting that this was a subject of special interest for youths, even more than the rider vases. There is also a strong selectivity at work in the type of youthful spectator represented on these vases, with five-sixths of the vases featuring the inert, mantled spectator (Y.1). The frequency of spear-bearing youths (Y.2) is very small compared with their frequency in the CVA census, as are the frequencies of both active and very active youthful spectators. Indeed, all four vases with active spectators have only type Y.3a, a more demonstrative configuration of the predominant Y.1a, suggesting that the spectator for this scene is expected to stand quietly and observe the runner, with, at most, a hand or forearm pointing toward the running figure. This is a scene that focuses on youth, both as performer and as spectator. The spectator in the picture is linked to the runner by belonging to the same gender grouping and partakes of his excellence through this association and his gaze.

Perhaps the highly active nature of the runners theme, especially compared with the more measured pace of action in scenes with riders, leads to the adoption of an antithetical figure who is still and calm as a spectator. Our literary picture of spectators at competitions, such as the funeral games of Patroklos in the *Iliad*, however, suggests that spectators could be far more animated than those on runner vases. In the footrace among Odysseus, the lesser Aias, and Antilochos, for example, "all the Achaians were shouting for his [Odysseus's] effort to win, and hallooed him hard along in his running."[77] Laughter, applause, wonder, and even arguments and anger are also reactions of the fans to various actions in the footrace, the throwing contest, and archery. Certainly, the seated spectators in figure 7 are demonstrative in their reaction to an athletic performance. It should be noted, however, that most of these spectators are mature men. For youths, who have yet to take their place as full citizens of the polis, we should perhaps see a different expectation of their reaction to an athletic contest. Here, the emphasis upon the mantled and closed figure points toward modesty (*aidos*) as an overriding quality of the spectator's behavior.[78]

Table 37. *Frequency of Spectator Categories in Wrestling and Boxing Vases*

Category	Wrestling and Boxing Vases with Men	CVA Vases with Men (223)	Category	Wrestling and Boxing Vases with Youths	CVA Vases with Youths (527)
M.1	45.5% (5/11)	31.8%	Y.1	48.0% (12/25)	49.1%
M.2	27.3% (3/11)	34.1%	Y.2	20.0% (5/25)	33.6%
M.3	9.1% (1/11)	12.1%	Y.3	12.0% (3/25)	11.4%
M.4	18.2% (2/11)	14.8%	Y.4	24.0% (6/25)	12.9%
M.5	0	8.1%	Y.5	10.0% (2/25)	5.3%
M.6	9.1% (1/11)	12.6%	Y.6	10.0% (2/25)	6.3%

Wrestlers and Boxers

Other athletic competitions with spectators include wrestling and boxing matches, which share the same basic configuration of two standing, striding figures with their arms projecting fully from their bodies (see figures 8 and 40).[79] There are a total 32 vases with scenes of either wrestling or boxing with spectators in the CVA census but, unlike runners, these scenes feature frequencies of men and youths as spectators that are more typical of the CVA vases generally, as can be seen in table 37. A little more than one-third of the wrestling/boxing vases have adult men as spectators; the only significant difference from the distribution of type categories from the CVA census is that nearly half of the vases have standing, mantled figures (M.1). Youths appear on a little more than three-fourths of the vases; spear-bearing youths are somewhat less frequent than in the CVA census, and very active spectators (Y.4) a bit more, but otherwise the distribution generally follows the CVA census.

Music Scenes

There are a large number of music scenes in the CVA, but many have been excluded from the spectator database if the spectator serves in the role of judge, as in a musical competition. Thus, figures that carry forked sticks like those used by trainers, or who seem to be about to intervene with the musician, have not been included because they have a potential structural impact on the narrative action. So, too, in symposion music scenes, there must be a clear division between performer and audience, without the implication that the audience will begin performing themselves or will take other actions with the musicians. With these exclusions, there are 36 vases with music scenes in the CVA census that we will consider.

Before turning our attention to the spectators, however, we need to distinguish several different types of music scenes with spectators.[80] First is what we might call the formal, public music performance, either a concert or a competition, as can be seen in figure 39. There, the aulist stands on a podium with another figure, likely a singer, while a man leaning on a stick listens with his head turned down. Another example,

Table 38. *Chronological Distribution of Types of Music Scenes*

Type of Music Scene	550–525	525–500	500–475	475–450	450–425	425–400	After 400
Formal public concert	1	9	1	0	0	0	0
Informal public concert	2	3	3	1	0	0	0
Symposion concert	0	1	3	2	5	1	3
Music school concert	0	0	0	3	0	0	0

with a kithara player, is seen in figure 52, flanked by two listeners with downturned heads. Another example of a kithara player is seen in figure 53 but here, the absence of a podium for the performer makes the setting more ambiguous. The listeners are stationary, but the occasion here may be more informal than a public competition. Given the fact that all three figures are youths, one might see this as a scene of practice or preparation rather than a public performance, not unlike the potential reading of the solitary runner discussed above. However, the music scene on figure 55 indicates a public performance, even when the podium is not present, as can be seen by the aulist's wreath and the seated youth on the right. We will call this type of scene an informal concert, where the performer is standing on the ground. A different kind of music performance can be found on the vase in figure 54, where we see a female aulist performing at a symposion. Here the context is domestic rather than public, but the formal arrangement and separation of performer and audience as well as differences in the use of clothing suggest a hired musician for a formal occasion.[81] All of these scenes have in common the presence of an instrumentalist or singer who performs; the audience is stationary but may move arms and head in response to the music. One final scene is the music school, in which a seated instrumentalist performs before a group of listeners, usually a mixture of boys and men.

The earliest of these types of music scenes with spectators is the informal concert. There are nine examples in all, two from the third quarter of the sixth century and continuing until the second quarter of the fifth century (see table 38). The formal concert develops alongside this other scene, beginning in the third quarter of the sixth century, but this scene is abandoned as a spectator scene after the early fifth century. Seven of the 11 examples of the scene belong to the last quarter of the sixth century, a time when it is clear that music performances were fully established as an important contest in the Panathenaic festival.[82] The symposion concert first appears in the last quarter of the sixth century and increases in frequency during the fifth century, with a zenith during the high classical period, when one-third of the 15 examples were made. Finally, there are only three examples of the music school scene, all from the second quarter of the fifth century.[83] This information suggests that there was a decided shift in music performances with spectators, with public performances dominating the late archaic period and symposion concerts replacing them during the classical period. This shift also signals a change in the position of the spectator, from standing while leaning on a stick or sitting upright to reclining on a couch.

Table 39. *Frequency of Spectator Categories in Music Vases*

Category	Music Vases with Men	CVA Vases with Men (223)	Category	Music Vases with Youths	CVA Vases with Youths (527)
M.1	0	31.8%	Y.1	16.0% (4/24)	49.1%
M.2	0	34.1%	Y.2	0	33.6%
M.3	3.8% (1/26)	12.1%	Y.3	4.0% (1/25)	11.4%
M.4	11.5% (3/26)	14.8%	Y.4	0	12.9%
M.5	19.2% (5/26)	8.1%	Y.5	28.0% (7/25)	5.3%
M.6	65.4% (17/26)	12.6%	Y.6	68.0% (17/25)	6.3%
M.6a	42.3% (11/26)	5.4%	Y.6a	48.0% (12/25)	2.5%
M.6b	23.1% (6/26)	7.2%	Y.6b	20.0% (5/25)	3.8%

Turning to the spectator types in music scenes, we find that there are fewer vases with youths as spectators (24) than men (27), a very unusual reversal of the pattern we have seen up to now. Only four of the 24 vases with youths have the standing, mantled figure (Y.1, see table 39), a frequency that is a little more than one-fourth of that for the CVA census. There are no examples of either spear-bearing or very active spectators, and only a single example of type Y.3. Whereas these "standard" types are low in frequency, we do see very high frequencies of the stick-leaning spectator (Y.5), the seated spectator (Y.6b), and the reclining spectator (Y.6a). Twenty-eight percent of the vases have the stick-leaning spectator, most of type Y.5c (see figure 53), in which the mantled figure leans lightly with the knobbed stick under one shoulder and the other arm and elbow drawn back and the glance turned downward. The pose suggests that the body is propped up and restrained in its movement as a reaction to the music. Certainly, the downturned head indicates active concentration on the music, and the averted gaze removes the distraction that seeing the performer would have on the psyche.[84] For these reasons, the stick-leaning figures should belong to the reactive mood of spectators, with the idea that the posture seeks to quell and channel the reaction, unlike the more demonstrative types of Y.4.

Spectators who are seated upright (Y.6b) are found on almost the same number of vases as leaning spectators. Two of the five examples are from music school concerts, and the other three from formal and informal concerts (see figure 55). The gaze of these spectators is turned toward the performer, and the hands are either tucked inside the mantle or else holding a short stick upright before them. The seated pose affords rest for the figure that a standing pose does not, and we might think that this affords more leisure both to listen and to watch the performance.

Reclining spectators show the greatest amount of head movement, as can be seen in figure 54, and perhaps the greatest signs of reverie. Most of these figures belong to the classical period, and a greater interest in pathos and ethos may be in part responsible for the popularity of this type of spectator, which occurs exclusively within a sympotic setting.

In contrast to youths, there are no vases with spectators from categories M.1 or M.2, so that the standard mantled figure is entirely absent for adult males in music scenes. Unlike youths, there are a few vases with more active spectators from categories M.3 and M.4, but their frequency is still lower than in the CVA census.

In the absence of what have been the standard types of spectator men in the previous scenes, we find an abundance of the last two categories, M.5 and M.6, for the first time. The stick-leaning figures are found on almost two-fifths of the vases with men, more than double the frequency in the CVA census. Most of these figures look down toward the ground, like the youths turning their gaze away from the performer in order to concentrate on the music. The earliest of these figures appears in the fourth quarter of the sixth century in the context of a formal concert, but the type also appears at informal concerts as well. Three-fourths of the seated-upright spectators (M.6b) are found with formal concerts, beginning in the third quarter of the sixth-century. Their number (eight) accounts for almost half of all seated men in the CVA census, demonstrating the importance of this pose for music scenes. The importance of seated and propped spectators for music concerts is, I would propose, a result of the concentration expected for a listener, who might otherwise be expected to move in response to the music.

Finally, the 11 examples of the reclining spectator all occur within the context of the symposion concert. There is only one example of the reclining spectator in the CVA census outside of the music scene, but it is a very early scene with komast dancers by the Taras Painter and still within a sympotic setting.[85] Frequently, the head is lifted up as in figure 54, which may indicate a deeper immersion into the music than the bowed head.[86]

Whereas early scenes of music in the symposion frequently have no visible boundary between performer and audience, with flute-girls being accosted for non musical entertainment or the audience becoming performers to the music, these later examples of symposion spectators on vases mark a clear restraint and separation on the part of the audience. Perhaps this change is tied to the increasing professionalization of music and a standard of performance during the fifth century that brings an expectation of focus and attention for the spectator, as S. Bundrick has argued.[87] If so, the impetus for representing spectators would differ in the fifth century than earlier, and the social significance of spectators would be different.

Erotic Scenes

One final subject we will examine encompasses erotic scenes.[88] Like music scenes, there are numerous examples from the archaic period and later in which figures watch two (or more) people courting or having sex, but fewer in which a structural boundary is maintained between the spectator and the actors. For example, the scene on a tripod pyxis at Yale University shows a man with a youth in the center of one panel (figure 58).[89] Both are nude and have a purple wreath draped over one of their forearms.

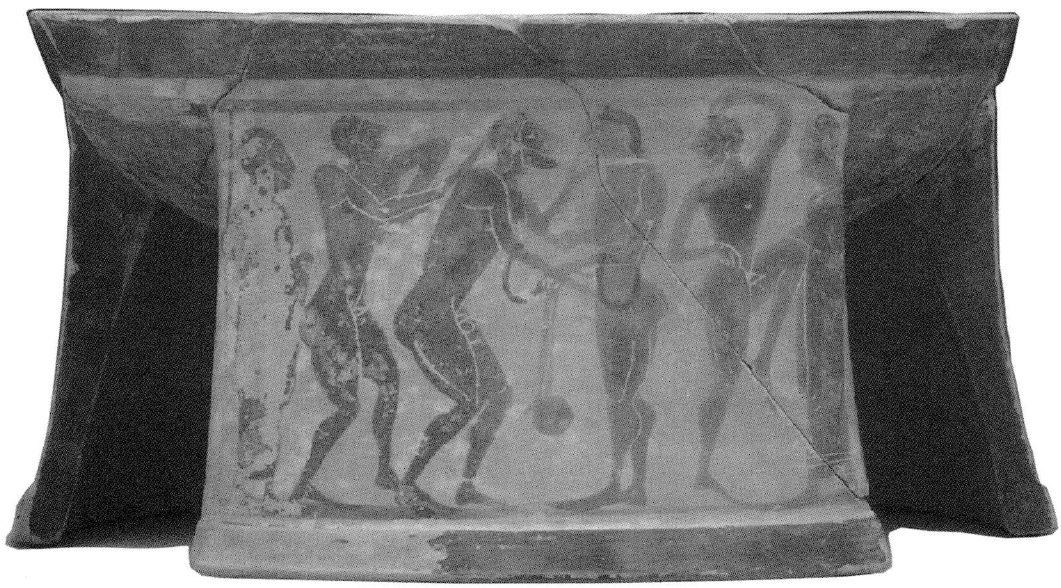

58. Attic black-figure tripod pyxis, c. 550. Side B: Courting scene. New Haven, Yale University Art Gallery, 1913.112. Stoddard Collection. (Photograph, Yale University Art Gallery)

The man crouches slightly, bringing his head level with the youth, and lifts his left hand up under the chin of the youth, while simultaneously stretching his right hand down to the youth's genitals. The youth, who holds an aryballos on a string, seems to place his hands in a gesture of gentle restraint, or perhaps subtle encouragement, on the forearm and elbow of the man.[90] To either side are two nude men who move or dance vigorously while watching the pair in the center. Although these figures are spectators in a sense, their nudity makes them visually equivalent to the *erastes* in the center, and hence interchangeable with him as potential lovers. Although their role is that of catalysts within the picture, placing the main action within a festive setting, they do not have the visual marker or boundary that would separate them from the main scene. Erotic scenes with only such figures have been excluded from the CVA census because they fall into the category of interested spectators at best, but the Yale pyxis also has two figures at the ends of the panel that do qualify as detached spectators. On the left is a mantled man, identified by the incision for his beard, and on the right is a mantled youth, the prototypical types M.1a and Y.1a respectively. Their dress and behavior set them apart from the action in the center of the panel, and in some sense make them appear closer to the modern idea of the voyeur.[91]

With this example in mind, there are a dozen vases with erotic scenes in the CVA census, six with men and eight with youths (see table 40). The number of examples with adult males is higher than the CVA census generally (50 percent compared with 30.1 percent), whereas the number of youths is about the same (66.7 percent versus

Table 40. *Frequency of Spectator Categories in Erotic Vases*

Category	Erotic Vases with Men	CVA Vases with Men (223)	Category	Erotic Vases with Youths	CVA Vases with Youths (527)
M.1	50.0% (3/6)	31.8%	Y.1	37.5% (3/8)	49.1%
M.2	16.7% (1/6)	34.1%	Y.2	12.5% (1/8)	33.6%
M.3	0	12.1%	Y.3	0	11.4%
M.4	16.7% (1/6)	14.8%	Y.4	12.5% (1/8)	12.9%
M.5	16.7% (1/6)	8.1%	Y.5	12.5% (1/8)	5.3%
M.6	16.7% (1/6)	12.6%	Y.6	37.5% (3/8)	6.3%

70.9 percent), but with the relatively small sample size it is uncertain whether the larger proportion of men as spectators is significant. Nine of the 12 vases have a narrative nucleus of one or more men courting a youth like the scene on the Yale pyxis; two scenes have a man and woman as the nucleus, one of which shows them courting and the other copulating. Finally, there is a unique scene of spectators watching two boars coupling. Even within this small group of vases, the preponderance of homoerotic courting scenes with spectators is particularly significant because it reflects the importance of pederastic relationships in the social development of aristocratic youth. With the addition of spectators to such scenes, the scene becomes enframed by the gaze of the onlookers as a model of behavior for the viewer.[92]

Among the vases with adult male spectators, half show mantled men who are quietly standing while watching, and one additional vase has an inert spear-bearing man watching. There are several examples of category M.4, all on a single vase. There is a notable presence of the last two categories of spectators, with one vase featuring a stick-leaning man and another showing a seated man (M.6b). Again, the small size of the group makes drawing a conclusion impossible, but the use of a pose that signifies both concentrated attention and restrained activity, such as we saw with the music scenes, suggests the strong emotional appeal for such scenes to the viewer, so that it is difficult to expect spectators to remain detached in such scenes, as the two dancing figures on the Yale pyxis indicate.

For youths, the frequency of the inert mood of spectator, spear-bearing and not, is 50 percent, well below the frequency in the CVA census. There is only a single example of an active or very active spectator, and this appears on a cup with inert spectators. Interestingly, this very active type of spectator occurs on the one vase with a heterosexual coupling, and the torsos of this pair of watching youths are positioned in exactly the same position as the man in the nucleus, making them somewhat mimetic in their reaction.[93] Half of all youthful spectators fall into the last two categories, with three vases having seated youths watching a courtship scene in the center. These figures, like those in music scenes, watch the main action closely, but seem to use their position to enforce a restraint in their behavior. The pattern that emerges for youthful spectators is that all of the eight vases have examples of immobile, watching youths. The only example with an active youth is also in the only heterosexual scene among the eight vases. It is tempting to consider whether this reflects a different code of behavior for relationships with men and women, with restraint and modesty expected for homoerotic relationships and mimicry accepted for heterosexual scenes, but the number of vases is too few to be certain of this pattern. It would, however, be worthwhile to consider the behavior not only of detached spectators, but also of interested spectators, excluded in this study, to explore this issue further.[94]

Given the importance of emotional and physical ties between men and youths as part of the socialization process, the category of erotic scenes is important to consider for spectator reactions, but the small number of scenes with structurally defined spectators makes drawing firm conclusions difficult. It is possible that a broader survey of such scenes beyond the CVA and the inclusion of a broader classification of spectators would provide sufficient numbers for such a discussion, but for now we may consider a few, tentative suggestions. First, it would seem that men are an important target audience for this scene, and that they see themselves as potential *erastes* like the figures in the nucleus of the composition. This would confirm the idea of reflection and identification discussed in chapter 3.3. Second, there is a decided tendency for youthful spectators not to react to the scene in front of them. The one example of a type Y.4 spectator is curiously a witness to a heterosexual coupling, rather than to a homosexual courtship. The behavior of the youthful spectator to the homosexual courtship scenes mimics the reaction of the *eromenos* in the nucleus, who, as we saw earlier, is expected to react with restraint to the attentions of the older *erastes*. Third, there is generally an expectation of restraint in terms of the behavior of spectators. One might think of this as a caution for the male viewer to behave with restraint in pursuing a relationship, and to contemplate his emotions and desires with control.

5.5 DISCUSSION

To end this chapter, I would like to offer some thoughts about what spectators suggest about the role of men and youth in archaic Athens. Clearly, inert spectators are the preferred behavioral mood of male spectators on vases, particularly for youth. The mantled youth is the most common type of spectator on all vases and, indeed, is an almost stereotypical spectator. When considered alongside the inert, spear-bearing youths, a calm, controlled contemplation of the narrative nucleus is the expected behavior for the young man. For the adult man, inert types are a majority of spectators, but they are not so predominant as their youthful counterparts. There is a split between the mantled and spear-bearing sorts in frequency, and the category of spear-bearers is, indeed, slightly higher overall than the mantled types. The spear signifies the status and role of the adult male as the citizen and leading group within the city, responsible for its well-being, but the controlled behavior that is necessary for that role is paramount in the behavior of the spectator.

The reactive behavioral mood constitutes a large number of adult male spectators, and it is significant that the most common types among these emphasize the position of men within the city. The most frequent types of reactive spectators are those who direct attention with the arm straight out (M.3a and M.4a). The leader types are found more frequently with heroic and battle images. The acclamation gestures direct the attention of other spectators as well as the viewer, and equate the adult man with the narrative ideal in the center of the picture. The relative frequency of stick-leaning and seated types (M.5, M.6) is also higher for men than for youths. These two categories are found primarily in what might be called civic scenes, such as musical performances and athletics, and signify social status.

Reactive spectators are less common among youth than men, and one can see the mantled youth as expressing the importance of *aidos*. The mantle and directed glance give youth protection during their temporarily subordinate social position. Among the reactive youthful spectators, the kouros type is noteworthy as being based on a sculptural type rather than public behavior, but it is only in the mimetic types that we see proportionally more youths than men. Often appearing with mantled counterparts, the combination of mimetic and inert types, frequently in the same picture, emphasizes the type of behavior that youth will need to follow so that they can become adult citizens: modest and decorous in observance and learning to act like their heroic exemplars when needed.

There is, then, a difference in the behavior of these two groups of spectators that reflects their position within the city. This selectivity also applies to the scenes that they witness. Several scenes have an affinity for men as spectators, especially those with Herakles, music, and erotica. Herakles is an adult, and so adult men gravitate to him as a metaphor. The man is also the dominant figure in erotic scenes, and so again targeting a male viewer, whereas the seated and stick-leaning postures common in music scenes emphasize the social standing of men. Youths are found more commonly in athletic and processional scenes that refer to activities within the city, scenes like the rider and the runner. The types of event they witness are the sort of activities that prepare the young men and demonstrate their excellence and readiness to assume a role in the city. The predominance of youth observing figures of Nike and the sphinx, as well as the dominance of youthful spectators on lekythoi, suggests their association with death and commemoration, in a manner like the use of the kouros statue at a tomb.

If we look at the distribution of spectator categories for youth and men by period, we can see that the selection of types changes during the course of the sixth century. Looking first at men, we can see that the mantled and spear-bearing types, M.1 and M.2, begin at equivalent frequencies as a percentage of vases from that period, but there is a strong dominance of the spear-bearing types during the last third of the century (chart 2). The frequency of active spectator types (M.3, M.4) is stronger early and subsides at the end of the sixth century, at the same time the seated and stick-leaning

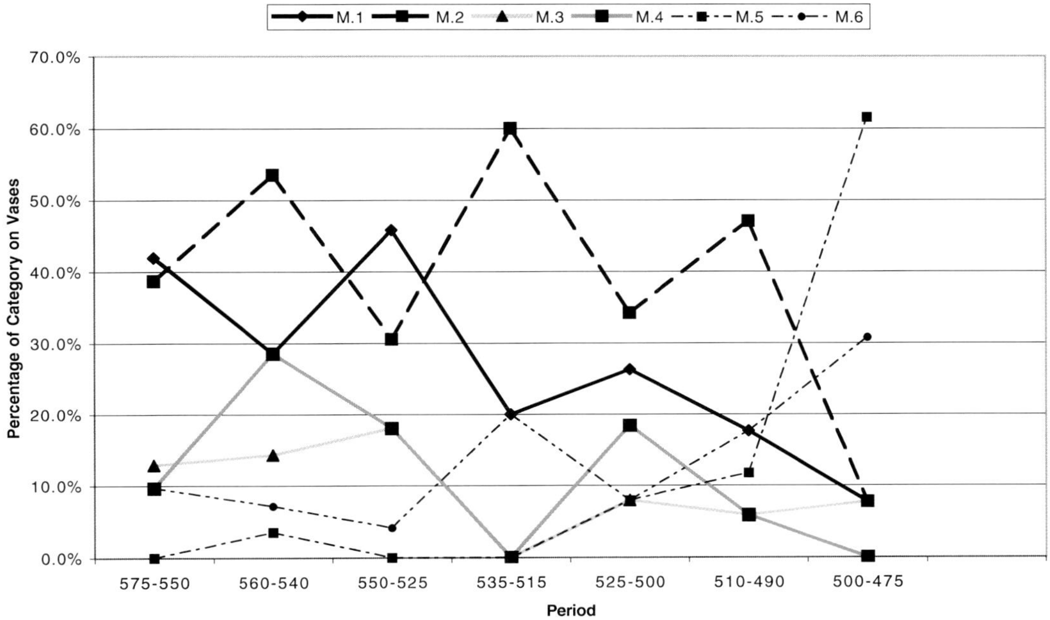

Chart 2. Adult Male Spectator Categories by Period.

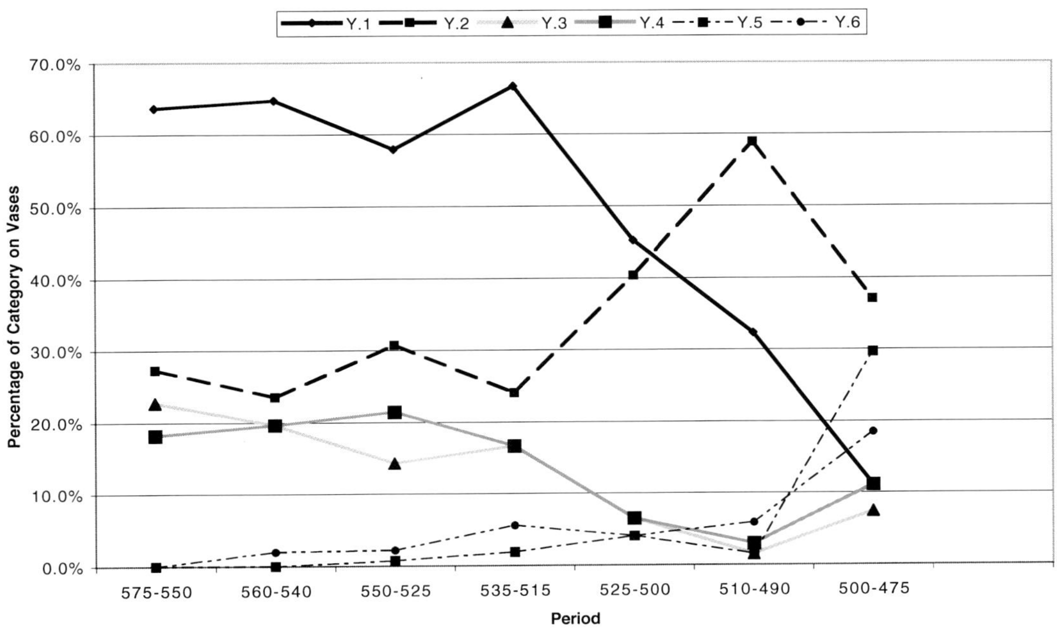

Chart 3. Youthful Spectator Categories by Period.

types (M.5, M.6) gain in frequency, becoming the predominant types in the early fifth century.

Turning to youthful spectators, we can see the strong dominance of the mantled youth through the third quarter of the sixth century, but that the spear-bearing youth achieves equal frequency and then predominance during the last part of the sixth and the early fifth centuries. The numbers of active spectators (Y.3 and Y.4) decline during the course of the sixth century, whereas the frequencies of seated and stick-leaning spectators become more common in the first quarter of the sixth century, although they do not become the most popular categories, as they do with men.

The shift to spear-bearing types in the latter part of the sixth century for both men and youths coincides with the development of the Greater Dionysia, which may have featured orphans being equipped with armor by the city and pyrrhic dances at this time (see chapter 4). The shift also coincides with the Kleisthenic reforms and projects an image of a stronger Athens. The rise of stick-leaning and seated spectators, especially of those seated upright (M.6b, Y.6b), also suggests a perception of privilege among groups within the city, at least among the citizens, especially in conjunction with civic scenes such as athletic competitions and musical contests. It is tempting to consider the greater popularity of these types as models for spectators at this time as reflecting the changing enfranchisement of the adult male citizens of Athens and their youthful protégés, expressing a sense of their entitlement. Such a conclusion, however, must be based on images of behavior outside of spectators on vases and must remain a hypothesis.

However, as we shall see in the next chapter, the selection of spectator types for men and youth does establish a very different pattern from the types for women spectators, and one can conclude that the underlying social expectations of gender behavior are encoded into the selection of spectator types. In this light, the idea of a more militant and privileged model of spectator behavior in the last part of the archaic period reflects a change from earlier in the sixth century, when the mantled, unarmed male figure was far more common, as was the reactive and expressive type of figure.

SIX

WOMEN AS SPECTATORS

Gender and Social Identity

Returning once more to look at the Minneapolis amphora, we can focus on the two women who are spectators to the fighting warriors (figure 59). Both make the same gesture, with the back forearm projecting from the body and the fingers and thumb of the hand extended. The near arm is crooked and held closer to the body, with the hand by the waist and the elbow projecting back. The women's gestures are markedly different from those of the two youths in the picture, and this raises a question: Are the reactions of female spectators influenced by definitions of gender roles in archaic Athens?

In this chapter, we will examine the reactions of women as spectators to the central scenes of the vase paintings, following the same approach used in the previous chapter for men and youths. Unlike males, there is no visual distinction of age among the pictures with female figures; most women wear a long garment, often belted at the waist, and frequently have a mantle. Their hair is usually shown long, with tresses falling down the back and often over the front of the shoulders. Figures may wear wreaths or diadems and there may be other jewelry represented, especially on larger scale figures. The clothing often shows a small degree of patterning, either dots, single lines, or cross-hatching. Despite this variety of dress and adornment, though, there is no clear distinction of age through the height of the figure, the size of the breasts, or the dressing of the hair.[1]

Not only is there no real age distinction among women, there was not in Athens a public initiation of girls into the status of women similar to the rituals for boys, as G. Ferrari has shown.[2] Marriage, although an action that is visible in public, is still a private affair, and the achievement of full womanly status depends finally on the production of children, a sign external to the woman herself, unlike the growth of a beard for men.[3] Yet the status of "wife" is one that can be lost and reacquired, as Ferrari points out, making the marriage rite and its associated ritual a marker of a change in

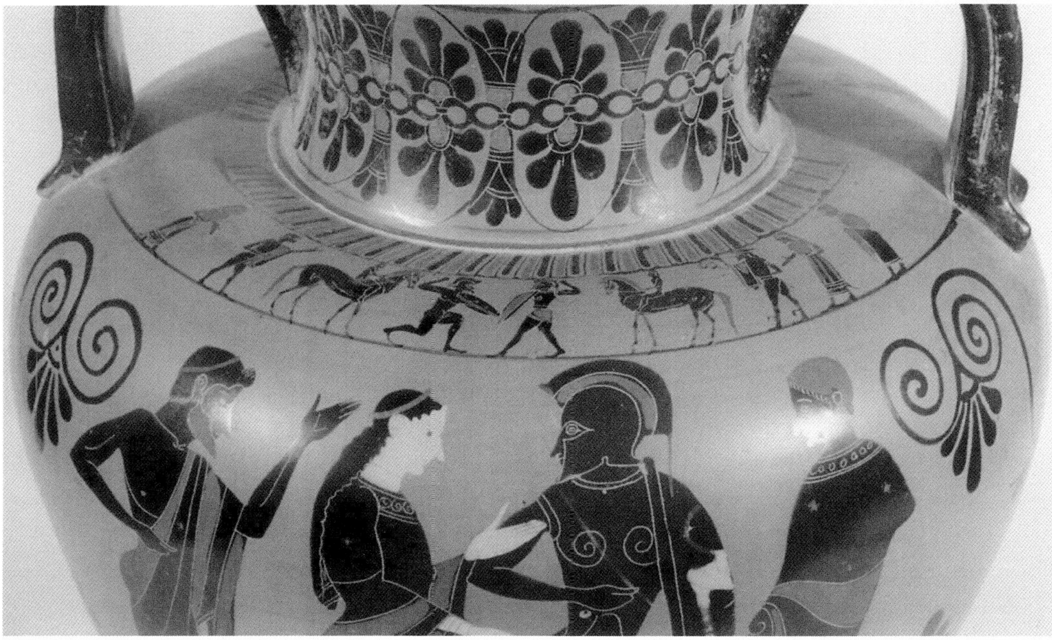

59. Attic black-figure amphora, attributed to the Painter of Vatican 359, c. 530. Side B: Detail of shoulder: warriors fighting. Minneapolis Institute of Arts, Ethel Morrison Van Derlip Fund, 57.1. (Photograph, The Minneapolis Institute of Arts)

position but not a change in social status such as what young boys experience in becoming citizen men. Indeed, one might speculate, based on ritualistic theory, that in the absence of a public initiation for girls similar to that for youths becoming men, a visual set of signs for female transition was not established as part of the archaic visual language. Even the rites of the cult of Artemis at Brauron, an important stage in the development of the Athenian maiden, were isolated from public view both by the remote location of the sanctuary from the city center and by the more cloistered and less public nature of the festivities and practices there. Whether or not the *arkteia*, or "playing the bear," at Brauron was an initiatory cult, an interpretation that has been recently challenged by C. Faraone, it was still not a public investiture of a new status in the same way that civic cults functioned for youths.[4] For these reasons, both visual and social, we will treat the female spectator as a single gender category without age distinction.

In the first section, we look at the types of gestures to be found among women spectators. In some categories, the gestures are the same as those for men, but in others there are significant differences. With this in mind, the categories of coding (W.1, W.2, etc.) remain the same as those for youths and men, but the specific types of gestures will not correspond in most cases (for example, W.1a does not equal M.1a

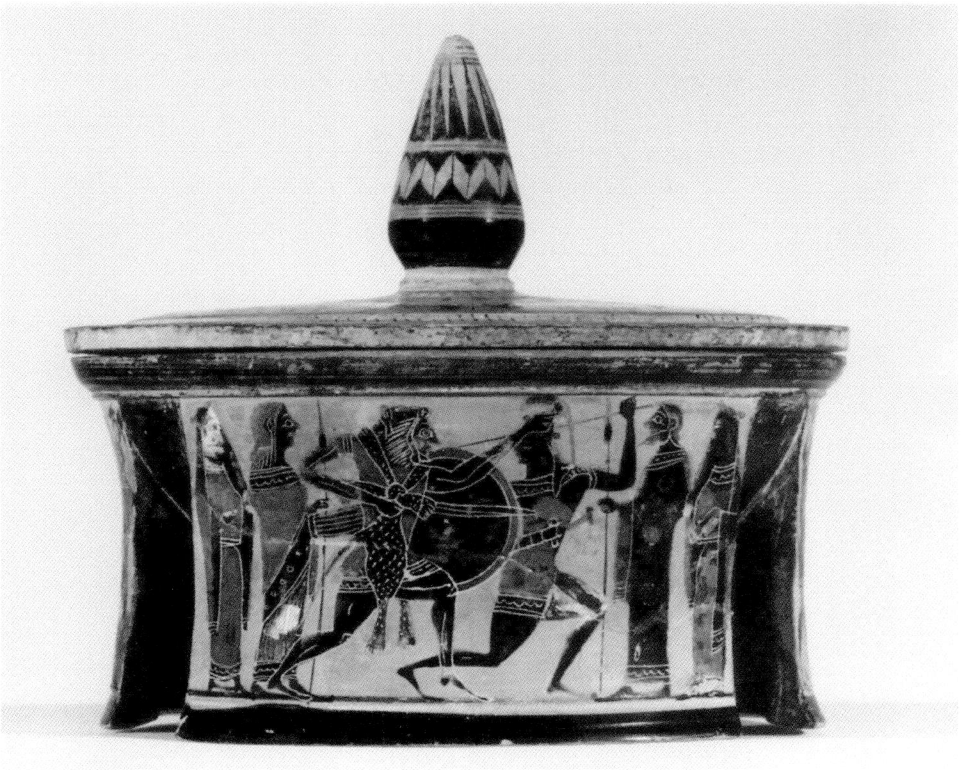

60. Attic black-figure tripod pyxis, c. 550. Side A: Herakles vs. Amazon. Berlin, Staatliche Museen zu Berlin – Preussischer Kulturbesitz Antikensammlung F3988. (Photograph: Bildarchiv Preussischer Kulturbesitz/Art Resource, NY)

or Y.1a). Following this examination of gesture types, we look at women as spectators to the same specific scenes that we examined in the previous chapter. Here, we will explore the questions of which scenes seem to have been focused on women spectators, and how their behavior changes depending on the type of action that they witness.

6.1 GESTURES AMONG WOMEN SPECTATORS

W.1: Inert/Inactive Spectators

The standing-still, heavily mantled figure that we found as the most prevalent single category for men and youth also exists for women, as can be seen at the ends of a panel on a pyxis in Berlin, where we see Herakles attacking an Amazon (figure 60, see chart of all female types at figure 61).[5] Both women wear a belted garment and a mantle that, unlike the man and youth in the same picture, is drawn up to cover the top of the head. The back hand of each woman holds the edge of the mantle at chest level

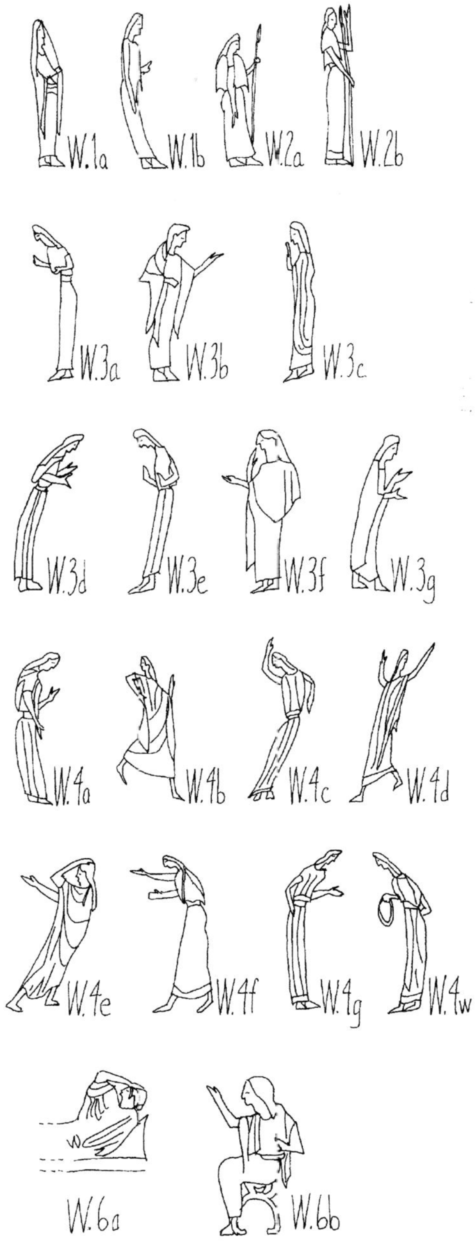

61. Chart of women spectator types. (Drawings, author)

and pulls it forward before the body, creating a deeper silhouette. Being found on 30 of 175 total vases with women spectators, it is the single most frequent type of female spectator, and has been coded as W.1a to parallel the ubiquitous mantled figure for men and youths, M.1a and Y.1a (see table 41).

Table 41. *Frequency of Types in Spectator Category W.1*

Type	Description	Number	Frequency of Total W in CVA Census (175)
W.1a	Mantle pulled forward ("*anakalypsis*-type")	30	17.1%
W.1b	Standing still, one hand projects from mantle	8	4.6%
		Total = 37	21.1%

This gesture is similar to the *anakalypsis*, or wedding gesture, in which the bride pulls forward her veil, revealing herself to the groom and signaling her acquiescence to the marriage.[6] That is not to say that the gesture of these spectators is the *anakalypsis* and that they are brides, but rather that they are mimicking the gesture that is the most important visual signal of a woman's change in condition from *kore* to *nymphe*, from maiden to bride. Whereas marriage is a private arrangement, the transport of the bride from the house of her parents to that of her new husband is an event that occurs in the public space and is perhaps the most visibly recognizable act of a woman in public.[7]

Despite its status as the most common single type of female spectator, the relative frequency of the "*anakalypsis*-type" does not match that for the standing mantled figure for either youths or men. The *anakalypsis*-type occurs on 17.1 percent of vases in the CVA census with women spectators. For vases with male spectators, the standing-still, mantled type (M.1a) occurs with a relative frequency of 28.7 percent; for vases with mantled youths (Y.1a), the relative frequency is 41.6 percent. Although it is the single most frequent type for women, the *anakalypsis*-type has a relative frequency less than two-thirds of that seen for the most common type for both men and youths. Whereas one might say of the youth and man on the Berlin pyxis that they are "typical" spectators for their group, bearing features that are found on more than half of all spectators in their group when including their spear-bearing counterparts, the *anakalypsis*-type for women is not sufficiently frequent to be considered as "typical." We shall return to this point later when considering more active gestures for women.

There are also examples of a female spectator who places her hand before her near the level of the waist, like the most common type of male mantled figure, as can be seen on a neck amphora in New York with a scene of Herakles and Acheloös (figure 62).[8] The woman behind Herakles on the left holds her right arm straight down, whereas her left hand projects in front of her, midway between chest and waist. As can be seen by comparing her with the woman on the far right of the picture, the gesture is distinct from that of pulling the mantle forward and is very much like the male types M.1a-b and Y.1a-b. Because it is less frequent than the *anakalypsis*-type, this spectator type has been coded as W.1b, noting its parallels to M.1a-b and Y.1a-b.

In the case of the New York amphora, Moore and von Bothmer raised the possibility that the figure behind Herakles is Athena.[9] There is, however, no distinguishing feature or sign that would make this figure Athena (compare figure 23), so that the figure should be regarded as more generic in intention and therefore a detached or, more likely, pure spectator. Still, the pose, especially the position of the projecting hand, is reminiscent of Athena holding a spear or shield before her. We should consider that the ambiguity of the woman's identity as Athena on this vase may be a reflection that this particular pose for a woman spectator is derived from figures of Athena, rather than that it is a common gesture or action expected of a woman in a social situation.[10]

Unlike the *anakalypsis*-type figure, the type W.1b is far more rare among women. It is found on just eight vases, or 4.6 percent of the vases with women spectators, compared with relative frequencies of 46.7 percent for Y.1a-b and 31.4 percent for M.1a-b. Although the overall form of the female figure may correspond to that for male spectators, the disparity in the relative frequency of its use shows that it is an action that is considered far more appropriate for males, especially youths, than for women. Rather than following the prototypical male in form, the ideal image of the inert, composed woman spectator is based instead on the imagery of the wedding and the notion that by pulling aside her mantle or veil, the woman accepts the situation that has been arranged for her as she is "given" to another.[11]

The overall disparity between males and females for the category W.1, the standing-still spectator, is noteworthy. Including all of the variants in the category, we see that Y.1 accounts for 49.1 percent of all vases in the CVA census with youthful spectators, and category M.1 accounts for 31.8 percent of all such vases with men. In comparison, category W.1 constitutes only 21.1 percent of the vases with women, a significantly lower frequency when compared with males generally. This disparity only increases if we consider all inert behavioral spectators, including the spear-bearing types. Adding the inert spear-bearing type W.2a that is described in the next section, we find that the total frequency of inert women spectators is only 27.4 percent of the total group of vases with women spectators. Including types 2a and 2b for men and youths, we find that the inert spectator accounts for 78 percent of all youthful spectators, and 56.1 percent of all adult male spectators (see table 11 in Chapter 2). The frequency for inert women spectators, then, is roughly half of that for men and one-third of that for youths, and clearly indicates that the behavioral pattern for women does not follow that for men and youths.

Although in sculpture one could say that the kore statue, perhaps the closest three-dimensional realization of type W.1b, is an idealized representation of the female form, we do not see its equivalent among spectator types having the same visual dominance of the imagery. One could argue that the kouros type of spectator is equally rare among youths as a spectator type, whether in the spear-bearing or simply nude form (Y.2e or Y.3d). This would affirm that the visual ideal or prototype being projected through spectators in general derives not from statuary, but from civic ritual and behavior.

This argument, however, would also lead to the conclusion that there does not appear to be a dominant, prototypical civic visual identity for females as there is for males. Although the marriage-related type W.1a is the most common single type of woman spectator and likely derives from aspects of the public behavior of the bride

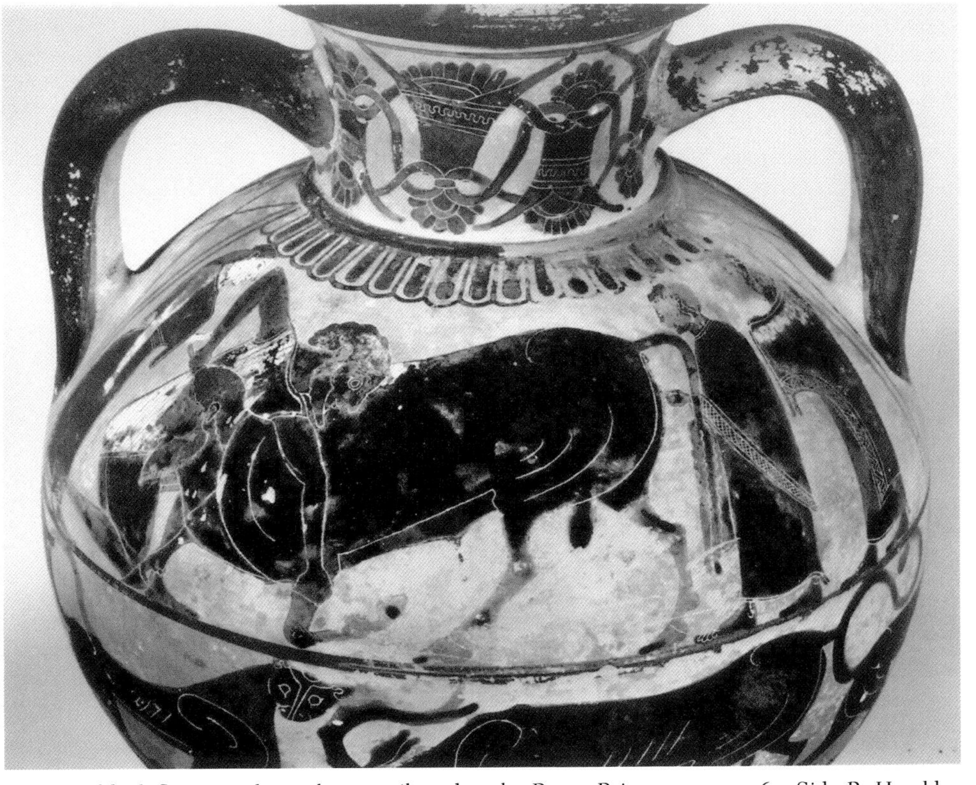

62. Attic black-figure neck amphora attributed to the Ptoon Painter, c. 570–560. Side B: Herakles and Acheloös. New York, The Metropolitan Museum of Art, Gift of Eugene Holman, 1959 (59.64). (Photograph, all rights reserved, The Metropolitan Museum of Art)

during the wedding festivities, it accounts for fewer than one-fifth of all CVA census vases with women spectators. The fact that this prototype does not translate into a dominant model for spectator behavior, as the inert, mantled figure does for both youth and men, testifies to the domestic and private rather than civic character of the wedding. The lack of dominance for category W.1 spectators among women spectators further suggests that the ideal of calm, restrained, and contemplative behavior that is characteristic of inert spectators is not a behavioral mood that is shared across gender categories in ancient Athens, a point to which we will return.

W.2: Spear-Bearing Spectators

In comparing the frequency of inert spectators across gender categories, we included the standing-still, spear-bearing types for men and youths because the pose and form of the figures are virtually identical, save for the presence of a spear. Spear-bearing female spectators also exist, but in much smaller numbers than either youths or men.

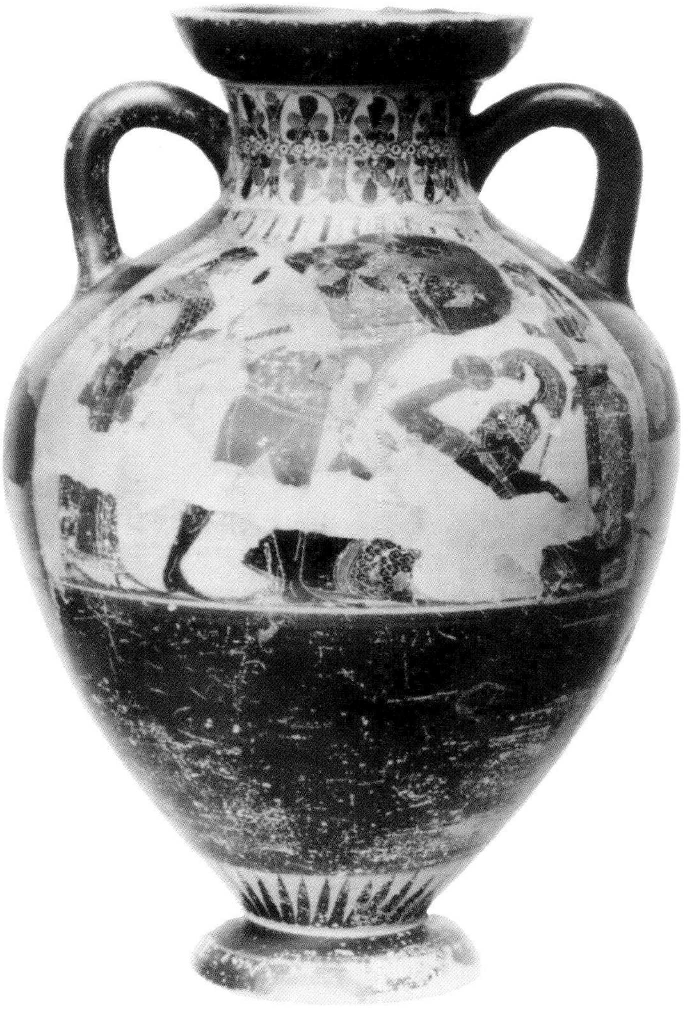

63. Attic black-figure Panathenaic amphora attributed to the Swing Painter, c. 550–525. Side A: Gigantomachy with Poseidon. Copenhagen, Department of Classical and Near Eastern Antiquities, National Museum of Denmark (Photo, museum) 3672.

The first type that we will look at, W.2a, is parallel to both M.2a and Y.2a and has the figure standing still while holding a spear before her and close to the body. This can be seen on a Panathenaic amphora by the Swing Painter in Copenhagen, on which we see Poseidon and a giant fighting, with the god holding a rock over his collapsing opponent (figure 63).[12] On either side are unidentified female figures with spears, each holding her hand slightly above her waist to grasp the spear haft. The other arm is bent slightly at the elbow and held along the front side of the body, within the silhouette.

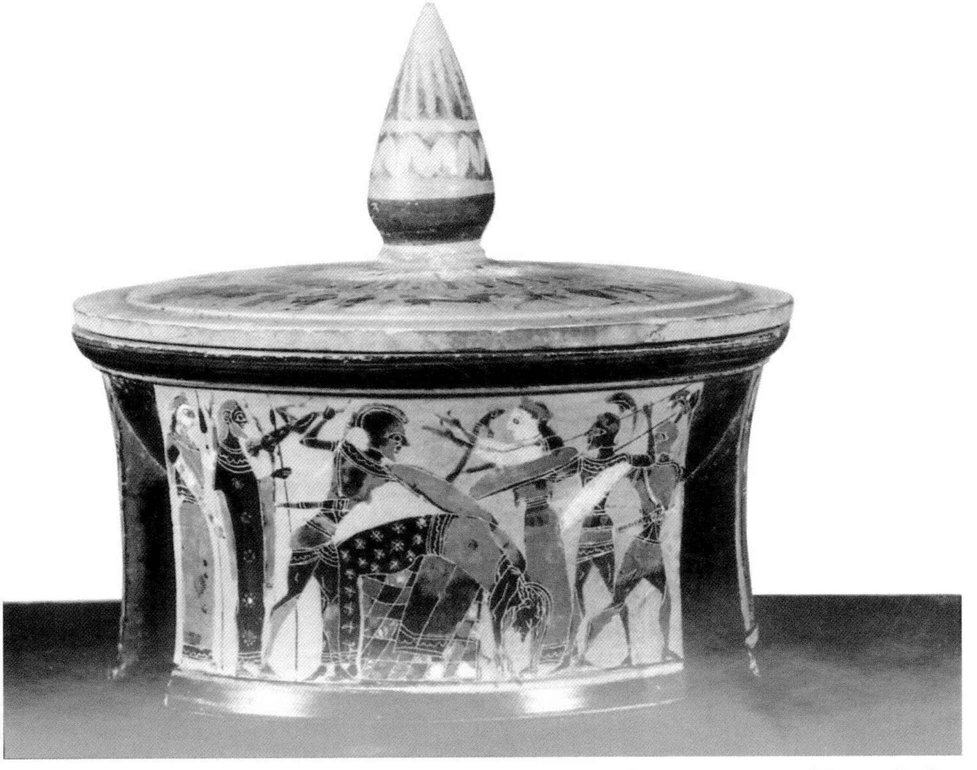

64. Attic black-figure tripod pyxis, c. 550. Side C: Neoptolemos slaying Astyanax and Priam. Berlin, Staatliche Museen zu Berlin – Preussischer Kulturbesitz Antikensammlung F3988. (Photograph, Bildarchiv Preussischer Kulturbesitz / Art Resource, NY)

A second type of spear-bearing woman raises either her spear-bearing or her free arm to gesture more vigorously, and occasionally takes a small stride. For example, on another side of the Berlin pyxis we see a spear-bearing woman and man watching Neoptolemos slaying Astyanax and Priam (figure 64).[13] To the left are a spear-bearing man and woman. The latter holds the spear in her right hand, while the left arm projects forward with the elbow bent 90° and the hand raised just over the head with the fingers and thumb extended fully. This gesture is similar to many of those in categories W.3 and W.4, but the feet here are held close together without the implication of movement. Although direct action is not implied, the gesture of the left arm here does suggest at least an emotional animation or stronger reaction to the scene, making her a reactive rather than inert spectator.

As might be expected from the lack of a military role for women in the city, the spear-bearing women spectators are very infrequent in appearance. There are 13 examples of type W.2a and four of W.2b (see table 42). As a category, the spear-bearing types account for a relative frequency of just 9.7 percent of the total CVA

Table 42. *Frequency of Types in Spectator Category W.2*

Type	Description	Number	Frequency of Total W in CVA Census (176)
W.2a	Standing still, holding spear before the figure	13	7.4%
W.2b	Standing-still, holding spear, one or both arms gesture strongly	4	2.3%
		Total = 17	9.7%

census vases with female spectators, far lower than the frequency found for youths and men (33.6 percent and 34.1 percent respectively). Type W.2a can be considered as belonging to the inert mood of women spectators, but the more active spear-bearing type does not fit into a single mood of behavior. Two of the four examples are mimetic, including the woman in figure 25, whose dress and attributes repeat those of Athena on the other side of Herakles.[14] The other two, including the woman on the Berlin pyxis, do not mimic the behavior of any of the figures in the nucleus and are reactive in mood.[15]

Given the lack of spear-bearing public roles that Athenian women had, this frequency of 9.7 percent would seem surprising, unless one were to consider Athena, rather than civic behavior, as the visual model for this type of spectator, as we did for type W.1b. Certainly Athena is normally seen with a spear as well as helmet and shield, and the strength of that association in the visual language leads to the speculation that at least an allusion to Athena is intended in scenes with a spear-bearing woman. This association can be seen more explicitly in figure 25, but it is important to emphasize that the spectator is not a surrogate for Athena. Athena's involvement in the deeds of heroes is well attested, so that the presence of a spear-bearing woman spectator in scenes from these narratives might be understandable as a metaphorical index. However, Athena does not appear in scenes with the slaying of Astyanax, perhaps in part because of the desecration of the sanctuary of the altar of Zeus that is taking place in the scene.[16] None of the spear-bearing women, then, are Athena, but they have an attribute and pose that is associated with her support for heroes like Herakles and for just wars like the Gigantomachy and Trojan War.

The use of the spear-bearing woman spectator as a pictorial index for Athena might be seen in light of the participation of women in the cult of Athena, even if this did not involve spears, and may provide the pretext for spear-bearing women as spectators. Certainly the idea of dressing up a woman as Athena to be paraded in the street is not novel, as the Phye incident of Peisistratos demonstrates (see chapter 4.1). That the relative frequency of spear-bearing women spectators, however, remains so small shows that it is not a category that caught on widely, not did it reflect the common civic and public behavior of women at rituals or elsewhere in the city.

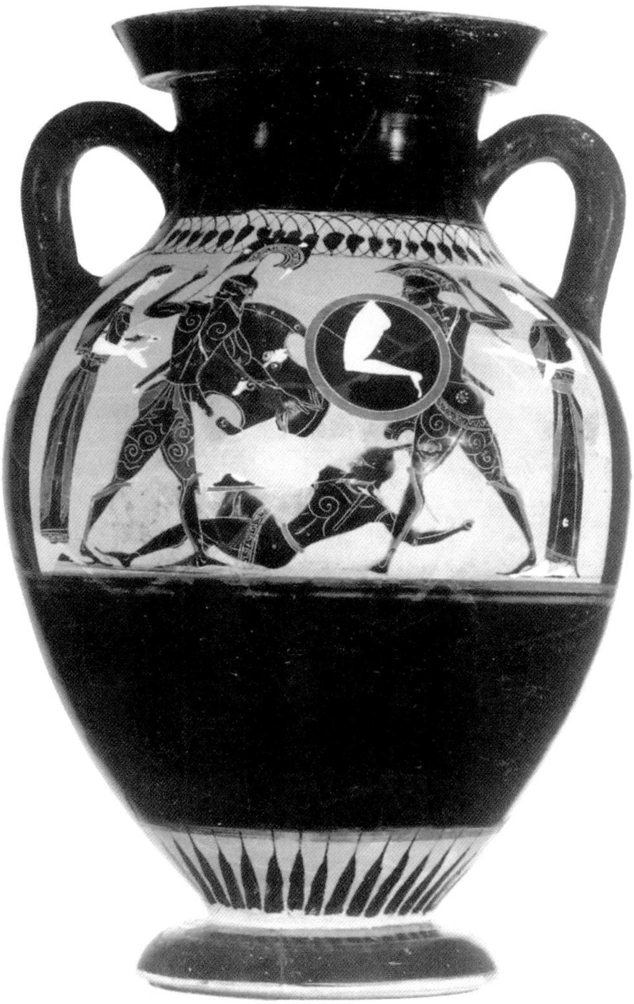

65. Attic black-figure amphora attributed to the Edinburgh Painter, c.510–500. Side A: Warriors fighting. Museum of Fine Arts, Boston. Contribution, 89.256. (Photograph © 2004 Museum of Fine Arts, Boston)

W.3: Active Spectators

Whereas the inert mood constitutes a minority of women spectators, the reactive mood, consisting mostly of categories W.3 and W.4, constitutes a majority. Looking first at category W.3, we can see two different types of active women spectators in the same scene on an amphora in Boston (figure 65).[17] In the center of the composition are two warriors fighting over a fallen soldier. To either side, female figures extend their hands and forearms from their body. There are no inscriptions to identify the warriors, making the scene a generalized heroic action rather than a mythological narrative like

Table 43. *Frequency of Types in Spectator Category W.3*

Type	Description	Number	Frequency of Total W in CVA Census (175)
W.3a	Forearm and hand extended at level of waist	11	6.3%
W.3b	Forearm and hand extended at 45° angle	18	10.3%
W.3c	Forearm and hand held vertically	9	5.1%
W.3d	Both forearms and hands extended at level of waist or slightly downward at the hips	28	16.0%
W.3e	Both hands held at the waist with palms up and facing out ("halt/stop gesture")	3	1.7%
W.3f	One forearm extended at waist, other forearm and hand held vertically near face or chin	7	4.0%
W.3g	Both forearms and hands held at different angles at or above the waist, making acute angle	16	9.1%
		Total = 75	42.9%

the fight of Achilles and Memnon with their mothers watching (see figure 6). The women on this vase are virtually identical in dress and hairstyle, with each wearing a belted peplos with incised and painted details. The woman on the right extends her right arm forward with the thumb extended and the palm facing upward. Her left arm is drawn back within the silhouette of her body; the left hand is fully extended vertically and pointed downward. This pose has been coded as W.3a, because of its similarity to the types of M.3a and Y.3a (see table 43 and compare figures 33 and 42).[18] As with those figures, the extended hand draws the viewer's attention to the action and acknowledges it.

The woman on the left side of the picture bends both arms at the elbow at a 90° angle and extends her forearms from her body, with both hands held straight and the fingers and thumb extended fully. This figure has been coded as W.3d, emphasizing the parallel extension of both arms and the hands held at slightly different positions.[19] The pose of this female figure is somewhat similar to that of types M.3d and Y.3d, but in most examples of men, the hands are drawn in closer to the body and usually below the hips, the elbows extend beyond the silhouette of the back, and the hands are kept parallel and synchronized. This makes the similarity across genders weaker than is the case with W.3a/M.3a/Y.3a.

The W.3d type is far more common than W.3a, with 28 examples in the CVA census, making it the second most common type of woman spectator, after W.1a. This prominence, however, again marks a difference in the attitude of female and male spectators. For men and youths, the runner-up in relative frequency, M.2a and Y.2a respectively, was a variation on the mantled figure (M.1a and Y.1a), simply adding a spear to the form; both the first and second most common types belonged to the inert mood of spectators. For women, however, the second most common figure is quite different in character from the most common type, presenting a more reactive picture of women as spectators. The male figures that are roughly analogous to W.3d, M.3d and Y.3d, are far less frequent for their groups, accounting for only 0.9 percent and 3.4 percent, compared with 16.0 percent for women. One can speculate from this that the gesture of placing both arms and hands in front of the body is more typical for women than for males, and that the concept of a reactive spectator finds greater acceptance for women than for men and youths, a point that we shall see confirmed in looking at other spectator types for women.

Looking more closely at the gesture of this figure (W.3d) on the Boston amphora, the extension of both hands and their configuration at different angles signals a certain distress or helplessness compared with the gesture of the woman on the right (W.3a), who maintains her left arm next to her body. Neumann distinguished the use of both arms as an action gesture, expressing strong emotions such as astonishment, shock, or fright.[20] The position of the hands confirms this idea of an emotional response, as opposed to a controlled reaction. Both hands are held vertically with thumb and fingers extended, a position from which one would expect them to grasp hold of an object, to carry it or to act with it. The empty hands, however, give the gesture a note of futility. Indeed, the fact that the hands are also not positioned together but are held at different angles from the body also implies a lack of purposefulness in their deployment, in that in order for them to act, the hands would have to be brought together first.

The empty hands of the woman on the left, then, signal an inability to act in the scene. In contrast, many of the male figures who have a similar extension of both forearms, as in types M.3d or Y.3d, have mostly closed hands, sometimes with a finger pointing, a gesture that points to the narrative but without conveying a notion of inaction. Further, for the male figures, it is important to note that the arms and hands are held in a rigidly parallel position, whereas the arms of the woman on the Boston amphora form an angle that makes the hands appear to be moving in different directions. Although some examples of type W.3d do not have open hands and others have arms held more parallel than in figure 65, most of the examples have one of these two features, distinguishing them from the behavior of male spectators who hold both hands forward. This difference signals a greater lack of control in the reaction of the figure, making it substantively different in intent.[21]

Two more category W.3 spectators can be seen on the shoulder of a hydria in Oxford (figure 66).[22] Once again, we have two warriors fighting over a fallen fighter, flanked by two female spectators. The figure on the left holds her left arm out and up at a 45° angle; the palm faces upward with the fingers extended. Her right arm is crooked back with the closed hand held in front of her garment. This pose is coded W.3b and is similar to the males types M.3b and Y.3b.[23] It is also the third most common spectator type for women, being found on 18 vases, one-tenth of the vases in the CVA census.

The other woman, on the right side of the picture, portrays an action different from her counterpart. One of her arms is held forward with the palm up and fingers extended. Her other arm is held vertically with the palm facing toward her face; both fingers and thumb are extended, but bent to meet together as the fingers are drawn

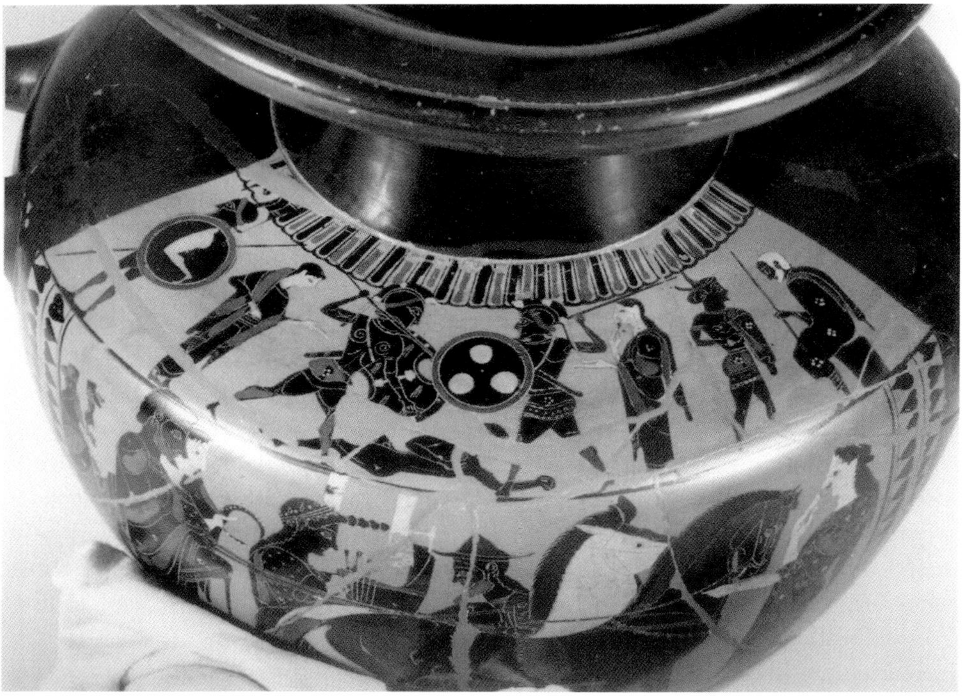

66. Attic black-figure hydria attributed to the manner of the Lysippides Painter, c. 530–520. Shoulder: Warriors fighting. Oxford, Ashmolean Museum 1965. 119. (Photograph, Ashmolean Museum, Oxford)

to her lips. This pose, with one arm extended straight at the waist and the other held vertically, is coded W.3f, and finds no real parallel among gestures for male spectators.[24] It is also less common than W.3b, appearing on seven vases.

Two additional examples of category W.3 spectators are seen on a Tyrrhenian amphora in Kassel (figure 67).[25] In the center, we see Herakles chasing Nessos, who holds Deianeira in his left arm. Three women flank the scene as spectators. The woman farthest to the right holds up one hand vertically before her chest, with the other arm held at her side. This positioning is similar to M.3c and Y.3c, and is similarly coded as W.3c, with nine examples.[26] On the Kassel amphora, the woman holds her palm toward herself with the thumb extended. Whether this is meant to use the hand as a shield from the sight of the action, or is a variation on the upturned palm as a gesture of acknowledgment and praise is unclear. Given the relative restraint of the figure, the idea of praise and acknowledgment might be more appropriate, whereas in the case of type W.3f in figure 66, who nearly touches her mouth, the hand position may indicate more a reaction of horror or shielding.

The other two women on the Kassel amphora show variations of another basic action, in which both forearms and hands are held before the body so that one or both are above the level of the waist. These figures are coded as W.3g, distinguishing the

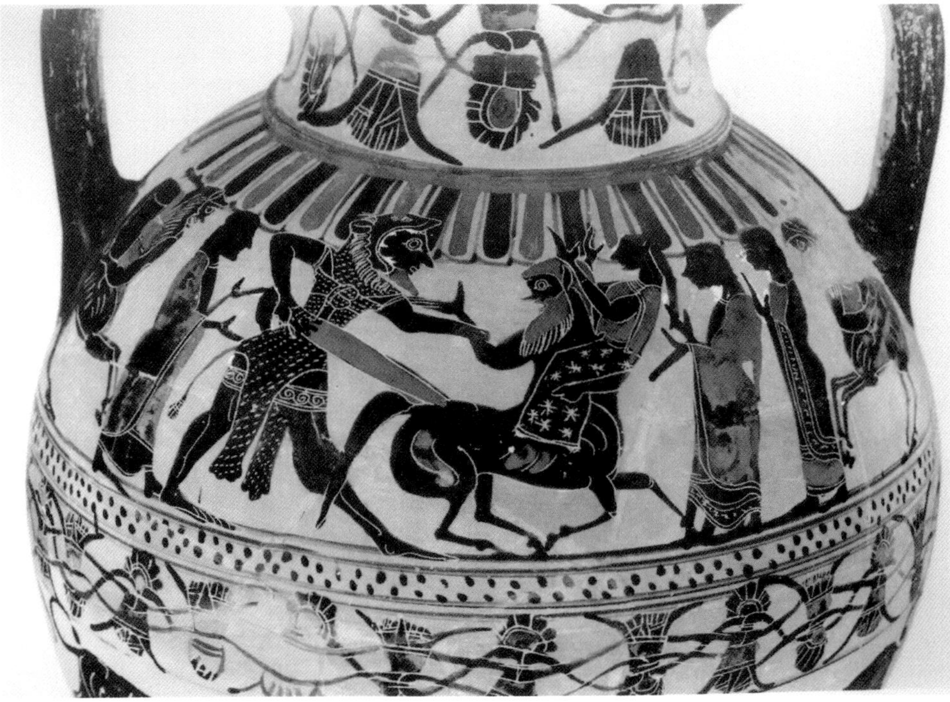

67. Attic black-figure amphora, c. 570–560. Side A: Herakles and Nessos with Deianeira. Kassel, Staatliche Museen, Antikensammlung T385. (Photograph, Copyright Staatl. Museen Kassel)

higher position of the arms than in type W.3d. In both of the examples on this vase, the forearms are arranged in a scissors-like configuration with an acute angle between them.[27] The fingers and thumb of both figures also extend fully, with the palms facing upward. Although singly the gesture of either hand might be associated with praise and acknowledgment, the lack of synchronization between the two hands and arms implies some lack of control, as we saw for type W.3d. Perhaps this indicates disquiet or fear on the part of the spectator, a restrained variation on the arms extended fully up in panic such as we will see subsequently in category W.4. Type W.3g is found on 16 vases.

One final type in this category of active spectators is on an amphora in Munich, on which two women flank a quadriga with charioteer and warrior (figure 68).[28] This scene may be referring to the idea of the warrior departing, but also resembles a pompe, with the warrior being displayed before the town and indicating a public rather than domestic context. The woman on the left holds one hand out and slightly down, and the other is crossed in front of her in a similar position, falling into type W.3d. The woman on the right holds both of her forearms level at the waist and projects her hands with the palms facing the scene in a gesture that is usually interpreted as indicating "stop" or "halt," as if pushing the sight away from oneself. This type, coded as W.3e, is found on only three vases in the CVA census.[29]

In reviewing generally the category of active women spectators, W.3, we can observe that they all fall into the class of reactive behavior. In total, there are 75 vases with figures from category W.3, accounting for 42.9 percent of all vases with women spectators. This is the largest single category for women spectators, and its relative frequency is double that of the inert spectators of category W.1. For men, this same category (M.3) constitutes only 12.1 percent of all vases with adult male spectators; similarly, active youths (Y.3) are only 11.4 percent of the total for their group. As the most common category of women spectators, W.3 has nearly the same relative frequency that the mantled youth (Y.1) has for its group, and is more frequent than either of the inert categories for men, M.1 and M.2a-b. Although no single type is as frequent as the *anakalypsis*-type (W.1a), as a category, W.3 is much more common than W.1 and W.2 combined, exactly the opposite pattern we found for reactive versus inert spectators for youth and men.

Of the seven types in category W.3, only three have a closely corresponding type among men and youths (W.3a/b/c). In each case, one arm is held along the side of the body and the other is used to gesture. The use of only one arm and the control exercised by holding the other arm against the body may indicate a more choreographed type of response such as we might expect from choral performance, and indeed, there are some parallels in frequency for these spectators across gender lines. The first type, W.3a/M.3a/Y.3a, accounts for 6.3 percent of all vases with women spectators, 7.8 percent for men, and 6.1 percent for youths. If derived from choral performance, this would explain the relatively similar proportions for the occurrence of these figures in the different gender groups. For the other common figures, W.3b/M.3b/Y.3b and W.3c/M.3c/Y.3c the frequency for the female version is far greater than in male groups. These two gestures, then, would appear to be more linked with women than with men and youths.

Of the remaining four types of active women spectators, W.3d/e/f/g, none has a close parallel among men or youths. Of particular significance among these types is that the spectator uses both arms, and that the arms are generally not synchronized in their deployment. Among active men, only one type uses both arms (M.3d), and the same is true of youths (Y.3d). In both cases, the hands are synchronized and parallel. This contrasts sharply with the two-arm types for women, which are less controlled in character. There is also a disparity in frequency. For both men and youths, the two-handed type (3d) appeared on a small proportion of vases (0.9 percent and 3.4 percent respectively). For women, 47 vases have active spectators using both hands (W.3d/e/f/g), 26.9 percent of the total. Thirty-seven vases have women using one-handed gestures, making them a minority within this category. Thus, at least for the majority of spectators in category W.3, the figure can be seen not only as reactive, but also as less controlled in its response and deviating from the ideal of a calm and focused witness, one who will see, identify with, and emulate the action of the scene.

To conclude, we can note that the greater overall variety of types for W.3, the frequent deployment of different types on the same vase, and the lack of a single, dominant type in this category indicate that there was no uniformity expected in the

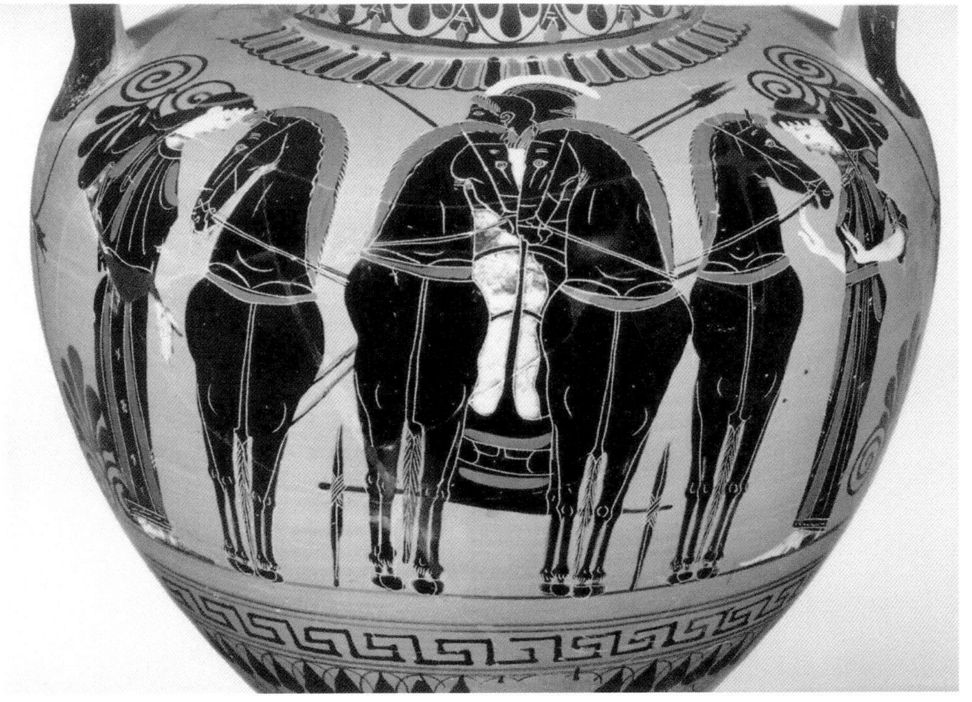

68. Attic black-figure neck amphora attributed to the Antimenes Painter, c. 520. Side B: Quadriga. Munich, Antikensammlung 1514. (Photograph, Staatliche Antikensammlungen und Glyptothek München)

reactions of women spectators to events. The high total frequency for the category W.3 demonstrates that reactive types were considered as more representative models for women spectators than inert types, and that overall, the reactions of women were less controlled than those of male spectators.

W.4: Very Active Spectators

Like category W.3, the very active spectators category, W.4, is more common for women spectators than is its counterpart for men and youths, and it contains a larger number of different types. We can begin looking at this category by examining two examples on an amphora in Munich (figure 69).[30] Once again, we have two unidentified warriors fighting in the center, with the one on the left apparently striking a mortal blow to his opponent, who has attempted to move away. On the left, we see a woman gesture with both arms. The left arm is held up at a 45° angle, whereas the right arm is extended straight and downward at a 45° angle. The placement of the arms at a 90°angle to each other is similar to type W.3g (see figure 67), but here the angle of separation is much wider and the arm is extended straighter. This wide separation of the arms indicates a more vigorous level of response than type W.3g. Therefore, this example

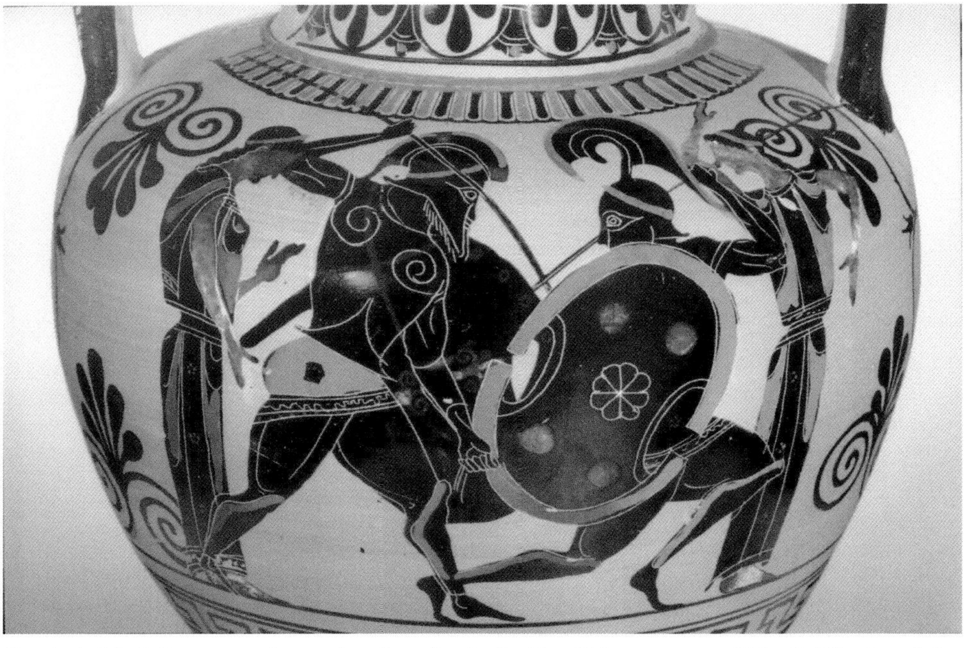

69. Attic black-figure amphora related to the Lysippides Painter, c. 520. Side B: Warriors fighting. Munich, Antikensammlung 1523. (Photograph, Staatliche Antikensammlungen und Glyptothek München)

has been placed into the very active category and coded as W.4a, with 14 examples (see table 44).[31] There is no similar type among adult male spectators, but there is among youths, type Y.4e (see chart at figure 42). However, there is only one example of Y.4e in the CVA census, on a vase by the Affecter, who seemed to favor this type of gesture for many of his non-spectator figures. It would seem that this type of gesture is primarily used for women spectators.

The figure on the right side of the vase seems even more distressed. Like the warrior in front of her, her feet are pointed away from the action, implying flight, but she twists her upper body back fully to look. Her right arm is bent and raised completely over her head; the left arm is similarly bent but is held down and away from the body, making a whirligig configuration for both arms. This figure is coded as W.4c, emphasizing that one arm is held above the head, and the other arm is down, whether held away from the body or closer to it.[32] This type is much more rare than W.4a, with just four examples, and has no parallel among men or youths. Because the warrior before her is collapsing under the attack, we can infer that the upraised arm and hand and fingers extended is an expression of great distress over his fate. That her hand is bent back toward her head recalls the gesture of grasping the hair and forehead in expressions of grief, heightening the sense of loss as well as distress.

Two other types of W.4 appear on the shoulder of a hydria in the British Museum (figure 70).[33] In the center of the frieze, two warriors fight, separated by a draped man.

Table 44. *Frequency of Types in Spectator Category W.4*

Type	Description	Number	Frequency of Total W in CVA Census (175)
W.4a	Both arms extended out at different angles, 90° angle of intersection, elbows may not project	14	8.0%
W.4b	One arm held up before body, tip of hand reaches above head; other arm crooked and down	15	8.6%
W.4c	One arm bent and raised above head, other held out or behind body	4	2.3%
W.4d	Both arms extended out to either side of body	5	2.9%
W.4e	One arm raised to forehead or hair in gesture associated with grief, second hand extended out forward or down behind figure depending on direction of movement	8	4.6%
W.4f	Both arms extended fully before body	11	6.3%
W.4g	One arm extended out at level of waist, other arm crooked behind back	14	8.0%
W.4w	Hand extended holding wreath	14	8.0%
		Total = 71	40.6%

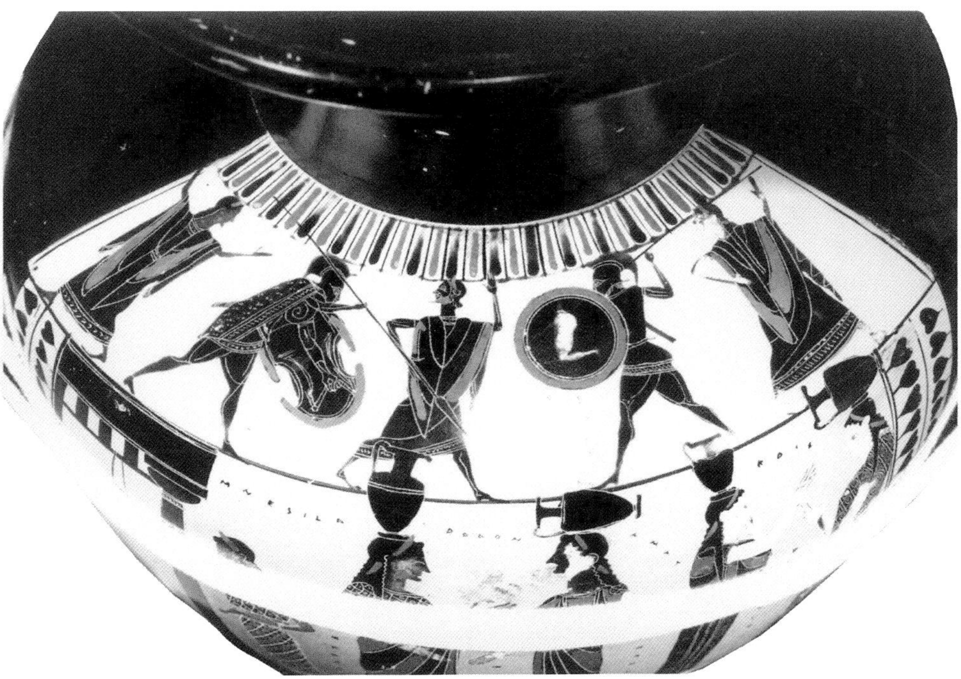

70. Attic black-figure hydria, c. 525–500. Shoulder: Warriors fighting. London, British Museum B333. (Photograph © Copyright The Trustees of The British Museum)

The composition recalls that of Herakles and Kyknos in which Zeus intervenes, but there is no specificity in any of these figures.[34] The draped man, however, must be a catalyst and part of the narrative, and the women running away should be considered as within the time and place of the fight, making them a rare example of a detached spectator at a combat scene. The woman on the right raises her left arm level with her shoulder, and bends her elbow 90° to set her forearm and hand vertically. Her right arm is held down and akimbo, with the hand crossing in front of her body. There are 15 vases with this type, coded W.4b.[35] This figure is close in configuration to W.4c (see chart at figure 61), but here the key feature is that one hand is held straight up and away from the head, rather than leaning in toward it like a mourning gesture. Whereas the woman here flees, more typically the type faces the action. The single upraised hand corresponds to the gesture found in types M.4b and Y.4b, except that in those cases the other arm is held alongside the body with sharp projection, making it more of a one-handed gesture. This type is also more common among women than either M.4b or Y.4b among males.

The woman on the left of the picture also flees, but raises both her arms up and extends them on opposite sides of her body, a gesture that is considered an expression of panic, especially placed in conjunction with her movement away from the action.[36] This figure (W.4d) is much less common than its companion, being found on five vases. There is no corresponding type among adult males, and only a single example of the type among youths (Y.4f, see figure 51), where it signals astonishment.

Another type has one or both arms brought back toward the head to grasp at the hair (see figure 61).[37] This is a gesture associated with mourning, and constitutes the key element for this type, W.4e, whether done with one hand or two.[38] There is no similar gesture of tearing/grasping the head among men and youths. There are eight examples of type W.4e in the CVA census. Like W.4c and W.4d, it can be seen as a reaction of panic and distress that moves into an acknowledgment of loss and death in the narrative nucleus.

An amphora in Los Angeles has yet another type of very active woman spectator (figure 71).[39] In the center is another combat; as in figure 69, the warrior on the right is collapsing before the attack. The woman to the left is another example of type W.4a. The woman on the right faces toward the scene and stretches out both arms at the level of the shoulders toward the action (W.4f).[40] There is no corresponding type among men and youths with both arms extended forward as they are here. The fully stretched arm is frequently associated with reaching for the chin of a threatening figure in a plea for mercy, and the daughters of Priam are so configured with both arms out in some representations of the deaths of Priam and Astyanax.[41] There is too much separation between the figures here for this woman to be seen as pleading directly for mercy, but the gesture would index that as well as acknowledging a helpless despair at the impending loss of the warrior. The type has some modest frequency, with 11 examples.

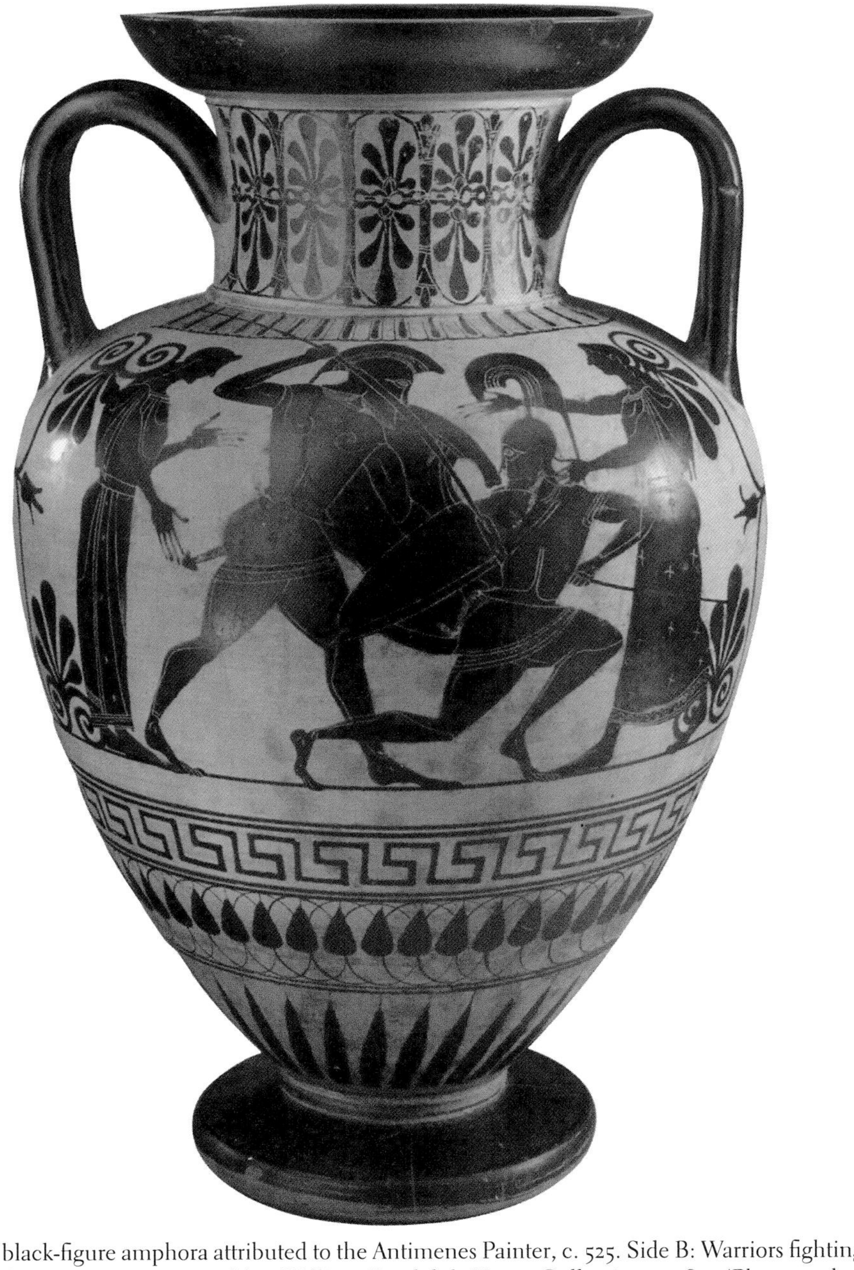

71. Attic black-figure amphora attributed to the Antimenes Painter, c. 525. Side B: Warriors fighting. Los Angeles County Museum of Art, William Randolph Hearst Collection, 50.8.1. (Photograph © 2005 Museum Associates/LACMA)

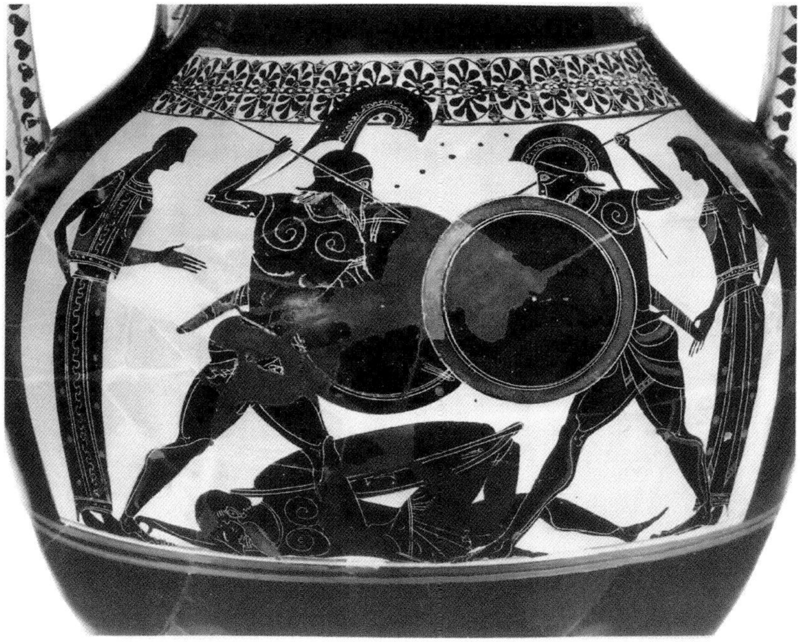

72. Attic black-figure amphora attributed to the Lysippides Painter, c. 520. Side B: Warriors fighting. New York, The Metropolitan Museum of Art, Gift of Colonel and Mrs. Lewis Landes, 1958 (58.32). (Photograph, all rights reserved, The Metropolitan Museum of Art)

Another gesture involves the extension of one arm at the level of the waist and the other arm pulled back, as can be seen on an amphora in New York (figure 72).[42] The woman on the left of the warrior combat extends her left arm and hand forward while pulling back her right arm. The type is similar to W.3a, but both arms project further from the front and back of the torso and there is usually an empty space between the back and arm. There is a loose parallel to the types M.4a and Y.4a for males, but in these cases, the arm is extended higher, at the level of the shoulder, and sometimes angled upward. A variation of this type has the projecting arm angled slightly downward with the hand below the level of the waist. This type is coded W.4g, and it represents perhaps the most restrained type in this category and one of only two types that make single-handed gestures. With 14 examples, it shares the status of second most frequent type in category W.4, along with W.4a and W.4w.

This last type, W.4w, is the other single-handed type in this category, a wreath-bearing figure, corresponding to the same types in both men and youth (M.4w and Y.4w). We can see one such example on an amphora in Adolphseck (figure 73).[43] The figure on the right of the fighting warriors extends her right hand and arm and holds a wreath forward. The woman on the other side also holds a wreath in a similar fashion, with the implication that both warriors are being recognized for their valor. With

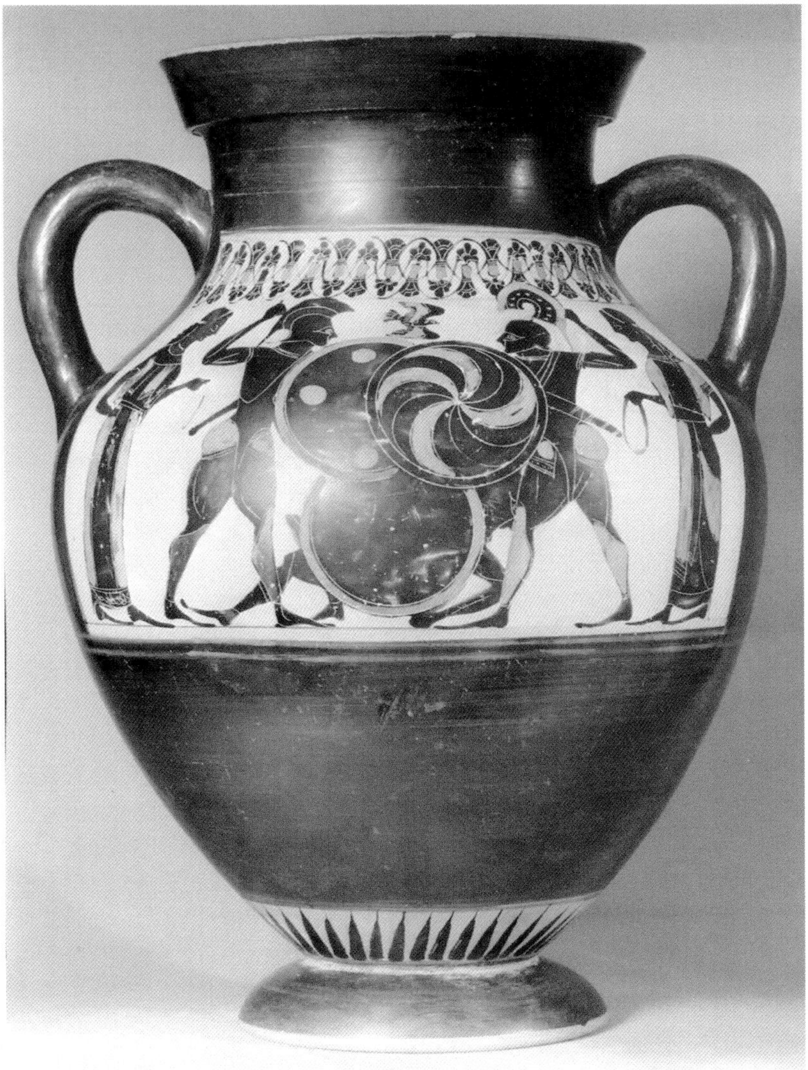

73. Attic black-figure amphora attributed to the Swing Painter, c. 540. Side B: Warriors fighting. Eichenzell/Fulda, Museum Schloss Fasanerie 1. (Photograph, Hessische Hausstiftung, Museum Schloss Fasanerie, Eichenzell/Fulda, Germany)

14 examples, the frequency of this type is higher for women (8.0 percent) than it is for men (2.7 percent) or youths (0.8 percent).

Looking more broadly at this category of very active female spectators, we find 71 vases with these figures, or 40.6 percent of the total group of vases with women spectators. This is only slightly less than the frequency for the category of active spectators, W.3 (42.9 percent), and far more than that for the inert types of W.1 (21.1 percent). Of the

Table 45. *One- and Two-Handed Types of W.3 and W.4 Spectators*

Gesture	Types	Number	Frequency of Total W in CVA Census (175)
One-Handed W.3	W.3a-c	37	21.1%
Two-Handed W.3	W.3d-f	47	26.9%
One-Handed W.4	W.4g, w	28	16.0%
Two-Handed W.4	W.4a-f	54	30.9%
One-Handed W.3-4		64	36.6%
Two-Handed W.3-4		94	53.7%

eight different types defined here, there are only two examples of parallels with men and youths: W.4b/M.4b/Y.4b and W.4w/M.4w/Y.4w. Not only are there more exclusive types of very active figures for women than men, there are twice as many types in this category for women than for men, and the relative frequency of vases with very active women spectators is almost triple that of men (40.6 percent versus 14.8 percent). In its varieties of types, category W.4 is similar to that of Y.4 for youths, and there are a few more parallels between these two genders. In addition to the parallel types found for both men and youths, two others apply just to youths: W.4a/Y.4e and W.4d/Y.4f. However, there is only two examples of each of these for youths, so that these parallels seem more coincidental than suggestive of shared patterns of behavior. Similarly, the relative frequency of vases with very active spectators is more than three times as high for women as it is for youths (40.6 percent versus 12.9 percent). Finally, there are no examples of a mimetic type in this category for women spectators, as there were for men and youths.

Only two of the types in this category use single-handed gestures (W.4g and W.4w), and they are found on 28 vases (see table 45). The other figures all use two-handed gestures, and appear on 54 vases, twice as frequently. We can conclude that this category demonstrates a tendency to show women spectators reacting with strong surprise or distress. The high relative frequency of this category emphasizes, even more than did the previous category of W.3, that women spectators are shown as behaving in a less controlled and contemplative manner than men and youths.

W.5, Stick-Leaning Spectators, and W.6, Seated Spectators

There is no example of the category of stick-leaning spectators for women (W.5), and only a handful of examples of women who are seated (W.6). For the reclining type (W.6a), only one example is found in the CVA census, on a kylix once in the Robinson Collection with a symposion (see table 46 and chart at figure 61).[44] For the seated-upright type of spectator (W.6b), there are five examples, all but one of which involve Herakles in the nucleus of the action.[45] For example, on a hydria in London we see Herakles wrestling the lion (figure 74).[46] To the left appears Athena, who is a catalyst in this picture and, because of her interest in the action, is not counted as a spectator.

Table 46. *Frequency of Types in Spectator Category W.6*

Type	Description	Number	Frequency of Total W in CVA Census (175)
W.5	Stick-leaning	0	0.0%
W.6a	Seated, reclining position	1	0.6%
W.6b	Seated upright	5	2.9%
		Total = 6	3.4%

Behind her is a youth with elbows out (Y.4c). He cannot be Iolaos, who stands on the other side of the picture holding a club, and so is a spectator to the action. On the right side, in front of Iolaos, sits a woman on a chair, holding up her right arm as if to acknowledge the action in the center. She is dressed in a chiton and mantle and wears a diadem, but bears no distinguishing feature, unlike Athena. Although it is possible she is a goddess, it is not certain and she falls more into the broad category of women spectators who are not goddesses and who watch Herakles, as we shall see in the next section. Similar types of seated women can be seen in late archaic paintings of women's ritual banquets that also make their appearance around this same time.[47]

In conclusion, the distribution pattern of spectator types among women indicates that a very active pattern of behavior was considered more typical for women than

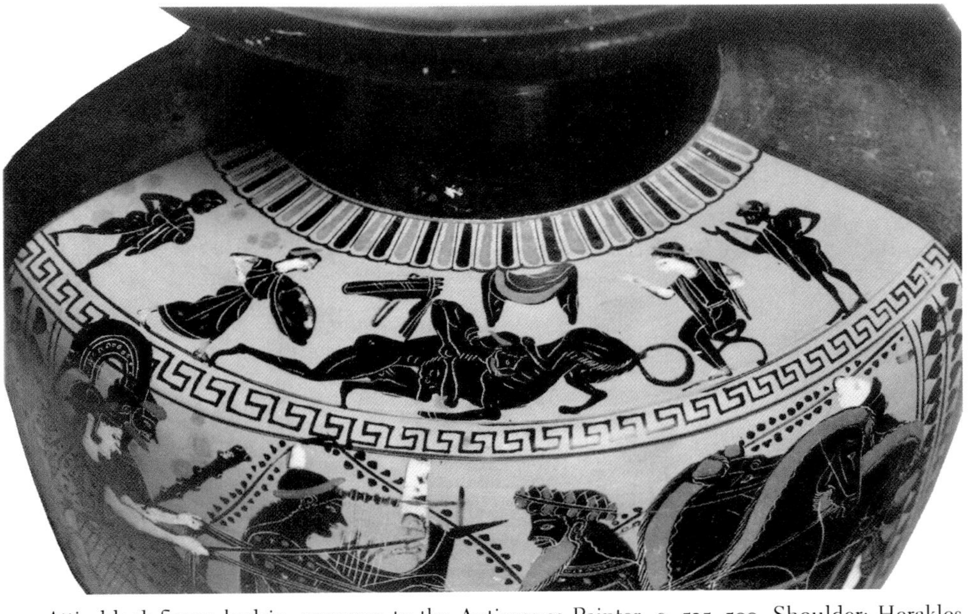

74. Attic black-figure hydria, compare to the Antimenes Painter, c. 525–500. Shoulder: Herakles and the lion. London, British Museum B319. (Photograph © Copyright The Trustees of The British Museum)

Table 47. *Women as Spectators by Mood*

Mood	Types	Number	Frequency of Total W in CVA Census (175)
Inert	W.1, W.2a	48	27.4%
Reactive	Some W.2b, all W.3, W.4, W.5, W.6	138	78.9%
Mimetic	Some W.2b	2	1.1%

a calm behavior, and that this distinguished them from both men and youths in the minds of the artist and viewer. Reactive women spectators are the overwhelming mood, appearing on approximately four out of five vases with women spectators (see table 47). This is strikingly different from the pattern for men and youths, where we found that the inert types appear on the majority of vases, 54.8 percent and 77.8 percent respectively. Conversely, the inert spectators appear on a minority of vases with women spectators, about one in four (27.7%), whereas for males the reactive types are a minority, 43.4 percent for men and 30.1 percent for youths. Thus, there is a reversal in frequency for the mood of spectators by gender, with men being primarily inert/quiet in their demeanor and women being primarily reactive. When one considers that many of the reactive types of women spectators also suggest emotional reactions of distress, agitation, panic, and lack of control, whereas many of the active types for males are mimetic in character, one can see that there is a clear stereotyping of behavior by gender taking place in the representation of spectators. This is a point to which we shall return at the end of the chapter.

6.2 THE REACTIONS OF WOMEN SPECTATORS TO SPECIFIC EVENTS

In the previous section, we examined the range of female spectator types, noting that the active and very active categories were far more prominent for women than for men and youths. The frequencies of each category and type established an overall baseline for the 175 vases in the CVA census with female spectators. In this section, we want to look at spectator reactions to individual scenes, looking for nuances in the patterns of behavior that may help us to construct a picture of archaic Athenian expectations of women's behavior and public role. We will look at the same scenes that were examined in the previous chapter (5.4), thus allowing us to compare behavior across gender. Some of the questions to be addressed include whether there are scenes in which women spectators figure more prominently, and others in which they are mostly excluded. How do their behaviors, as we have defined them by category and type, differ from those of men and youth? What do the results suggest about social attitudes toward women in archaic Athens?

In order to illuminate this issue for each of the scenes, we look at two sets of numbers. In the first case, we look at how many vases of an individual scene contain

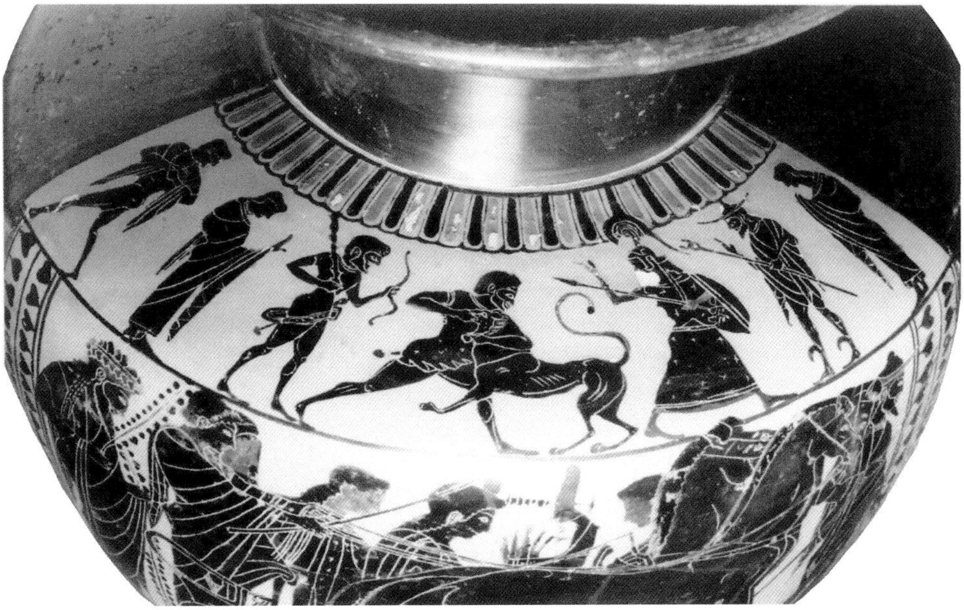

75. Attic black-figure hydria attributed to the Antimenes Painter, c. 520–510. Shoulder: Herakles and the lion. San Antonio Museum of Art, Gift of Gilbert M. Denman, Jr., 86.134.42. (Photograph, Courtesy of the San Antonio Museum of Art)

women spectators. Then, we calculate the relative frequency of these vases among all vases within the gender group. In other words, we determine the relative frequency for women spectators in, for example, scenes of Herakles and the lion by calculating the number of such vases as a percentage of all CVA census vases with women spectators (175). Doing the same as we did in the previous chapter for men and youths and comparing the figures will allow us to consider whether or not the scene has a particular significance for one gender group. As a second measure, we compare the relative frequencies for the different categories of women spectators within a specific scene to the frequencies for the entire group of CVA census vases with women spectators. Thus, we compare the relative frequencies for types and categories that we described in the previous section with the relative frequency within the group of vases with only that subject. This comparison shows whether specific types of behavior are more prevalent for a particular scene, and hence express an expectation of women's reactions to such narratives.

Herakles and the Lion

To begin as we did in the previous chapter, we will first look at scenes with Herakles wrestling the lion, such as is found on the shoulder of a hydria by the Antimenes Painter in San Antonio (figure 75; for other representations see figures 4, 37, 74).[48] Athena is readily recognized by her armor and spear, raising her right arm toward Herakles; Iolaos is identified by the club on his shoulder. Behind Iolaos is a woman

Table 48. *Gender Distribution on Vases with Scenes of Herakles and the Lion*

Gender Category	# Vases with Gender	# of all CVA Census Vases with Gender	% of all CVA Census Vases with Gender (c2/c3)	% of Vases with Subject (c2/75)	Comparison % of CVA Census Vases w/Gender (from table 8)
W.	36	175	20.6	48.0	23.6
M.	20	223	9.0	26.7	30.1
Y.	51	527	9.7	68.0	71.0

who raises up her back, left arm with fingers extended and thumb and palm pointed outward, an example of spectator type W.3e. On the far right of the panel is another female spectator, whose hand, wrapped within her mantle, is drawn up toward her face, a variation on type W.3c. When female figures are found in these scenes, it is not unknown to label them as Athena, or Nemea if a second female is present, even if there is no distinguishable attribute. On this vase, it is unambiguous that Athena is present, and even if one of the other women were Nemea, there is still another female spectator, demonstrating that pure female, as well as male spectators, were a feature of scenes with Herakles and the lion.

Women spectators are found on 36 vases with Herakles and the lion in the CVA census. Therefore, of the 175 vases with women spectators, Herakles and the lion account for 20.6 percent of the total (see table 48). In comparison, adult male spectators in scenes of Herakles and the lion are found on 9 percent of the total vases with men and youthful spectators on 9.7 percent of the vases with youths. From these figures, we can see that the story is of roughly equal importance for men and youths as spectators, but that the relative frequency of women spectators on these vases is double, indicating that it is a more important narrative for female than for male spectators. From another angle, we note that of all the vases with Herakles and the lion (75), 48 percent have women spectators, whereas 26.7 percent have men and 68 percent have youths. The frequencies for men and youths are nearly those for both groups in the CVA census, affirming that this scene is part of the standard repertoire for men and youths. However, the relative frequency for women is double that for the entire CVA census (23.6 percent), again suggesting that this scene was particularly significant for the woman spectator.

In looking at specific categories and types of women spectators for Herakles and the lion, we find that the relative frequency of category W.1 and W.2 spectators is slightly lower than that for all CVA census vases with women spectators (see table 49). The appearance of spear-bearing types of spectators would fit with the common appearance of Athena at these scenes, as we see in figure 75, and confirms the earlier suggestion that the category may be derived from images of the goddess rather than from common social behavior. The relative frequency of category W.3 is almost the same as for the entire group of vases. However, one particular type, W.3b, with the arm raised 45°, is found on eight vases, almost one-fourth of the Herakles/lion scenes and double the

Table 49. *Distribution of Spectator Categories on Vases with Herakles and the Lion*

Type	# of Vases	% of Vases with Subject (c2/36)	Comparison % of Category for all CVA Census Vases w/Women Spectators
W.1	5	13.9	21.1
W.2	3	8.3	9.7
W.3	16	44.4	42.9
W.4	11	30.6	40.6
W.6	3	8.3	3.4

type's frequency in the CVA census; the most common type in this category, W.3d, is found only half as frequently on Herakles vases. Looking at category W.4, we find a lower relative frequency (30.6 percent) than in the CVA census, and a preference for the more restrained type, W.4g.[49] One final type, W.6b, the seated spectator, is found on three vases, 8.3 percent of the group, more than double the frequency of the CVA group. Indeed, the seated women spectators in these scenes account for half of all seated women spectators.

In summary, we can note that women spectators are a particularly important feature of scenes with Herakles and the lion. Further, the proportion of scenes with active/reactive spectators is slightly lower than for the CVA census, and those that fall into this category can be said to be among the more restrained types. Most of the reactive spectators (16 of 28) use only one arm for gesturing, exhibiting a greater degree of control in their reaction. This proportion is different from the CVA census generally, where roughly three out of five reactive spectators use two hands. For men and youths as spectators to Herakles and lion, we noted in the previous chapter that active types had a higher relative frequency in this scene compared with the CVA census, particularly among the mimetic types of spectators for youths and the leader type for men (see chapter 5.4). Herakles is less a model for emulation for women in terms of their action, but their behavior does show a higher degree of restraint as they watch the prototypical hero dealing with a scourge.

Herakles and Nessos

Less common than Herakles and the lion, scenes of Herakles and Nessos (see figures 56 and 67) are found on 35 vases, 14 of which have women spectators (see table 50). This number represents a relative frequency of 8 percent of all vases with women spectators, equivalent to that for men (8.1 percent), and double that for youths (4.0 percent). This suggests that the scene is of greater importance for both women and adult men than for youths, as would be in keeping with its theme of the abduction of a wife and the threat to the *oikos*. Looking at the distribution of spectators within the subject group, we see that women are found on 40 percent of Nessos vases, much

Table 50. *Gender Distribution on Vases with Scenes of Herakles and Nessos*

Gender Category	# Vases with Gender	# of all CVA Census Vases with Gender	% of all CVA Census Vases with Gender (c2/c3)	% of all Vases with Subject (c2/35)	Comparison % of CVA Census Vases w/ Gender (from table 8)
W.	14	175	8.0	40.0	23.6
M.	18	223	8.1	51.4	30.1
Y.	21	527	4.0	60.0	71.0

higher than the frequency of 23.6 percent for the entire CVA census. Men also appear in higher numbers, whereas youths are less frequent, again showing that the narrative has a particular resonance for women and adult males. Most of the vases with women spectators also include Deianeira in the narrative nucleus, and perhaps we should consider her importance in the story as the abducted wife as being the reason for this scene's prominence for women spectators. This element would make her a potential model for the woman spectator, just as Herakles offered a model for the adult male spectator in the picture.

Deianeira's response usually consists of turning back toward Herakles and reaching both arms straight out from the shoulder toward her husband. She models, then, a very active type of behavior that is similar to spectator type W.4f. Curiously, none of the women spectators mimic her gesture and the pattern of responses for this scene follows broadly that for the entire CVA group. For example, category W.1 is found on 21.4 percent of the vases in this group, almost exactly the same frequency as in the CVA group (see table 51). The relative frequencies for categories W.2, W.4, and W.6 are slightly lower than for the CVA group, whereas that of W.3 is higher. Looking at individual types, the number of women using two-handed gestures is about equal to those using one-handed gestures.[50] Overall in the CVA census, the number of vases with two-handed spectators outnumbers those with one-handed figures by more than five to three (see table 45), so the near equivalence of the two groups on Nessos vases actually represents a more controlled response than is found generally.

Although one might expect that the role of Deianeira in the narrative would heighten a sense of identification between spectator and victim, and elicit a similarly

Table 51. *Distribution of Spectator Categories on Vases with Herakles and Nessos*

Type	# of Vases	% of Vases with Subject (c2/14)	Comparison % of Category for all Vases w/ Women Spectators
W.1	3	21.4	21.1
W.2	1	7.1	9.7
W.3	7	50.0	42.9
W.4	5	35.7	40.6
W.6	0	0	3.4

Table 52. *Gender Distribution on Vases with Scenes of Warriors Fighting*

Gender Category	# Vases with Gender	# of all CVA Vases with Gender	% of all CVA Census Vases with Gender (c2/c3)	% of all Vases with Subject (c2/168)	Comparison % of CVA Census Vases w/Gender (from table 8)
W.	70	175	40.0	41.7	23.6
M.	35	223	15.7	20.8	30.1
Y.	98	527	18.6	58.3	71.0

active response in a female viewer, we find that women spectators exhibit more control than the victim, and a level of control similar to those with scenes of Herakles and the lion. It would seem that Herakles elicits a more controlled response from women spectators than is typical. Although women spectators do not emulate the actions of heroes, the prototypical hero might be said to inspire a calmer response, one that is significantly more restrained than that of Deianeira. The responses of women spectators might be said to fall more into the pattern of acclamation, acknowledging the worthiness of the heroic model in a manner like the chorus of Alkman recognizing the excellence of its leaders and its mythic exemplars (see chapter 4.3).

Warriors Fighting

As we have already seen in this chapter, the theme of warriors fighting is very common for vases on which we find women spectators (see figures 65–66 and 69–73). Frequently, they appear without any male spectators, and in this configuration, the structure of the composition recalls the scenes of heroes fighting with their mothers intervening behind, particularly the theme of Achilles and Memnon (see figure 6). In most of these scenes, however, there is no way to identify the warriors or the spectators, and we have to conclude that the female figures are removed from the place of the combat. Unlike goddesses who can see what is happening to their sons, these spectators react to an event that is removed from their view, although its impact is no less given that in most cases one of the warriors will not return home, impacting the situation of the woman. Given the reality of death on the battlefield for a contemporary viewer of the vase, the theme epitomizes the risks inherent to the household and its women from war.

The importance of this theme for women spectators is reflected in the numbers. Of the 175 vases that have women spectators, 70 have the theme of warriors fighting, a frequency of 40 percent for the group (see table 52). By comparison, the frequency of such scenes on vases with men and youths is less than half. This is further reflected in the warrior vases as a group. Of the 168 vases with warriors fighting, 41.7 percent have women, 20.8 percent have men, and 58.3 percent have youths as spectators. Although there are more vases with youths than women, the proportion of youths is less than

Table 53. *Distribution of Spectator Categories on Vases with Warriors Fighting*

Type	# of Vases	% of Vases with Subject (c2/70)	Comparison % of Category for all Vases w/ Women Spectators
W.1	8	11.4	21.1
W.2	6	8.6	9.7
W.3	37	52.9	42.9
W.4	34	48.6	40.6
W.6	0	0	3.4

the average of 71 percent for that group, whereas that for women is almost double their CVA census frequency of 23.6 percent. These numbers suggest that the theme of warriors fighting rivals Herakles and the lion in terms of its significance for women spectators.

Looking at the types of women spectators watching warriors, we find that category W.1 is found on about one-tenth of vases, about half the frequency for the CVA census as a whole (see table 53). The frequency of spear-bearing types is close to that for the CVA census, but the frequencies for both active (W.3) and very active (W.4) spectators are notably higher. Spectators from category W.3 occur on more than half of all vases with women spectators, and very active spectators on nearly half. One can conclude from this that women spectators are far more active than usual in these scenes. Further, more than two-thirds of these reactive spectators use two hands in their response, again an increase over the pattern found in the CVA census (see table 45). In particular, types W.3d, W.3f, W.3g, and W.4f occur at significantly higher frequencies than in the CVA census as a whole.[51] Of the most extreme gestures with both arms extended, such as types W.4c, W.4d, and W.4e, almost half of all examples are found on vases with warriors fighting.

As we saw in the previous chapter, the frequency of inert, nonreactive male spectators in scenes of warriors fighting is higher than it is generally in the CVA census; there is a corresponding decrease in the reactive types of spectators (see chapter 5.4). For women spectators, the opposite trend occurs; there is a higher frequency of reactive types and a lower frequency of inert types. What is striking, then, about the warriors fighting theme is not only that it is proportionally more important for women spectators, but that the responses of women spectators are much more reactive. Thus, in the face of a life-and-death battle, one might say that the stereotypical conception of archaic Athenian artists and viewers is that women will react more demonstrably and with some degree of distress or panic, whereas men will face the scene with reserve and detachment or, if they react, that it will be in a mimetic, warrior-like fashion.

Of all of the scenes with spectators, that of warriors fighting represents the one theme that has the greatest, potentially negative, impact as an action on the spectator and on the viewer of the vase. The loss that the death of a husband or son represents to a wife or mother respectively is significant, and would certainly justify the strength of a woman's response to a combat scene in which the warrior before her might well be facing death. However, for male spectators and viewers, the death of the warrior also represents a significant loss of a father or perhaps a brother or son, which jeopardizes the smooth transition of property in the household and inheritance. Youths, however, are clearly expected to react with control and detachment, whereas women are expected to react with strong emotion and grief. This contrast between the behavior of male and female corresponds to the patterns of mourning in ancient Greece, and to the concern that behavior at such events represented a potential threat to the city. As N. Loraux has succinctly summarized:[52]

> According to Plutarch, Solon wanted to check women's disorderliness and license. He thus prohibited them from lacerating their skin (by which mourning women attempted to reproduce on their own cut-up bodies the injury done by death to the corpse), from using *thrênoi* in verse, and from lamenting any other dead.

Grief and its attendant public behavior were regarded as threatening the order of the city, so that women's participation was generally limited to the prothesis inside the house and to laments at the tomb, but only by members of the deceased's family. That such displays were both gender-specific and a threat to the city can be seen in the office of the *gunaikonómos*, who is charged in Solon's law with punishing those who transgressed the statutes. What is of particular interest in Plutarch's description of the duties of the *gunaikonómos* is that he is charged not just with regulating the behavior of women, but also of men in public, especially those who "indulge in unmanly and effeminate extravagances of sorrow when they mourn."[53] Mourning is feminine, and for a man to indulge in grief is unmanly and a danger to the social order.

More than in the scenes with Herakles, women spectators to fighting warriors can be seen as epitomizing the extreme stereotypes of women as emotional, uncontrolled, and a potential threat to the civic order. That youths react with control and calmness in the face of an action that threatens their well-being too, demonstrates the gendered patterns of behavior that were expected of men and women in archaic Athens. As Loraux aptly puts it:[54]

> What is true of mourning is true of women, and it is only natural that Plato, in book 3 of the *Republic*, defining the ban on mímesis (thus on theater, and especially on tragedy), specifies that guardians are prohibited from imitating women, "being men"; and we find surrender to grief and lamentation among the feminine forms of behavior that are not to be imitated.

The patterns of behavior found among women and youthful spectators to scenes of warriors fighting are only a visualization of these stereotyped social patterns, but one

Table 54. *Gender Distribution on Vases with Scenes of Amazon Combats*

Gender Category	# Vases with Gender	% of Vases with Subject (c2/49)	Comparison % of CVA Census Vases w/Gender (from table 8)
W.	9	18.4	23.6
M.	10	20.4	30.1
Y.	40	81.6	71.0

that establishes a quickly recognized dichotomy between the gendered expectations of men and women in archaic Athens.

Amazons

Another combat scene with women spectators is that between Greek men and Amazons.[55] Compositionally, these follow the same basic formula as warriors fighting, as we can see looking back at figures 15 and 60. The reactions of women in these scenes, however, form a sharp contrast to their reactions in scenes of warriors fighting. This can be seen by analyzing the supplemental database of 49 vases for Amazon combats used in chapter 5.4. Of these, nine vases have women spectators, or 18.4 percent of the total. This makes their frequency comparable but slightly lower than the general CVA census frequency, but almost equal to men (see table 54).[56]

Of the nine vases with women spectators, five show the *anakalypsis*-type, W.1a, (W.1a, see figures 15 and 60, table 55). In addition, one vase has a quietly standing, spear-bearing woman (W.2a), so that inert spectators are found on two-thirds of the vases with Amazons, a total that is more than double the frequency of 27.4 percent for the CVA census generally (see table 11 in chapter 2), and triple that for scenes with warriors fighting. Active types of spectators, W.3, are found on four vases, two of which include type W.1a in the same picture. Three of the four vases that have active spectators are of type W.3c, a single-handed gesture that could be linked to acclaim for the hero fighting the Amazon. Although the number of vases with active spectators is near the frequency for the entire CVA census, there is a proportionally higher number of the more composed, single-handed types than two-handed types, a reversal of the

Table 55. *Distribution of Spectator Categories on Vases with Amazon Combats*

Type	# of Vases	% of Vases with Subject (c2/9)	Comparison % of Category for all Vases w/Women Spectators
W.1	5	55.6	21.1
W.2	1	11.1	9.7
W.3	4	44.4	42.9
W.4	2	22.2	40.6
W.6	0	0	3.4

pattern in the warriors fighting vases discussed previously. For the very active spectator types (W.4) there are only two vases, 22.2 percent of the total compared to 40.6 percent within the CVA census generally. One of these vases also includes a less reactive type of category W.3, so that a total of five vases show either W.3 or W.4 spectators, compared with six vases showing W.1 or W.2.

In a striking departure from the pattern of the warriors fighting vases, women spectators to Amazon combats can be characterized as composed in their demeanor, with more vases showing inert than reactive spectators. Women spectators in these scenes could be said to conform more closely with a civic ideal for women as represented by the *anakalypsis*-type (W.1a) than with any of the other themes we have examined. We might consider whether it is the quality of the Amazon narrative itself that elicits this response among painters for using the women spectators as an antithesis to the behavior of the female warrior. When showing Amazons fighting, painters have Athenian women acknowledge the heroic struggle against them and signal their own acceptance of their role within the city by alluding to the *anakalypsis* gesture of the wedding. Whereas Amazons reject living in a city and the social conventions of urban life, women spectators acclaim their role within the city and behave with a calm that is the opposite of the Amazon's action. The women spectators are not "man-hating," but submit to men in their actions. In this role, they reflect a change in attitudes toward the Amazon that Hardwick and Blok have detected in the epithets used for Amazons. Whereas Homer applied the term *antianerai* to Amazons, "a match for men," later writers such as Aeschylus emphasized their femininity and their hostility to men with epithets such as *stuganoor*, or "man-hating."[57] By acting with reserve and deliberation, the women spectators become the antithesis of the Amazon, standing by their men rather than against them and serving as a sign of social and civic order rather than its opposite.

It is curious that it is only in the presence of the ultimate womanly wildness of the Amazon that the woman spectator behaves in a manner similar to that of youths and men for the same scene: calm, detached, resolute in her demeanor. That the spear-bearing male and the mantle-pulling female are equivalent civic ideals is brought home by their dominance as spectator types to Amazon combats, as can be seen in figure 60, but it also points out the disparity between the civic position of men and women within the city. Whereas men, or youths as they mature, can assume a civic identity that guards the city against aggression, women defend the polis by their submission to men and being the antithesis of the Amazon. Given that their reactions are decidedly against the trend for women spectators, however, only emphasizes the dangers that men saw in women's stereotyped, reactive nature, which, in excess, could be as dangerous to the social harmony as the Amazon. Although women spectators rise above their preconceived nature in response to Amazons, the anomaly only confirms the dominant ideology's view of women's nature compared with men. Whether women in archaic Athens saw things in this light is another question, but the imagery of Amazons and spectators is set up to provide a model for such beliefs.

Table 56. *Gender Distribution on Vases with Scenes of Riders*

Gender Category	# Vases with Gender	# of all CVA Census Vases with Gender	% of all CVA Census Vases with Gender (c2/c3)	% of all Vases with Subject (c2/76)	Comparison % of CVA Census Vases w/ Gender (from table 8)
W.	6	175	3.4	7.9	23.6
M.	24	223	10.8	31.6	30.1
Y.	62	527	11.8	81.6	71.0

Other Scenes

Whereas women spectators are prominently featured in scenes of Herakles and the lion and warriors fighting and are common in the other mythological themes that we examined, they are notably absent from a range of scenes that we saw were important for men or youths. For example, of the 14 vases with a sphinx as the nucleus discussed in the previous chapter, none shows a woman spectator. Similarly, there is no woman spectator among the 18 vases with the Nike-type figure.

Among spectators to athletic scenes, there is no example of a woman spectator on the 32 vases with wrestlers or boxers. There is only one vase out of a total of 59 with a runner that has a woman spectator, an *anakalypsis*-type (W.1a).[58] Because foot races would take place in a more open setting because of the distance involved, it is certainly more possible that a woman might observe part of a race, but the inference is that women were not common or prominent as spectators at athletic competitions. Athletic figures were objects of intense scrutiny and admiration, evoking erotic emotions in the observer, as we saw in chapter 3, but with only one example of a woman spectator it would appear that the performances of the athletes were, above all, of interest to men and to youths, either to admire or to emulate, or both.[59]

Women spectators do show up a little more frequently in display or parade scenes such as those with a rider. Six of the 76 vases with riders have women spectators, including an amphora in the Getty Museum showing two nude riders and a walking youth, all holding spears, arriving before three spectators, a man in a mantle and two *anakalypsis*-type women (figure 76).[60] These vases account for 3.4 percent of all vases with women spectators, less than one-third the frequency for men and youths, showing the relative insignificance of this scene for women (see table 56). This is a type of scene that is apparently less appropriate for a woman spectator and suggests the limited role that women might have had in observing public ceremonies and processions in archaic Athens.

The highly ceremonial nature of the rider scene, with or without a procession, and the decorum expected of its witnesses can be seen in the distribution of spectator types (see table 57). Four belong to the type W.1a, with single examples of W.2a, W.3c, and W.4w. Both of the W.3 and W.4 spectators, although reactive, fall into the restrained,

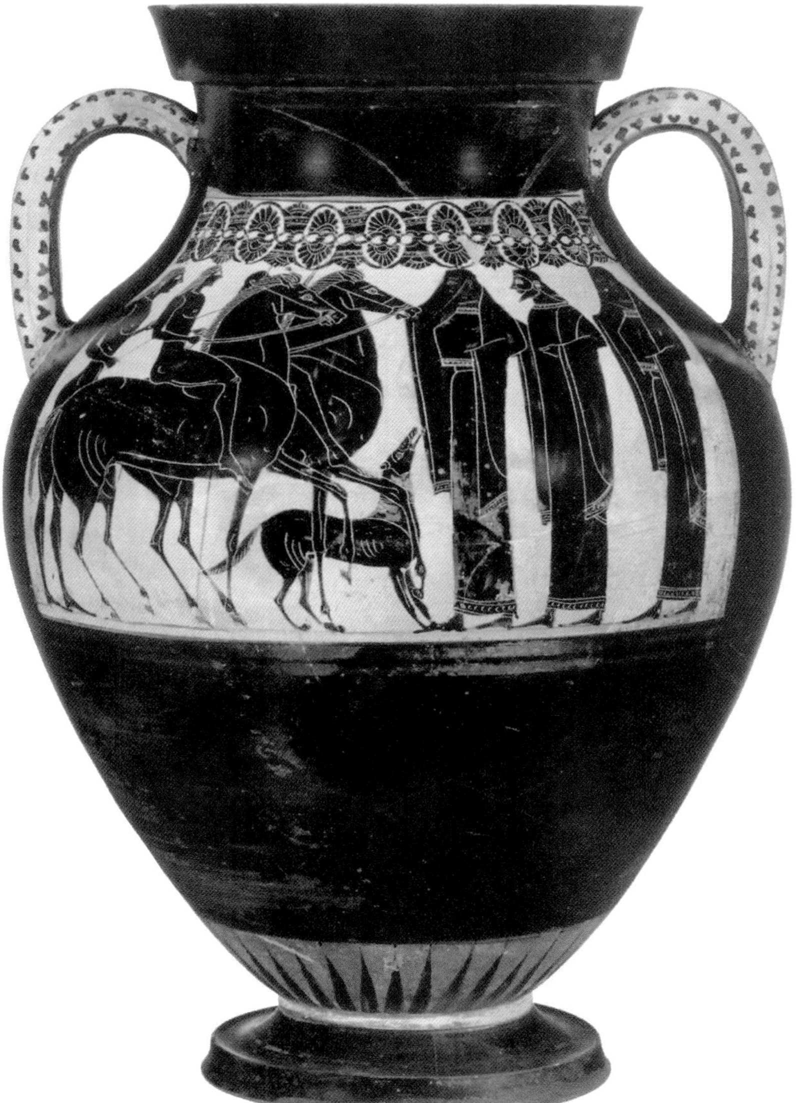

76. Attic black-figure amphora attributed to Lydos or a painter close to Lydos, c. 550–540. Side B: Rider. Malibu, California, The J. Paul Getty Museum, 86.AE.60. (Photograph, © The J. Paul Getty Museum)

one-handed types and exhibit movement that would be appropriate for a choral or other group acknowledgment of the figures being honored. The predominance of the "*anakalypsis*-type" does match the idea of the victorious athlete being the object of admiration for both men and women, as D. T. Steiner has discussed.[61]

Turning to erotic scenes, there is only one scene among the 12 examples included in the CVA census that includes a woman spectator.[62] This is on a truly unusual lekythos

Table 57. *Distribution of Spectator Categories on Vases with Riders*

Type	# of Vases	% of Vases with Subject (c2/6)	Comparison % of Category for all Vases w/Women Spectators
W.1	4	66.7	21.1
W.2	1	16.7	9.7
W.3	1	16.7	42.9
W.4	1	16.7	40.6
W.6	0	0	3.4

showing boars copulating, with a man and woman observing to either side. Even in heterosexual scenes of lovemaking, women are participants or objects of attention and not detached observers, and this would suggest that the representation of such scenes was meant for a male viewer.

Finally, women are also less frequent as spectators in scenes featuring music. There are 36 vases featuring scenes with music, including musicians performing at a symposion, or musicians performing in public on a podium, perhaps as part of a competition (see chapter 5.4). Even with this wide range of subjects, only two vases have women spectators: one shows a woman seated on a rock while listening to a satyr play the aulos, and another, a woman reclining on a symposion couch listening to an aulos player.[63]

From this examination of athletic competitions, parades, music scenes, and erotic themes, one can conclude that women spectators generally played a less significant or nonexistent role, unlike their male counterparts. Most of these scenes fall into the broad category of contemporary civic activities, rather than actions from a remote, heroic past or location, making the spectators "detached" in their structural role within the picture, present at the scene but separated from it individually as well as conceptually. These, then, are the scenes of the polis and representative of its culture and excellence, scenes in which women are notably marginalized as spectators.

6.3 DISCUSSION

Democratic Athens was a men's club, as P. Vidal-Naquet phrased it, and it is an arrangement that extends back into the archaic polis as well.[64] Gender distinction as a moralizing dichotomy clearly exist in the misogynistic views of Hesiod, who sees the value of a woman only in producing an heir, because otherwise she only consumes the productivity of her husband; and of Semonides, who likens different kinds of women to various animals selected for their vices rather than their virtues as exemplars.[65] Gender not only defines women as different from men, but also lowers them in the social hierarchy. Citizens – that is, adult Athenian men – occupy the highest position in the polis, with all others below them. Children, youths, women, slaves, and foreigners all occupy subservient positions in the hierarchy, but with some differences. Boys can become men, changing their position in the hierarchy, and it is possible for adult men to lose their status, particularly if they offend the sexual morality of the city.[66] Women are perhaps slightly higher than slaves, at least in the case of women who belong to citizen men as wives, mothers, and daughters, but it is possible for women to become slaves and then doubly lower on the scale.

The precise position of women in archaic Athens is not well documented and we should be wary of drawing a too black-and-white picture. However, during this period, there does appear to have been a shift from bride price to dowry in connection with marriage. The dowry helped the bride's family to maintain protection for her, but this conversely points out that the bride was likely in a weaker position than she had experienced earlier.[67] We can see some more specific examples of changes in laws that restricted the actions and status of women in the sixth century by looking at later testimony about Solon.[68] According to Plutarch, Solon permitted men greater latitude in naming beneficiaries in their wills, as long as wills or gifts "were not made under the influence of sickness, or drugs, or imprisonment, or when a man was the victim of compulsion or yielded to the persuasions of his wife."[69] Both compulsion and wifely persuasion are counter to reason and tantamount to deceit. Selling children into slavery in order to meet debts had been a social problem prior to Solon's reforms, and his laws did forbid the practice, but with a loophole: "no man is allowed to sell a daughter or a sister, unless he finds that she is no longer a virgin."[70] Plutarch also tells us that Solon was very explicit in his regulation of women's public behavior:[71]

> He also subjected the public appearances of the women, their mourning and their festivals, to a law that did away with disorder and license. When they went out, they were not to wear more than three garments, they were not to carry more than an obol's worth of food or drink, nor a pannier more than a cubit high, and they were not to travel about by night unless they rode in a wagon with a lamp to light their way. Laceration of the flesh by mourners, and the use of set lamentations, and the bewailing of any one at the funeral ceremonies of another, he forbade.

As Pomeroy and others have pointed out, the Solonian laws do not seem to have been directed against women *per se*, but were "aimed at eliminating strife among men . . . Women are a perennial source of friction among men. Solon's solution to this problem was to keep them out of sight and to limit their influence."[72] The laws had the effect of being primarily anti-sumptuary, and limited not only women's behavior but also the amount of grave goods and markers. However, the legislation equates sumptuous displays and women's unregulated behavior as disruptive to the social order. The testimony reveals that although women may have had necessary functions in public, especially for religion and funerals, their appearance must be strictly controlled.

Women were not, however, completely without virtue according to literary sources, but even here their difference from men, even for the same virtue, is apparent. Aristotle, for example, compares the importance of excellent young men and women for the state:[73]

> The blessing of good children and numerous children needs little explanation. For the commonwealth it consists in a large number of good young men, good in bodily excellences, such as stature, beauty, strength, fitness for athletic contests; the moral excellences of a young man are self-control and courage. For the individual it consists in a number of good children of his own, both male and female, and such as we have described. Female bodily excellences are beauty and stature, their moral excellences self-control and industrious habits, free from servility. The object of both the individual and of the community should be to secure the existence of each of these qualities in both men and women."

Thus women can possess self-control (*sophrosyne*) and be productive, in contrast to the picture painted of them by Hesiod and Semonides. However, as G. Ferrari points out, women's productivity (*philergia*) is set in apposition to courage (*andreia*) in young men.[74] This implies that men are to maintain their self-control when confronted with a dangerous or challenging situation, a degree of resolve that apparently does not belong to the *sophrosyne* of women, who can only demonstrate their virtue within the confines of the house or city. Indeed, the addition of "free from servility" (*aneu aneleutherias*) to the moral virtues of women implies that slavish or mean-spirited behavior occur easily for women in Aristotle's mind and are a part of their nature, but not men's.

What, then, do women spectators add to this picture? The *anakalypsis*-type (W.1a) presents a picture of women in public that epitomizes the ideal. She has self-control, and the allusion to bridal ritual also signifies the ideal of the harmonious and productive household. The full mantle completely envelopes her body and serves as a shield to protect her from the public gaze, serving to demonstrate her modesty and chastity.[75] This type, and the other types of inert women spectators (W.1b, W.2a) show women in a decorous light and one that does not disturb the harmony of the city. Some of the active women spectators could also be equated with their appearance in civic and religious ritual, dancing and singing as members of a chorus. These types of spectators (W.3a-c) all show control by using only one arm in their gestures, but they are found on fewer than half the vases within category W.3. In contrast to these images of self-control, we find others that are histrionic in their behavior, using both arms in gestures that could be said to represent a range of moods ranging from excitement to panic. Most of category W.4 falls into this group, as do a large number of types in W.3.

Which group represents the dominant social view of women in archaic Athens? As we have seen, the *anakalypsis*-type is found on just 17 percent of vases with women spectators, and inert women spectators overall on only 27 percent. This relative frequency is far less than that for the inert spear-bearing youth or man on his own, and far, far less than the inert spectator for both men and youths (see table 11 in chapter 2).

Rather than restrained, the image of women is one of active response to a scene, from acute distress in many of the women witnessing warriors fighting, to a more controlled but still reactive response in scenes with Herakles.

The spectators do not document actual behavior by any of the gender groups in archaic Athens, but they do represent the social expectations of their behavior. Like the laws of Solon, there is a presumption that extreme behavior is waiting to manifest itself in women, behavior that has the potential to disrupt the social order. That the examples of histrionic behavior are found on more than half the vases with women spectators (table 45 earlier) reveals the underlying male attitude about women's nature and role within the city. I would suggest that this split represents an underlying belief, at least of the citizen men of Athens, that women do not have courage and control by their nature, and that the virtuous behavior that women can and do display in public is only too easily undermined in response to the actions they witness.

Because the pots are painted by men, we have to assume that they represent the outlook of the painter and the male agenda more broadly.[76] There is a decided preference for strong emotional responses by women spectators to warriors fighting, which only demonstrates their lack of self-control and courage and their general helplessness, virtues that youths learn and men possess.[77] Yet we have seen that other motives can alter this presentation of women. Amazons may possess courage in battle, but they represent a more fundamental challenge to the civic order. In such cases, the frequency of the *anakalypsis*-type rises dramatically whereas the examples of histrionic behavior decline. Yet here it must be noted that the *anakalypsis*-type, although representing the ideal woman described by Aristotle, is still one that functions differently from its male counterpart, the mantled youth and man. The *anakalypsis*-type, with its pulling forward of the mantle, signifies the acquiescence of the woman to her marriage, and to the bridegroom's address to her as he takes control from her father.[78] The mantled youth does not imply this sense of submission and, indeed, his garment serves as a shield for the figure, protecting the youth's modesty but also symbolically a weapon to bolster his courage. In the Amazon pictures, we can see that the social order finds expression through women's self-control within her subordination to male control of the *oikos* and polis.

If we look at the deployment of the three main spectator categories for women over time, we can also see that there is a shift in attitude about women's behavior from the second quarter of the sixth century to the beginning of the fifth. Comparing the utilization of each spectator category as a percentage of vases with women spectators from that period, we see the relative frequencies shown in table 58.

The shift in relative popularity from inert to active types can be seen more clearly in a chart from the data (chart 4). As is seen in the chart, category W.1, primarily the *anakalypsis*-type, is on the majority of vases with women spectators during the second quarter of the sixth century. Their popularity, however, declined steadily in the following periods, while the relative frequency for active and very active women spectators rose sharply and dominated. Toward the end of the century, very active women

Table 58. *Distribution of Women Spectators by Category as Percentage of Vases with Women Spectators during Period*

Type	575–550	560–540	550–525	535–515	525–500	510–490	500–475
W.1	60.0%	33.3%	19.4%	0.0%	6.7%	10.0%	12.5%
W.3	25.0%	54.5%	44.4%	66.7%	48.9%	20.0%	12.5%
W.4	25.0%	27.3%	33.3%	46.7%	44.4%	70.0%	75.0%

spectators become the dominant type, although this is the period when spectators generally declined rapidly in the frequency of their appearance.

I can only offer speculation regarding this pattern, but it does match the trend that many scholars have found toward a curtailing of women's status as the rights of men increased under the democratic reforms beginning in the late sixth century. I would suggest that if we consider that spectators in archaic Attic vase-painting are a phenomenon that is, at least in part, stimulated by the expansion of ritual and sanctuaries in the first half of the sixth century, then the predominance of the *anakalypsis*-type in the earliest phases of spectators would be a reflection of this development of new and expanded rituals. Ritual performance emphasizes discipline and harmony as individuals perform in a group, and the expression of self-control found in the *anakalypsis*-type signifies the participation of women in rituals like the Panathenaia. However, I would also suggest that as spectators mature as a pictorial construct to reflect a broader

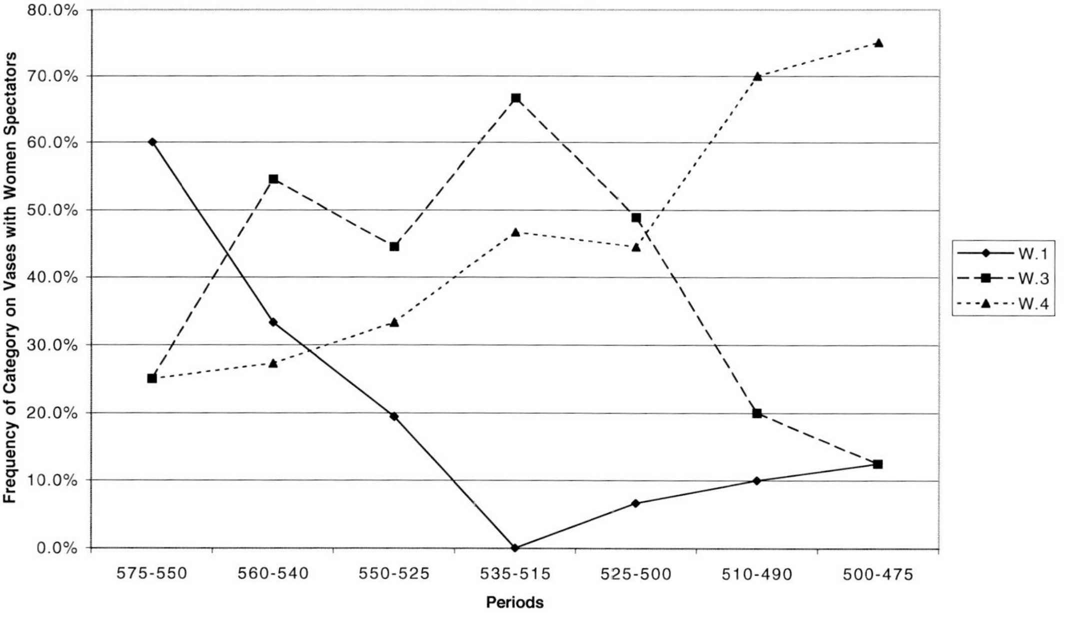

Chart 4. Frequency of Women Spectator Categories by Period

picture of social identity, the representation of women spectators begins to reflect the social/male view of their nature as different from men, as susceptible to emotions and extreme forms of behavior that were antithetical to the values and virtues of men as citizens and rulers of the polis. If we consider that archaic art holds up models of behavior and praises or blames individuals based on how well they match those models, then we can see that women move from praise to blame as the century progresses, a harbinger of things to come in the classical period.[79]

CONCLUSION

I hesitate to offer a "conclusion" because much of this study was based on descriptive statistics, and not a true random sample or a complete census. Still, the quantity of vases with spectators offers sufficient material to at least propose some thoughts about their development and significance. Above all, the data show that we must think about spectators in the context of archaic, and primarily pre-democratic, Athens, but we can use the phenomenon to consider in general terms the experience of the viewer.

The spectators on vases demonstrate that what we see, what the original viewers saw, matters. This is not to say that Athenians stood or sat around and discussed these images in detail as if they were a revealed truth that required their closest attention. Rather, the importance of viewing was twofold. First, like Plato's young man who is unaware of why his feelings are being stirred (chapter 3.2), what one sees affects one subconsciously. Second, because what one sees enters into the soul, it has the potential to affect what we are and how we act. The images that surround one establish a tone, even if they are in the background, and serve as signs for how one sees oneself, and how one would like to be seen by others.

The predominance of inert spectators overall suggests that calm reflection is the basic mode for contemplating narrative images, at least those of a serious nature (excepting comedy, parody, etc.). Acclaim is also important, and would have been common as part of choral performances on the same types of themes. Images may prompt one to act, as mimetic spectators suggest, but the frequency of these types indicates that the connection between image and act is indirect. Narrative images encode values and ideas, not plans for action.

The appearance of spectators in pictures indicates that observation and public behavior were important, but it is still a strange pictorial construct within ancient art, having people see things that are not really before them. We cannot know exactly how or why they begin to appear in large numbers in the second quarter of sixth-century Athens, but I would like to offer some speculation. Among the earliest work with spectators, as Carpenter and Brijder noted, are Siana cups by the C Painter, who, according to Brijder, was active between 575 and 555.[1] The earliest works with spectators, like the cup at Washington University (see figure 4.3), belong to the middle phase of the C Painter's work, which Brijder places in the 560s. The spectators are identical to the stock figures that the painter had used in earlier gatherings of men, youth, and women without a narrative nucleus. By redeploying them at the margins of narrative subjects like warriors fighting, the painter creates a different kind of pictorial construct than either of the earlier types of scenes from which they are drawn. The new formula was adopted and expanded by other painters of Siana cups, such as the Taras Painter and particularly the Heidelberg Painter, who was active about 10 years later than the C Painter.

Whether or not the C Painter "invented" the pictorial construct with spectators, two factors about the appearance of spectators on the cups are important. First, the construct was not a radical innovation, but resulted from a realignment of existing pictorial elements. This suggests that there was not a single "cause," such as an individual patron or commission that led to the development of spectators, but that there was a broader contextual change that prompted it. The coincidence of the appearance of spectators with the reorganization of the Panathenaic festival is certainly suggestive, but the connection must be more general than specific, particularly because many of the works by the C Painter were exported. Nevertheless, I would suggest that the reorganization of a major civic festival, with its impact on ritual performance and display, provided a heightened civic awareness in Athens, one that might be said to prompt a new conception of the spectator as signifying this enhanced image of Athenians. The second factor is that nearly two-thirds of known findspots for the work of the C Painter are sanctuaries.[2] For the Heidelberg Painter, the association of the cups with sanctuaries is even stronger, with almost three-quarters coming from such contexts. The link with sanctuaries, whether or not they are in Athens, is striking, and strengthens the notion that we should consider spectators within a ritualistic context.

The effect of including spectators in a picture with a narrative nucleus is to transform the image into a model of choral and civic ritual performance, and thereby into a model of social values and behavior. Although subjects such as heroic duels might be seen as aristocratic, the addition of spectators to the scene makes the subject more public, and can, perhaps, be seen as expressing the development of the "middling" culture in Athens.[3] By a series of transpositions, we can see the spectators on the vase as a chorus, with the narrative as the subject of their song. Shifting the point of view, we can then see the narrative nucleus as a sign for the chorus, who, by singing about the ideal, become identified with it; the spectators then become the audience that witnesses the choral performance. In one final shift, the spectator also becomes a sign for the viewer and user of the vase, representing his or her public image as a member of the polis.

The fact that most of the vases with spectators for which we have findspots are outside of Athens suggests that this image of its citizens as pious, exemplary, and prosperous was important as a symbol of the city and its desired Hellenic status. In a sense, the self-proclamation was as much for others as it was for themselves, and we might see spectators, like the Panathenaic amphorae, as creating a kind of "brand" awareness for Athens. As a newcomer commercially as well as politically, such promotion is understandable, but we should not view spectators as an explicitly political form sponsored by a specific individual or group. The ritualistic elaboration of archaic Athens was broadly based and continuous, and reflects a sense of what it meant to be Athenian.

We can see that the spectators encode expectations of behavior that match the role of different groups within the polis, particularly according to gender. The prevalence of inert spectators among men and youths, especially the mantled figure, signifies the importance of a modest and decorous behavior in public, and in the contemplation of narrative. Men are expected to be leaders, and a high proportion have spears, lean on a stick, sit, or use directive gestures, all indicating their status among spectators and generally within the city. Youthful spectators are overwhelmingly inert, but also have a significant component of mimetic types, alluding to their position of preparing for the requirements of adult status. Civic scenes are particularly focused on youths, a reflection of the importance of civic rituals in making their transition from child to ephebe to citizen.

Women, in contrast, are much more reactive than inert in their actions as spectators. Rather than mimetic or directive types of gestures, we saw that more than half of the reactive types consisted of two-handed gestures that signaled a heightened emotional state and lack of self-control. Women also watch scenes removed in time and/or place, such as heroic deeds and battles, and are notably absent from civic scenes like athletic contests. Still, women could be calm and controlled in the face of a civic threat like Amazons, but it is yet clear that the spectators confirm the gendered expectations of behavior in archaic Athens.

The impact of gender can also be seen other ways. Women appear more frequently on shapes that would be in general use around the household, such as the amphora and hydria, and less on those associated with the male symposion like the kylix and other drinking cups. The emergence of lekythoi as a spectator shape in the last third of the sixth century points to a new association of spectators with funerary ritual or elegiac remembrance, with a focus on youths as both spectator and narrative subject. Such changes show how a pictorial construct shifts to meet a new or altered agenda.

Spectators begin to decline as a pictorial construct in the later part of the sixth century and early fifth century. Although they do not disappear completely, their context and meaning apparently shift. Just as it is hard to say how and why something begins, it is equally so to suggest how it ends. Certainly the democratic reforms of the last decade of the sixth century had a significant impact on Athenian culture and art, and it is perhaps significant that the last great flourish of spectators occurs on funerary lekythoi; its associations with larger scale public rituals and choral performances is weaker. Perhaps we might consider that the political and ritualistic changes taking place in fifth-century Athens made the spectator an outdated concept, as did changes in the nature of Attic art. As we move into the fifth century, there is a much greater degree of naturalism in the representation of the human figure and a more coordinated representation of time and space. Spectators, especially pure spectators, are an artificial presence in the picture, at odds with these developments. Athenian culture needed new images to represent itself, like the Tyrannicides and Theseus, leaving spectators as archaic in both time and function.

GLOSSARY

Catalyst	Pictorial element that elaborates on the nucleus, but is not essential to the main action.
Category (of spectator)	Distinction of spectators on the basis of their gesture, action, and gender (see chapters 5.1, 5.2, and 6.1).
Class (of spectator)	Distinction of spectators on the basis of their role within the narrative (see invested, interested, detached, and pure).
Detached spectator	A spectator who is a catalyst in the narrative, has a weak indexical role and is often in the same time and place as the action.
Index	Pictorial element that refers to an event, idea, or person outside of the immediate narrative.
Inert spectators	A type of mood in which the spectator has no reaction or action.
Informant	Pictorial element that identifies participants or locates the narrative in time and place.
Interested spectator	A spectator who is a catalyst in the narrative, having also a strong indexical role, but no potential to intervene in the action.
Invested spectator	A spectator who is a catalyst in the narrative, having also a strong indexical role and the potential to intervene in the action.
Mimetic spectator	A type of mood in which the action of the spectator partially imitates an action of the hero, particularly in the position of arms or legs.

Mood (of spectator)	Distinction of spectators on the basis of the type of behavior shown by the spectator in response to the narrative action (see inert, mimetic, and reactive).
Nucleus	The essential action and its participants on which a narrative hinges.
Pure spectator	A type of spectator who is not a catalyst in the narrative and has a weak indexical role. Usually is removed from the action in time and/or place.
Reactive spectator	A type of mood in which the spectator responds animatedly to the main action.

NOTES

CHAPTER 1: SEEING SPECTATORS

1. Minneapolis Institute of Arts 57.1. Attic black-figure neck amphora attributed to the Painter of Vatican 359, c. 530. *Para.* 59.2; *Add.*[2] 38; Beazley Archive 350448. See Beazley (1958); Moon and Berge (1979) 70–1, no. 43 (entry by M. B. Moore); Stansbury-O'Donnell (1999) 32–3 and 51–2.
2. Scheibler (1988) 548 notes the ambiguous identity of the woman and young man on such scenes. Lewis (2002) 38–42 argues for the identity of the figures as mothers rather than wives, as they are called in many discussions. On warrior departures more generally, see Scheibler (1987) 83–8.
3. The rider was, in the archaic period, a part of the departing warrior theme, but became disassociated from it when he lost his weapons, as Scheibler (1987) 84 points out. The meaning of the riders themselves is controversial, and the existence of riders in vase painting has suggested to some that there was a cavalry in archaic Athens. Bugh (1988) 3–38 reviews the scholarship and evidence, arguing for the existence of cavalry but admitting that certainty is not possible. With regard to riders in images with spectators, in most cases the riders do not bear any weapon, nor do they play any active role in battle scenes such as figure 2. I would suggest that the horse is a sign of elite status, as can be seen in Solon naming the second of his four classes of Athenians as *hippeis*, or horsemen, and that the rider is a figure worthy of admiration, whether for his racing ability, his fighting ability, or simply his excellence.
4. Beazley (1931) 258–9. The vase is illustrated in Bothmer (1985) 75, fig. 57; *ABV* 150.1. For a different example, see here fig. 16.
5. Bothmer (1971) 124–5. The term "supernumeraries" is used in Bothmer (1985) 70.
6. Korte-Konte (1979). Scenes of Theseus and the Minotaur: 70 Attic black-figure, 19 Attic red-figure, 6 non-Attic. Herakles and the lion: 40 Attic black-figure; 3 Attic red-figure. Other labors of Herakles: 20 Attic black-figure; 3 Attic red-figure. Combat duels: 45 Attic black-figure, 1 non-Attic.
7. Ibid. (1979) 168–70.
8. Carpenter (1986) 32–54.
9. Ibid., 40 for both quotations.

10. Scheibler (1988).
11. Kaeser (1990).
12. Brijder (1991) 337–40.
13. Ibid., 337, n. 13.
14. Van Wees (1997) 353–4.
15. Barringer (2001) 118. See also Scheibler (1988) 547.
16. See Eagleton (2003) on the state of theory and its application in the last few decades, and its continuing importance. Eagleton (1996) remains the fundamental introduction to the historiography and philosophy of literary theory.
17. *Critical Inquiry* 30 (winter 2004). See especially the summary of Mitchell (2004) and the comments about theory and art history by Neer (2004). On the futility of theory, see Fish (2004), and on its "professionialization," Harootunian (2004).
18. On the historiography of Greek archaeology, see Morris (1994), esp. 42–3 on "alternative archaeologies."
19. See, for example, the report of E. Eakin, "The Latest Theory Is That Theory Doesn't Matter," *The New York Times*, April 19, 2003, section D, p. 9, and of C. Shea, "2003: The 3rd Annual Year in Ideas; Theory is Finished," *The New York Times Magazine*, December 14, 2003, p. 94.
20. Poovey (2004) 430.
21. So similarly did Scheibler (1987) consider the rider and warrior theme on the belly amphora in the context of the military and political machinations of Hippias. On the question of local/ethnic interpretation, see Antonaccio (2003), esp. 64–5.

CHAPTER 2: DEFINING SPECTATORS

1. See Stansbury-O'Donnell (1999) 18–31 for definitions and discussions of these terms and their derivation from the work of Barthes.
2. Chicago, Art Institute 1978.114. Beazley Archive 5170. See Moon and Berge (1979) 52–3 (entry by D. von Bothmer); Bothmer (1985) 51. On the iconography of Herakles and the lion see: *LIMC* V.1, 16–27 and 31–3, s.v. Heracles 1762–1914 (J. Boardman); Brommer (1973) 109–43; Brommer (1986) 7–11; Uhlenbrock (1986).
3. Bothmer in Moon and Berge (1979) 53.
4. On the possibility of combining individual actions into multiple nuclei see Stansbury-O'Donnell (1999) 22–6. On Nereid iconography see Barringer (1995) 69–77.
5. See, for example, *Iliad* 13.43–90, where Poseidon takes the form of the seer Kalchas to spur on the two Ajax.
6. The J. Paul Getty Museum, Malibu, California 86.AE.142.1–2. Not in Beazley lists or Beazley Archive. CVA United States 25, The J. Paul Getty Museum 2 (Malibu, 1990) 18–20 and pl. 71 with earlier bibliography (A. Clark).
7. New York, Metropolitan Museum of Art 59.11.25. *Para.* 40; *Add.*[2] 28; Beazley Archive 250772. CVA United States 16, New York, Metropolitan Museum of Art 4 (New York, 1976) 2–4 and pl. 3.1 with earlier bibliography (M. B. Moore and D. von Bothmer). See also Kluiver (1995) 60, no. 30; Knittlmayer (1997) 54. 60, no. 30.
8. *Iliad* 1.493–530.
9. See gesture W.4a in chapter 6.1.
10. Paris, Cabinet des Médailles 243. Beazley Archive 1047. CVA France 10, Paris, Bibliothèque nationale, Cabinet des Médailles 2 (Paris, 1931), III.H.e p. 68 and pl. 88.4 (E. Pottier). See also Reed (1987) 61–2; Shapiro (1989) 32–3; Maul-Mandelartz (1990) 168–72, no. KA1; Shapiro (1992) 56.

11. See Shapiro (1989) 33; Shapiro (1992) 56; Kyle (1992) 89–91.
12. Translation from Shapiro (1989) 33. On the gesture see ch. 5.2, M.4a.
13. See the dinos with the funeral games of Patroklos by Sophilos, Athens, National Museum 15499 (*ABV* 39.16; *Para.* 18; *Add.*² 10; Beazley Archive 305075). There are, however, only a handful of such representations with stands.
14. Cleveland Museum of Art 16.1062. *Para.* 179.6; *Add.*² 109; Beazley Archive 351293. CVA United States 16, Cleveland Museum of Art 1 (Princeton, 1971) 11–2 and pl. 17.2 (C. G. Boulter).
15. New York, Metropolitan Museum of Art 61.11.16. *Para.* 141.6; *Add.*² 87; Beazley Archive 351044. CVA United States 16, New York, Metropolitan Museum of Art 4 (New York, 1976) 27–9 and pl. 29.2 with earlier bibliography (M. B. Moore and D. von Bothmer).
16. On the idea of generalized heroic, see Snodgrass (1979); idem (1980b) 54–8. On the idea of generic narrative, relying on a formula with elaborations to provide specificity, see Stansbury-O'Donnell (1999) 44–53. A similar blurring of the lines between mythological and non-mythological also exists in hunting scenes; see Barringer (2001) 32–42.
17. Brijder (1991) 337.
18. New York 56.171.18. *ABV* 137.61; *Para.* 55; *Add.*² 37; Beazley Archive 310321. CVA United States 16, New York, Metropolitan Museum of Art 4 (New York, 1976) 13–4 and pl. 14–5 with earlier bibliography (M. B. Moore and D. von Bothmer).
19. On races at the Panathenaic games, see Kyle (1992) 91 with figs. 41–2.
20. On the identity of the figures as grooms see Mommsen (2002) 30 and 34. On these as training scenes for runner and riders, see Maul-Mandelartz (1990) 173.
21. On the arrangement of the *chlamys* and its role in hunt imagery, see Barringer (2001) 26–32 and 52–3.
22. New Haven, Yale University Art Gallery 1913.110. See Baur (1922) 74–6, no. 110; Vian (1945) 22, no. 61 (with earlier bibliography); Matheson Burke and Pollitt (1975) 27–28, no. 31 (entry by J. N. Blanchard); Bothmer (1969) 40–42; Uhlenbrock (1986) 101, no. 1 (entry by H. A. Shapiro); *LIMC* VII.1, 973, s.v. Kyknos I no. 27. Bothmer reattributed the fabric of the vase as Euboean rather than Attic. Shapiro notes that the presence of onlookers in scenes of Herakles and Kyknos is unusual in Attic work, but there are two elderly males watching the same combat on a hydria by the Antimenes Painter in the Minneapolis Institute of Arts (inv. 59.1, *Para.* 119.8ter, *Add.*² 69; Beazley Archive 340469 (with pictures); see Burow (1989) pls. 108–10.
23. This behavior has been noted of some spectators by Barringer (2001) 37.
24. See ch. 1.1.
25. I would like to acknowledge the comments of the anonymous readers for Cambridge University Press about using the CVA as the main data source. As a result, I have included the excavation material from Athens and the random sample of the Beazley Archive. On the construction of a census for Corinthian vase painting and its analysis, see Shanks (1999), esp. 40–2.
26. As published in *ABV* (1956) and *ARV*² (1963) and updated in *Para.* (1971) and *Add.*² (1989).
27. See Hannestad (1988) 224 and Hannestad (1989) 114–5.
28. As accessed at http://www.beazley.ox.ac.uk/test/Vases/ASP/default.asp on August 17, 2004. On the limitations of the Beazley Archive as of 1990, see Bazant (1990) 94–5, nn. 4 and 7. On the basis of the random sample of 354 vases from the Beazley Archive described in section 2.4, 50.3 percent of the sample vases were listed in *ABV*, *ARV*², or *Para*; 22.6 percent of the vases were also found in volumes of the CVA; 31.9 percent of the vases were

unattributed. According to search results, the total number of black-figure vases was almost equal to that of red-figure vases (27,000 versus 27,834).

29. However, many excavation reports, out of necessity, do not illustrate all pieces; see Moore and Philippides (1986) 3 on Attic black-figure pottery from the Agora in Athens.
30. On the history of the CVA, see Rouet (2001) 124–37 and Bentz (2002).
31. Search for "onlooker" in the "Term Words (Subject)" field at http://www.beazley.ox.ac.uk/test/vases/asp/BookSearch.asp yielded 50 vases on August 17, 2004. Search for "onlookers" in the "Term Words (Subject)" field at the same URL on the same date yielded 428 vases. The search did include figures 7 and 11, as well as the reverse side of the amphora in figure 4, but not the obverse with Herakles.
32. See also the arguments for using the CVA by Scheffer (2001) 128.
33. An analogous approach of combining the Beazley lists with selected excavation materials was developed by Curry (2000), esp. 88, nn. 2–3. Here, however, I prefer not to merge the data from the two sources.
34. Sources for the Athens census: Graef and Langlotz (1925) and (1931); Knigge (1976); Kunze-Götte, Tancke, and Vierneisel (1999); Moore (1997); Moore and Philippides (1986).
35. Bazant (1990) argues for the validity of an approach using relative frequency of iconographic themes based on data from the Beazley Archive. See also, for example, Stewart (1995) 87–8 for the tabulation of the pursuit theme using the Beazley lists.
36. On the need to focus on the perspective of the viewer, see Stissi (1999) 95–7.
37. On the general requirements for a database and describing the data, see Fletcher and Lock (1991) 2–49.
38. Scheibler (1987). She does the same for the Heron-class skyphos in Scheibler (2000), and Shapiro (1997) follows her method for the black-figure pelike.
39. A recent review of the bibliography and controversy over chronology can be found in Neer (2002) 186–205, with focus on the late archaic period. Because the disparity in dating decreases significantly for the fifth century, following the traditional chronologies for the database has little impact on the phasing out of the spectator depictions, although it would affect the timing of their initial appearance in the sixth century.
40. The use of overlapping periods can be found in the study of Bazant (1990) and Tuna-Nörling (1995) 103–5, who adds the single straddling period of "Ende 6./Anf. 5. Jh.," which is equivalent to the range of 510–490 used in this study. For the periods of 560–540 and 510–490, there is a relatively large number of artists, but many fewer fall into the period 535–515. In this case, there seems to be a much stronger tendency to place artists either in the third quarter of the century, at the end of the high archaic period, or in the fourth quarter, at the beginning of the late archaic. As the number of vases from 550–525 and 525–500 shows, however, there was a steady production of spectator vases right through the transitional period of 535–515, with a real decline in production only beginning during the period 510–490.
41. Equivalent would be the assignation of the Droop cup shape to 525–500 in Tuna-Nörling (1995) 103, even though the dates in the literature range between 540 and 510.
42. Eleusis 741. See Stansbury-O'Donnell (1999) 36–7 and fig. 15 with earlier bibliography.
43. Athens, National Museum 3961: 'Melian' amphora from Melos. See Boardman (1998) fig. 250.
44. Two of the three examples before 600 are Protocorinthian (Taranto 4173; Paris, Louvre CA617); one is Attic Geometric (Paris, Louvre CA2509). For the period 600–575, the one example is Corinthian (Basel, BS 425).

45. Kerameikos Inv. 706; see Kunze-Götte, Tancke, and Vierneisel (1999) 64, no. 234.8. The tally for the undetermined vase (Kerameikos VII.8.1) is split into 0.5 for each fabric in the table.
46. Other shapes include the aryballos (3), amphoriskos (1), chous (1), dinos (1), kotyle (2), lebes (2), lekanis (1), mastoid cup (4), plate (2), stamnos (6). "Cup" refers generally to a kylix type. Pitchers include both the olpe and oinochoe.
47. Like the CVA census, the majority (22 of 33) of pitchers belong to the periods 550–525 and 525–500. Their production is, however, heavier between 510–475 (6/33) than earlier, 575–540 (2/33).
48. Thirteen of the 25 kraters in the CVA census date after 475. These scenes are discussed more fully in ch. 5.
49. See Shapiro (1997) on the pelike and its subject matter. Eight of the 11 pelikai fall between 525 and 475.
50. Scheibler (2000) esp. 33. Twelve of the 22 skyphoi in the CVA census belong to the combined periods, 525–490.
51. See Clark in CVA United States 25, The J. Paul Getty Museum 2 (Malibu, 1990); 19. 9 of the 11 pyxides date to the combined periods 575–525.
52. There has been some debate as to whether or not Tyrrhenian-style amphorae are Attic productions. See most recently in favor of the Attic origins Kluiver (1992) and (1995) and Curry (2000); contra, Ginge (1988). Carpenter (1983) proposes lowering the traditional dates of the group from 575–550 to 560–530 based on iconography and inscriptions, but Curry proposes that the iconographic variations could be attributed to the immigrant status of the painters/potters. I have chosen to follow the more traditional chronology and have dated some of the works to the period 575–550 and others to 560–540 based on the attributions and discussion in the CVA and in Kluiver (1995) and (1996).
53. For a compilation of the distribution of wares by various painters in the Mediterranean world, see Scheffer (1988); Tuna-Nörling (1995) 144–8 and Abb. 31.
54. Three hundred sixty-five vases have some place of origin with a degree of firmness. I have included vases that simply state the vase is "from Italy," etc., but have excluded those under the rubric "said to be from . . ." or "thought to be from. . . ." Vases indicated as being purchased in Athens or Rome or another city were not included as from that country unless specifically indicated.
55. On the scale of production, see Scheibler (1983)116–9, Hannestad (1988) 222–3, and Cook (1997) 259–62. Arafat and Morgan (1989) 328 point out that we cannot necessarily assume that workshops produced steadily year-round, and may have fluctuated along with the agricultural cycle.
56. There are a number of detailed studies on the production and distribution of Attic pottery. For general overview see Beazley (1989) 39–59, Scheibler (1983) 137–86, Arafat and Morgan (1989), Boardman (1991b), Johnston (1991), and Osborne (1996b), as well as the more detailed studies listed subsequently. Arguments on the low value of traded pottery can be found in Gill (1994), and a review of scholarly opinions on the Etruscan trade in Spivey (1991) and Sparkes (1996) 140–51 and 160–7.
57. Curry (2000) 81–5.
58. See Osborne (1996b) 32–3 and Stissi (1999) 94.
59. Tuna-Nörling (1995) 146.
60. Scheffer (1988) 538–9.
61. See Hannestad (1989) 128, Arafat and Morgan (1989) 340–1, Osborne (1996b) 39. On trademarks generally, see Johnston (1979).

62. See Hannestad (1999) 306, also Small (1994) 40–1. On the popularity of the lekythos in the western Greek colonies, see Hannestad (1999) 314.
63. See Johnston (1984) 210 on neck amphora. See also Scheffer (1988) 543–4.
64. See the summary in Reusser (2002) 204–6. Contra, see Small (1994) 45–53.
65. See the conclusions of Scheffer (1988) 544, Arafat and Morgan (1989) 337, Hannestad (1999) 308–9, Mehren (2001) 46 and 52.
66. Reusser (2002) 188–9. On the comprehension of imagery generally, see Naerebout (1997) 229–33.
67. Barringer (2001) 3. See also Boardman (1991b) 80–1 and Stissi (1999) 98.
68. On these painters, see Brijder (1983) and (1991).
69. On the Tyrrhenian Group, see especially Kluiver (1992) 74–80 and (1995) 77–83. See also von Bothmer (1944) and Tuna-Nörling (1997), who shows that these vases were also exported to the east in addition to Etruria, although the latter is the main destination for the work.
70. Carpenter (1986) 33–5 also noted that the early Siana Cups came mainly from Greek findspots, whereas later band cups show an increased share coming from Etruria. He uses these data, as well as the increase in the number of painters and workshops, to suggest a change that took place in Attic production around 550, with increased production destined for the export market. Thus, the imagery on the cups, particularly the use of stock figures, is found early on vases meant primarily for a Greek market, but continues to be used when the Etruscan market expands. Shapiro (1990) has also shown that the mythological repertory of Attic vase painters also underwent a shift in the period 570–550, with old themes abandoned and a significant number of new themes introduced. These developments in production and iconography during the second quarter of the sixth century coincide with the introduction of spectators on vases on a large scale, and the correlation suggests that spectators were developed as part of the changes in vase shapes, subject matter, and expanded markets in Athens in this period.
71. See Junker (2002), esp. 12–15 on the use of vases for grave ritual. For the interpretation of sympotic-shaped vases as grave goods, see Langlotz (1957), esp. the conclusion on 419–21. On the functional interpretation of the vase shape within a sympotic context, see Beazley (1961) 55, Bazant (1985) 55–8, and Lissarrague (1996) 238. Hoffmann considers the vase from a symbolically functional point of view, its shape serving the function of drinking, but the decoration and the use of white-ground technique as specifically funerary; see Hoffmann (1988), (1989), and (1994) 71.
72. Hannestad (1988) 226.
73. On the use of lekythoi, see Knigge (1976) 15 and Houby-Nielsen (1996) 239–40. On grave offerings generally, see Kurtz and Boardman (1971) 203–17.
74. On the deployment of votive cups in sanctuaries, see Stissi (2003); on the symbolic use of the cup in the grave, see Hoffmann citation in note 71.
75. On the function of the hydria in funerary ritual, see Diehl (1964) 128–41, and also Kurtz and Boardman (1971) 149–50, 161; Houby-Nielsen (1996) 239; Junker (2002) 21. On the hydria generally, see A. Steiner (2004) 447–57.
76. See Ferrari (2002) 90–5, who argues strongly that we should regard this as the existence of three separate gender classes for ancient Greece.
77. See Kurtz (1975) on lekythoi; Fantham et al. (1994) 96–7.
78. On the importance of the belly amphora for this reason, see Scheibler (1987).
79. For this table, the following individual types of spectators, as described in chs. 5 and 6, are included in each classification:

Inert: M.1; M.2a-b; Y.1; Y.2a-b; W.1; W.2a
Mimetic: M.2c; M.4c-d; Y.2c; Y.4c-d; W.2b.
Reactive: M.3; M.4a-b; M.4w; M.5; M.6; Y.2d-e; Y.3; Y.4a-b; Y.4e-f; Y.4w; Y.5; Y.6; W.2b; W.3; W.4; W.6.

One should note that W.2b does not always mimic the action of the figures in the nucleus, but because the action with a spear suggests an active and positive response, at least with regard to a threat, it has been considered as mimetic. As we shall see in ch. 6.1, however, this pose probably derives from the goddess Athena, rather than the behavior of mortal women.

80. These vases are Como, Museo Archeological Civico D3359 (see figure 25 with references) and Paris, Musée du Louvre CP10676 (Beazley Archive 12192; CVA France 18, Paris, Musée du Louvre 11, III.H.e pl. 146.6).
81. Accessed at http://www.beazley.ox.ac.uk/test/vases/asp/BookSearch.asp. The figures for black-figure (27,000) and red-figure (27,834) were the results of a search using those terms under the pull-down menu for "technique."
82. On hypothesis testing, see Fletcher and Lock (1991) 51–62.
83. A search for the terms "cup," "amphora," and "lekythos" under "shape" in the Beazley Archive on September 4, 2004 yielded a total of 17,549 cups (32.0 percent of the 54,834 vases), 12,831 lekythoi (23.4 percent) and 6,663 amphora (12.2 percent). The three shapes account for 67.6 percent of the vases in the Beazley Archive, lower than the total frequency for these three shapes in both the Beazley Archive sample and the CVA census.
84. So similarly did Scheibler (1987) consider the rider and warrior theme on belly amphora in the context of the military and political machinations of Hippias. On the question of local/ethnic interpretation, see Antonaccio (2003), esp. 64–5.

CHAPTER 3: VISION AND THE CONSTRUCTION OF IDENTITY

1. Minneapolis Institute of Arts 57.1; see references at figure 1. The material in this chapter was presented to a colloquium at the University of Kansas in September 2002. I am grateful to Pam Gordon and the Classics Department for the opportunity to discuss this approach.
2. Lacan's work was part of the subject of a joint AIA/APA symposium on psychoanalysis and classics at the 2004 Annual Meeting in San Francisco (January 5).
3. See the critique of duBois (1988) 7–17.
4. On the range of pyschoanalytic uses, see Eagleton (1996) 155–66; see also Lacan (1978) 109 and Gay (1976) 14–32.
5. I am mindful of duBois's argument that gender in ancient Greece was not defined in terms of the possession and lack of possession of the phallus (A and −A) as psychoanalysis regards modern gender construction, as well as Ferrari's argument that we should consider that there were three gendered groups in ancient Greece – men, youthful males, and women. The analysis of gender here will be based on the analysis of spectators' reactions in chs. 5 and 6. See duBois (1988) 18–36 and Ferrari (2003) 88–99.
6. Wilden's commentary in Lacan (1968) 157–311; Rose (1986); Jay (1993), especially 329–80; Eagleton (1996) 140–55.
7. See glossary by A. Sheridan in Lacan (1977) x; Rose (1986) 54.
8. See Wilden in Lacan (1968) 175; Jay (1993) 344–6.
9. Wilden in Lacan (1968) 160–2.
10. Ibid., 161–3.

11. Jay (1993) 361.
12. Ibid., 351.
13. Wilden in Lacan (1968) 165 and 186; Rose (1986) 61.
14. Lacan (1968) 40–2.
15. Rose (1986) 50–1 and 66–9; see also Wilden in Lacan (1968) 286.
16. Quotations in this paragraph are from Lacan (1977) 1–2.
17. Rose (1986) 173.
18. Ibid., 53.
19. Ibid., 176; Jay (1993) 349.
20. Lacan (1978) 73.
21. Ibid., 72–5.
22. Ibid., 74, commenting on Valéry.
23. Ibid., 83.
24. Rose (1986) 181.
25. Ibid., 184; Jay (1993) 361.
26. Lacan (1968) 48: "The Symbolic function presents itself as a double movement within the subject: man makes an object of his action, but only in order to restore to this action in due time its place as a grounding. In this equivocation, operating at every instant, lies the whole process of a function in which action and knowledge alternate . . . [in a historical example:] phase one, the man who works at the level of production in our society considers himself to rank amongst the proletariat; phase two, in the name of belonging to it, he joins in a general strike."
27. On the diagrams, see Lacan (1978) 105–6; Rose (1986) 190–3; Jay (1993) 364–8.
28. For example, Lacan (1978) 86.
29. Lacan (1978) 89, 92, and 96.
30. Ibid., 101.
31. On visual language in narrative see Stansbury-O'Donnell (1999) 92–103.
32. Lacan (1978) 113.
33. Ibid., 116.
34. Lacan (1968) 17.
35. Lindberg (1976) 1–17. The following section is based on Lindberg as well as the following: Ronchi (1957) 12–33; Lloyd (1987) 299–301; Simon (1988); Plantzos (1997) 459–64; Laks (1999), esp. 262–8.
36. See Lindberg (1976) 11–17. See also Simon (1988) 52–53.
37. See discussion in Lindberg (1976) 2–3 and Simon (1988) 37–8. On Democritus generally, see Lloyd (1970) 45–9.
38. As seen in Aristotle's critique of Democritus: "Democritus and the majority of natural philosophers who discuss perception are guilty of a great absurdity; for they represent all perception as being by touch; *de sensu* 4, 442a29, tr. Kirk, Raven, and Schofield (1983) 428, no. 587. See also Stewart (1997) 16 and Gordon (2002) 92.
39. Aetius 4.8.10, tr. Kirk, Raven, and Schofield (1983) 428, no. 588.
40. Theophrastus, *de sensu* 50, tr. Kirk, Raven, and Schofield (1983) 428, no. 589.
41. Aristotle, *de sensu* 2 (438a5–12) refutes while reporting on Democritus's position.
42. See critique in Ronchi (1957) 25–6 and on 28–9, the solution of Ibn al-Haitham in the eleventh century C.E.
43. As quoted by Theophrastus, *de sensu* 26, tr. Stratton (1917) 89.
44. Plato, *Timaeus* 45b-d, tr. R. G. Bury (1966) 101–3.
45. Aristotle *De anima* 2.7; 419a18–21, tr. Hamlyn (1968) 28.
46. See Frede (1992) 280–1.

47. Tr. from Lindberg (1976) 9–10.
48. Laks (1999) 264.
49. Simon (1988) 193.
50. Plato, *Phaedrus* 255c-d, tr. Fowler (1966) 501.
51. D. T. Steiner (2001) 203–4. See also Stewart (1997) 19.
52. See Frontisi-Ducroux (1995) 20 and 25–7; Stewart (1997) 16; D. T. Steiner (2001) 150–1, 198–204, Barringer (2001) 104–9.
53. Gorgias, *Hel.*17; tr. Waterfield (2000) 230. For a recent discussion of Gorgias, see D. T. Steiner (2001) 286–90.
54. Aeschylus, *Eumenides* 34–37, tr. Lattimore (1953) 136.
55. Pindar, *Olympian* 10.99–105, tr. D. T. Steiner (1998) 140, with discussion.
56. See D. T. Steiner (2001) 229–32. On public modesty and the mantle, see Ferrari (2003) 54–5.
57. Aristotle, *Poetics* 4, tr. Halliwell (1987) 34.
58. D. T. Steiner (2001) chap. 4.
59. Thucydides 2.43.1, tr. Smith (1980) I, 335. See D. T. Steiner (2001) 209; Loraux (1993) 14–15.
60. As Stewart (1997) 18 comments, "When I enjoy an image constructed to satisfy the public eye, I implicitly align my glance with the gaze that shaped it."
61. As Gay (1976) 21–2 emphasizes, however, the goal of the theories is to explain normal development. Pathology, however, seems to bring the normal into sharper focus by its contrast.
62. On these aspects of the viewing context, see Stansbury-O'Donnell (1999) 70–9.
63. Paris, Musée du Louvre A478. *ABV* 66.54; *Para.* 26; *Add.*² 18; Beazley Archive 300597. CVA France 12, Musée du Louvre 8, III.H.e p. 59 and pl. (508) 76.2–3 (E. Pottier). See Brijder (1991) 447–8, no. 357 with earlier bibliography; see also Boardman (2001) 57.
64. See Pollitt (1985) and the recent discussions in Stewart (1997) 14–6, D. T. Steiner (2001) 32–44, and Ferrari (2003) 59–60 and 87–92.
65. Aristotle, *Rhetoric* I.5.6 (1361a3–5), tr. Freese (1982) 51. See Ferrari (2003) 59–60 and 87–8.
66. See Barringer (2001) 118.
67. On the parallels between praise in poetry and statuary, see D. T. Steiner (2001) ch. 5.
68. See Stewart (1997) 14.
69. On the "shooting" of the eye, see Lacan (1978) 72.
70. Munich, Antikensammlung 1384. *ABV* 299.2; Beazley Archive 320426. CVA, Germany 3, Munich, Antikensammlung, 1 (Munich, 1939) 16–7 and pl. 18.2 & 20.1 (R. Lullies).
71. Omaha, Joslyn Art Museum 1963.480. *Para.* 34, no. 2; *Add.*² 24; Beazley Archive 350215. CVA, United States 21, Omaha 1, 6–8 and pls. 10–11 (A. Steiner). See Moon and Berge (1979) 40–1, no. 25, where the spectators are identified as the gods and goddesses on Olympos, but they belong more clearly in the group of spectators that are typical of Amazonomachies; compare Bothmer (1957) 47.
72. On the guardian or *kyrios*, see Just (1989) 26–39.
73. On Amazons, see chs. 5.4 and 6.2; see also Bothmer (1957), duBois (1982), Tyrrel (1984), Hardwick (1990), Blok (1995), Stewart (1997) 118–20.
74. The gender arrangement of the Greek house is a subject of some debate, ranging from isolation and separation to a more fluid organization with overlapping spheres. See Walker (1983); Fantham et al. (1994) 103–4; Nevett (1999) 12–20 and 154–6; Lewis (2002) 130–8.
75. Mainz, Universität 88. *Para.* 67; *Add.*² 46; Beazley Archive 350482. CVA Germany 15, Mainz, Universität, 1 (Munich, 1959) 43 and pl. 41.2 (R. Hampe and E. Simon). See Bothmer (1985) 215–6, no. 59; Maul-Mandelartz (1990) 172–5, no. RL2; Junker (1999) 34–8; Junker (2003) 22–8.

76. On generic narrative, see Stansbury-O'Donnell (1999) 44–53.
77. See Bérard et al. (1989) 39–44 and 61–70, Barringer (2001) 22–32.
78. See Stewart (1997) 7–10; Barringer (2001) 103–4 with earlier references.
79. Barringer (2001) 104 and 117–8.
80. Bonn, Akademisches Kunstmuseum 74. *ARV*[2] 816.5; Beazley Archive 210095. CVA, Germany 1, Bonn, Akademisches Kunstmuseum, 1 (Munich, 1938) 9–10 and pl. 4.4 and 6.1–3 (A. Greifenhagen), where attributed to the School of Makron.
81. For a recent discussion of *aidos* and the gaze, see Ferrari (2002) 54–5.
82. See Frontisi-Ducroux (1996) 84; Stewart (1997) 14–5.
83. See bibliography note 2 of ch. 2 at figure 4. On the structural qualities of this particular episode, see Stansbury-O'Donnell (1999) 93–5.
84. For an illustration, see Boardman (1996) fig. 278. On mask and identity, see Frontisi-Ducroux (1995) 40.
85. See generally Lissarrague (1990) ch. 1.
86. Rose (1986) 184.

CHAPTER 4: RITUAL PERFORMANCE, SPECTATORS, AND IDENTITY

1. See the critique of Skinner (1993), esp. 129.
2. Tarquinia, Museo Nazionale Tarquiniese RC4194. Beazley Archive 397. On the kylix, see especially Barringer (1995) 83–6 and 212, no. 224 with bibliography. On the three-dimensional, semi-circular arrangement of a frieze of figures in the Parthenon, see Neils (2001) 61–6.
3. On the history of Peisistratos, see Andrewes (1982b). On the general history of sixth-century Athens, see also Andrewes (1982a), Murray (1993) 181–200 and 268–73; on the archaeology of archaic Attica, see Whitley (2001) 233–43 and 255–65, Camp (2001) 23–47.
4. On the interpretation of this incident, see Boardman (1972) and McGlew (1993) 74–8.
5. Herodotos 1.60, tr. D. Grene (1987). For an evaluation of Herodotus as a source on Peisistratos, see Lavelle (1993) 61–2.
6. The following is based on Sinos (1998), originally published in 1993. On the Phye incident as civic spectacle, see also Connor (1987) and Ferrari (1995). Sinos notes three elements of special importance: the use of the chariot, a figure impersonating the goddess, and the messengers. Boardman (1972) 62–5 argued that the incident led to the interest of Athenian vase painters in scenes showing the introduction of Herakles to Olympos as a metaphor for Peisistratos being returned to Athens by Athena, a view to which Ferrari (1995) provides more nuance – that it was Peisistratos imitating ritual in the Panathenaic festival in his dramatic entry, and that scenes of Herakles in a chariot are initially stimulated by the festival rather than Peisistratos.
7. See generally Stahl (1987) and Manville (1990).
8. See generally Andrewes (1982a), McGlew (1993) 87–123.
9. Manville (1990) 149.
10. On the cults at the time of Solon, see Connor (1987) 49–50 and Shapiro (1996), who discusses the cult of Aphrodite Pandemos.
11. Shapiro (1989). I follow his synthesis (pp. 19–42) of the history and development of the Panathenaic festival. See also Kolb (1977), Shear (1978), and Stahl (1987) 229–55 for building activity of this era.
12. See Shapiro (1989) 19–21 on chronology and sources and Neils (1992) 13–27 for a broad description of the festival with earlier bibliography. See also Simon (1983) 55–72.

13. See Neils (1992) 29 and fig. 19. On the development of sports at the Panathenaia see Kyle (1987) 22–31.
14. See Wickersham (1991) and Hopper (1961) 208–17.
15. Shapiro (1989) 20.
16. On the archaeology of the Acropolis between 575 and 510, see Hurwit (1999) 94–121. Hurwit places the architectural and sculptural fragments of the Archaic temple to c. 560.
17. On Panathenaic amphorae, see Neils (1992) 29–51, with earlier bibliography. Bentz (1998) provides an exhaustive documentation and discussion, including findspots and secondary uses of the amphora after the games. For a recent analysis of the image of Athena, see Marx (2003).
18. On the idea of branding in Corinthian pottery, see Rasmussen (1991) 66.
19. Sourvinou-Inwood (2003) 68–72, 99–100, 106–8, 145–56.
20. On the location of the Old Agora, see now Papadapoulos (2003) 280–5.
21. Shapiro (1989) 85–7 reviews the possible connections of Peisistratos to the developments of the cults of Dionysos. Whereas the seating of spectators and organization of the dithyrambic choirs follows the social and political reorganization of Athens by Kleisthenes into 10 tribes, it is possible that earlier practices were organized around phratery or Solonian class and that the performances themselves are not new.
22. Aristotle, *Poetics* 4, tr. Halliwell (1987) 35.
23. See Calame (1994/95) for a brief summary of this evolution and discussion of the changes that took place in one form of choral song in the process; see also Else (1957). On recent discussions of development of the early City Dionysia, see Winkler (1990), Barringer (2001) 53–7, and Sourvinou-Inwood (2003) 67–200; contra, see Connor (1990).
24. For a discussion of the impact of tragic performance on Athenian democracy and identity, see Calame (1999) and Kavoulaki (1999).
25. Winkler (1990) 24–5; Barringer (2001) 53–8. For a discussion of early social organization, see Manville (1990) 55–69. For a debate on early Athenian democracy, see Wallace (1994); Raaflaub (1994a and 1994b); Ober (1994).
26. Aristotle, *Poetics* 4, tr. Halliwell (1987) 35.
27. On the pre-Kleisthenic elements, see generally Winkler (1990); Sourvinou-Inwood (2003) 67–200; Ceccarelli (2004) 93–9.
28. de Polignac (1995) 83–86.
29. On autochthony, see Rosivach (1987) 300–3. On the importance of this myth and its gender implications for classical Athens, see Loraux (1993). For autochthony and questions of ethnic identity, see Konstan (2001) 34–5 and Hall (1997) 51–6, esp. 53–4.
30. Frost (1990) 5–6.
31. Osborne (1994) 160.
32. Kavoulaki (1999) 299–300.
33. See Calame (2001) 130–4. See also Stehle (1997) 60 and the description of the Panathenaia from Euripides's *Herakleidae* in ch. 4.3.
34. McClure (1999) 55. Alkman's other *partheneion* names Astymeloisa; see Alcman 3 in Campbell (1988) 379. Perikles's admonition (Thuc. 2.45.2) that greatest will be the glory of the woman who is least talked about among men also suggests anonymity in public.
35. Plutarch, *Solon* 21, see also ch. V.3. See Loraux (1998) 15–6 and 21–5; Alexiou (2002) 14–19. See McClure (1999) 40–7 on the lament as a speech genre for women.
36. Sourvinou-Inwood (2003) 181, also 69–70 and 79.
37. Sch. Ael. Arist. 13.189–4–5; see the discussion in Shapiro (1989) 20.
38. Stehle (1997) 61–63; see also Else (1957) 35–6. On Solon's use of myth and poetry to instill a civic consciousness, see Stahl (1987) 231–2, Wickersham (1991) 23–7.

39. As Else (1957) 36 and Hurwit (1999) 101 reiterate, this is the "histrionic period" of Athenian history.
40. Morris (2000) 161–91, quote on p. 162; Kurke (1999) 19–21 and 68 on the use of Peisistratid coinage for this purpose; Dougherty and Kurke (2003) 26–7 (quote on p. 26). See also Hall (2003) 26–7.
41. Shapiro (1989) 164–5.
42. Dougherty and Kurke (1998) 1–5; Dougherty and Kurke (2003) 1–13.
43. Greenblatt (1980) 1–9, quotes are from pages 2 and 4.
44. See the discussion of Bell (1997) 12–16 for a summary of the psychoanalytic approaches to ritual.
45. For a discussion of the ethological approach that sees ritual as stereotyped and remote, see Naerebout (1997) 307–8 et passim.
46. Geertz (1973) 6–14.
47. Ibid., 89.
48. Ibid., 93 and generally 91–97.
49. Ibid., 112 and generally 112–22.
50. Ibid., 127.
51. Ibid., 142.
52. Ibid., 143–4.
53. Sahlins (1981) 5–8.
54. Ibid., 9–28.
55. Ibid., 14.
56. Ibid., 13, 52.
57. Ibid., 67–69, quote from p. 68.
58. Bell (1992) 21–7.
59. Ibid., 32.
60. Ibid., 171–8.
61. Along these lines, see Burkert (1979) 35–45, where social behavior replaces instinct.
62. Bell (1992) 186. On consent in Greek cultures, see Hall (2003) 25–6.
63. Ibid., 197. On ideology and physical force, see 189–93.
64. Ibid., 204.
65. Ibid., 206–7.
66. Ibid., 207. On consent see 208–10.
67. Ibid., 220–221.
68. Naerebout (1997) 324–404. On mobilization, see 344ff; on communication, see 346ff and 377ff; on performances, see 371ff.
69. Ibid., 377.
70. Ibid., 343.
71. Ibid., 349.
72. De Polignac (1995) 20; see generally Hurwit (1985) 73–85, Osborne (1996a) 88–104, and Whitley (2001) 134–64. See also the essays in Alcock and Osborne (1994).
73. Stehle (1997) 57. In this section, I have relied heavily on the work of Stehle (1997) and Calame (2001), both of whom synthesize our knowledge of Archaic choral performances and their role in gender identity.
74. Calame (2001) 26–30.
75. Plato, *Laws* 664cd, tr. Bury (1967) 127–9. See also Stehle (1997) 27.
76. See Stehle (1997) 26–7, who follows Fairbanks on the responsiveness included in the paian.
77. Plato, *Laws* 665d, tr. Bury (1967) 131.

78. Euripides *Heracleidae* 777–783, tr. R. Gladstone in Grene and Lattimore (1955) 146.
79. Calame (2001) 78 and 130–1; see also Stehle (1997) 59–60.
80. Sappho 44.24–34, tr. Lombardo (2002) no. 24. My thanks to Pamela Gordon for comments on this passage. See also Calame (1996) 119–20.
81. On this passage and the *ololuge*, see McClure (1999) 52–3.
82. Lardinois (2001) 79, notes that the mythological references of Sappho promote identification of mortal women with goddesses.
83. Stehle (1997) 28. See also Kowalzig (2004) 42–4.
84. Stehle (1997) 25, 29, 136. See also Sourvinou-Inwood (2003) 15–16; Kowalzig (2004) 54.
85. Plato, *Laws* 660a, tr. Bury (1967) 113.
86. Stehle (1997) 27; Calame (2001) 222–3; see also Lonsdale (1993) 174 and Cleary (2003).
87. Plato *Laws* 653bc, tr. Bury (1967) 91; see also 653a–654b and 659d–660a.
88. Plato *Laws* 656a, tr. Bury (1967) 99. On the need for censorship, see 656b–657b.
89. Plato *Laws* 669c, tr. Bury (1967) 145.
90. Calame (2001) 11, and generally, 11–5. See also De Polignac (1995) 62.
91. See generally Lonsdale (1993) 194–203; Clark (1996); Stehle (1997) 30–9; Calame (2001) 1–8 and passim; Pomeroy (2002) 4–9 and 142–6.
92. The mythic past is also combined with the present in some other fragments, such as Tyrtarios and Korinna; see Stehle (1997) 69 and 102. On the narrative within the choral poem, see Seagal (1985) 126, Calame (2001) 15, Clark (1996) 146.
93. Stehle (1997) 33–4; Calame (2001) 4; Hutchinson (2001) 85.
94. Alkman 1.39–57, tr. Campbell (1988) 365.
95. Alkman 1.16–17, tr. Campbell (1988) 363; Stehle (1997) 32. Stehle 26–7 also notes that some forms such as the paian seem to insist on a response from the audience.
96. See Calame (1999) 149, on the function of the tragic chorus that replicates that of the archaic chorus: "the actual spectator, because of his situation in the theatre in relationship to members of the choros, seems above all invited to assume the position of the choral *I/we*; that position is the position of a performer who is engaged in *mimesis* and therefore 'virtual.'"
97. Alkman 1.64–69, tr. Campbell (1988) 367.
98. Alkman 1.84–87, tr. Campbell (1988) 367–9.
99. See Stehle (1997) 12, 86, 127.
100. Calame (2001) 34–5; see also Lonsdale (1993) 120; Sourvinou-Inwood (2003) 146–7.
101. *Hymn to Aphrodite* 119–120; tr. Stehle (1997) 32.
102. Calame (2001) 36.
103. On *pompe* see Pickard-Cambridge (1968) 61–3; Burkert (1985) 99–101; Graf (1996).
104. De Polignac (1995) 83–6; Kavoulaki (1999) 294–8.
105. Sourvinou-Inwood (2003) 118 and 145–7. See also Pickard-Cambridge (1968) 57–67. The position of the Old Agora has been reviewed most recently by Papadapoulos (2003) 280–5, who places it east or southeast of the Acropolis, in contrast to the classical Agora, located to the northwest.
106. On the importance of mobilization as part of performance, see Naerebout (1997) 344 and 347–9.
107. See Naerebout (1997) 348–9 on the importance of "joining," even if this does not result in full-fledged conversion.
108. See Goldhill in Goldhill and Osborne (1999) 5–7. See also Gadamer (1985) 111. Bassi (1998) 16–17 offers the definition of spectatorship as "the representation of attentive or disciplined watching," and that it must take place in a civic venue.

109. Kavoulaki (1999) 311. See also Winkler (1990) 57 and Graf (1996) 57–8.
110. See the discussion of *theoroi* by Rutherford (2004), esp. 67–9 and 89. That these Athenian delegations were primarily male matches the preponderance of male spectators on vases.
111. See Murray (1990) 3–11, Lissarrague (1990) 19–46 and 123–39, and Schmitt-Pantel (1997) 17–52 for a synthesis of the history and structure of the symposion. For the symposion as a communal performance, see Stehle (1997) 213–27; on komasts at the symposion, see Smith (2000). On the history of the *syssiton*, or public symposion, see Schmitt-Pantel (1997) 53–113, and Steiner (2002) for links between public and private dining during the fifth century.
112. See Junker (2002) 12–5 and the discussion of context in ch. 2.3.
113. See the discussion of Morris (2000) and Dougherty and Kurke (2003) on this use of the symposion for the "middling culture." On potential subversion, see Stehle (1997) 224–7. The relationship of aristocratic symposia to the "middling culture" is usually seen as one of exclusion and rejection on the part of the elite, especially in terms of practices like pederasty. However, the focus on heroic themes or athletic excellence observed by spectators would serve to confirm the ideals of the elite as well as the polis, and an artistocrat could imagine himself as the object of the envious gaze of the non-elite as he identified with the heroic ideal represented on the cup. I would argue that as a ritual, however, the symposion would still reflect a surface acquiescence to the social order, even if it were highly critical of the non-elite.
114. New York, Metropolitan Museum of Art, 25.78.33. *ABV* 70.3; Beazley Archive 300634. CVA United States 11, New York, Metropolitan Museum of Art, 2 (Cambridge, MA, 1953), 2–3 and pl. 3a (G. M. A. Richter). See also Ellinghaus (1997) fig. 14.
115. On the V-shape of choral representations as a convention for the circular arrangement of the chorus, see Crowhurst (1963) 292–3. On the spatial arrangement of the chorus, see ch. 4.3 in this book.
116. See Crowhurst (1963) 268–74, who discourages the idea of singing being represented in pictures of the choruses. However, because choruses sing as well as dance, one should understand singing as being semiotically included within the collective sign of a chorus. On the representation of a chorus singing, see the arguments of Ferrari (1987) for the seventh-century Menelaos stand inscription as representing the words of the Doric choral song, as opposed to a label identifying the figure, and of Ferrari (1995) 224–5, suggesting that the inscription HERAKLEOUS KORE are the first words of a ritual song sung at the Panathenaia. Even Achilles and Aias on Exekias's famous amphora in the Vatican have speech words coming from their lips, but keep their mouths closed (Vatican 344, *ABV* 144.7, and Beazley Archive 310395 with images; see Boardman (1974) fig. 100).
117. Winkler (1990) 50 notes the later placement of the *koryphaios* in the middle of the ranks of fifth-century tragic choruses.
118. The Homeric *Hymn to Aphrodite* mentioned in section 4.2 explicitly states that the spectators encircled the performing maidens. Later in dithyrambic performances of the City Dionysia, the audience would be arranged in the theater as wedges by tribe, with prominent citizens in the front, lower seats; see Winkler (1990) 39. Perhaps some type of arrangement by Solonian social/economic class preceded this, which must date to after the Kleisthenic reforms of 508/7.
119. Boardman (1972) 60–6.
120. Boardman (1978) 17–24.
121. Williams (1980) 144, n. 55.
122. See the comments of Whitley (2001) 257–8.
123. Karlsruhe, Badisches Landesmuseum B2423. *ABV* 100.65; *Add*[2] 27; Beazley Archive 310064. CVA Germany, 7, Karlsruhe, 1 (Munich, 1951) 15 and pl. 5.5 & 6.3 (G. Hafner).

Maul-Mandelartz (1990) no. A17; Kluiver (1996) 8, no. 152. On the idea that spectators to a heroic scene represent a dithyrambic chorus, see Ghiron-Bistagne (1976) 283–6.

124. A similar gesture is found on a breastplate found at Olympia showing a woman holding up the back of her hand behind Apollo playing a lyre; see Neumann (1965) 42–3 and Abb. 19. The gesture would seem closest to L31B4 in McNiven (1982) 80–2 and pl. 7a in terms of arm position. It is important to note, however, that the position of the hand in figure 22 suggests that the palm is up but facing toward the spectator, an arrangement more like McNiven's L11E (p. 70–2 and pl. 6a). The hand can also be held upright with the palm facing to the side, but this gesture seems more conversational in nature.
125. See Stehle (1999) 120 and 158–9; Calame (1997)131. On the crane dance, see Crowhurst (1963) 169.
126. Naples, Museo Archeologico Nazionale 81186 (H2503). *ABV* 305.26; *Add.*[2] 80; Beazley Archive 301506. CVA Italy 20, Naples, Museo Nazionale 1 (Rome, 1950) III.H.e p. 4 and pl. 3.1–2 (A. Adriani). See Böhr (1982) 37, 50, and 78, no. 8, pl. 6.
127. The figure of Athena is decidedly not, however, that of the Panathenaic vases, which several scholars have linked to a sculpture of Athena on the Acropolis. See discussions in Shapiro (1989) 28–9; Ridgway (1992)127–30; Connelly (1993) 101; and Marx (2003).
128. Como, Museo Archeologico D3359 (C.22 in CVA). Beazley Archive 1793 (not in *ABV*). CVA Italy 47, Como, Civico Museo Archeologico 1 (Rome, 1970) III.H p. 1 and pl. 1.1–2 (T. P. Porten Palange).
129. The CVA and Beazley Archive identify these figures as Nereids, but they are not included in Barringer (1995). It would be highly unusual for Nereids to accompany a scene of Herakles and the lion, nor do Nereids carry spears routinely, as does the similarly dressed figure on side A. I prefer to call these figures dancers, companions to the spectator on side A.
130. See Ghiron-Bistagne (1976) 265–96, who sees the types as representing dithyrambic dances; Fantham et al. (1994) 17–8 and fig. 1.1.
131. Paris, Musée du Louvre E850. *ABV* 97.31; *Para.* 37; *Add*[2] 26; Beazley Archive 310031. CVA France 1, Paris, Musée du Louvre 1 (Paris, 1922) III.H.d p. 5 and pl. 5.2 and 7.2 (E. Pottier). See Kluiver (1996) 8, no. 168; Schauenburg (1973) 23–4; and esp. Ghiron-Bistagne (1976) 283–6 for the use of these figures as representing a dithyrambic chorus.
132. Shapiro (1989) 145–147; on Theseus and the Minotaur see LIMC VII.1, 940–1, s.v. Theseus 228–242 (S. Woodford), Brommer (1973) 226–43; Brommer (1982) 35–64.
133. See the summary of the evidence in Shapiro (1989) 48–9, which includes Herodotos 1.64.2, Thucydides 3.104.1, Plutarch, *Theseus* 21.1–2. See also Robertson (1992) 128–33.
134. On the ritualistic place of the komos dancers within the City Dionysia, see most recently Sourvinou-Inwood (2003) 78–9.
135. On Panathenaic music contests, see Shapiro (1992); on athletic contests, see Kyle (1992), both with bibliography. On athletics in general, see Kyle (1987) and Tzachou-Alexandri (1988).
136. Munich, Antikensammlung 1471. *ABV* 137.60; *Para.* 55; *Add*[2] 37; Beazley Archive 310320. CVA Germany 32, Munich, Antikensammlung 7 (Munich, 1970) 50–1 and pl. 346 (E. Kunze-Götte).
137. See also the famous dinos fragment by Sophilos: Athens, National Museum 15499; *ABV* 39.16; *Para.* 18; *Add*[2] 10; Beazley Archive 305075.
138. D. T. Steiner (2001) ch. 4; see discussion earlier in this book in chs. 3.2 and 3.3.
139. See Garland (1985) 21–37; Shapiro (1991); McClure (1999) 40–7.
140. Cambridge, Harvard University, Sackler Museum 60.320. Beazley Archive 13404 (not in *ABV*). CVA United States 4, Baltimore, The Robinson Collection 1 (Cambridge, MA, 1934) 40–1 & pl. 19.2a–b (D. M. Robinson).

141. Svenbro (1993) ch. 1; Osborne (1998) 81; Lissarrague (1999) 360–1.
142. On elegy as both sympotic and public, as well as funerary lament, see Bowie (1986).
143. McClure (1999) 42–4; Alexiou (2002) 102–5.
144. See Shapiro (1991) figs. 1, 5–6, 7–9, and 11; Alexiou (2002) 4–7.
145. See ch. 5.4 and 6.2 for the distribution of spectators by subject.
146. One hundred seventy-three of 742 vases in the CVA census (see ch 2.3). Where a specific archaeological context is known, the lekythoi are mostly from tombs in the Greek world, including Athens, Marathon, Rhitsona, and Taranto. For additional excavated examples not in the CVA, see Moore and Philippides (1986) for the Agora in Athens; Ure (1927) for Rhitsona; and D'Amicis (1994) for Taranto. On black-figure lekythoi, see Haspels (1936). Hannestad (1988) 226 remarks that black-figure lekythoi may also be important in daily life.
147. New Haven, Yale University Art Gallery 1993.46.16. Not in *ABV* or Beazley Archive; not in the CVA census.
148. For examples of relief stelai, see Stewart (1990) figs. 130, 131, 143, 146 and Boardman (1991a) figs. 230, 231, 233, 235, 239.
149. Heidelberg, Universität L55. Attic black-figure lekythos, c. 550. Beazley Archive 3250 (not in *ABV*). See CVA Germany 31, Heidelberg, Universität 4 (Munich, 1970) 55 & pl. 169.2, 5–6 (H. Gropengiesser).
150. Shapiro (1991) fig. 1, 6, 7, 11. See also Alexiou (2002) 6.
151. The J. Paul Getty Museum, Malibu, California 86.AE.135. Beazley Archive 41310 (not in *ABV*). CVA United States 25, Malibu, The J. Paul Getty Museum 2 (Malibu, 1990) 15–6 & pl. 69.1–3 (A. Clark).
152. See Stewart (1990) fig. 146, Boardman (1991) figs. 230, 231, 234, 235.
153. For the Athena Gigantomachy pediment see Shapiro (1989) 38–9 and pl. 4d–e; Stewart (1990) 129–30 and figs. 205–7; Boardman (1991a) 155 and fig. 199.
154. See Winkler (1990), esp. 28 and 33.
155. Translation from Stehle (1997) 119.
156. On such a flattering self-image, see Bazant (1985) 58–61.
157. For a review of these changes, see Manville (1990) 124–56 and Manville (1994) 25–6.
158. Manville (1990) 144 and 162. Manville (1994) 27 states this another way, with citizenship as an "ideology emerging from people's everyday social, economic, and political experience."
159. Frost (1994) 51.
160. Manville (1990) 149.
161. Brijder (1984).
162. Plutarch, *Sol.* 18.5, tr. (Perrin 1967) 453.

CHAPTER 5: MEN AND YOUTHS: GENDER AND SOCIAL IDENTITY

1. Neumann (1965).
2. Boegehold (1999).
3. McNiven (1982). Another classification scheme was developed by Salomé (1980) 50–52, but without the implementation in McNiven's study.
4. McNiven (2000).
5. Boston, Museum of Fine Arts 1970.8. *ABV* 140.2; *Add.*[2] 38; Beazley Archive 310353. CVA United States 14, Boston, Museum of Fine Arts 1 (Boston, 1973) 4–5 and pl. 6.2 (H. Hoffmann). See Scheibler (1987) 83.
6. Similar to McNiven's types L31B9 and R31B9; see McNiven (1982) 82–4 and 125–7.

7. M.1c is found on Munich 2420, a red-figure hydria attributed to the Pezzino Group; *ARV*[2] 32.3; *Add.*[2] 157; Beazley Archive 200172 (with illustration); see CVA Germany 20, Munich, Antikensammlung 5 (Munich, 1961) 14–5 and pl. 218.3 (R. Lullies).
8. St. Louis, Washington University WU 3272. *ABV* 52.17; *Para.* 23; *Add.*[2] 13; Beazley Archive 300394 (the Beazley publications reference the inventory number as 673). Moon and Berge (1979) 42–3, no. 26 with previous bibliography; Brijder (1983) 240, no. 48. This vase is not in the CVA census.
9. Aristotle, *Rhetoric* 1361a2–4, tr. Freese (1982) 51. See Ferrari (2002) 59–60 and 87–8ff for a discussion of this passage.
10. See D. T. Steiner (2001) 229–32.
11. Ferrari (2002) 113.
12. Copenhagen, National Museum 6585. *ABV* 115.5; Beazley Archive 310238. CVA Denmark 3, Copenhagen, National Museum 3 (Copenhagen, n.d.) 94 and pl. 113.4a–b (C. Blinkenberg and K. Friis Johansen).
13. Generally similar to McNiven (1982) 139–43, type T32B4W.
14. By the Affecter; see Kassel, Staatliche Museen, Antikensammlung T679: *Para.* 111.25bis, *Add.*[2] 61, Beazley Archive 340429 (with pictures); Boston, Museum of Fine Arts 99.516: *ABV* 239.11, *Para.* 110. 61, *Add.*[2] 61, Beazley Archive 301299. The third example is a Protocorinthian pointed aryballos, Louvre CA617; see CVA France 12, Musée du Louvre 8, pl. III.C.a.14.3. The gesture is similar to McNiven (1982) 72–4, type L21B9 and 115–7, type R21B9.
15. See references in note 123 of ch. 4. The short stick seen here was considered as a minor prop, being much smaller than a spear or long staff and not integral to the posture of the figure as in category M.5 or Y.5 (it is also shorter than these).
16. M.3a corresponds most closely to McNiven (1982) 84–5, type L32B9 and 127–8, type R32B9; M.3b corresponds to McNiven (1982) 80–2, type L31B4 & 123–5, type R31B4; M.3c to McNiven (1982) 78–80, type L31B3 and 121–3, type R31B3; see McNiven (1982) 78–82, 84–5, 121–5, 127–8. For M.3b, in most cases, the palm of the hand is out or upward, but in a few cases the thumb is below and the palm is facing downward.
17. Trieste S406 (*Para.* 134.21.6; *Add.*[2] 80; Beazley Archive 340561; CVA Italy 43, Trieste 1, pl. III.H.1.2); Los Angeles, Getty 86.AE.70 (*Para.* 112.85ter; CVA United States 23, Getty Museum 1, pl. 13.1). The type corresponds to McNiven (1982) 85–7, type L33e and 128–31, type R33e. There may be a degree of alarm also associated with this gesture that is lacking in the others.
18. Boegehold (1999) 15.
19. Munich, Antikensammlung 1385 . *ABV* 310; *Add.*[2] 84; Beazley Archive 301590. CVA Germany 3, Munich, Antikensammlung 1 (Munich, 1939) 17 and pl. 25.1 (R. Lullies). Bohr (1982) 109–10, no. P2 and pl. 164c and 165 (circle of the Princeton Painter).
20. That the figure wears armor would distinguish him as an adult citizen, hence a man. On the gesture, see McNiven (1982) 70–2, type L11E & 113–5, type R11E; Neumann (1965) 18–19 and fig. 7 characterizes this as a pointing gesture implying an acclamation on the part of the figure. See also the discussion of Athena's gesture on the vote over the arms of Achilles on the Douris kylix in Vienna (Kunsthistorisches Museum 3695) at Boegehold (1999) 30–31 and fig. 22. Neumann (1965) 99 interprets this gesture as one of warning, but Boegehold 31 argues convincingly that this is a "case of a public announcement, where long-range visibility was the aim, the sweep and direction of the arm motion carried the message." This, I think, fits the notion of the spectator using this gesture as a choral or group leader.

21. See Shapiro (1991) 635–6, fig. 1, 5, 7, 11.
22. On the effect of using both arms to express a stronger emotional reaction, see the discussion of astonishment by Neumann (1965) 97–102.
23. See Boston, Museum of Fine Arts 98.918: *ABV* 306.41; *Para.* 132, *Add.*[2] 81; Beazley Archive 301521; CVA United States 14, Boston, Museum of Fine Arts 1, pl. 4.1. The gesture is more widespread outside of spectators; see McNiven (1982) 72–4, type L21B9 and 115–7, type R21B9; Neumann (1965) 41–8 , fig. 19–21.
24. Munich, Antikensammlung 1471. *ABV* 137.60; *Para.* 55; *Add.*[2] 37; Beazley Archive 310320. CVA Germany 32, Munich, Antikensammlung 7 (Munich, 1970) 50–1 and pl. 346–7 (E. Kunze-Götte). For the gesture, see McNiven (1982) 139–43, gesture T32B4W.
25. See Paris, Louvre F33: *ABV* 141.3, *Para.* 50, *Add.*[2] 38, Beazley Archive 310363 (with picture), CVA France 4, Paris, Musée du Louvre 3, pl. III.H.e.15.7; Geneva, Musée d'Art et d'Histoire 3.1870: Beazley Archive 5659 (not in *ABV*) CVA Switzerland 3, Geneva, Musée d'art et d'histoire 2, pl. 71.9–11. On this gesture, see McNiven (1982) 74–8, type L22E and 117–21, type R22E; Neumann (1965) 10–11; Boegehold (1999) 22 and fig. 13, who illustrates a similar gesture on an Apulian krater in New York (Metropolitan Museum of Art 24.97.104). This has an inscription next to it, making the speaker (a male actor dressed as an old woman) say "I shall provide." The gesture, undoubtedly, has a range of meanings, but it does suggest a strong response on the part of the figure to the action, and we might infer this also for the arm in a more raised position as in type M.4a.
26. See, for example, Heidelberg S1 (*ABV* 51.3; *Add.*[2] 13; Beazley Archive 300378 (with picture); CVA Germany 31, Heidelberg 4, pl. 152.1).
27. London, British Museum B188. Beazley Archive 2932 (with bibliography). CVA Great Britain 4, London, British Museum 3 (London, 1927) III.H.e p. 10 and pl. 45.10 (H. B. Walters).

    On many of the vases with such male spectators, it is difficult to determine whether the figure is a spectator or is, instead, a judge or trainer, who would not be counted as a spectator for this study because they can affect the result of the central action. If the figure holds up a stick or wand in the direction of the player or appears to intervene, he has been excluded as a spectator. This has resulted in the exclusion of many of these figures from the CVA census. In the case of figure 39, the bema provides a separation between performer and listener that places him in the realm of the spectator.
28. For M.5b and M.5c, see the kylix by the Foundry Painter in Berlin (Antikensammlung F2294, *ARV*[2] 400.1; *Para.* 370; *Add.*[2] 230; Beazley Archive 204340; CVA Germany 21, Berlin, Antikensammlung 2, pl. 72.2). M.5b corresponds to McNiven (1982) 85–7, type L33E and 128–31, type R33E; M.5c corresponds to McNiven (1982) 97–100, type M10wrL and M10wrR.
29. See McNiven (1982) 64–5, type H30; Neumann (1965) 145–8, although his examples feature the bent head supported by the hand or arm.
30. Kansas City, Nelson-Atkins Museum 52.22. *ABV* 219.23; *Para.* 104.23; *Add.*[2] 58; Beazley Archive 302772. Moon and Berge (1979) 64–5, no. 38. This vase is not in the CVA census.
31. Pictures in which the spectator holds a forked stick, such as trainers frequently use, have been excluded, even if they make no gesture toward the nucleus. In such cases, the special form of stick is a sign of the holder's involvement with the acting figures, making them interested or invested spectators.
32. Munich, Antikensammlung 1369. *ABV* 126.53; *Add.*[2] 34; Beazley Archive 300949. CVA Germany 3, Munich, Antikensammlung 1 (Munich, 1939) 9–10 and pl. 6.1, 7.3 (B. Lullies).
33. Ceccarelli (1998) 45–52 places the beginning of the iconographic tradition for the pyrrhic dance proper in the last quarter of the sixth century, with most examples dating from

red-figure work of the fifth century. The crouching position of the figure and its 180° twist in direction are similar to later black-figure representations of pyrrhic dancers, especially by the Athena Painter (see her plate III), but the Munich amphora lacks either an aulist or other dancers that are part of the group performance of the pyrrhic. The nucleus here should be seen as signifying a performance or demonstration by a warrior within a civic setting, whether a pyrrhic dance itself or some other type of display that was perhaps not competitive. On weapons dances see also Poursat (1968), Wheeler (1982) 229–32, Brommer (1989).

34. See, for example, the tondo of the kylix attributed to the Veii Painter in Bologna, Pell. 384; *ARV*[2] 903.57, *Add.*[2] 303, Beazley Archive 211982. On the mantle figure and *aidos*, see Ferrari (1990).
35. See Ferrari (2002) 54 and 80 on the mantle as a shield for *aidos*. On the behavior expected of an eromenos who might be dressed like this, see ch. 3.2.
36. New York, Metropolitan Museum of Art 06.1021.159. *ABV* 199.1, 689; *Para.* 80; Beazley Archive 302573. CVA United States 11, New York, Metropolitan Museum of Art 2 (Cambridge, MA, 1953) 13–4 and pl. 23 (G. M. A. Richter).
37. London, British Museum B339. *ABV* 264.1; Beazley Archive 302301. CVA Great Britain 8, London, British Museum 6 (London, 1931) III.H.e p. 10 and pl. 92.3, 95.1 (H. B. Walters).
38. On the chlamys as a shield, see Barringer (2001) 22–6. Y.2c corresponds generally to McNiven (1982) 139–43, type T32B4W.
39. See McNiven (1982) 72–4, type L21B9 and 115–7, type R21B9.
40. See Winkler (1990) 55, discussing the testimony of Athenaios, on the ephebes (18–20 year olds) who would dance the *pyrrhikhe* in partial armor, and the 16–18 year olds who danced the *gymnopaidike* that imitated wrestling. The presence of a spear suggests a weapon dance or performance, but not the fully equipped or trained *pyrrhikhe*. See also Barringer (2001) 56–7.
41. Mainz, Universität 75. *Para.* 85.34; Beazley Archive 350851. CVA Germany 15, Mainz, Universität 1 (Munich, 1959) 41–2 and pl. 40.1 (R. Hampe & E. Simon). See also Bothmer (1957) 47, no. 100; Junker, ed. (1999) 43–6.
42. Tübingen, Antikensammlung des Archäologischen Instituts der Universität S705. Beazley Archive 6060 (not in *ABV*). CVA Germany 47, Tübingen, Antikensammlung des Archäologischen Instituts der Universität 3 (Munich, 1980) 14 and pl. 6.3 (J. Burow).
43. Paris, Musée du Louvre F99. *ABV* 228; *Para.* 107; *Add.*[2] 59; Beazley Archive 303477. CVA France 5, Paris, Musée du Louvre 4 (Paris, n.d.) III.H.e p. 18–9 and pl. 32.6 (E. Pottier).
44. Karlsruhe, Badisches Landesmuseum B3048. *ABV* 626.1; Beazley Archive 306378. CVA Germany 7, Karlsruhe, Badisches Landesmuseum 1 (Munich, 1951) 20–1 and pl. 11.6–7 (G. Hafner).
45. See Chiusi, Museo Archeologico Nazionale 1840; *ARV*[2] 904.60, *Add.*[2] 303, Beazley Archive 211985 (with picture); CVA Italy 60, Chiusi, Museo Archeologico Nazionale 2, pl. 26.
46. Berlin, Antikensammlung F1905. *ABV* 332.23; *Para.* 146; *Add.*[2] 90; Beazley Archive 301801. CVA Germany 61, Berlin, Antikensammlung 7 (Munich, 1991) 28–9 and pl. 22.1 (H. Mommsen). See also Shapiro (1989) pl. 23. The youth on the right does have a scabbard, but no spear.
47. McNiven (1982) 70–4. Y.4a = McNiven (1982) 70–2, type L11E and 113–5, type R11E; Y.4b = McNiven (1982) 72–4, type L21B9 and 115–7, type R21B9.
48. Munich, Antikensammlung 1471. For bibliography see above n. 24. Y.4c = McNiven (1982) 139–43, type T32B4W.
49. Y.4d = McNiven (1982) 75–8, type L22E and R22E.

50. Pointing, though, usually involves the extension of only one or two fingers and not the full hand; see Neumann (1965) 17–22 and Boegehold (1999) 22–3. On hunting, see Barringer (2001) 24, fig. 11.
51. See, for example, Hannover, Kestner Museum 1936.107; Beazley Archive 1854 (with picture). See CVA Germany 34, Hannover, Kestner Museum 1, pl. 7.1.
52. See New York, Metropolitan Museum of Art 56.171.17; *ABV* 239.8, *Para.* 110, *Add.*[2] 60, Beazley Archive 301296 (with picture). See CVA United States 16, New York, Metropolitan Museum of Art 4, pl. 10.2–3. On the gesture, see McNiven (1982) 134–5, type T11EY.
53. Boston, Museum of Fine Arts 67.861. *Para.* 107; *Add.*[2] 56; Beazley Archive 340249. CVA United States 19, Boston, Museum of Fine Arts 2 (Boston, 1978) 48 and pl. 106.2–3 (M. True). On the gesture, see McNiven (1982) 136 T22EW.
54. Lonsdale (1993) 137–8; Winkler (1990) 55–6. On pyrrhic and weapons dances see Poursat (1968), Wheeler (1982) 229–32, Brommer (1989), Ceccarelli (1998).
55. Lonsdale (1993) 139.
56. Lonsdale (1993) 141.
57. These combined totals eliminate duplications from tables 5.5 and 5.11.
58. Berlin, Antikensammlung F1873. *ABV* 407; *Add.*[2] 106; Beazley Archive 303074. CVA Germany 45, Berlin, Antikensammlung 5 (Munich, 1980) 50–1 and pl. 34.4, 38 (H. Mommsen).
59. London, British Museum E254. *ARV2* 31.3; Beazley Archive 200166. CVA Great Britain 4, London, British Museum 3 (London, 1927) III.I.c p. 3 and pl. 2.2b (H. B. Walters). For type Y.5b, see for example, Cleveland, Museum of Art 1976.89: *ARV*[2] 7.7 and 38.8; *Para.* 321; *Add.*[2] 151, Beazley Archive 200027 (with pictures), CVA United States 35, Cleveland Museum of Art 2, pl. 76.
60. For Y.4d, see Amsterdam, Allard Pierson Museum 8211; *ARV*[2] 959.4, Beazley Archive 212999; CVA Netherlands 6, Amsterdam, Allard Pierson Museum 1, pl. 55. For Y.4e, see New York, Metropolitan Museum of Art 56.171.17: *ABV* 239.8, *Para.* 110, *Add.*[2] 60, Beazley Archive 301296 (with pictures), CVA United States 16, New York, Metropolitan Museum of Art 4, pl. 10.2–3.
61. Baltimore, Walters Art Gallery 48.67. *ARV*[2] 1098.29; Beazley Archive 216093. CVA United States 28, Baltimore, Walters Art Gallery 1, pl. 17 (J. H. Oakley). On this particular gesture, see McNiven (1982) 92–3, type M10hr.
62. Munich, Antikensammlung 1411. *ABV* 311.2; *Add.*[2] 84; Beazley Archive 301594. CVA Germany 3, Munich, Antikensammlung 1 (Munich, 1939) 28–9 and pl. 41.3, 43.3 (R. Lullies). See Bohr (1982)17 and pl. 183.
63. Winkler (1990) 22 notes the Kleisthenic seating by tribes in wedges, with the prominent citizens in front, and the reserved seating for the ephebes in the Dionysiac festival (p. 37–8). He also ascribes (p. 31–3) the classical period practices to developments from the earlier archaic period, so that the recognition of the ephebes and their importance for the city would be a feature, in some form, of earlier Dionysiac rituals. See also Goldhill (1990)105–6; Barringer (2001) 53–4.
64. For Herakles and the lion, see LIMC V.1, 16–27 and 31–3, s.v. Heracles 1762–1914 (J. Boardman); Brommer (1973) 109–43; Korte-Konte (1979) 186–92; Brommer (1986) 7–11; Uhlenbrock (1986); A. Steiner (2004) 437–44.
65. See Korte-Konte (1979) 186–92 for the inclusion of these figures as spectators. See also the discussion for figure 4.
66. On Herakles and Nessos, see LIMC VI.1, 838–47, s.v. Nessos (F. Díez de Velasco). See also Fittschen (1970), Schauenburg (1973), Korte-Konte (1979) 195–6, Brommer (1984b) 48–53, Stansbury-O'Donnell (1999) 93–6.

67. Copenhagen, National Museum 5180. *ABV* 69.5, *Add.*[2] 18; Beazley Archive 300624. CVA Denmark 3, Copenhagen, National Museum 3 (Copenhagen, n.d.) 94 and pl. 114.1a (C. Blinkenberg & K. Friis Johansen). See also LIMC VI.1, 838–47, s.v. Nessos 40.
68. On the social function of pictures of warriors, see Bazant (1981) 29 and Bérard (1989) 46–51. Snodgrass (1980b) 52; idem (1987) 153 used the term "generalized heroic" for such scenes. On the relationship of generic and mythological narrative, see Stansbury-O'Donnell (1999) 44–51. Some of these scenes, especially those in which two women are spectators, have been likened to the duel of Achilles and Memnon watched by their mothers, but in the pictures included in the CVA census, there is no effort to distinguish either the warriors or the spectators as being mythological.
69. On Amazons, see LIMC I.1, 586–653, s.v. Amazones 1–482 (P. Devambez), Bothmer (1957), duBois (1982), Tyrrel (1984), Hardwick (1990), Blok (1995), Stewart (1997) 118–20. Preliminary results of this study were presented at the Annual Meeting of the Archaeological Institute of America in San Francisco on January 3, 2004.
70. Four of the 40 vases with youths. See, for example, Toronto, Royal Ontario Museum 919.5.145 (*ABV* 428.1; *Add.*[2] 110; Beazley Archive 303280; CVA Canada 1, Toronto, Royal Ontario Museum 1 (Oxford, 1981) 20 and pl. 26.6–7 (J. W. Hayes)).
71. London, British Museum B387. Beazley Archive 13234; CVA Great Britain 2, British Museum 2, pl. III.H.e.16.1.
72. On Nike, see LIMC VI.1, 850–9, s.v. Nike 1–93 (A. Moustaka), esp. Nike 72–86; Isler-Kerényi (1969), esp. 18–47. On the sphinx, see LIMC VIII.1, 1149–65, s.v. Sphinx 1–234 (N. Kourou), esp. Sphinx 193–205. On winged figures and death see Vermeule (1979) 145–77. On spectators and sirens, see Hofstetter (1990) 104–5.
73. On the rider theme, see Vedder (1990); Mommsen (2002). The depictions of riders in vase painting also become involved in the issue of the existence of an Athenian cavalry in the Archaic period; on this question, see Bugh (1988) with review of earlier literature. On scenes of "life," see generally Bazant (1981) 13–22 and (1985) 7–33.
74. See Scheibler (1987) 83–5.
75. Vedder (1990) 128.
76. On the footrace see Kyle (1987) 178–80; Tzachou-Alexandri (1988) 243–52, see especially nos. 137 and 140; Kyle (1992) 82–3.
77. *Iliad* 23.766–7, tr. Lattimore (1951) 470. See *Iliad* 23.448–97 for the argument of the lesser Aias and Idomeneus, who had to be calmed by Achilles himself in their dispute over who was leading in the chariot race. Certainly the boisterous spectators on the dinos by Sophilos on the same subject match this quality of animation; Athens, National Museum 15499 (*ABV* 39.16; *Para.* 18; *Add.*[2] 10; Beazley Archive 305075). On laughter, see *Il.* 23.784 and 840; on thundering approval see *Il.* 23.869; on gazing with wonder, see *Iliad* 23.881.
78. On reactions to athletes, see D. T. Steiner (2001) 222–9.
79. On wrestling and boxing, see Kyle (1987) 183–4; Poliakoff (1987) 23–53 and 68–88;Tzachou-Alexandri (1988) 266, no. 158, 270–7, nos. 162–6, 282–8, no. 169–77 (see especially no. 158, 170, 172); Pfisterer-Haas (1990); Kyle (1992) 86–8.
80. On musical activity during this period, see Shapiro (1989) 41–3, Hamdorf (1990), Shapiro (1992), West (1992) 14–28 and 336–40, Anderson (1994) 113–44 , Landels (1999) 1–23, Bundrick (forthcoming 2005).
81. See Bundrick (forthcoming 2005) ch. 3.
82. See Shapiro (1992) 61–70. Shapiro shows that music performances associated with the Panathenaic festival begin shortly after the reorganization of 566. The only specific change during this period is the change in the rhapsode competition under Hippias, in which the accuracy of the recital was measured against a texts of the *Iliad* and *Odyssey*; see

Shapiro 72–5. The bubble of popularity in the last quarter of the sixth century for formal music concerts or competitions may reflect some change in the festival, or may simply reflect a passing fad of interest for vase-painting. Without more precise documentation, it is impossible to know whether there was some stimulus for the increased incidence of the subject during a short period.

83. Bundrick (forthcoming 2005) ch. 1 links the appearance of music school scenes generally to the role of mousike in the schools that emerged in Athens during the early fifth century. The symposion concerts also seem to reflect a change that she detects in the shift to the use of professional musicians in the second half of the fifth century, replacing the idea of the symposiast-musician earlier. See also Bundrick ch. 3.
84. On the gesture, McNiven (1982) 64–5, type H30.
85. See Amsterdam, Allard Pierson Museum 13.3-8: Beazley Archive 21183 (not in *ABV*); CVA Netherlands 8, Amsterdam, Allard Pierson Museum 2, pl. 69.1–2, 75.3.
86. See McNiven (1982) 64, type H30.
87. On the changes in musicianship, see Bundrick (forthcoming).
88. On erotic scenes generally see Keuls (1985) 274–99, Schnapp (1989) 71–87, Reinsberg (1989), Hoesch (1990), Dierichs (1993), Stewart (1997) 156–71, with extensive bibliography on 255–8; Barringer (2001) 70–124; Lewis (2002) 116–28.
89. New Haven, Yale University Art Gallery 1913.122. Beazley Archive 9439 (not in *ABV*). Matheson Burke and Pollitt (1975) no. 30; Baur (1922) 81–3, no. 122; Wescoat (1986) 26–7, no. 4. This vase is not in the CVA census.
90. On the behavior of *erastes* and *eromenos* see Dover (1989) 91–100; Reinsberg (1989)163–215 Barringer (2001) 70–124.
91. Frontisi-Ducroux (1996) 90.
92. It is curious, however, that one of the 12 vases is a tripod-pyxis (Getty 86.AE.142) from about the same date as the Yale pyxis. If one associates the pyxis with a female user, then the use of male spectators for a homoerotic courtship is an odd choice of subject. Perhaps one should consider that the users of these early pyxides were not so gender specific as later red-figure examples that feature wedding and related imagery. See Lewis (2002) 133–4.
93. Leipzig T3359: Beazley Archive 3385; CVA Germany (East) 2, Leipzig 1, pl. 31.1–2.
94. Aspects of the voyeuristic element here have been discussed by Frontisi-Ducroux (1996) 89–95. On pederasty in archaic Athens, see also Percy (1996) 171–82.

CHAPTER 6: WOMEN AS SPECTATORS: GENDER AND SOCIAL IDENTITY

1. See Sourvinou-Inwood (1988) 33–9 on the age distinctions for the Artemis imagery. Such distinctions belong mostly to the fifth century and the lack of nudity and heavy clothing among female spectators makes distinctions like the breasts more difficult for the archaic period.
2. Ferrari (2003).
3. On stages of women's lives, see Fantham et al. (1994) 12–39, Reeder (1995) 20–6.
4. Faraone (2003), esp. 62–3.
5. Berlin, Antikensammlung F3988. Attic black-figure tripod pyxis, c. 550. Beazley Archive 360. CVA Germany 61, Berlin, Antikensammlung 7 (Munich, 1991) 54–6 and pl. 42 (H. Mommsen). See Bothmer (1957) 47f, later discussion.
6. On the gesture, see McNiven (1982) 103–6, type N10. On the interpretation of the *anakalypsis*, see Oakley and Sinos (1993) 25–6 and 30, Bérard et al. (1989) 97–103; Reeder (1995) 127; Ferrari (2002) 186; Ferrari (2003) 32–5.

7. On wedding imagery generally, see Oakley and Sinos (1993) 22–38, and esp. 28–30 on black-figure processions.
8. New York, Metropolitan Museum of Art 59.64. *Para.* 31; *Add.*[2] 23; Beazley Archive 350203. CVA United States 16, New York, Metropolitan Museum of Art 4 (New York, 1976) 1–2 and pl. 2b (M. B. Moore and D. von Bothmer). See Isler (1970) 134, no. 67 et passim. On the iconography of Acheloös, see LIMC I.1, 12–36, s.v. Acheloos (H. P. Isler), esp. Acheloos 213–218; Isler (1970).
9. Moore and von Bothmer, ibid., 1. Isler (1970) 14–5 names the figures as Deianeira, Oineus, and Deianeira's mother. The Beazley Archive describes both figures as onlookers, a position that I also take. On the Athena-like quality of the spectator, see the discussion of category W.2.
10. See the comments in ch. 5.3 for figures Y.2e and Y.3d being derived from the kouros statue, rather than public behavior.
11. On the acquiescence or assent in the *anakalypsis*, see Patterson (1991) 55, Oakley and Sinos (1993) 30.
12. Copenhagen, National Museum 3672. *ABV* 307.58; *Add.*[2] 82; Beazley Archive 301538. CVA Denmark 3, Copenhagen, National Museum 3 (Copenhagen, n.d.) 84 and pl. 105.1a–b (C. Blinkenberg & K. Friis Johansen); Bohr (1982) 18, 32, 92, no. 90 and pl. 88. On the Gigantomachy, see LIMC IV.1, 191–270, s.v. Gigantes (F. Vian), esp. pp. 226–7 and Gigantes 268–288.
13. Berlin, Antikensammlung F3988. For bibliography, see figure 60. On the death of Astyanax see LIMC II.1, 929–37, s.v. Astyanax I (O. Touchefeu), esp. Astyanax I 7–14. Astyanax I 932 notes the female figure as "Andromache?", but the lack of a spear for the figure in later painting, where the identity of Andromache is more certain, makes this identification of the spectator here very uncertain.
14. Como, Museo Archeologico Civico D3359; see references in note 128 of ch. 4. The other mimetic W.2b is found on a hydria by the Antimenes Painter: Paris, Louvre CP10676; see Beazley Archive 12191, CVA France 18, Paris, Musée du Louvre 11, pl. III.H.e 146.6.
15. The second vase is an amphora in Leiden (PC 53): see *ABV* 101.87; *Add.*[2] 27, Beazley Archive 310086 (with picture); CVA Netherlands 3, Leiden 1, pl. 3.
16. On Athena's roles in the Trojan War, see LIMC I.1, 1007–9, s.v. Athena B.3.h 551–564.
17. Boston, Museum of Fine Arts 89.256. *Para.* 115, no. 4bis; *Add.*[2] 67; Beazley Archive 340448. CVA United States 14, Boston, Museum of Fine Arts 1 (Boston, 1973) 7 and pl. 10.1 (H. Hoffmann).
18. On the gesture, see McNiven (1982) 84–5, type L32B9 and 127–8, type R32B9.
19. The gesture is related to two in McNiven's list; see McNiven (1982) 143–4, type T32B9Y and 144–5, type T33EY.
20. Neumann (1965) 97–105. See also Houby-Nielsen (1996) 237 on the use of a single hand as a mark of control. Boegehold (1999) 31 notes that Odysseus throws up both of his hands in surprise and joy in seeing the vote granting him the arms of Achilles, but this does convey the sense of powerlessness, that the decision is in the hand of others.
21. On the lack of control, see McNiven (2000) 72–3.
22. Oxford, Ashmolean Museum 1965.119. *ABV* 261.35; *Para.* 115; *Add.*[2] 68; Beazley Archive 302267. CVA Great Britain 14, Oxford, Ashmolean Museum 3 (Oxford, 1975) 23–4 and pl. 38.3 (J. Boardman).
23. See McNiven (1982) 80–2, type L31B4 and 123–5, type R31B4.
24. This is a combination of two gestures in McNiven: R31B3 (vertical hand) and L32B9 (horizontal arm); see McNiven (1982) 84–5 and 121–3. The hand to chin or mouth is associated with perplexity and a reaction to death; see Neumann (1965) 109–12.

25. Kassel, Staatliche Museen, Antikensammlung T385. *ABV* 105.2; *Para.* 35; *Add.*[2] 28; Beazley Archive 310136. CVA Germany 35, Kassel, Antikensammlung der Staatlichen Kunstsammlungen 1 (Munich, 1972) 40–1 and pl. 16, 18.1 (R. Lullies). Kluiver (1996) 35 lists the vase as questionably Tyrrhenian.
26. See McNiven (1982) 78–80, type L31B3.
27. This is closest to McNiven (1982) 139, type T31B9Y, for which he lists only five examples. However, it is important to note that the forearms are held at different angles in this type.
28. Munich, Antikensammlung 1514. *ABV* 272.90; *Add.*[2] 71; Beazley Archive 320101. CVA Germany 37, Munich, Antikensammlung 8 (Munich, 1973) 40–1 and pl. 387.2 (E. Kunze-Götte). See Beazley (1927) 74; Burow (1989) no. 5; Vierneisel and Kaeser (1990) 378.
29. See McNiven (1982) 74 , type L22E under 1b, and 83, type L31B9 under 1d.
30. Munich, Antikensammlung 1523. *ABV* 262.1; *Add.*[2] 68; Beazley Archive 302284. CVA Germany 37, Munich, Antikensammlung 8 (Munich, 1973) 14–5 and pl. 366.1 (E. Kunze-Götte).
31. This is a combination of McNiven (1982) 78–80, type L31B3 (or R31B3) and 85–7, type L33E (or R33E).
32. See McNiven (1982) 100–1, type M30hr and 138, type T31B4W. In general on the raising of arms, see McNiven (2000) 80–1 and Neumann (1965) 97–105, where he links these gesticulations to emotions of astonishment, fright, and shock.
33. London, British Museum B333. *ABV* 676, 7, 8; Beazley Archive 306483. CVA Great Britain 8, London, British Museum 6 (London, 1931) III.H.e p. 9 and pl. 91.3 (H. B. Walters).
34. On Herakles and Kyknos, see LIMC VII.1, 970–90, s.v. Kyknos I (A. Cambitoglou and S. A. Paspalas); see also Vian (1945) and Shapiro (1984).
35. On this gesture, see McNiven (1982) 70–2, type L11E and 113–5, type R11E.
36. See McNiven (1982) 134, type T11EW or 136, type T22EW.
37. See Toledo, Museum of Art 63.27, Attic black-figure skyphos attributed to the Theseus Painter; *Para.* 257; *Add.*[2] 130; Beazley Archive 351546. CVA United States 17, Toledo, Museum of Art 1 (Toledo, 1976) 22–3 and pl. 32 (C. G. Boulter & K. T. Luckner); Boardman (1974) fig. 245.
38. On the gesture, see McNiven (1982) 92–3, type M10hr. The stretched out hand here is McNiven's L22E. On funerary gestures and practices during the archaic period, see Shapiro (1991) 631–44
39. Los Angeles, County Museum of Art 50.8.1. *ABV* 273.108; *Add.*[2] 71; Beazley Archive 320119. CVA United States 18, Los Angeles, County Museum of Art 1 (Berkeley/Los Angeles, 1977) 9–10 and pl. 7.2 (P. M. Packard and P. A. Clement).
40. See McNiven (1982) 136–7, type T22EY. On pleading, see Neumann (1965) 67–72 and Boegehold (1999) 19.
41. For the daughters of Priam, see for example the amphora once in Berlin by Lydos: Berlin F1685 (*ABV* 109.24; *Add.*[2] 30, Beazley Archive 310170 (with pictures); see Stansbury-O'Donnell (1999) 166–8 and fig. 71.
42. New York, Metropolitan Museum of Art 58.32. *ARV*[2] 2, n. 1; *Para.* 114.10bis; *Add.*[2] 66; Beazley Archive 340445. CVA United States 12, New York, Metropolitan Museum of Art 3 (New York, 1963) 23–4 and pl. 29.2 (D. von Bothmer).
43. Adophseck, Schloss Fasanerie 1. *ABV* 693.3bis; *Para.* 132, *Add.*[2] 79; Beazley Archive 306597. CVA Germany 11, Adolphseck, Schloss Fasanerie 1 (Munich, 1956) 7–8 and pl. 2 (F. Brommer). Bohr (1982) 103, no. U1 and pl. 146 (Circle of the Swing Painter).
44. Cambridge (MA), Harvard University, Arthur M. Sackler Museum 1959.124 (formerly Robinson Collection, no number). *ARV*[2] 438.140; Beazley Archive 205186. CVA United

States 6, Baltimore, The Robinson Collection 2 (Cambridge, MA, 1937) 16–17 and pl. 14.1 (D. M. Robinson).

45. This on a hydria by a pupil of the Niobid Painter, showing a satyr playing the aulos with maenads: Oxford (MS), University of Mississippi, University Museums 1977.3.88 (formerly in the Robinson Collection). *ARV*[2] 611.35; Beazley Archive 207082. See CVA United States 6, Baltimore, The Robinson Collection 2, pl. 36, and Robinson (1932) 6–7 and pl. XVI. The woman is wrapped fully and dressed in a mantle, so that dress, position, and action all distinguish her from the maenads in the picture, who belong to the nucleus of the picture.
46. London, British Museum B319. *Para.* 124; *Add.*[2] 73; Beazley Archive 340507. CVA Great Britain 8, London, British Museum 6 (London, 1931) III.H.e p. 6 and pl. 83.4 (H. B. Walters).
47. See Pingiatoglou (1994). One of the vases in the Villa Giulia illustrated by Pingiatoglou includes a musician, suggesting performance in association with the activities of seated women.
48. San Antonio, Kimball Art Museum 86.134.42. Beazley Archive 19192. See Shapiro et al. (1995) 108–10, no. 53. This work is not in the CVA census.
49. Numbers: W.4a = four; W.4b = three; W.4d = one; W.4g = five; W.4w = one (no examples of W.4c, W.4e, W.4f).
50. Numbers: W.3b = two; W.3c = two; W.3d = one; W.3e = one; W.3g = three. For very active spectators: W.4b = one; W.4c = one; W.4d = one; W.4g = one; W.4w = two.
51. Numbers for category W.3: W.3a = six (8.8%); W.3b = six (8.8%); W.3c = three (4.4%); W.3d = 16 (23.5%); W.3e = one (1.5%); W.3f = six (8.8%); W.3g = 12 (17.6%). Category W.4: W.4a = nine (13.2%); W.4b = nine (13.2%); W.4c = two (2.9%); W.4d = two (2.9%); W.4e = two (2.9%); W.4f = six (8.8%); W.4g = four (5.9%); W.4w = five (7.4%).
52. Loraux (1998) 21. See Plutarch, *Solon* 21.5–7. On funerary customs generally, see Kurtz and Boardman (1971) 142–61; Garland (1985) 21–37, Shapiro (1991); Houby-Nielsen (1996) 236–9.
53. Plutarch, *Solon* 21.5, tr. (Perrin 1967) 465. See Loraux (1998) 23.
54. Loraux (1998) 10–1.
55. On Amazons, see LIMC I.1, 586–653, s.v. Amazones (P. Devanbez); see also Bothmer (1957), duBois (1982), Tyrrel (1984), Hardwick (1990), Blok (1995), Stewart (1997) 118–20.
56. Three of these nine vases occur in the CVA census. Thus, Amazon vases account for 1.7% of all CVA census vases with women spectators, compared with 1.4 percent (3/219) for men and 3.6% for youths (19/522), showing that the theme has slightly less importance for men and women than for youths, who would seem to be the main target audience for the group.
57. See Hardwick (1990) 15–8; Blok (1995) 164–85.
58. Brussels, Musée Royaux A2128, Attic black-figure lekythos attributed to the Group of Vatican G52; *ABV* 461.28; Beazley Archive 330302. See CVA Belgium 2, Brussels, Musée Royaux 2, pl. 21.20; Haspels (1936) pl. 17.2.
59. See ch. 3.2; Steiner (2001) ch. 4.
60. Los Angeles, Getty Museum 86.AE.60. Beazley Archive 10143. CVA United States 23, Malibu, The J. Paul Getty Museum 1 (Malibu, 1988) 1–3 and pl. 2.2 (A. J. Clark), with bibliography.
61. Steiner (1998) 140–3.
62. Zurich, University 2472. Attic black-figure lekythos attributed to the Hähne Class; Beazley Archive 1473. See CVA Switzerland 2, Zurich 1, pl. 16.8–10. See also Reinholdt (1994) 171–2.

63. Both vases were in the Robinson Collection. Oxford (MS), University of Mississippi, University Museums 1977.3.88; see citation in n. 41. Cambridge (MA), Harvard University, Arthur M. Sackler Museum 1959.124; see n. 44.
64. Vidal-Naquet (1986) 206. See also Stewart (1997) 10.
65. For a discussion of these two poets' positions on women, see Pomeroy (1975) 48–52, Fantham et al. (1994) 39–44.
66. For discussions of the continuum of gender and social hierarchy, see Stewart (1997) 7–12; Ferrari (2002) 138–61. On transgression of pederastic relationships in vase-painting, see Sutton (2000).
67. On bride price and dowry, see Blundell (1995) 68–9.
68. On Solon and the status of women, see Pomeroy (1975) 57–60 et passim, Fantham et al. (1994) 74–5, Blundell (1995) 75.
69. Plutarch, *Solon* 21.3, tr. Perrin (1967) 463.
70. Plutarch, *Solon* 23.2, tr. Perrin (1967) 467. On the issue of slavery, see *Solon* 13.2–3.
71. Plutarch, *Solon* 21.4, tr. Perrin (1967) 463.
72. Pomeroy (1975) 57. See also Fantham et al. (1994) 74–5, Blundell (1995) 75, and Pomeroy (1995).
73. Aristotle, *Rhetoric* 1361a1–8, tr. Freese (1982) 51. On an alternative philosophical model of Pythagorean female virtue, see Lambropoulou (1995).
74. Ferrari (2002) 88.
75. Ibid., 59, 80, et passim. On *aidos* and women, see Cairns (1993) 120–5.
76. On artist and agenda, see Osborne (1991) and Boardman (1991b).
77. There are some parallels here between the appearance of spectator women in scenes of warriors fighting and Herodotos's use of passive women as victims of warfare and strife; see Dewald (1981).
78. Ferrari (2002) 186. On how the honor of a woman is bound up in that of a man, see Cairns (1993) 186–8.
79. On praise and blame, see Fantham et al. (1994) 10.

CONCLUSION

1. See Brijder (1983) 109–42 and catalogue on 236–46; Carpenter (1986) 32–40. On dating, see Brijder 110 and 139–42. On the connection of the C Painter and Taras Painter themes to the Panathenaic reforms, see Brijder (1984).
2. Brijder (1991) 424: "Provenances are known for 56.7 percent of the [C Painter's] cups, roughly the same percentage as the Heidelberg Painter's workshop (60 percent). Of these, a smaller percentage comes from sanctuaries (62 percent, compared with 73 percent); the reverse holds for graves (33.5 percent, compared with 20.5 percent). Houses and settled areas have yielded 4.5 percent (compared with 6.5 percent)." Only one cup fragment by the C Painter comes from the Acropolis, an early battle scene that does not include the section where spectators, if any, might have occurred (Brijder (1991) no. 15). A few other cup fragments by the Taras and Heidelberg Painters are from the Acropolis, but again are missing the sections where spectators would be found (Brijder (1991) nos. 153, 161, 165–66, 380).
3. On the conservative character of the heroic duel, see Bazant (1981) 29ff. On the development of middling culture, see Morris (2000) 111ff and 162ff.

APPENDIX

Museum & Accession Number	Object Type	CVA Reference	Beazley Reference
Adolphseck, Schloss Fasanerie 1	amphora	Germany 11, Schloss Fasanerie 1, pl. 2	ABV 693.3BIS; BA 306597
Adolphseck, Schloss Fasanerie 10	lekythos	Germany 11, Schloss Fasanerie 1, pl. 12.3–4	Para. 208; BA 340673
Adolphseck, Schloss Fasanerie 12	lekythos	Germany 11, Schloss Fasanerie 1, pl. 13.4–6	ABV 491.60; BA 303575
Adolphseck, Schloss Fasanerie 24	cup	Germany 11, Schloss Fasanerie 1, pl. 21.1	BA 11523
Adolphseck, Schloss Fasanerie 3	amphora	Germany 11, Schloss Fasanerie 1, pl. 9.1	ABV 692.34bis; BA 306590
Adolphseck, Schloss Fasanerie 6	hydria	Germany 11, Schloss Fasanerie 1, pl. 10	BA 7985
Adolphseck, Schloss Fasanerie 8	lekythos	Germany 11, Schloss Fasanerie 1, pl. 12.1	Para. 238; BA 361199
Adria, Museo Archeologico Nazionale A108; I.G. 22690	lekythos	Italy 65, Adria 2, pl. 26.8	BA 43738
Adria, Museo Archeologico Nazionale A110; I.G. 22689	lekythos	Italy 65, Adria 2, pl. 26.6–7	
Adria, Museo Archeologico Nazionale A141; I.G. 22777	lekythos	Italy 65, Adria 2, pl. 24.2	BA 11006
Adria, Museo Archeologico Nazionale A216; I.G. 22451, I.G. 22660	hydria	Italy 65, Adria 2, pl. 13.2	BA 9118
Adria, Museo Archeologico Nazionale A225; I.G. 22276	lekythos	Italy 65, Adria 2, pl. 26.2–4	BA 21060

(continued)

Appendix *(continued)*

Museum & Accession Number	Object Type	CVA Reference	Beazley Reference
Adria, Museo Archeologico Nazionale A236; I.G. 22585	amphora	Italy 65, Adria 2, pl. 6	ABV 244.47; BA 301335
Adria, Museo Archeologico Nazionale A259–A316–A437; I.G. 22778 v	lekythos	Italy 65, Adria 2, pl. 21.6–7	BA 44567
Adria, Museo Archeologico Nazionale A334; I.G. 22724	lekythos	Italy 65, Adria 2, pl. 26.5	BA 21059
Adria, Museo Archeologico Nazionale A59; I.G. 22910	lekythos	Italy 65, Adria 2, pl. 23.6	BA 11005
Adria, Museo Archeologico Nazionale A63; I.G. 23877	lekythos	Italy 65, Adria 2, pl. 23.5	BA 12061
Agrigento, Museo Archeologico Regionale C774	lekythos	Italy 61, Agrigento 1, pl. 41.1–2	BA 10522
Agrigento, Museo Archeologico Regionale C779	lekythos	Italy 61, Agrigento 1, pl. 44.3–4, 45.4	BA 15767
Agrigento, Museo Archeologico Regionale C783	lekythos	Italy 61, Agrigento 1, pl. 48.1–3	
Agrigento, Museo Archeologico Regionale C788	lekythos	Italy 61, Agrigento 1, pl. 47.3–4	Para. 210; BA 340712
Agrigento, Museo Archeologico Regionale C790	lekythos	Italy 61, Agrigento 1, pl. 38.2	Para. 202; BA 340578
Agrigento, Museo Archeologico Regionale C791	lekythos	Italy 61, Agrigento 1, pl. 38.3	Para. 202; BA 340581
Agrigento, Museo Archeologico Regionale C792	lekythos	Italy 61, Agrigento 1, pl. 38.4	Para. 202; BA 340579
Agrigento, Museo Archeologico Regionale C793	lekythos	Italy 61, Agrigento 1, pl. 38.5	Para. 202; BA 340582
Agrigento, Museo Archeologico Regionale C794	lekythos	Italy 61, Agrigento 1, pl. 38.7–8	Para. 202; BA 340595
Agrigento, Museo Archeologico Regionale C795	lekythos	Italy 61, Agrigento 1, pl. 38.6	Para. 202; BA 340583
Agrigento, Museo Archeologico Regionale C797	lekythos	Italy 61, Agrigento 1, pl. 38.1	Para. 201; BA 351488

Museum & Accession Number	Object Type	CVA Reference	Beazley Reference
Agrigento, Museo Archeologico Regionale C847	lekythos	Italy 61, Agrigento 1, pl. 71.1–2	BA 15724
Agrigento, Museo Archeologico Regionale R144	pitcher	Italy 61, Agrigento 1, pl. 30.1	ABV 418.3; BA 303171
Agrigento, Museo Archeologico Regionale R151	lekythos	Italy 61, Agrigento 1, pl. 37.1–2	BA 15761
Agrigento, Museo Archeologico Regionale R152	lekythos	Italy 61, Agrigento 1, pl. 37.3–4	BA 15762
Agrigento, Museo Archeologico Regionale R154	cup	Italy 61, Agrigento 1, pl. 33.2	BA 15754
Altenburg, Staatliches Lindenau–Museum 200	lekythos	Germany 17, Altenburg 1, pl. 42.7–9	Para. 254; BA 361505
Altenburg, Staatliches Lindenau-Museum 203	pitcher	Germany 17, Altenburg 1, pl. 33–34	BA 10443
Altenburg, Staatliches Lindenau-Museum 210	pitcher	Germany 17, Altenburg 1, pl. 35.1–3	BA 12112
Altenburg, Staatliches Lindenau-Museum 222	hydria	Germany 17, Altenburg 1, pl. 30.1	ABV 268.27; BA 320037
Altenburg, Staatliches Lindenau-Museum 225	cup	Germany 17, Altenburg 1, pl. 38.8	BA 12098
Ampurias, Museo Monografico 424 (once Barcelona)	lekythos	Spain 3, Barcelona 1, pl. 13.2	ABV 70.5; BA 300636
Amsterdam, Allard Pierson Museum 10.000	cup	Netherlands 8, Amsterdam, Pierson 2, pls. 79–80	BA 12934
Amsterdam, Allard Pierson Museum 13.348	cup	Netherlands 8, Amsterdam, Pierson 2, pl. 104	BA 20535
Amsterdam, Allard Pierson Museum 13.367	cup	Netherlands 8, Amsterdam, Pierson 2, pl. 69.1–2 & 75.3	BA 21183
Amsterdam, Allard Pierson Museum 2709	cup	Netherlands 8, Amsterdam, Pierson 2, pl. 112.1	BA 2761
Amsterdam, Allard Pierson Museum 3343 (once Hague)	lekythos	Netherlands 1, Hague 1, III H d & e, pl. 4.7	ABV 461.35; BA 330309
Amsterdam, Allard Pierson Museum 3461 (once Hague)	cup	Netherlands 1, Hague 1, III H e/L 5.7 Netherlands 8, Amsterdam, Pierson 2, pl. 113.1	BA 14080
Amsterdam, Allard Pierson Museum 400 (once Hague)	cup	Netherlands 1, Hague 1, III H d & e, pl. 1.3 Netherlands 8, Amsterdam, Pierson 2, pl. 120–1	ABV 199.2; BA 302574
Amsterdam, Allard Pierson Museum 8211 (Six 31)	cup	Netherlands 6, Amsterdam, Pierson 1, pl. 55	ARV2 959.4; BA 212999

(continued)

Appendix *(continued)*

Museum & Accession Number	Object Type	CVA Reference	Beazley Reference
Amsterdam, Allard Pierson Museum 8693	cup	Netherlands 8, Amsterdam, Pierson 2, pl. 115.2	BA 19180
Amsterdam, Allard Pierson Museum RALS 529	cup	Netherlands 8, Amsterdam, Pierson 2, pl. 103.5	
Amsterdam, Allard Pierson Museum RALS 829	cup	Netherlands 8, Amsterdam, Pierson 2, pl. 129.2	BA 18636
Amsterdam, Allard Pierson Museum RALS523	cup	Netherlands 8, Amsterdam, Pierson 2, pl. 68.4	BA 21181
Amsterdam, Allard Pierson Museum RALS801a–b	cup	Netherlands 8, Amsterdam, Pierson 2, pl. 102.1–2	BA 18549
Athens, National Museum 1116	kotyle	Greece 3, Athens 3, pl. 47.4–6	Para. 90.43; BA 350950
Athens, National Museum 1152	cup	Greece 3, Athens 3, pl. 36.3–4	BA 30526
Athens, National Museum 12708	cup	Greece 3, Athens 3, pl. 31	BA 31922
Athens, National Museum 12910	skyphos	Greece 4, Athens 4, pl. 51.4–6	BA 46529
Athens, National Museum 16286	cup	Greece 3, Athens 3, pl. 36.1–2	BA 45041
Athens, National Museum 17302	cup	Greece 2, Athens 2, pl. 13.3–4	ARV2 835.4; BA 212155
Athens, National Museum 20813	cup	Greece 3, Athens 3, pl. 22	BA 9530
Athens, National Museum 21025	cup	Greece 3, Athens 3, pl. 32.5–6	BA 30518
Athens, National Museum 21027	cup	Greece 3, Athens 3, pl. 38.1–2	BA 30523
Athens, National Museum 21030	cup	Greece 3, Athens 3, pl. 32.1–4	BA 30519
Athens, National Museum 21031	cup	Greece 3, Athens 3, pl. 36.5–6	BA 30525
Athens, National Museum 21033	kotyle	Greece 3, Athens 3, pl. 47.1	BArch 30495
Athens, National Museum 22658	skyphos	Greece 4, Athens 4, pl. 46.4	BA 46522
Athens, National Museum 22838	skyphos	Greece 4, Athens 4, pl. 13.1–2	BA 46465
Athens, National Museum 443	skyphos	Greece 4, Athens 4, pl. 17	Para. 85.32; BA 350849
Athens, National Museum 445	cup	Greece 3, Athens 3, pl. 48	ABV 113.83; BA 310229
Athens, National Museum 500	pyxis	Greece 1, Athens 1, pl. 1.3–4	ABV 302.2; BA 301468
Athens, National Museum 636	skyphos	Greece 4, Athens 4, pl. 46.1–3	BA 46521

Museum & Accession Number	Object Type	CVA Reference	Beazley Reference
Athens, National Museum 638	skyphos	Greece 4, Athens 4, pl. 15	ABV 120.2; BA 300862
Athens, National Museum 9711	cup	Greece 3, Athens 3, pl. 42	BA 15090
Austin, TX, Blanton Museum 1980.32 (once Castle Ashby)	amphora	Great Britain 15, Castle Ashby 1, pl. 15.6	BA 25
Baltimore, Johns Hopkins University B11 (once Robinson)	cup	United States 6, Baltimore, Robinson 2, pl. 18.1b	ARV2 340.65; BA 203498
Baltimore, Walters Art Museum 48.67	krater	United States 28, Baltimore, Walters 1, pl. 17	ARV2 1098.29; BA 216093
Baltimore, Walters Art Museum 48.93	cup	United States 28, Baltimore, Walters 1, pl. 49.1–2	ARV2 960.23; BA 213019
Basel, Antikenmuseum und Sammlung Ludwig BS1921.330	amphora	Switzerland 4, Basel 1, pl. 46.1–2	BA 7073
Basel, Antikenmuseum und Sammlung Ludwig BS1921.335	lekythos	Switzerland 4, Basel 1, pl. 34.11, 35.1	BA 7078
Basel, Antikenmuseum und Sammlung Ludwig BS1921.336	lekythos	Switzerland 4, Basel 1, pl. 35.9, 35.14	BA 7055
Basel, Antikenmuseum und Sammlung Ludwig BS1921.344	pitcher	Switzerland 4, Basel 1, pl. 31.1	BA 7691
Basel, Antikenmuseum und Sammlung Ludwig BS1921.346	pitcher	Switzerland 4, Basel 1, pl. 31.14	BA 42137
Basel, Antikenmuseum und Sammlung Ludwig BS1953.8	cup	Switzerland 4, Basel 1, pl. 25.2	ABV 68.1; BA 300617
Basel, Antikenmuseum und Sammlung Ludwig BS408	hydria	Switzerland 4, Basel 1, pls. 26.1–2 & 27.2	BA 6916
Basel, Antikenmuseum und Sammlung Ludwig BS425	aryballos	Switzerland 4, Basel 1, pl. 11.10	
Basel, Antikenmuseum und Sammlung Ludwig Z339	amphora	Switzerland 4, Basel 1, pl. 30.1, 30.3	BA 6912
Basel, Antikenmuseum und Sammlung Ludwig Z357	lekythos	Switzerland 4, Basel 1, pl. 34.12, 35.2	BA 7069
Basel, Antikenmuseum und Sammlung Ludwig Z395	amphora	Switzerland 4, Basel 1, pl. 42.1, 43.1	BA 7076
Basel, Antikenmuseum und Sammlung Ludwig Z560	lekythos	Switzerland 4, Basel 1, pl. 34.14, 35.4	BA 7067
Basel, Antikenmuseum und Sammlung Ludwig Z561	lekythos	Switzerland 4, Basel 1, pl. 34.13, 35.3	BA 7068

(continued)

Appendix *(continued)*

Museum & Accession Number	Object Type	CVA Reference	Beazley Reference
Berlin, Antikensammlung 5844	amphora	Germany 33, Berlin 4, pl. 175	
Berlin, Antikensammlung F1702	amphora	Germany 45, Berlin 5, pl. 17	BA 6098
Berlin, Antikensammlung F1717	amphora	Germany 45, Berlin 5, pl. 19.1	ABV 141.7; BA 310367
Berlin, Antikensammlung F1722	krater	Germany 61, Berlin 7, pls. 6–8	ABV 104.124; BA 310123
Berlin, Antikensammlung F1728	pyxis	Germany 61, Berlin 7, pl. 44.4	BA 6899
Berlin, Antikensammlung F1736	pitcher	Germany 61, Berlin 7, pl. 30.1–2	ABV 462.41; BA 330315
Berlin, Antikensammlung F1873	amphora	Germany 45, Berlin 5, pl. 34.4 & 38	ABV 407; BA 303074
Berlin, Antikensammlung F1905	hydria	Germany 61, Berlin 7, pl. 22.1	ABV 332.23; BA 301801
Berlin, Antikensammlung F2294	cup	Germany 21, Berlin 2, pl. 72.2	ARV2 400.1; BA 204340
Berlin, Antikensammlung F3988	pyxis	Germany 61, Berlin 7, pl. 42	BA 360
Berlin, Antikensammlung F4009	pyxis	Germany 61, Berlin 7, pl. 46.6	BA 41987
Berlin, once Antikensammlung F2308	cup	Germany (East) 3, Berlin 1, pl. 22.1	ARV2 818.25; BA 210125
Bologna, Museo Civico Archeologico 384	cup	Italy 33, Bologna 5, pl. 124.1	ARV2 903.57; BA 211982
Bologna, Museo Civico Archeologico 41292 (69)	pitcher	Italy 7, Bologna 2, pl. 38.1	ABV 447.5; BA 330113
Bologna, Museo Civico Archeologico C161	cup	Italy 5, Bologna 1, pl. 10.1	
Bologna, Museo Civico Archeologico C177 (362)	cup	Italy 5, Bologna 1, pl. 5	ARV 357; BA 203759
Bologna, Museo Civico Archeologico C179	cup	Italy 5, Bologna 1, pl. 6	
Bologna, Museo Civico Archeologico C50	lekythos	Italy 7, Bologna 2, pl. 39.4	
Bologna, Museo Civico Archeologico C64 (65)	pitcher	Italy 7, Bologna 2, pl. 38.2	BA 13022
Bologna, Museo Civico Archeologico PU199	pelike	Italy 7, Bologna 2, pl. 25	ABV 393.14; BA 302930
Bonn, Akademisches Kunstmuseum 74	cup	Germany 1, Bonn 1, Taf. 6.3	ARV2 816.5; BA 210095
Boston, Museum of Fine Arts 00.331	amphora	United States 14, Boston 1, pl. 35.4	ABV 307.62; BA 301542
Boston, Museum of Fine Arts 03.852	cup	United States 19, Boston 2, pl. 109.5	ABV 51.2; BA 300379

Museum & Accession Number	Object Type	CVA Reference	Beazley Reference
Boston, Museum of Fine Arts 13.76	amphora	United States 14, Boston 1, pl. 19.2–3	ABV 240.17; BA 301305
Boston, Museum of Fine Arts 1970.8	amphora	United States 14, Boston 1, pl. 6.2	ABV 140.2; BA 310353
Boston, Museum of Fine Arts 28.46	hydria	United States 19, Boston 2, pl. 79.3	ABV 261.38; BA 302270
Boston, Museum of Fine Arts 60.1	amphora	United States 14, Boston 1, pl. 7.2	Para. 107.7bis; BA 340413
Boston, Museum of Fine Arts 62.1185	hydria	United States 19, Boston 2, pl. 84.1	Para. 171.10; BA 351265
Boston, Museum of Fine Arts 67.861	cup	United States 19, Boston 2, pl. 106.2–3	Para. 100.7; BA 340249
Boston, Museum of Fine Arts 89.256	amphora	United States 14, Boston 1, pl. 10.1	Para. 115.4bis; BA 340448
Boston, Museum of Fine Arts 98.918	amphora	United States 14, Boston 1, pl. 4.1	ABV 306.41; BA 301521
Boston, Museum of Fine Arts 99.516	amphora	United States 14, Boston 1, pl. 20	ABV 239.11; BA 301299
Boston, Museum of Fine Arts 99.519	cup	United States 19, Boston 2, pl. 87.5	ABV 69.1; BA 300620
Bourges, Museé D.863.1.37	amphora	France 30, Bourges 1, pl. 3	BA 5591
Bourges, Musée D.863.1.38	lekythos	France 30, Bourges 1, pl. 4	BA 5590
Brussels, Musées Royaux A1578	cup	Belgium 1, Brussels 1, pl. III. H.e.1.2	ABV 63.7; BA 300551
Brussels, Musées Royaux A2128	lekythos	Belgium 2, Brussels 2, pl. 21.20	ABV 461.28; BA 330302
Brussels, Musées Royaux A2192	lekythos	Belgium 3, Brussels 3, pl. III H e 24.6	ABV 464.11; BA 330347
Brussels, Musées Royaux A2292	lekythos	Belgium 3, Brussels 3, pl. III H e 24.7	ABV 464.12; BA 330348
Brussels, Musées Royaux A712	amphora	Belgium 1, Brussels 1, pl. III H e 9.3a	ABV 320.3; BA 301674
Brussels, Musées Royaux A717	stamnos	Belgium 2, Brussels 2, pl. III I c 12	ARV2 20.1; BA 200102
Brussels, Musées Royaux A910	lekythos	Belgium 2, Brussels 2, pl. 21.14	ABV 464.1; BA 330353
Brussels, Musées Royaux R289	amphora	Belgium 2, Brussels 2, pl. 16.4	ABV 133.3; BA 301037
Brussels, Musées Royaux R317	amphora	Belgium 1, Brussels 1, pl. 8.3a	BA 12074
Brussels, Musées Royaux R333	lekythos	Belgium 2, Brussels 2, pl. 21.13	ABV 460.2; BA 330273
Brussels, Musées Royaux R334	cup	Belgium 1, Brussels 1, pl. III H e 5	BA 12087
Cambridge (MA), Harvard University, Sackler Museum 1959.124 (once Robinson)	cup	United States 6, Baltimore, Robinson 2, pl. 14	ARV2 438.140; BA 205186
Cambridge (MA), Harvard University, Sackler Museum 2214	lekythos	United States 8, Fogg/Gallatin, pl. 11.9	BA 13580

(continued)

Appendix *(continued)*

Museum & Accession Number	Object Type	CVA Reference	Beazley Reference
Cambridge (MA), Harvard University, Sackler Museum 2271	amphora	United States 8, Fogg/Gallatin, pl. 7.1	Para. 50.1; BA 350384
Cambridge (MA), Harvard University, Sackler Museum 60.320	cup	United States 4, Baltimore, Robinson 1, pl. 19.2a–b	BA 13404
Cambridge, Fitzwilliam Museum 101	lekythos	Great Britain 6, Cambridge 1, pl. 22.6	Para. 238, BA 361201
Cambridge, Fitzwilliam Museum 19.17	amphora	Great Britain 6, Cambridge 1, pl. 11.2a	BA 12771
Cambridge, Fitzwilliam Museum G51	amphora	Great Britain 6, Cambridge 1, pl. 12.2b	ABV 340.1; BA 301877
Cambridge, Fitzwilliam Museum G54	hydria	Great Britain 6, Cambridge 1, pl. 16.2	BA 12709
Cambridge, Fitzwilliam Museum G55	hydria	Great Britain 6, Cambridge 1, pl. 17.2	BA 12770
Cambridge, Fitzwilliam Museum G67	cup	Great Britain 6, Cambridge 1, pl. 19.3	BA 3706
Cambridge, Fitzwilliam Museum G80a	lekythos	Great Britain 6, Cambridge 1, pl. 22.3	ABV 516.6; BA 330658
Cambridge, Fitzwilliam Museum GR.20.1929	cup	Great Britain 11, Cambridge 2, pls. 23.1, 24.1	ABV 54.55; BA 300432
Cambridge, Fitzwilliam Museum GR6.1937	lekythos	Great Britain 11, Cambridge 2, pl. III H 2.1a–b	ABV 310; BA301592
Capua, Museo Campano 157	amphora	Italy 23, Capua 2, pl. 5.3	
Capua, Museo Campano 162	mastoid	Italy 23, Capua 2, pl. 12.1–3	BA 14004
Castle Ashby 21 (once)	hydria	Great Britain 15, Castle Ashby 1, pl. 21.3	ABV 277.13; BA 320175
Champaign–Urbana, University of Illinois, Krannert Art Museum AM 70.9.3	amphora	United States 24, Illinois 1, pl. 9.1	BA 5172
Champaign–Urbana, University of Illinois, Krannert Art Museum W77.1.1683	hydria	United States 24, Illinois 1, pl. 7.3–4	BA 18458
Charlottesville, University of Virginia, Bayly Art Museum 1988.62 (once Castle Ashby)	krater	Great Britain 15, Castle Ashby 1, pl. 20.4	BA 2415
Chiusi, Museo Archeologico Nazionale 1804	amphora	Italy 59, Chuisi 1, pl. 7.1–2	ABV 101.83; BA 310082
Chiusi, Museo Archeologico Nazionale 1840	cup	Italy 60, Chiusi 2, pl. 26	ARV2 904.60; BA 211985
Chiusi, Museo Archeologico Nazionale 269	lekythos	Italy 59, Chuisi 1, pl. 22	BA 6848
Chiusi, Museo Archeologico Nazionale P476	cup	Italy 60, Chiusi 2, pl. 32	BA 6981

Museum & Accession Number	Object Type	CVA Reference	Beazley Reference
Chiusi, Museo Archeologico Nazionale P814	lekythos	Italy 59, Chuisi 1, pl. 23	BA 6847
Christchurch, Canterbury Museum AR 431.2	lekythos	New Zealand 1, pl. 20.5–6	Para 210; BA 340713
Christchurch, University of Canterbury 39.57	cup	New Zealand 1, pl. 25	Para. 24.59bis; BA 350162
Christchurch, University of Canterbury 43/57	amphora	New Zealand 1, pl. 7.1–2	Para. 58.2bis; BA 350443
Christchurch, University of Canterbury 55/58	cup	New Zealand 1, pl. 29.1–4	BA 6702
Christchurch, University of Canterbury AR431.1	amphora	New Zealand 1, pl. 13.5–6	ABV 244.53; BA 301341
Cleveland, Museum of Art 16.1062	pitcher	United States 15, Cleveland 1, pl. 17.2	Para. 179.6; BA 351293
Cleveland, Museum of Art 1971.46	dinos	United States 35, Cleveland 2, pl. 64–65	BA 5166
Cleveland, Museum of Art 1976.89	cup	United States 35, Cleveland 2, pl. 76	ARV2 38.8, BA 200027
Cleveland, Museum of Art 23.645	amphora	United States 15, Cleveland 1, pl. 5	BA 1498
Cleveland, Museum of Art 65.78	cup	United States 15, Cleveland 1, pl. 21.1	BA 758
Columbia, University of Missouri 57.9	lekythos	United States 36, Columbia 1, pl. 20.4–6	
Columbia, University of Missouri 61.3	pelike	United States 36, Columbia 1, pl. 15	Para. 256; BA 351532
Columbia, University of Missouri 66.309	pitcher	United States 36, Columbia 1, pl. 16.3–4	BA 44059
Como, Museo Archeologico C.27	lekythos	Italy 47, Como 1, pl. 6.1a–b	BA 2219
Como, Museo Archeologico C.28	lekythos	Italy 47, Como 1, pl. 6.2a–b	BA 2218
Como, Museo Archeologico C.22	amphora	Italy 47, Como 1, pl. 1.1–2	BA 1793
Compiègne, Musée Vivenel 1044	lekythos	France 3, Compiègne 1, pl. 3.9.	ABV 461.25; BA 330299
Compiègne, Musée Vivenel 1055	hydria	France 3, Compiègne, pl. 6.2	BA 11155
Compiègne, Musée Vivenel 1094	cup	France 3, Compiègne 1, pl. 5.2	BA 11157
Copenhagen, National Museum 1408	lekythos	Denmark 3, Copenhagen, Nat. Mus. 3, pl. 110.5	ABV 467.7; BA 330416
Copenhagen, National Museum 3672	amphora	Denmark 3, Copenhagen, Nat. Mus. 3, pl. 105.1a–b	ABV 307.58; BA 301538
Copenhagen, National Museum 5180	cup	Denmark 3, Copenhagen, Nat. Mus. 3, pl. 114.1a	ABV 69.5; BA 300624

(continued)

Appendix *(continued)*

Museum & Accession Number	Object Type	CVA Reference	Beazley Reference
Copenhagen, National Museum 597	skyphos	Denmark 8, Copenhagen, Nat. Mus. 8, pl. 351	ARV2 1301.5; BA 219000
Copenhagen, National Museum 6585	cup	Denmark 3, Copenhagen, Nat. Mus. 3, pl. 113.4a–b	ABV 115.5; BA 310238
Copenhagen, National Museum 809	hydria	Denmark 3, Copenhagen, Nat. Mus. 3, pl. 123.4b	ABV 324.29; BA 301715
Copenhagen, National Museum Chr.VIII.317	amphora	Denmark 2, Copenhagen, Nat. Mus. 2, pl. 92	
Copenhagen, National Museum Chr.VIII.387	lekythos	Denmark 3, Copenhagen, Nat. Mus. 3, pl. 110.9	
Copenhagen, Thorvaldsens Museum H540	amphora	Denmark 9, Copenhagen, Thorvaldsens 1, pl. 6a–b	
Copenhagen, Thorvaldsens Museum 50 or H550	mastoid	Denmark 9, Copenhagen, Thorvaldsens 1, pl. 60	ABV 614.2; BA 306188
Copenhagen, Thorvaldsens Museum 67 or H567	cup	Denmark 9, Copenhagen, Thorvaldsens 1, pl. 66	BA 9939
Copenhagen, Thorvaldsens Museum H544	amphora	Denmark 9, Copenhagen, Thorvaldsens 1, pl. 9b	ABV 485; BA 303494
Copenhagen, Thorvaldsens Museum H552 or 52	amphora	Denmark 9, Copenhagen, Thorvaldsens 1, pl. 15A	BA 9955
Copenhagen, Thorvaldsens Museum H554 or 54	hydria	Denmark 9, Copenhagen, Thorvaldsens 1, pl. 29.2	ABV 267.20; BA 320030
Cork, University College GP 74	lekythos	Ireland 1, University College Dublin/Cork, pl. 51.1–3	
Cork, University College GP 76	lekythos	Ireland 1, University College Dublin/Cork, pl. 51.11–13	
Cracow, National Museum FK6195	lekythos	Poland 2, Cracow 1, Nat. Mus. pl. 1.3	BA 14183
Dublin, University College 104	cup	Ireland 1, University College Dublin/Cork, pl. 21.1–3	
Dublin, University College 113	cup	Ireland 1, University College Dublin/Cork, pl. 20.1–5	
Dublin, University College 546	lekythos	Ireland 1, University College Dublin/Cork, pl. 16.12–14	
Dunedin, Otago Museum E39.80	amphora	New Zealand 1, pl. 10.1–3	BA 6733
Dunedin, Otago museum E48.149	amphora	New Zealand 1, pl. 10.4–5	ABV 462.55; BA 330329
Dunedin, Otago Museum E48.226	pelike	New Zealand 1, pl. 17.4	ABV 386.12; BA 302889
Edinburgh, National Museums of Scotland 1881.44.26	stamnos	Great Britain 16, Edinburgh 1, pl. 18.4	ARV2 814.100; BA 210082
Edinburgh, National Museums of Scotland 1938.508	lekythos	Great Britain 16, Edinburgh 1, pl. 13.7–8	BA 31443

Museum & Accession Number	Object Type	CVA Reference	Beazley Reference
Edinburgh, National Museums of Scotland 1956.431 v	pitcher	Great Britain 16, Edinburgh 1, pl. 11.1–2	BA 31433
Ferrara, Museo Nazionale de Spina 2505	pitcher	Italy 37, Ferrara 1, pl. 23.3	ARV2 1206.3; BA 215960
Ferrara, Museo Nazionale de Spina T212BVP or 9351	cup	Italy 37, Ferrara 1, pl. 32.1	ARV2 880.12; BA 211576
Fiesole, Coll. Costantini	amphora	Italy 57, Fiesole 1, pl.7.2	Para. 134.28bis; BA 340566
Fiesole, Coll. Costantini	mastoid	Italy 57, Fiesole 1, pl. 35.3–5	BA 6800
Florence, Museo Archeologico Etrusco 285–287	cup	Italy 38, Florence 4, pl. 156	ARV2 1397.1; BA 250106
Florence, Museo Archeologico Etrusco 3792	hydria	Italy 42, Florence 5, pl. 18.2	BA 8054
Florence, Museo Archeologico Etrusco 3793	hydria	Italy 42, Florence 5, pl. 19.1	BA 8098
Florence, Museo Archeologico Etrusco 3799	hydria	Italy 42, Florence 5, pl. 8.1	BA 8094
Florence, Museo Archeologico Etrusco 3803	hydria	Italy 42, Florence 5, pl. 27.2	BA 8102
Florence, Museo Archeologico Etrusco 3825	hydria	Italy 42, Florence 5, pl. 13.1	BA 6100
Florence, Museo Archeologico Etrusco 3944	cup	Italy 30, Florence 3, pl. 85.3	ARV2 353.4; BA 203686
Florence, Museo Archeologico Etrusco 3967	hydria	Italy 42, Florence 5, pl. 32.2	ABV 364.58; BA 302053 (under 3867)
Florence, Museo Archeologico Etrusco 70800	cup	Italy 30, Florence 3, pl. 98.1	ARV2 413.25; BA 204507
Florence, Museo Archeologico Etrusco 70994	hydria	Italy 42, Florence 5, pl. 5.1	BA 8093
Florence, Museo Archeologico Etrusco 74356	cup	Italy 38, Florence 4, pl. 147	ARV2 904.59; BA 211984
Florence, Museo Archeologico Etrusco 75590	cup	Italy 38, Florence 4, pl. 121.1	ARV2 419.47; BA 204592
Florence, Museo Archeologico Etrusco 94314	hydria	Italy 42, Florence 5, pl. 36.2	ABV 386.14; BA 302891
Florence, Museo Archeologico Etrusco 94315	hydria	Italy 42, Florence 5, pl. 34.2	ABV 289.29; BA 320332
Florence, Museo Archeologico Etrusco 94345	hydria	Italy 42, Florence 5, pl. 39.4–5	BA 8074
Florence, Museo Archeologico Etrusco PD56	cup	Italy 38, Florence 4, pl. 126.1	ARV2 412.6; BA 204488
Frankfurt, Liebieghaus 532	lekythos	Germany 30, Frankfurt 2, pl. 49.8–10	BA 5133
Frankfurt, Museum für Kunsthandwerk WM015	amphora	Germany 25, Frankfurt 1, pl. 28.2	BA 12554

(continued)

Appendix *(continued)*

Museum & Accession Number	Object Type	CVA Reference	Beazley Reference
Frankfurt, Museum für Vor– und Frühgeschichte B345	hydria	Germany 25, Frankfurt 1, pl. 38	ABV 267.16; BA 320026
Frankfurt, Museum für Vor– und Frühgeschichte B285	amphora	Germany 25, Frankfurt 1, pl. 24.2	Para. 40.35; BA 350269
Frankfurt, Museum für Vor– und Frühgeschichte B292	lekythos	Germany 30, Frankfurt 2, pl. 47.1–2	BA 11894
Frankfurt, Museum für Vor– und Frühgeschichte B293	lekythos	Germany 30, Frankfurt 2, pl. 47.6–7	BA 11899
Frankfurt, Universität 79	lekythos	Germany 66, Frankfurt 4, pl. 17.11–13	
Gela, Museo Archeologico (no number)	lekythos	Italy 56, Gela 4, pls. 16.3 & 6–8	BA 5209
Gela, Museo Archeologico N15	lekythos	Italy 56, Gela 4, pls. 35.8, 36.7–9	BA 5255
Gela, Museo Archeologico 18 (N18)	lekythos	Italy 56, Gela 4, pl. 15.2 & 15.4	BA 10529
Gela, Museo Archeologico 25 (N25)	lekythos	Italy 56, Gela 4, pl. 10.1–2 & 10.9	BA 5220
Gela, Museo Archeologico 37 (N37)	lekythos	Italy 54, Gela 3, pl. 4.1 & 4, 5.1	BA 1195
Gela, Museo Archeologico 4	lekythos	Italy 54, Gela 3, pl. 8.3–4	BA 11248
Gela, Museo Archeologico 53 (N53)	lekythos	Italy 56, Gela 4, p. 17.1,3,5	BA 10526
Gela, Museo Archeologico N153	amphora	Italy 56, Gela 4, pl. 11.1–3, 12.1–2	BA 5217
Gela, Museo Archeologico N155.B	lekythos	Italy 56, Gela 4, pl. 36.1–3	BA 5256
Gela, Museo Archeologico N324	lekythos	Italy 56, Gela 4, pl. 10.4–6	BA 5219
Gela, Museo Archeologico N55	lekythos	Italy 56, Gela 4, pls. 18.4 & 8, 19.5–6	BA 5206
Geneva, Musée d'Art et d'Histoire 14047	cup	Switzerland 3, Geneva 2, pl. 66.1–2	BA 5678
Geneva, Musée d'Art et d'Histoire 14985	cup	Switzerland 1, Geneva 1, pl. 8.3–4	ARV2 420.58; BA 204603
Geneva, Musée d'Art et d'Histoire 15041.1937	krater	Switzerland 3, Geneva 2, pl. 61.1	BA 5686
Geneva, Musée d'Art et d'Histoire 20599.1967	lekythos	Switzerland 3, Geneva 2, pl. 71.7–8	BA 5657
Geneva, Musée d'Art et d'Histoire 3.1870	lekythos	Switzerland 3, Geneva 2, pl. 71.9–11	BA 5659
Geneva, Musée d'Art et d'Histoire 4793	pelike	Switzerland 1, Geneva 1, pl. 20.5	BA 14814
Geneva, Musée d'Art et d'Histoire I529	cup	Switzerland 1, Geneva 1, pl. 7.4	ARV2 154.7; BA 201410
Geneva, Musée d'Art et d'Histoire I736	lekythos	Switzerland 3, Geneva 2, pl. 71.1–3	BA 5660

Museum & Accession Number	Object Type	CVA Reference	Beazley Reference
Geneva, Musée d'Art et d'Histoire I758	lekythos	Switzerland 3, Geneva 2, pl. 71.14–15	BA 5655
Geneva, Musée d'Art et d'Histoire MF 143	lekythos	Switzerland 3, Geneva 2, pl. 71.12–13	BA 5656
Geneva, Musée d'Art et d'Histoire MF149A	lekythos	Switzerland 3, Geneva 2, pl. 73.12–13	BA 5653
Geneva, Musée d'Art et d'Histoire MF241	cup	Switzerland 3, Geneva 2, pl. 64.3–4	BA 5682
Geneva, Musée d'Art et dHistoire P698.1889	lekythos	Switzerland 3, Geneva 2, pl. 72.1–4	BA 5654
Genoa, Museo Civico 1165	amphora	Italy 19, Genoa 1, pl. III H 1.1–2	ABV 129.4; BA 300997
Giessen, Justus–Liebig–Universität KIII–102	lekythos	Germany 68, Giessen 1, pl. 20	
Giessen, Justus–Liebig–Universität KIII–31	cup	Germany 68, Giessen 1, pl. 23	BA 29764
Gioia del Colle, Museo Archeologico MG 1469	cup	Italy 68, Gioia del Colle 1, pl. 25	
Gioia del Colle, Museo Archeologico MG 2300	krater	Italy 68, Gioia del Colle 1, pl. 27.1	
Glasgow, Hunterian Museum D198	lekythos	Great Britain 18, Glasgow 1, pl. 22.4–6	BA 19934
Glasgow, Hunterian Museum D1981.12	lekythos	Great Britain 18, Glasgow 1, pl. 22.1–3	BA 19935
Glasgow, Sir William Burrell Collection 19.103	skyphos	Great Britain 18, Glasgow 1, pl. 19.1	BA 19955
Glasgow, Sir William Burrell Collection 19.163	amphora	Great Britain 18, Glasgow 1, pl. 13.5	ABV 225.5; BA 302823
Göteborg, Rohsska Museum 27.49	lekythos	Sweden 3, Gotha, Public Collections, pl. 29.3–5	BA 14659
Göteborg, Rohsska Museum 71.58	cup	Sweden 3, Gotha, Public Collections, pl. 31	BA 14660
Gotha, Schlossmuseum 36	hydria	Sweden 3, Gotha, Public Collections, pl. 30.1–2	Para. 219; BA 360886
Gotha, Schlossmuseum ZV2380	pyxis	Sweden 3, Gotha, Public Collections, pl. 29.3–4	ABV 455.2; BA 330212
Hamburg, Museum für Kunst und Gerwerbe 1917.226	cup	Germany 41, Hamburg 1, pl. 36.2 & 38.1–2	BA 1169
Hamburg, Museum für Kunst und Gerwerbe 1917.230	pyxis	Germany 41, Hamburg 1, pl. 47.6	ABV 455.4; BA 330214
Hamburg, Museum für Kunst und Gerwerbe 1960.1	amphora	Germany 41, Hamburg 1, pl. 12 & 14.3–4	Para. 40.35; BA 350268
Hamburg, Museum für Kunst und Gewerbe 1917.225	mastoid	Germany 41, Hamburg 1, pl. 48.4–6	BA 1015
Hannover, Kestner Museum 1966.36	lekythos	Germany 34, Hannover 1, pl. 23.7–8	BA 3111
Hannover, Kestner Museum (no number)	lekythos	Germany 34, Hannover 1, pl. 23.1–2	BA 1020

(continued)

Appendix *(continued)*

Museum & Accession Number	Object Type	CVA Reference	Beazley Reference
Hannover, Kestner Museum 1936.107	amphora	Germany 34, Hannover 1, pl. 7.1	BA 1854
Hannover, Kestner Museum 1984.29	cup	Germany 72, Hannover 2, pl. 3–5	ARV2 437.115; BA 205161
Hannover, Kestner Museum 755, 1966.64	lekythos	Germany 34, Hannover 1, pl. 21.3–5	BA 1024
Heidelberg, Ruprecht-Karls-Universität 169	cup	Germany 10. Heidelberg 1, pl. 25.3	
Heidelberg, Ruprecht-Karls-Universität 226	amphora	Germany 10. Heidelberg 1, pl. 34.11	BA 11563
Heidelberg, Ruprecht-Karls-Universität 229	amphora	Germany 10. Heidelberg 1, pl. 35.1	ABV 305.28; BA 301508
Heidelberg, Ruprecht-Karls-Universität 252	hydria	Germany 10. Heidelberg 1, pl. 39.1	Para. 200.4; BA 351473
Heidelberg, Ruprecht-Karls-Universität 254	pitcher	Germany 10. Heidelberg 1, pl. 39.4	ABV 698.1bis; BA 306658
Heidelberg, Ruprecht-Karls-Universität 256	pitcher	Germany 10. Heidelberg 1, pl. 39.6	Para. 179.7; BA 351294
Heidelberg, Ruprecht-Karls-Universität 68.2	plate	Germany 31, Heidelberg 4, pl. 164.1–4	BA 2186
Heidelberg, Ruprecht-Karls-Universität L55	lekythos	Germany 31, Heidelberg 4, pl. 169.2 & 5–6	BA 3250
Heidelberg, Ruprecht-Karls-Universität S1	cup	Germany 31, Heidelberg 4, pl. 152.1	ABV 51.1; BA 300378
Heidelberg, Ruprecht-Karls-Universität S10a/b	cup	Germany 31, Heidelberg 4, pl. 157.1–4	BA3819
Heidelberg, Ruprecht-Karls-Universität S12	cup	Germany 31, Heidelberg 4, pl. 156.5	BA 3825
Japan, Museum for Ancient Mediterranean Culture 4	cup	Japan 2, pl. 41.2–6	
Karlsruhe, Badisches Landesmuseum 61.89	amphora	Germany 60, Karlsruhe 3, pl. 12.2 & 13.2	ABV 311.693; BA 351011
Karlsruhe, Badisches Landesmuseum 65.45	amphora	Germany 60. Karlsruhe 3, pl. 19.1	Para. 61.8bis; BA 350447
Karlsruhe, Badisches Landesmuseum 67.90	cup	Germany 60. Karlsruhe 3, pl. 24	BA 355
Karlsruhe, Badisches Landesmuseum 75.36	pelike	Germany 60. Karlsruhe 3, pl. 46.1–2	BA 6195
Karlsruhe, Badisches Landesmuseum B2423	amphora	Germany 7, Karlsruhe 1, pl. 6.3–4	ABV 100.65; BA 310064
Karlsruhe, Badisches Landesmuseum B29	lekythos	Germany 7, Karlsruhe 1, pl. 14.3–4	Para. 253; BA 361486
Karlsruhe, Badisches Landesmuseum B3048	skyphos	Germany 7, Karlsruhe 1, pl. 11.6–7	ABV 626.1; BA 306378
Kassel, Staatliche Museen T384	amphora	Germany 35, Kassel 1, pl. 21.1	ABV 137.57; BA 310317

Museum & Accession Number	Object Type	CVA Reference	Beazley Reference
Kassel, Staatliche Museen T675	pelike	Germany 35, Kassel 1, pl. 24.1	Para 167.223bis; BA 351233
Kassel, Staatliche Museen T679	amphora	Germany 35, Kassel 1, pl. . 19.1	Para. 111.25bis; BA 340429
Kassel, Staatliche Museen T385	amphora	Germany 35, Kassel 1, pl. 18.1	ABV 105.2; BA 310136
Kassel, Staatliche Museen T664	cup	Germany 35, Kassel 1, pl. 37.1–2 & 40.3	ARV2 401.10bis; BA 204351
Kassel, Staatliche Museen T674	amphora	Germany 35, Kassel 1, pl. 23.3	Para 56.31 bis; BA 350427
Kiel, Antikensammlung B44	lekythos	Germany 55, Kiel 1, pl. 18.1–3	BA 28007
Kiel, Antikensammlung B507	amphora	Germany 55, Kiel 1, pl. 6.1 & 7.1–2	BA 7921
Kiel, Antikensammlung B510	amphora	Germany 55, Kiel 1, pl. 10.1–3	BA 8322
Kyoto, Hashimoto Collection 130	amphora	Japan 2, pl. 8.2	BA 37
Kyoto, Hashimoto Collection 70	cup	Japan 2, pl. 11.2–3	BA 23622
Laon, Musée Archéologique Municipal 37.891	lekythos	France 20, Laon 1, pl. 13.3–5	BA 12438
Laon, Musée Archéologique Municipal 37.895	lekythos	France 20, Laon 1, pl. 14.5–6	Para. 207; BA 340666
Laon, Musée Archéologique Municipal 37.921	lekythos	France 20, Laon 1, pl. 15.1–2	ABV 702.40ter; BA 306749
Laon, Musée Archéologique Municipal 37.971	hydria	France 20, Laon 1, pl. 9.2	BA 12346
Laon, Musée Archéologique Municipal 37.976	lekythos	France 20, Laon 1, pl. 14.7–8	BA 12348
Laon, Musée Archéologique Municipal 37.978	pelike	France 20, Laon 1, pl. 9.4	BA 12353
Laon, Musée Archéologique Municipal 37.982	cup	France 20, Laon 1, pl. 21.1 & 6	BA 12373
Laon, Musée Archéologique Municipal 37.983	cup	France 20, Laon 1, pl. 21.2 & 5	
Laon, Musée Archéologique Municipal CP 60	lekythos	France 20, Laon 1, pl. 14.3–4	ABV 698.25bis; BA 306664
Leiden Rijksmuseum van Ouheden ROIII23	hydria	Netherlands 3, Leiden 1, pl. 17.1–2	BA 624
Leiden, Rijksmuseum van Ouheden ROII35	lekythos	Netherlands 4, Leiden 2, pl. 86.6–7	BA 7284
Leiden, Rijksmuseum van Ouheden 1954.2.1	krater	Netherlands 3, Leiden 1, pl. 19.1	ABV 263.9; BA 302292
Leiden, Rijksmuseum van Ouheden I.1934.11.4	lekythos	Netherlands 4, Leiden 2, pl. 86.9–10	BA 1233
Leiden, Rijksmuseum van Ouheden I.1958.1.2	lekythos	Netherlands 4, Leiden 2, pl. 106.7–9	BA 1487

(continued)

Appendix *(continued)*

Museum & Accession Number	Object Type	CVA Reference	Beazley Reference
Leiden, Rijksmuseum van Ouheden K94.9.14	cup	Netherlands 4, Leiden 2, pl. 60.2 & 4	BA 600
Leiden, Rijksmuseum van Ouheden PC2	hydria	Netherlands 3, Leiden 1, pl. 11.3	BA 626
Leiden, Rijksmuseum van Ouheden PC39	pitcher	Netherlands 4, Leiden 2, pl. 80.1–2	ABV 443.16; BA 303208
Leiden, Rijksmuseum van Ouheden PC53	amphora	Netherlands 3, Leiden 1, pl. 3	ABV 101.87; BA310086
Leiden, Rijksmuseum van Ouheden ROII43	lekythos	Netherlands 4, Leiden 2, pl. 85.1–2	BA 1239
Leiden, Rijksmuseum van Ouheden ROII89	plate	Netherlands 4, Leiden 2, pl. 70.1.	ABV 131.1; BA 301015
Leipzig, Antikenmuseum der Universität T4485	amphora	Germany (East) 2, Leipzig 2, pl. 13.1–4	BA 1907
Leipzig, Antikensammlung der Universität T3127	lekythos	Germany (East) 2, Leipzig 2, pl. 36.1–3	BA 3270
Leipzig, Antikensammlung der Universität T3323	amphora	Germany (East) 2, Leipzig 2, pl. 6 & 7.3–4	ABV 96.9; BA 310009
Leipzig, Antikensammlung der Universität T3324	amphora	Germany (East) 2, Leipzig 2, pl. 4 & 5.2	ABV 98.36; BA 310035
Leipzig, Antikensammlung der Universität T3359	cup	Germany (East) 2, Leipzig 2, pl. 31.1–2	BA 3385
Leipzig, Antikensammlung der Universität T4757	lekythos	Germany (East) 2, Leipzig 2, pl. 35.8–9	BA 3384
Limoges, Musée Adrien Doubouche 78.97	pitcher	France 24, Limoges 1, pl. 8.3	BA 8687
London, British Museum 1848.6–19.7	cup	Great Britain 17, London 9, pl. 59.1	ARV2 371.24; BA 203923
London, British Museum 1894.11–1.105	cup	Great Britain 2, London 2, pl. III H e 15.5 & 8	BA 11802
London, British Museum 1894.11–1.207	cup	Great Britain 2, London 2, pl. III H e 15.5	BA 11800
London, British Museum 1906.12–15.2	cup	Great Britain 2, London 2, pl. III H e 17.3	ABV 196.3; BA 302558
London, British Museum B151	amphora	Great Britain 4, London 3, pl. III H e 25.1a–b	ABV 226.7; BA 302844
London, British Museum B157	amphora	Great Britain 4, London 3, pl. III H e 26.3b & d	BA 11916
London, British Museum B160	amphora	Great Britain 4, London 3, pl. III H e 28.1b	ABV 134.15; BA 301049
London, British Museum B175	amphora	Great Britain 4, London 3, pl. III H e 45.8b	ABV 453.8; BA 330190
London, British Museum B188	amphora	Great Britain 4, London 3, pl. III H e 45.10	BA 2932
London, British Museum B201	amphora	Great Britain 4, London 3, pl. III H e 40.1a	ABV 323.22; BA 301708

Museum & Accession Number	Object Type	CVA Reference	Beazley Reference
London, British Museum B214	amphora	Great Britain 5, London 4, pl. III H e 50.3a	ABV 141; BA 310368
London, British Museum B223	amphora	Great Britain 5, London 4, pl. III H e 55.2a	ABV 284.7; BA 320266
London, British Museum B224	amphora	Great Britain 5, London 4, pl. III H e 54.2a	Para. 141.4; BA 351048
London, British Museum B23	amphora	Great Britain 4, London 3, pl. III H e 23.4	ABV 127.63; BA 300959
London, British Museum B233	amphora	Great Britain 5, London 4, pl. III H e 54.3b	BA 4750
London, British Museum B244	amphora	Great Britain 5, London 4, pl. III H e 59.4a	ABV 271.74; BA 320085
London, British Museum B263	amphora	Great Britain 5, London 4, pl. III H e 64.4b	ABV 271.73; BA 320084
London, British Museum B300	hydria	Great Britain 8, London 6, pl. III H e 75.1	ABV 324.39; BA 301725
London, British Museum B302	hydria	Great Britain 8, London 6, pl. III H e 75.3	ABV 261.40; BA 302272
London, British Museum B311	hydria	Great Britain 8, London 6, pl. III H e 78.4	BA 13294
London, British Museum B312	hydria	Great Britain 8, London 6, pl. III H e 79.1	BA 6493
London, British Museum B319	hydria	Great Britain 8, London 6, pl. III H e 83.4	Para. 124; BA 340507
London, British Museum B331	hydria	Great Britain 8, London 6, pl. III H e 91.1	ABV 261.41; BA 302273
London, British Museum B333	hydria	Great Britain 8, London 6, pl. III H e 91.3	ABV 676; BA 306483
London, British Museum B339	hydria	Great Britain 8, London 6, pl. III H e 95.1	ABV 264.1; BA 302301
London, British Museum B341	hydria	Great Britain 8, London 6, pl. III H e 96.1	BA 13298
London, British Museum B379	cup	Great Britain 2, London 2, pl. III H e 8.2c	ABV 60.20; BA 300525
London, British Museum B387	cup	Great Britain 2, London 2, pl. III H e 16.1	BA 13234
London, British Museum B397	cup	Great Britain 2, London 2, pl. III H e 16.3	BA 13236
London, British Museum B404	cup	Great Britain 2, London 2, pl. III H e 12.1a	BA 13248
London, British Museum B457	cup	Great Britain 2, London 2, pl. III H e 16.7	
London, British Museum B460	cup	Great Britain 2, London 2, pl. III H e 22.2a	ABV 212.1; BA 302683
London, British Museum E172	hydria	Great Britain 7, London 5, pl. III I c 77.2	ARV2 565.42; BA 206472

(continued)

Appendix *(continued)*

Museum & Accession Number	Object Type	CVA Reference	Beazley Reference
London, British Museum E254	amphora	Great Britain 4, London 3, pl. III I c 2.2b	ARV2 31.3; BA 200166
London, British Museum E453	stamnos	Great Britain 4, London 3, pl. III I c 23.4	ARV2 1039.8; BA 213506
London, British Museum E454	stamnos	Great Britain 4, London 3, pl. III I c 24.1a	ARV2 1028.14; BA 213395
London, British Museum E811	lebes	Great Britain 8, London 6, pl. III I c 104.1	ARV2 1334.26; BA 217487
London, British Museum GR 1836.2–24.173 (E818)	cup	Great Britain 17, London 9, pl. 78.1	ARV2 412.10; BA 204492
London, British Museum GR 1895.5–13.1	cup	Great Britain 17, London 9, pl. 70	ARV2 405.2; BA 204396
Los Angeles, County Museum 50.8.34	krater	United States 18, Los Angeles 1, pl. 32.1	ARV2 1422.2; BA 260039
Los Angeles, County Museum 50.8.1	amphora	United States 18, Los Angeles 1, pl. 7.2	ABV 273.108; BA 320119
Los Angeles, County Museum 50.9.36	amphora	United States 18, Los Angeles 1, pl. 8.4	BA 4645
Los Angeles, Getty Museum 86. AE.112	krater	United States 23, Getty 1, pl. 50.1	BA 32055
Los Angeles, Getty Museum 86. AE.128	pitcher	United States 25, Getty 2, pl. 62.2	BA 3892
Los Angeles, Getty Museum 86. AE.135	lekythos	United States 25, Getty 2, pl. 69.1–3	BA 41310
Los Angeles, Getty Museum 86. AE.142.1–2	pyxis	United States 25, Getty 2, pl. 71	BA 8113
Los Angeles, Getty Museum 86. AE.145	cup	United States 25, Getty 2, pl. 74	BA 11076
Los Angeles, Getty Museum 86. AE.150	skyphos	United States 25, Getty 2, pl. 80.1–2	
Los Angeles, Getty Museum 86. AE.329	cup	United States 33, Getty 8, pl. 449.7	BA 24176
Los Angeles, Getty Museum 86. AE.53	amphora	United States 30, Getty 5, pl. 253.1	BA 15387
Los Angeles, Getty Museum 86. AE.60	amphora	United States 23, Getty 1, pl. 2.2	BA 10143
Los Angeles, Getty Museum 86. AE.63	amphora	United States 23, Getty 1, pl. 4.2	Para. 130.5bis; BA 340543
Los Angeles, Getty Museum 86. AE.64	amphora	United States 23, Getty 1, pl. 7.2	Para. 134.21.5; BA 340560
Los Angeles, Getty Museum 86. AE.67	amphora	United States 23, Getty 1, pl. 11.1	BA 79
Los Angeles, Getty Museum 86. AE.70	amphora	United States 23, Getty 1, pl. 13.1	Para. 112.85ter; BA 340437
Los Angeles, Getty Museum 86. AE.75	amphora	United States 23, Getty 1, pl. 19.1	Para. 111.14bis; BA 340428

Museum & Accession Number	Object Type	CVA Reference	Beazley Reference
Los Angeles, Getty Museum 86. AE.96.4	amphora	United States 23, Getty 1, pl. 45.3–4	Para 105.21bis; BA 340400
Madrid, Museo Arqueologico Nacional 10942	cup	Spain 1, Madrid 1, III H e pl. 2.2a–b	BA 14434
Madrid, Museo Arqueologico Nacional 19492	lekythos	Spain 1, Madrid 1, III H e pl. 29.6ab	ABV 467.6; BA 330415
Mainz, Johannes–Gutenberg–Universität 75	skyphos	Germany 15, Mainz 1, pl. 40.1	Para. 85.34; BA 350851
Mainz, Johannes–Gutenberg–Universität 86	cup	Germany 15, Mainz 1, pl. 44.2	BA 12032
Mainz, Johannes–Gutenberg–Universität 88	cup	Germany 15, Mainz 1, pl. 41.2	Para. 67; BA 350482
Mainz, Romisch–Germanisches Zentralmuseum 0.29882	lekythos	Germany 42, Mainz RGZ 1, pl. 33.1–3	BA 1265
Mainz, Romisch–Germanisches Zentralmuseum 0.35997	cup	Germany 42, Mainz RGZ 1, pl. 30.6–8	BA 1777
Mainz, Romisch–Germanisches Zentralmuseum 21962	lekythos	Germany 42, Mainz RGZ 1, pl. 33.6–8	BA 1263
Mainz, Romisch–Germanisches Zentralmuseum 35996	lekythos	Germany 42, Mainz RGZ 1, pl. 30.6–8	BA 1267
Mannheim, Reiss–Museum 41	amphora	CVA Germany 13, Mannheim 1, pl. 16.1–3	ABV 588.4; BA 331245
Mannheim, Reiss–Museum 58	amphora	Germany 13, Mannheim 1, pl. 14.2	Para. 126; BA 340522
Mannheim, Reiss–Museum Cg342	hydria	Germany 75, Mannheim 2, pl. 10	BA 83
Marathon, Museum K 215	lekythos	Greece 7, Marathon 1, pl. 12.1–3	
Marathon, Museum K 419	lekythos	Greece 7, Marathon 1, pl. 9.4–5	BA 24850
Marathon, Museum K 460	lekythos	Greece 7, Marathon 1, pl. 9.1–3	BA 24849
Marathon, Museum K 678	lekythos	Greece 7, Marathon 1, pl. 8	BA 24822
Milan, Collection H.A. C387	amphora	Italy 51, Milan, Coll. H.A. 2, pl. 1.1–2	BA 8690
Minneaoplis Institute of Arts 57.1	amphora	Not in CVA	Para. 59.2; BA 350448
Munich, Antikensammlung 1367	amphora	Germany 3, Munich 1, pl. 4.3 & 5.5	ABV 127.61; BA 300957
Munich, Antikensammlung 1368	amphora	Germany 3, Munich 1, pl. 4.4	ABV 126.51; BA 300947
Munich, Antikensammlung 1369	amphora	Germany 3, Munich 1, pl. 6.1 & 7.3	ABV 126.53; BA 300949
Munich, Antikensammlung 1370	amphora	Germany 3, Munich 1, pl. 6.2 & 7.4	ABV 303.3; BA 301475

(continued)

Appendix *(continued)*

Museum & Accession Number	Object Type	CVA Reference	Beazley Reference
Munich, Antikensammlung 1380	amphora	Germany 3, Munich 1, pl. 14.1	ABV 135.34; BA 310294
Munich, Antikensammlung 1381	amphora	Germany 3, Munich 1, pl. 16.2 & 17.2	ABV 142.5; BA 310373
Munich, Antikensammlung 1382	amphora	Germany 3, Munich 1, pl. 18.1	ABV 135.47; BA 310307
Munich, Antikensammlung 1384	amphora	Germany 3, Munich 1, pl. 18.2 & 20.1	ABV 299.2; BA 320426
Munich, Antikensammlung 1385	amphora	Germany 3, Munich 1, pl. 25.1	ABV 310; BA 301590
Munich, Antikensammlung 1387	amphora	Germany 3, Munich 1, pl. 25.4	ABV 304.7; BA 301487
Munich, Antikensammlung 1397	amphora	Germany 3, Munich 1, pl. 30.2	ABV 134.20; BA 301054
Munich, Antikensammlung 1411	amphora	Germany 3, Munich 1, pl. 41.3 & 43.3	ABV 311.2; BA 301594
Munich, Antikensammlung 1428	amphora	Germany 32, Munich 7, pl. 323	ABV 98.40; BA 310039
Munich, Antikensammlung 1430	amphora	Germany 32, Munich 7, pl. 321	ABV 101.92; BA 310091
Munich, Antikensammlung 1433	amphora	Germany 32, Munich 7, pl. 319	ABV 98.37; BA 310036
Munich, Antikensammlung 1439	amphora	Germany 32, Munich 7, pl. 337	ABV 240.20; BA 301308
Munich, Antikensammlung 1443	amphora	Germany 32, Munich 7, pl. 334.1	ABV 241.27; BA 301315
Munich, Antikensammlung 1468	amphora	Germany 32, Munich 7, pl. 343	ABV 315.3 & 326.5; BA 301629
Munich, Antikensammlung 1471	amphora	Germany 32, Munich 7, pl. 346–7	ABV 137.60; BA 310320
Munich, Antikensammlung 1492	amphora	Germany 37, Munich 8, pl. 416.2	BA 1017
Munich, Antikensammlung 1502A	amphora	Germany 37, Munich 8, pl. 371.1	ABV 263.2; BA 302285
Munich, Antikensammlung 1514	amphora	Germany 37, Munich 8, pl. 387.2	ABV 272.90; BA 320101
Munich, Antikensammlung 1523	amphora	Germany 37, Munich 8, pl. 366.1	ABV 262.1; BA 302284
Munich, Antikensammlung 1537	amphora	Germany 37, Munich 8, pl. 403.3 & 405.2	BA 1580
Munich, Antikensammlung 1541	amphora	Germany 48, Munich 9, p. 28a	BA 4820
Munich, Antikensammlung 1628	amphora	Germany 48, Munich 9, pl. 63.4	BA 7419
Munich, Antikensammlung 1758	pitcher	Germany 65, Munich 12, pl. 8.3–4	BA 19437

Museum & Accession Number	Object Type	CVA Reference	Beazley Reference
Munich, Antikensammlung 1764	pitcher	Germany 65, Munich 12, pl. 25.3–4	BA 19446
Munich, Antikensammlung 1777	pitcher	Germany 65, Munich 12, pl. 25.1–2	BA 19449
Munich, Antikensammlung 1780A	pitcher	Germany 65, Munich 12, pl. 26.1–2	BA 19439
Munich, Antikensammlung 1788	pitcher	Germany 65, Munich 12, pl. 12	Para. 179.8; BA 351295
Munich, Antikensammlung 2218	cup	Germany 57, Munich 11, pl. 50.1–3	BA 31977
Munich, Antikensammlung 2220	cup	Germany 57, Munich 11, pl. 30.6	BA 31912
Munich, Antikensammlung 2221	cup	Germany 57, Munich 11, pl. 26.4 & 27.1	BA 31976
Munich, Antikensammlung 2222	cup	Germany 57, Munich 11, pl. 32.1–3	BA 31972
Munich, Antikensammlung 2222A	cup	Germany 57, Munich 11, pl. 10.6	BA 45080
Munich, Antikensammlung 2226	cup	Germany 57, Munich 11, pl. 49.1–3	BA 31953
Munich, Antikensammlung 2229	cup	Germany 57, Munich 11, pl. 44.5	BA 31910
Munich, Antikensammlung 2240	cup	Germany 57, Munich 11, pl. 55.2	BA 31971
Munich, Antikensammlung 2241	cup	Germany 57, Munich 11, pls. 22.9, 23.1–3	BA 7975
Munich, Antikensammlung 2407	stamnos	Germany 20, Munich 5, pl. 241	ARV2 274.35; BA 202871
Munich, Antikensammlung 2420	hydria	Germany 20, Munich 5, pl. 218.3	ARV2 32.3; BA 200172
Munich, Antikensammlung 596	hydria	Germany 28, Munich 6, pl. 280.1 & 281	
Munich, Antikensammlung 6199	pyxis (kothon)	Germany 9, Munich 3, pl. 147.3–6	
Munich, Antikensammlung 8600	pyxis (kothon)	Germany 9, Munich 3, pl. 138.3–5	BA 4515
Munich, Antikensammlung 9438	cup	Germany 57, Munich 11, pl. 27.4–6	BA 45109
Munich, Antikensammlung 9440	cup	Germany 57, Munich 11, pl. 31.5–6	BA 45108
Munich, Antikensammlung 9441	cup	Germany 57, Munich 11, pl. 32.8	BA 45107
Munich, Antikensammlung 9449	cup	Germany 57, Munich 11, pl. 43.4	BA 45094
Munich, Antikensammlung J1271	amphora	Germany 37, Munich 8, pl. 373.4	BA 1159

(continued)

Appendix *(continued)*

Museum & Accession Number	Object Type	CVA Reference	Beazley Reference
Munich, Antikensammlung J636	cup	Germany 57, Munich 11, pl. 19	BA 31913
Munich, Antikensammlung M1913	pitcher	Germany 65, Munich 12, pl. 3.4–5	BA 19431
Munich, Antikensammlung M425	pitcher	Germany 65, Munich 12, pl. 8.1–2	BA 19435
Nantes, Musée Dobrée D863.1.74	lekythos	France 36, Nantes 1, pl. 9.4–5	BA 28932
Nantes, Musée Dobrée D974.2.21	lekythos	France 36, Nantes 1, pl. 9.6–8	BA 28933
Nantes, Musée Dobrée D974.2.39	lekythos	France 36, Nantes 1, pl. 9.1–3	BA 28931
Naples, Museo Nazionale Archeologico 112849	amphora	Italy 20, Naples, Mus. Naz. 1, pl. 5.3	ABV 138.2; BA 310334
Naples, Museo Nazionale Archeologico 164163 (Sp. 149)	amphora	Italy 71, Naples, Mus. Naz., Collezione Spinelli 2, pl. 11.2	
Naples, Museo Nazionale Archeologico 164165 (Sp.1955)	lekythos	Italy 71, Naples, Mus. Naz., Collezione Spinelli 2, pl. 29	Para. 205; BA 340626
Naples, Museo Nazionale Archeologico 81083	pelike	Italy 20, Naples, Mus. Naz. 1, pl. 13.1–2	ABV 338.3; BA 301859
Naples, Museo Nazionale Archeologico 81104	hydria	Italy 20, Naples, Mus. Naz. 1, pl. 41.4	BA 14156
Naples, Museo Nazionale Archeologico 81142	cup	Italy 20, Naples, Mus. Naz. 1, pl. 19.4	BA 14222
Naples, Museo Nazionale Archeologico 81186	amphora	Italy 20, Naples, Mus. Naz. 1, pl. 3.1–2	ABV 305.26; BA 301506
Naples, Museo Nazionale Archeologico 86335	lekythos	Italy 69, Naples, Mus. Naz. 5, pl. 59.2,5,8	ABV 701.13bis; BA 306738
Naples, Museo Nazionale Archeologico 86344 or RC201	lekythos	Italy 69, Naples, Mus. Naz. 5, pl. 55.4–6	ABV 489.8; BA 303523
Naples, Museo Nazionale Archeologico 86345	lekythos	Italy 69, Naples, Mus. Naz. 5, pl. 57.4–6	Para. 330; BA 361031
Naples, Museo Nazionale Archeologico 86358	pitcher	Italy 69, Naples, Mus. Naz. 5, pl. 50.3–4	
Naples, Museo Nazionale Archeologico 86359	pitcher	Italy 69, Naples, Mus. Naz. 5, pl. 50.1–2	ABV 699.43ter; BA 306667
Naples, Museo Nazionale Archeologico Sant. 126	cup	Italy 20, Naples, Mus. Naz. 1, pl. 32.1	BA 14096
Naples, Museo Nazionale Archeologico Sant. 130	cup	Italy 20, Naples, Mus. Naz. 1, pl. 45.1–3	ABV 609.4; BA 306109
Naples, Museo Nazionale Archeologico STG144	amphora	Italy 20, Naples, Mus. Naz. 1, pl. 1.5–6	ABV 298.13; BA 320412
New York, Metropolitan Museum of Art 06.1021.153	cup	United States 11, New York 2, pl. 17	BA 13416

Museum & Accession Number	Object Type	CVA Reference	Beazley Reference
New York, Metropolitan Museum of Art 06.1021.159	cup	United States 11, New York 2, pl. 23	ABV 199.1; BA 302573
New York, Metropolitan Museum of Art 14.147.3	cup	United States 11, New York 2, pl. 16	ABV 227.1; BA 302856
New York, Metropolitan Museum of Art 17.230.14	amphora	United States 16, New York 4, pl. 18.2	ABV 144.3; BA 310385
New York, Metropolitan Museum of Art 21.88.76	amphora	United States 12, New York 3, pl. 23.1	BA 13297
New York, Metropolitan Museum of Art 25.78.33	cup	United States 11, New York 2, pl. 3a	ABV 70.3; BA 300634
New York, Metropolitan Museum of Art 41.162.129 (once Gallatin)	cup	United States 8, Fogg/Gallatin, pl. 48.1b	ARV2 92.66; BA 200763
New York, Metropolitan Museum of Art 41.162.133 (once Gallatin)	cup	United States 8, Fogg/Gallatin, pl. 49.1b	ARV2 151.47; BA 201371
New York, Metropolitan Museum of Art 41.162.222 (once Gallatin)	cup	United States 11, New York 2, pl. 33	BA 13403
New York, Metropolitan Museum of Art 41.162.32	amphora	United States 12, New York 3, pl. 48.9	ABV 676; BA 306477
New York, Metropolitan Museum of Art 56.171.17	amphora	United States 16, New York 4, pl. 10.2–3	ABV 239.8; BA 301296
New York, Metropolitan Museum of Art 56.171.18	amphora	United States 16, New York 4, pl. 14.1	ABV 137.61; BA 310321
New York, Metropolitan Museum of Art 58.32	amphora	United States 12, New York 3, pl. 29.2	Para. 114.10bis; BA 340445
New York, Metropolitan Museum of Art 59.64	amphora	United States 16, New York 4, pl. 2b	Para. 31; BA 350203
New York, Metropolitan Museum of Art 61.11.16	amphora	United States 16, New York 4, pl. 29.2	Para. 141.6; BA 351044
New York, Metropolitan Museum of Art 67.44.1	amphora	United States 16, New York 4, pl. 34.3	ABV 328.5; BA 301762
New York, Metropolitan Museum of Art 96.9.34	amphora	United States 16, New York 4, pl. 37.5–8	BA 3763
Omaha, Joslyn Art Museum 1963.480	amphora	United States 21, Omaha 1, pl. 10, 11	Para. 34.2; BA 350215
Omaha, Joslyn Art Museum 44.1953	hydria	United States 21, Omaha 1, pl. 20.1	Para. 119.7bis; BA 340468
Orvieto, Museo Civico 1042	cup	Italy 16, Orvieto 1, pl. 14.4–6	ARV2 938.18; BA 212628
Orvieto, Museo Civico 2491	pyxis	Italy 41, Orvieto Faina 1, pl. 1.2	BA 9704
Orvieto, Museo Civico 2547	cup	Italy 41, Orvieto Faina 1, pl. 4.3, 5	BA 8048
Orvieto, Museo Civico 2548	cup	Italy 41, Orvieto Faina, pl. 3.1	BA 8046
Oslo, Museum of Applied Art 5816	lekythos	Norway 1, pl. 24.1	Para. 205; BA 340633

(continued)

Appendix *(continued)*

Museum & Accession Number	Object Type	CVA Reference	Beazley Reference
Oslo, University (anonymous deposit)	lekythos	Norway 1, pl. 23.4	Para. 209; BA 340703
Oxford (MS), Robinson Collection	cup	United States 4, Baltimore, Robinson 1, pl. 20.1	ABV 70.1; BA 300632
Oxford (MS), University of Mississippi 1977.3.88	hydria	United States 6, Baltimore, Robinson 2, pl. 36	ARV2 611.35; BA 207082
Oxford, Ashmolean Museum 1924.3	amphora	Great Britain 3, Oxford 1, pl. 15.3–4	ARV2 200.45; BA 201833
Oxford, Ashmolean Museum 1925.14	amphora	Great Britain 9, Oxford 2, pl. III H 6 2	BA 11824
Oxford, Ashmolean Museum 1928.573	cup	Great Britain 9, Oxford 2, pl. III I 56.3	ARV2 920.15; BA 211185
Oxford, Ashmolean Museum 1929.19	pitcher	Great Britain 9, Oxford 2, pl. III H 3.28	ABV 153.38; BA 310465
Oxford, Ashmolean Museum 1965.116	amphora	Great Britain 14, Oxford 3, pl. 10.1	ABV 273.111; BA 320122
Oxford, Ashmolean Museum 1965.119	hydria	Great Britain 14, Oxford 3, pl. 38.3	ABV 261.35; BA 302267
Oxford, Ashmolean Museum 1965.124	amphora	Great Britain 14, Oxford 3, pl. 31.3	ABV 300.6; BA 320430
Oxford, Ashmolean Museum 1965.135	amphora	Great Britain 14, Oxford 3, pl. 2–3	ABV 137.59; BA 310319
Oxford, Ashmolean Museum 1965.141	amphora	Great Britain 14, Oxford 3, pl. 31.2 & 4	ABV 299.1; BA 320425
Oxford, Ashmolean Museum 563	pelike	Great Britain 9, Oxford 2, pl. III H 8.8	ABV 396.21; BA 302990
Oxford, Ashmolean Museum V517	cup	Great Britain 3, Oxford 1, pl. 8.2	ARV2 785.8; BA 209671
Palermo, Mormino Collection 109	lekythos	Italy 50, Palermo 1, pl. 3.7–8	BA 2779
Palermo, Mormino Collection 120	lekythos	Italy 50, Palermo 1, pl. 3.9–10	BA 2777
Palermo, Mormino Collection 121	lekythos	Italy 50, Palermo 1, pl. 5.2–3	BA 3146
Palermo, Mormino Collection 124	lekythos	Italy 50, Palermo 1, pl. 1.6–8	BA 2786
Palermo, Mormino Collection 126	lekythos	Italy 50, Palermo 1, pl. 2.1–3	BA 2784
Palermo, Mormino Collection 133	lekythos	Italy 50, Palermo 1, pl. 10.3–4	BA 3068
Palermo, Mormino Collection 135	lekythos	Italy 50, Palermo 1, pl. 10.9–10	BA 3186
Palermo, Mormino Collection 160	lekythos	Italy 50, Palermo 1, pl. 2.4–5	BA 3144
Palermo, Mormino Collection 295	lekythos	Italy 50, Palermo 1, pl. 11.11–12	BA 3064

Museum & Accession Number	Object Type	CVA Reference	Beazley Reference
Palermo, Mormino Collection 32	lekythos	Italy 50, Palermo 1, pl. 3.5–6	BA 2780
Palermo, Mormino Collection 629	lekythos	Italy 50, Palermo 1, pl. 14.5–6	BA 2974
Palermo, Mormino Collection 664	lekythos	Italy 50, Palermo 1, pl. 1.1–3	BA 2787
Palermo, Mormino Collection 770	lekythos	Italy 50, Palermo 1, pl. 3.1	BA 2783
Palermo, Mormino Collection 889	lekythos	Italy 50, Palermo 1, pl. 11.9–10	BA 3063
Paris, Cabinet des Médailles 206	amphora	France 7, Paris, Bibliothéque nationale 1, pl. 34.2	ABV 109.27; BA 310173
Paris, Cabinet des Médailles 207	amphora	France 7, Paris, Bibliothéque nationale 1, pl. 34.3	ABV 296.6; BA 320385
Paris, Cabinet des Médailles 214	lekanis	France 7, Paris, Bibliothéque nationale 1, pls. 82.15, 83.8–9	BA 390249
Paris, Cabinet des Médailles 243	amphora	France 10, Paris, Bibliothéque nationale 2, pl. 88.4	BA 1047
Paris, Cabinet des Médailles 278	lekythos	France 7, Paris, Bibliothéque nationale 1, pl. 46.7–9	BA 10992
Paris, Cabinet des Médailles 300	lekythos	France 10, Paris, Bibliothéque nationale 2, pl. 85.6–8	BA 11336
Paris, Cabinet des Médailles 308	lekythos	France 10, Paris, Bibliothéque nationale 2, pl. 86	BA 7586
Paris, Cabinet des Médailles 314	cup	France 7, Paris, Bibliothéque nationale 1, pl. 45.3	ABV 65.41; BA 300584
Paris, Cabinet des Médailles AVH 3388	amphora	France 10, Paris, Bibliothéque nationale 2, pl. 75.2	BA 11348
Paris, Louvre A478	cup	France 12, Louvre 8, pl. III H e 76.2–3	ABV 66.54; BA 300597
Paris, Louvre CA2252	amphora	France 26, Louvre 17, pl. 51.1	
Paris, Louvre CA2509	pitcher	France 25, Louvre 16, pl. III H b 16	
Paris, Louvre CA3279	amphora	France 26, Louvre 17, pl. 31.1	
Paris, Louvre CA2918	cup	France 14, Louvre 9, pl. III H e 84.1–2	ABV 157.85; BA 310514
Paris, Louvre CA576	cup	France 12, Louvre 8, pl. III H e 75.7	ABV 63.3; BA 300547
Paris, Louvre CA617	aryballos	France 12, Louvre 8, pl. III C a 14.3	
Paris, Louvre CA6243	hydria	France 39, Louvre 26, pl. 32	
Paris, Louvre Camp. 11259	krater	France 19, Louvre 12, pl. III H e 165.1	
Paris, Louvre Camp. 11266	krater	France 19, Louvre 12, pl. III H e 170.6	
Paris, Louvre Cp10654	hydria	France 18, Louvre 11, pl. III H e 137.3	ABV 304.2; BA 301480

(continued)

Appendix *(continued)*

Museum & Accession Number	Object Type	CVA Reference	Beazley Reference
Paris, Louvre Cp 12632	cup	France 38, Louvre 25, pl. 15.2	
Paris, Louvre Cp10649	hydria	France 18, Louvre 11, pl. III H e 134.3	ABV 313.2; BA 301620
Paris, Louvre Cp10651	hydria	France 18, Louvre 11, pl. III H e 135.1	BA 12421
Paris, Louvre Cp10661	hydria	France 18, Louvre 11, pl. III H e 142.2	BA 12166
Paris, Louvre Cp10675	hydria	France 18, Louvre 11, pl. III H e 145.12	BA 12193
Paris, Louvre Cp10676	hydria	France 18, Louvre 11, pl. III H e 146.6	BA 12192
Paris, Louvre Cp10684	hydria	France 18, Louvre 11, pl. III H e 148.5	BA 15382
Paris, Louvre E831	amphora	France 1, Louvre 1, pl. III H d 2.10	ABV 103.108; BA 310107
Paris, Louvre E835	amphora	France 1, Louvre 1, pl. III H d 2.6	ABV 101.82; BA 310081
Paris, Louvre E845	amphora	France 1, Louvre 1, pl. III H d 4.5	ABV 102.93; BA 310092
Paris, Louvre E852	amphora	France 1, Louvre 1, pl. III H d 5.14	ABV 96.13; BA 310013
Paris, Louvre E853	amphora	France 1, Louvre 1, pl. III H d 5.7	ABV 101.90, 94; BA 310089
Paris, Louvre E854	amphora	France 1, Louvre 1, pl. III H d 5.3	ABV 101.89; BA 310088
Paris, Louvre EL 173	cup	France 14, Louvre 9, pl. III H e 89.8 & 11	BA 10926
Paris, Louvre F1	amphora	France 4, Louvre 3, pl. III H e 10.2	Para. 132.3; BA 340549
Paris, Louvre F107	amphora	France 5, Louvre 4, pl. III H e 34.3 & 34.7	ABV 221.39; BA 302788
Paris, Louvre F108	amphora	France 5, Louvre 4, pl. III H e 34.4 & 34.8	ABV 220.30; BA 302779
Paris, Louvre F112	amphora	France 5, Louvre 4, pl. III H e 36.13	ABV 219.28; BA 302777
Paris, Louvre F14	amphora	France 4, Louvre 3, pl. III H e 11.5, 11.8	BA 10708
Paris, Louvre F235	amphora	France 5, Louvre 4, pl. III H e 45.3	ABV 395.8; BA 302962
Paris, Louvre F282	amphora	France 8, Louvre 5, pl. III H g 2.5	BA 10730
Paris, Louvre F291	hydria	France 9, Louvre 6, pl. III H e 70.1	BA 11295
Paris, Louvre F31	amphora	France 4, Louvre 3, pl. III H e 11.9	ABV 313.1; BA 301613
Paris, Louvre F33	amphora	France 4, Louvre 3, pl. III H e 15.7	ABV 141.3; BA 310363
Paris, Louvre F35	amphora	France 4, Louvre 3, pl. III H e 15.3	BA 10709
Paris, Louvre F36	amphora	France 4, Louvre 3, pl. III H e 15.5.	ABV 150.6; BA 310433
Paris, Louvre F40	hydria	France 9, Louvre 6, pl. III H e 64.4	BA 11270
Paris, Louvre F41	hydria	France 9, Louvre 6, pl. III H e 64.6	ABV 310; BA 301588
Paris, Louvre F43	hydria	France 9, Louvre 6, pl. III H e 65.2	ABV 130.4; BA 301002
Paris, Louvre F45	hydria	France 9, Louvre 6, pl. III H e 65.3	ABV 92.3; BA 300857

Museum & Accession Number	Object Type	CVA Reference	Beazley Reference
Paris, Louvre F46	hydria	France 9, Louvre 6, pl. III H e 66.1	BA 4799
Paris, Louvre F47	hydria	France 9, Louvre 6, pl. III H e 66.3	ABV 309.100; BA 301579
Paris, Louvre F50	hydria	France 9, Louvre 6, pl. III H e 67.2	ABV 277.8; BA 320170
Paris, Louvre F57	amphora	France 5, Louvre 4, pl. III H e 31.1	ABV 316.3; BA 301644
Paris, Louvre F6	hydria	France 9, Louvre 6, pl. III H e 59.2	ABV 123.3; BA 300899
Paris, Louvre F62	lebes	France 2, Louvre 2, pl. III H e 1.2	BA 10095
Paris, Louvre F7	hydria	France 9, Louvre 6, pl. III H e 59.5	BA 11265
Paris, Louvre F76	cup	France 14, Louvre 9, pl. III H e 82.1 & 3	BA 10884
Paris, Louvre F77	cup	France 14, Louvre 9, pl. III H e 82.6	BA 164
Paris, Louvre F78	cup	France 14, Louvre 9, pl. III H e 82.2 & 5	BA 10893
Paris, Louvre F91	cup	France 14, Louvre 9, pl. III H e 86.6–7	BA 10901
Paris, Louvre F93	cup	France 14, Louvre 9, pl. III H e 86.9–10	BA 10904
Paris, Louvre F99	amphora	France 5, Louvre 4, pl. III H e 32.6	ABV 228; BA 303477
Paris, Louvre G103	krater	France 1, Louvre 1, pl. III I c 4.1	ARV2 14.2; BA 200064
Paris, Louvre G182bis	stamnos	France 2, Louvre 2, pl. III I c 15.6	ARV2 251.29; BA202506
Paris, Louvre G228	pelike	France 9, Louvre 6, pl. III.I.c 44.1, 45.2–3	ARV2 250.14; BA 202517
Paris, Louvre G355	krater	France 5, Louvre 4, pl. III I d 25.9	ARV2 563.10; BA 206435
Paris, Louvre G485	krater	France 8, Louvre 5, pl. III I d 32.3	BA 10872
Paris, Louvre G499	krater	France 38, Louvre 25, pl. 6.2	
Paris, Louvre G520	krater	France 8, Louvre 5, pl. III I e 5.2	ARV2 1190.29; BA 215763
Paris, Louvre G522	krater	France 8, Louvre 5, pl. III I e 5.4	ARV2 1426.25; BA 260085
Paris, Louvre G525	krater	France 8, Louvre 5, pl. III I e 6.2	BA 10869
Paris, Louvre N3163/MN 706	amphora	France 8, Louvre 5, pl. III H g 5.8	ABV 415.3; BA 303149
Paris, Louvre N3223 (F91)	cup	France 14, Louvre 9, pl. 86.6–8	BA 10901
Paris, Louvre S1258 (F35)	amphora	France 4, Louvre 3, III H e, pl. 14.9	BA 10709
Paris, Musée du Petit Palais 312	hydria	France 15, Petit Palais 1, pl. 10.4	ABV 130.3; BA 301001
Paris, Musée du Petit Palais 432	lekythos	France 15, Petit Palais 1, pl. 3.9	ABV 465.30; BA 330382
Paris, Musée Rodin TC 237	lekythos	France 16, Rodin 1, pl. 14.7–8	ABV 70.6; BA 300637
Paris, Musée Rodin TC 959	amphora	France 16, Rodin 1, pl. 11.5	BA 10845
Paris, Musée Rodin TC 979	skyphos	France 16, Rodin 1, pl. 13.4–6	ABV 120.4; BA 300864
Parma, Museo Nazionale di Antichita C118	amphora	Italy 45, Parma 1, pl. 5.1	BA 965

(continued)

Appendix *(continued)*

Museum & Accession Number	Object Type	CVA Reference	Beazley Reference
Parma, Museo Nazionale di Antichita C120	amphora	Italy 45, Parma 1, pl. 2.1	BA 967
Parma, Museo Nazionale di Antichita C124	lekythos	Italy 45, Parma 1, pl. 18.1–2	BA 3318
Pilsen, Museum of Western Bohemia 8408	lekythos	Czech Republic 4, Pilsen 1, pl. 1	ABV 463.5; BA 330341
Prague, Charles University 22.76	lekythos	Czech Republic 1, Prague, Univ. 1, pl. 30.4–6.	ABV 499.39; BA 305366
Prague, Charles University 60.41	lekythos	Czech Republic 1, Prague, Univ. 1, pl. 30.1–3	BA 1707
Prague, National Museum 3790	lekythos	Czech Republic 2, Prague, Nat. Mus. 1, pl. 40.6–8	BA 21421
Prague, National Museum 4484	lekythos	Czech Republic 2, Prague, Nat. Mus. 1, pl. 50.1–3	BA 18517
Prague, National Museum 4607	lekythos	Czech Republic 2, Prague, Nat. Mus. 1, pl. 39.1 & 5	BA 21425
Prague, National Museum 4757	cup	Czech Republic 2, Prague, Nat. Mus. 1, pl. 33	ABV 682.71; BA 306522
Providence, Rhode Island School of Design 14.432 (C2155)	pitcher	United States 2, Providence 1, pl. 12.3	BA 4538
Providence, Rhode Island School of Design 23.303	amphora	United States 2, Providence 1, pl. 9.2a–2c	ABV 220.34; BA 302873
Reading, University 25.viii.6	lekythos	Great Britain 12, Reading 1, pl. 11.10	ABV 698.11bis; BA 306665
Reading, University 26.xii.12	skyphos	Great Britain 12, Reading 1, pl. 10.12	BA 14365
Rhodes, Archaeological Museum 10.480	pitcher	Italy 9, Rodi 1, pl. 13.3	ABV 449.1; BA 330149
Rhodes, Archaeological Museum 11.822	cup	Italy 9, Rodi 1, pl. 18.2	BA 14405
Rhodes, Archaeological Museum 12471	skyphos	Italy 10, Rodi 2, pl. 20.3	ABV 620.87; BA 306299
Rhodes, Archaeological Museum 13105	cup	Italy 9, Rodi 1, pl. 18.6	ABV 194.2; BA 302545
Rhodes, Archaeological Museum 1346	amphora	Italy 10, Rodi 2, pl. 22.1	ABV 298.7; BA 320406
Rome, Musei Capitolini 136	amphora	Italy 36, Rome, Capitolini 1, pl. 13.3	Para. 39; BA 350218
Rome, Musei Capitolini 47	amphora	Italy 36, Rome, Capitolini 1, pl. 18.2	ABV 134.19; BA 301053
Rome, Musei Capitolini 49	amphora	Italy 36, Rome, Capitolini 1, pl. 18.3–4	BA 13757
Rome, Musei Capitolini 71	lekythos	Italy 36, Rome, Capitolini 1, pl. 207.3–4	BA 13761
Rome, Musei Capitolini 84	amphora	Italy 36, Rome, Capitolini 1, pl. 19.1	ABV 125.38; BA 300934

Museum & Accession Number	Object Type	CVA Reference	Beazley Reference
Rome, Musei Capitolini 98	amphora	Italy 36, Rome, Capitolini 1, pl. 20.1	ABV 300.5; BA 320429
Rome, Villa Giulia 1204	pitcher	Italy 3, Villa Giulia 3, pl. 51.6	ABV 441; BA 330045
Rome, Villa Giulia 1394	lekythos	Italy 3, Villa Giulia 3, pl. 51.9	ABV 470.92; BA 330501
Rome, Villa Giulia 23333	lekythos	Italy 2, Villia Giulia 2, pl. 14.4,6,7	ABV 516.2; BA 330654
Rome, Villa Giulia 24997	lekythos	Italy 3, Villa Giulia 3, pl. 50.5	ABV 459.3; BA 330261
Rome, Villa Giulia 26358	lekythos	Italy 3, Villa Giulia 3, pl. 50.14	BA 13013
Rome, Villa Giulia 3559	cup	Italy 3, Villa Giulia 3, pl. 27.4 & 28	ABV 195.1; BA 302556
Rome, Villa Giulia 7847	cup	Italy 3, Villa Giulia 3, pl. 25.12–13	BA 13066
Rome, Villa Giulia 995	lekythos	Italy 2, Villia Giulia 2, pl. 14.5,8	BA 13048
Schwerin, Staatliches Museum 706	krater	Germany (East) 1, Schwerin 1, pl. 36	ARV2 618.6; BA 207154
Schwerin, Staatliches Museum 707	hydria	Germany (East) 1, Schwerin 1, pl. 23	ARV2 565.41; BA 206471
Schwerin, Staatliches Museum 713	amphora	Germany (East) 1, Schwerin 1, pl. 4.2	
Stuttgart, Württembergisches Landesmuseum KAS69	skyphos	Germany 26, Stuttgart 1, pl. 18.7–9	Para. 90.3; BA 350969
Stuttgart, Württembergisches Landesmuseum KAS78	lekythos	Germany 26, Stuttgart 1, pl. 21.1–2	Para. 208; BA 340675
Stuttgart, Württembergisches Landesmuseum KAS79	lekythos	Germany 26, Stuttgart 1, pl. 21.6–7	BA 11985
Stuttgart, Württembergisches Landesmuseum KAS83	lekythos	Germany 26, Stuttgart 1, pl. 22.7–8	Para. 202; BA 340589
Syracuse, Museo Archeologico Regionale Paolo Orsi 10599	amphora	Italy 17, Syracuse 1, pl. 1a	ABV 100.67; BA 310066
Syracuse, Museo Archeologico Regionale Paolo Orsi 12063	amphora	Italy 17, Syracuse 1, pl. 7.4	ABV 131.6; BA 301022
Taranto, Museo Archeologico Nazionale 143476	lekythos	Italy 70, Taranto 4, pl. 10.1–3	
Taranto, Museo Archeologico Nazionale 143483	lekythos	Italy 70, Taranto 4, pl. 10.4–6	
Taranto, Museo Archeologico Nazionale 20132 (117187)	cup	Italy 18, Taranto 2, pl. 3.1–3	BA 13870
Taranto, Museo Archeologico Nazionale 20274A	cup	Italy 35, Taranto 3, pl. III H e 18.3	Para. 46; BA 350352
Taranto, Museo Archeologico Nazionale 4173	aryballos	Italy 18, Taranto 2, pl. III C d 1.1–3	
Taranto, Museo Archeologico Nazionale 4320	amphora	Italy 18, Taranto 2, pl. III H e 1.4	ABV 139.11; BA 310343
Taranto, Museo Archeologico Nazionale 4359	amphora	Italy 18, Taranto 2, pl. III H e 1.2	ABV 109.26; BA 310172
Taranto, Museo Archeologico Nazionale 4365	cup	Italy 18, Taranto 2, pl. III H e 6.2	BA 13839

(continued)

Appendix *(continued)*

Museum & Accession Number	Object Type	CVA Reference	Beazley Reference
Taranto, Museo Archeologico Nazionale 51320	cup	Italy 18, Taranto 2, pl. III H e 5.1	BA 4252
Taranto, Museo Archeologico Nazionale 51323	cup	Italy 18, Taranto 2, pl. III H e 5.2	BA 13885
Taranto, Museo Archeologico Nazionale 52.128 or 52128	lekythos	Italy 18, Taranto 2, pl. 14.4	BA 13865
Taranto, Museo Archeologico Nazionale 52155	cup	Italy 35, Taranto 3, pl. III H e 24.1–2	BA 219
Taranto, Museo Archeologico Nazionale 8.7.1921	lekythos	Italy 18, Taranto 2, pl. III H e 12.1	ABV 464; BA 330352
Taranto, Museo Archeologico Nazionale I.G. 4342	cup	Italy 35, Taranto 3, pl. III H e 26.2	ABV 65.55; BA 300598
Taranto, Museo Archeologico Nazionale I.G. 4362	cup	Italy 35, Taranto 3, pl. 17.1–2	ABV 113.72; BA 310218
Taranto, Museo Archeologico Nazionale I.G. 4363	cup	Italy 35, Taranto 3, pl. 17.1–2	ABV 113.71; BA 310217
Taranto, Museo Archeologico Nazionale I.G. 4408	cup	Italy 35, Taranto 3, pl. III H e 28.1	ABV 65.43; BA 300586
Taranto, Museo Archeologico Nazionale I.G. 4492	cup	Italy 35, Taranto 3, pl. III H e 19.1–2	ABV 113.73; BA 310219
Tarquinia, Museo Nazionale Tarquiniese 690	cup	Italy 26, Tarquinia 2, p. III I 21.2	ARV2 818.17; BA 210117
Tarquinia, Museo Nazionale Tarquiniese P39	amphora	Italy 25, Tarquinia 1, pl. 16.3	
Tarquinia, Museo Nazionale Tarquiniese RC1550	amphora	Italy 26, Tarquinia 2, pl. 23.1 & 4	ABV 137.63; BA 310323
Tarquinia, Museo Nazionale Tarquiniese RC3984	amphora	Italy 26, Tarquinia 2, pl. 25.2	Para. 132.4; BA 340550
Tarquinia, Museo Nazionale Tarquiniese RC6846	cup	Italy 25, Tarquinia 1, pl. III I 5	ARV2 369.4; BA 203903
Tarquinia, Museo Nazionale Tarquiniese RC6992	amphora	Italy 26, Tarquinia 2, pl. 28.2	BA 13831
Thebes, Archaeological Museum 17078 (R.15)	skyphos	Greece 6, Thebes 1, pl. 46	BA 24457
Thebes, Archaeological Museum 22540	cup	Greece 6, Thebes 1, pl. 31	
Thebes, Archaeological Museum 6010 (R.31.160)	lekythos	Greece 6, Thebes 1, pl. 58.4–6	BA 330537
Thebes, Archaeological Museum 6011 (R.31.176)	skyphos	Greece 6, Thebes 1, pl. 40	Para. 84.8; BA 350827
Thebes, Archaeological Museum 6016 (R.31.181)	skyphos	Greece 6, Thebes 1, pl. 54.1–3	BA 24561
Thebes, Archaeological Museum 6074 (R.51.229)	lekythos	Greece 6, Thebes 1, pl. 58.1–3	Para. 201.1; BA 351483
Thebes, Archaeological Museum 6104 (R.49.265)	skyphos	Greece 6, Thebes 1, pl. 25	

Museum & Accession Number	Object Type	CVA Reference	Beazley Reference
Thebes, Archaeological Museum 6113 (R.49.261)	cup	Greece 6, Thebes 1, pl. 30	ABV 70.2; BA 300633
Thebes, Archaeological Museum Th.P. 700	krater	Greece 6, Thebes 1, pl. 16	
Thessaloniki, Archaeological Museum 14900	krater	Greece 5, Thessaloniki 1, pl.43.2	
Thessaloniki, Archaeological Museum 14906 (T289)	cup	Greece 5, Thessaloniki 1, pl. 54.3–5	BA 24857
Thessaloniki, Archaeological Museum 9290	krater	Greece 5, Thessaloniki 1, pl. 26.5 & 27	BA 24483
Thessaloniki, Archaeological Museum 13452	krater	Greece 5, Thessaloniki 1, pl.41.1	
Tokyo, Bridgestone Museum 135	amphora	Japan 2, pl. 39.3–4	BA 18449
Tokyo, Bridgestone Museum 81	pitcher	Japan 1, pl. 27.1–2	BA 7218
Tokyo, Matsuoka Museum of Art 351	lekythos	Japan 2, pl. 49.1–4	BA 3469
Tokyo, University 50/16	lekythos	Japan 2, pl. 19.5–7	
Toledo, Museum of Art 55.42	hydria	United States 17, Toledo 1, pl. 25.1	Para. 161; BA 306994
Toledo, Museum of Art 63.27	skyphos	United States 17, Toledo 1, pl. 32	Para. 257; BA 351546
Toronto, Royal Ontario Museum 919.5.133	hydria	Canada 1, Toronto 1, pl. 25.4	ABV 277.10; BA 320172
Toronto, Royal Ontario Museum 919.5.136	amphora	Canada 1, Toronto 1, pl. 18.4	ABV 588.2; BA 331248
Toronto, Royal Ontario Museum 919.5.145	pitcher	Canada 1, Toronto 1, pl. 26.6–7	ABV 428.1; BA 303280
Toronto, Royal Ontario Museum 919.5.146	amphora	Canada 1, Toronto 1, pl. 3.1	BA 5445
Toronto, Royal Ontario Museum 919.5.176	amphora	Canada 1, Toronto 1, pl. 2.1	ABV 134.11; BA 301045
Toronto, Royal Ontario Museum 925.97	amphora	Canada 1, Toronto 1, pl. 20.1	Para. 141.2; BA 351046
Toronto, Royal Ontario Museum 929.22.9	cup	Canada 1, Toronto 1, pl. 31.2–3	ABV 54.54; BA 300431
Toronto, Royal Ontario Museum 959.17.212	krater	Canada 1, Toronto 1, pl. 28.1	BA 5992
Toronto, Royal Ontario Museum 959.17.74	cup	Canada 1, Toronto 30, pl. 34.1–3	BA 6033
Tours, Musée des Beaux–Arts 863.2.64	hydria	France 30, Bourges 1, pl. 5.1	BA 5600
Trieste, Museo Civico S406	amphora	Italy 43, Trieste 1, pl. 1.2	Para. 134.21.6; BA 340561
Trieste, Museo Storia ed Arte S405	hydria	Italy 43, Trieste 1, pl. 2.2	ABV 350; BA 301979
Trondheim, J. Utheim	lekythos	Norway 1, pl. 23.3	Para 199.55bis; BA 351466

(continued)

Appendix *(continued)*

Museum & Accession Number	Object Type	CVA Reference	Beazley Reference
Tübingen, Eberhard-Karls-Universität 7434	lekythos	Germany 47, Tübingen 3, pl. 38.5–7	Para. 66; BA 350474
Tübingen, Eberhard-Karls-Universität H.10.1202	amphora	Germany 47, Tübingen 3, pl. 6.1	BA 5924
Tübingen, Eberhard-Karls-Universität S702	amphora	Germany 44, Tübingen 2, pl. 36.1	BA 2848
Tübingen, Eberhard-Karls-Universität S705	cup	Germany 47, Tübingen 3, pl. 6.3	BA 6060
Turin, Museo di Antichita 4100	amphora	Italy 40, Turin 2, pl. 3.1	ABV 274.128; BA 320139
Turin, Museo di Antichita 4105 or 2366	lekythos	Italy 40, Turin 2, pl. 15.3–4	BA 8727
Turin, Museo di Antichita 4109	lekythos	Italy 40, Turin 2, pl. 15.5 & 7	BA 10402
Turin, Museo di Antichita 4112 or 5776	cup	Italy 40, Turin 2, pl. 2.1	ABV 214.50; BA 302732
Verona, Museo Civico 18	amphora	Italy 34, Verona 1, pl. 1.2a–b & 2	BA 14191
Vibo Valentia, Museo Statale Vita Capialbi C20	lekythos	Italy 67, Vibo Valentia 1, pl. 14.1–3	BA 18512
Vibo Valentia, Museo Statale Vita Capialbi C21	lekythos	Italy 67, Vibo Valentia 1, pl. 14.4	BA 21246
Vienna, Kunsthistorisches Museum 1049	krater	Austria 3, Vienna 3,pl. 130.3	ARV2 1437.7; BA 218066
Vienna, Kunsthistorisches Museum 984	krater	Austria 3, Vienna 3, pl. 104.4	BA 2196
Vienna, Matsch Collection	cup	Germany 5, Vienna 1, pl. 4.2 & 4.5	BA 12529
Warsaw, Collection Binental	cup	Poland 3, Various Collections IIIG/IIIH e pl. 1.3a–b	BA 14979
Warsaw, National Museum 138487	amphora	Poland 4, Warsaw 1, pl. 11	Para. 131.14bis; BA 340545 (as 13847)
Warsaw, National Museum 140359	pelike	Poland 6, Warsaw 3, pl. 22	Para. 482; BA 340056
Warsaw, National Museum 142191	cup	Poland 4, Warsaw 1, pl. 37.3–4	BA 15035
Warsaw, National Museum 198552	lekythos	Poland 4, Warsaw 1, pl. 25	Para. 66; BA 350476
Wellington, National Museum 1957.2	pitcher	New Zealand 1, pl. 19.1–3	Para. 194; BA 351430
Wellington, Victoria University 1950A20	lekythos	New Zealand 1, pl. 20.1–2	BA 6742
Winchester, College Museum 11	skyphos	Great Britain 19. Winchester 1, pl. 3.1–4.	BA 14986
Winchester, College Museum 6	cup	Great Britain 19, Winchester, pl. 1.8–9	BA 13245
Würzburg, Universität, Martin von Wagner Museum H4455	pyxis	Germany 46, Würzburg 2, pl. 34.4–5	ARV2 1133.196; BA 215006

Museum & Accession Number	Object Type	CVA Reference	Beazley Reference
Zurich, Eidgenossische Technische Hochschule 7	amphora	Switzerland 2, Zurich 1, pl. 12.1	ABV 256.17; BA 302227
Zurich, University 13	lekythos	Switzerland 2, Zurich 1, pl. 17.7–9	BA 1532
Zurich, University 2466	amphora	Switzerland 2, Zurich 1, pl. 8.1–2	ABV 305.27; BA 301507
Zurich, University 2472	lekythos	Switzerland 2, Zurich 1, pl. 16.8–10	BA 1473
Zurich, University 2494	lekythos	Switzerland 2, Zurich 1, pl. 20.1–4	BA 1519
Zurich, University ET9	hydria	Switzerland 2, Zurich 1, pl. 7.4	ABV 92.1; BA 300855
Zurich, University ETH12	amphora	Switzerland 2, Zurich 1, pl. 10.3	ABV 226.6; BA 302843

BIBLIOGRAPHY

ABBREVIATIONS

ABV	J. D. Beazley, *Attic Black-figure Vase-Painters* (Oxford, 1956).
Add.[2]	T. H. Carpenter with T. Mannack and M. Mendonça, *Beazley Addenda. Additional References to ABV, ARV*[2] *& Paralipomena*, 2nd edition (Oxford, 1989).
AJA	*American Journal of Archaeology*
AM	*Mitteilungen des Deutschen Archäologischen Instituts, Athenische Abteilung*
AntK	*Antike Kunst*
ARV[2]	J. D. Beazley, *Attic Red-figure Vase-Painters*, 2nd edition (Oxford, 1963).
Beazley Archive	Beazley Archive (http://www.beazley.ox.ac.uk/BeazleyAdmin/Script2/default.htm).
BABesch	*Bulletin antieke beschaving. Annual Papers on Classical Archaeology.*
CAH	J. Boardman and N. G. L. Hammond, eds. *The Cambridge Ancient History*, 2nd edition, vol. 3, pt. 3: *The Expansion of the Greek World, Eighth to Sixth Centuries* B.C. (Cambridge, 1982).
ClAnt	*Classical Antiquity*
CVA	Corpus Vasorum Antiquorum
JdI	*Jahrbuch des Deutschen Archäologischen Instituts*
JHS	*Journal of Hellenic Studies*
LIMC	*Lexicon Iconographicum Mythologia Classicae* (Zurich and Munich, 1981–1997).
OJA	*Oxford Journal of Archaeology*
Para.	J. D. Beazley, *Paralipomena* (Oxford, 1971).

SOURCES AND TRANSLATIONS

Note: Translations without full citations are found in the main bibliography.

Aeschylus, *Eumenides*: tr. Lattimore, R. (1953) *Aeschylus* 1: *Oresteia* (Chicago).
Aetius: tr. Kirk, Raven, and Schofield (1983).

Alkman: tr. Campbell, D. A., ed. (1988) *Greek Lyric II: Anacreon, Anacreontea, Choral Lyric from Olympus to Alcman* (Cambridge, MA/London).
Aristotle, *De anima*: tr. Hamlyn, D.W. (1968) *Aristotle's De Anima, Books II and III (with Certain Passages from Book I)* (Oxford).
Aristotle, *De sensu* 4: tr. Kirk, Raven, and Schofield (1983).
Aristotle, *Poetics*: tr. Halliwell, S. (1987) *The Poetics of Aristotle* (Chapel Hill).
Aristotle, *Rhetoric*: tr. Freese, J. H. (1982) Aristotle, *The "Art" of Rhetoric* (Cambridge, MA/London).
Euripides, *Heracleidae*: tr. Grene, D. and R. Lattimore (eds). (1955). *Euripides I* (Chicago).
Gorgias, *The Encomium of Helen*: tr. Waterfield (2000).
Herodotos: tr. Grene, D. (1987) *Herodotus. The History* (Chicago).
Homer: tr. Lattimore, R. (1951) *The Iliad of Homer* (Chicago).
Hymn to Aphrodite: tr. Stehle (1997).
Pindar, *Ol.* 10: tr. Steiner (1998) 140.
Plato, *Laws*: tr. Bury, R. G. (1967) *Plato: Laws* (Cambridge, MA/London).
Plato, *Phaedrus*: tr. Fowler, H. N. (1966) *Plato: Euthyphro, Apology, Crito, Phaedo, Phaedrus* (Cambridge, MA/London).
Plato, *Timaeus*: tr. Bury, R. G. (1966) *Plato: Timaeus, Critias, Cleitophon, Menexenus, Epistles* (Cambridge, MA/London).
Plutarch, *Solon*: tr. Perrin, B. (1967) *Plutarch's Lives, 1: Theseus and Romulus, Lycurgus and Numa, Solon and Publicola* (Cambridge, MA/London).
Sappho: tr. Lombardo, S. (2002) *Sappho. Poems and Fragments* (Indianapolis).
Theophrastus, *de sensu* 26: tr. Stratton, G. M. (1917) *Theophrastus and the Greek Physiological Psychology before Aristotle* (London/New York).
Theophrastus, *de sensu* 50: tr. Kirk, Raven, and Schofield (1983).
Thucydides: tr. Smith, C. F. (1980) *Thucydides* (Cambridge, MA/London).

MAIN

Alexiou, M. (2002) *The Ritual Lament in Greek Tradition*, 2nd edition revised by D. Yatromanolakis and P. Roilos (Lanham, MD).
Alcock, S. E. and R. Osborne, eds. (1994) *Placing the Gods. Sanctuaries and Sacred Space in Ancient Greece* (Oxford).
Alföldi, A. (1967) "Die Herrschaft der Reiterei in Griechenland und Rom nach dem Sturz der Könige." In M. Rohde-Leigle, H. A. Cahn, and H. C. Ackermann, eds. *Gestalt und Geschichte. Festschrift Karl Schefold zu seinum sechzigsten Geburtstag am 26. Januar 1965* (Bern) 13–47.
Anderson, W. D. (1994) *Music and Musicians in Ancient Greece* (Ithaca).
Andrewes, A. (1982a) "The Growth of the Athenian State." In *CAH* (1982) 360–91.
(1982b) "The Tyranny of Pisistratus." In *CAH* (1982) 392–416.
Antonaccio, C. (2003) "Hybridity and the Cultures within Greek Culture." In Dougherty and Kurke (2003) 57–74.
Arafat, K. and C. Morgan (1989) "Pots and Potters in Athens and Corinth: A Review." *OJA* 8: 311–46.
Barringer, J. M. (1995) *Divine Escorts. Nereids in Archaic and Classical Greek Art* (Ann Arbor).
(2001) *The Hunt in Ancient Greece* (Baltimore).
Bassi, K. (1998) *Acting Like Men: Gender, Drama, and Nostalgia in Ancient Greece* (Ann Arbor).
Baur, P. V. C. (1922) *Catalogue of the Rebecca Darlington Stoddard Collection of Greek and Italian Vases in Yale University* (New Haven).

Bazant, J. (1981) *Studies on the Use and Decoration of Athenian Vases* (Prague).
(1985) *Les citoyens sur les vases athéniens du 6 au 4 siècle av. J.C.* (Prague).
(1990) "The Case for a Complex Approach to Athenian Vase Painting." *Metis* 5: 93–111.
Beazley, J. D. (1927) "The Antimenes Painter." *JHS* 47: 63–92.
(1931) "Amasea." *JHS* 51: 275–85.
(1958) "An Attic Black-Figured Vase." *Minneapolis Institute of Arts Bulletin* 47 (3): 40–1.
(1961) "An Amphora by the Berlin Painter." *AntK* 4: 49–67.
(1989) *Greek Vases. Lectures by J. D. Beazley*, D. C. Kurtz, ed. (Oxford).
Bell, C. (1992) *Ritual Theory, Ritual Practice* (Oxford).
(1997) *Ritual. Perspectives and Dimensions* (Oxford).
Bentz, M. (1998) *Panathenäische Preisamphoren. Eine athenische Vasengattung und ihre Funktion vom 6.-4. Jahrhundert v. Chr.* (Basel).
(2002) "Zur Geschichte des CVA." In M. Bentz, ed., *Vasenforschung und Corpus Vasorum Antiquorum. Standortbestimmung und Perspektiven* Beihefte zum CVA Deutschland, 1 (Munich) 9–15.
Bérard, C. (1989) *A City of Images: Iconography and Society in Ancient Greece*, D. Lyons, tr. (Princeton).
Blok, J. (1995) *The Early Amazons. Modern and Ancient Perspectives on a Persistent Myth* (Leiden).
Blundell, S. (1995) *Women in Ancient Greece* (Cambridge, MA).
Boardman, J. (1972) "Herakles, Peisistratos and Sons." *Revue archéologiqúe* 1972: 57–72.
(1974) *Athenian Black Figure Vases* (London).
(1978) "Exekias." *AJA* 82: 11–25.
(1984) "Image and Politics in Sixth Century Athens." In Brijder, ed. (1984) 239–47.
(1985) *Greek Sculpture. The Classical Period. A Handbook* (London).
(1991a) *Greek Sculpture. The Archaic Period. A Handbook* (London).
(1991b) "The Sixth-Century Potters and Painters of Athens and Their Public." In Rasmussen and Spivey (1991) 79–102.
(1996) *Greek Art*, 4th edition (London).
(1998) *Early Greek Vase Painting, 11th–6th Centuries* BC (London).
(2001) *The History of Greek Vases: Potters, Painters and Pictures* (London).
Boegehold, A. L. (1999) *When a Gesture Was Expected. A Selection of Examples from Archaic and Classical Literature* (Princeton).
Boegehold, A. L. and A. C. Scafuro, eds. (1994) *Athenian Identity and Civic Ideology* (Baltimore).
Böhr, E. (1982) *Der Schaukelmaler*, Kerameus 4 (Mainz).
Bothmer, D. von (1944) "The Painters of 'Tyrrhenian' Vases." *AJA* 48: 161–70.
(1957) *Amazons in Greek Art* (Oxford).
(1969) "Euboean Black-figure in New York." *Metropolitan Museum of Art Journal* 2: 27–44.
(1971) "Three Vases by the Amasis Painter." *Madrider Mitteilungen* 12: 123–30.
(1985) *The Amasis Painter and his World. Vase-Painting in Sixth-Century* B.C. *Athens* (Malibu).
Bowie, E. L. (1986) "Early Greek Elegy, Symposium, and Public Festival." *JHS* 106: 13–35.
Brijder, H. A. G. (1983) *Siana Cups I and Komast Cups* (Amsterdam).
(1984) "Changing the Subject: Evidence on Siana Cups." In Brijder, ed. (1984) 248–51.
(1986) "A Pre-Dramatic Performance of a Satyr Chorus by the Heidelberg Painter." In H. A. G. Brijder, A. A. Drukker, and C. W. Neeft, eds. *Enthousiasmos. Essays on Greek and Related Pottery presented to J. M. Hemelrijk* (Amsterdam) 69–82.
(1991) *Siana Cups II: The Heidelberg Painter* (Amsterdam).
(2003) "The Study of Attic Black-Figure Vases over the Past Thirty Years." In Schmaltz and Söldner (2003) 13–21.

Brijder, H. A. G., ed. (1984) *Ancient Greek and Related Pottery. Proceedings of the International Vase Symposium in Amsterdam 12–15 April 1984* (Amsterdam).
Brommer, F. (1973) *Vasenlisten zur griechischen Heldensage*, 3rd edition (Marburg).
(1982) *Theseus. Die Taten des griechischen Helsen in der antiken Kunst und Literature* (Darmstadt).
(1984a) "Themenwahl aus örtlichen Gründen." In Brijder, ed. 178–84.
(1984b) *Herakles II. Die unkanonischen Taten des Helden* (Darmstadt).
(1986) *Herakles* (New Rochelle, NY).
(1989) "Antike Tänze." *Archäologischer Anzeiger* 1989: 483–94.
Bryson, N. (1983) *Vision and Painting. The Logic of the Gaze* (New Haven).
Bugh, G. R. (1988) *The Horsemen of Athens* (Princeton).
Bundrick, S. (2005) *Music and Image in Classical Athens* (Cambridge).
Burkert, W. (1979) *Structure and History in Greek Mythology and Ritual* (Berkeley).
(1985) *Greek Religion*, J. Raffan, tr. (Cambridge, MA).
Burow, J. (1989) *Der Antimenesmaler* (Mainz).
Cairns, D. L. (1993) *Aidos. The Psychology and Ethics of Honour and Shame in Ancient Greek Literature* (Oxford).
Calame, C. (1989) *Les chœurs de jeunes filles en Grèce ancienne* (Lausanne).
(1994/95) "From Choral Poetry to Tragic Stasimon: The Enactment of Women's Song." *Arion* series 3, 3.1: 136–54.
(1996) "Sappho's Group: An Initiation into Womanhood." In E. Greene, ed. *Reading Sappho. Contemporary Approaches* (Berkeley/Los Angeles) 113–24.
(1999) "Performative Aspects of the Choral Voice in Greek Tragedy: Civic Identity in Performance." In Goldhill and Osborne (1999) 125–53.
(2001) *Choruses of Young Women in Ancient Greece. Their Morphology, Religious Role, and Social Function*, new and revised edition, D. Collins and J. Orion, trs. (Lanham, MD).
Camp, J. M. (1992) *The Athenian Agora. Excavations in the Heart of Classical Athens*, updated edition (London).
(2001) *The Archaeology of Athens* (New Haven).
Carpenter, T. H. (1983) "On the Dating of the Tyrrhenian Group." *OJA* 2: 279–93.
(1986) *Dionysian Imagery in Archaic Greek Art. Its Development in Black-Figure Vase Painting* (Oxford).
Ceccarelli, P. (1998) *La Pirrica nell'Antichità Greco Romana. Studi sulla Danza Armata* (Pisa/Rome).
(2004) "Dancing the *Pyrrhiche* in Athens." In Murray and Wilson (2004) 91–117.
Christiansen, J. and T. Melander, eds. (1988) *Proceedings of the 3rd Symposium on Ancient Greek and Related Pottery. Copenhagen, August 31–September 4, 1987* (Copenhagen).
Clark, C. A. (1996) "The Gendering of the Body in Alcman's *Partheneion* 1: Narrative, Sex, and the Social Order in Archaic Sparta." *Helios* 23: 143–72.
Cleary, J. J. "*Paideia* in Plato's *Laws*." In S. Scolnicov and L. Brisson, eds. *Plato's Laws: From Theory into Practice. Proceeding of the IV Symposium Platonicum. Selected Papers* (Sankt Augustin) 165–73.
Cohen, B., ed. (2000) *Not the Classical Ideal. Athens and the Construction of the Other in Greek Art* (Leiden).
Connelly, J. B. (1993) "Narrative and Image in the Attic Vase Painting-Ajax and Kassandra at the Trojan Palladion." In. P. J. Holliday, ed., *Narrative and Event in Ancient Art* (Cambridge) 88–129.
Connor, W. R. (1987) "Tribes, Festivals and Processions: Civic Ceremonial and Political Manipulation in Ancient Greece." *JHS* 107: 40–50.

(1989) "City Dionysia and Athenian Democracy." *Classica et mediaevalia. Revue danoise de philologie et d'histoire* 40: 7–32.
(1990) "City Dionysia and Athenian Democracy." In W. R. Connor, et al. *Aspects of Athenian Democracy*, Classica et Mediaevalia Dissertationes XI (Copenhagen) 7–32.
Cook, R. M. (1997) *Greek Painted Pottery*, 3rd edition (London/New York).
Copjec, J. (1989) "The Orthopsychic Subject: Film Theory and the Reception of Lacan." *October* 49: 53–71.
Coulsen, W. D., ed. (1994) *The Archaeology of Athens and Attica under the Democracy. Proceedings of an International Conference Celebrating 2500 Years since the Birth of Democracy in Greece, Held at the American School of Classical Studies at Athens, December 4–6, 1992* (Oxford).
Crary, J. (1990) *Techniques of the Observer: On Vision and Modernity in the Nineteenth Century* (Cambridge, MA).
Crielaard, J. P., V. Stissi, and G. J. van Wijngaarden, eds. (1999) *The Complex Past of Pottery. Production, Circulation and Consumption of Mycenaean and Greek Pottery (Sixteenth to Early Fifth Centuries* BC*). Proceedings of the ARCHON International Conference, Held in Amsterdam, 8–9 November 1996* (Amsterdam).
Crowhurst, R. (1963) *Representations of Performance of Choral Lyric on the Greek Monuments, 800–350* B.C., diss. (London).
Curry, M. (2000) "The Export of Attic Black-Figure Pottery in the Early Sixth Century BC." In Tsetskhladze, Prag, and Snodgrass (2000) 80–8.
D'Amicis, A., (1994) *Catalogo del Museo Nazionale Archeologico di Taranto*, I.3: *Atleti e Guerrieri, Tradizioni aristocratische* (Taranto).
Dewald, C. (1981) "Women and Culture in Herodotus' Histories." In Foley (1981) 91–125.
Diehl, E. (1964) *Die Hydria. Formgeschichte und Verwendung im Kult des Altertums* (Mainz).
Dierichs, A. (1993) *Erotik in der Kunst Griechenlands* (Mainz).
Dodd, D. B. (2003) "Adolescent Initiation in Myth and Tragedy. Rethinking the Black Hunter." In Dodd and Faraone (2003) 71–84.
Dodd, D. B. and C. A. Faraone, eds. (2003) *Initiation in Ancient Greek Rituals and Narratives. New Critical Perspectives* (London/New York).
Dougherty, C. and L. Kurke, eds. (1998) *Cultural Poetics in Archaic Greece. Cult, Performance, Politics* (Oxford) 92–107.
(2003) *The Cultures within Ancient Greek Culture* (Cambridge).
Dover, K. J. (1989) *Greek Homosexuality*, updated edition (Cambridge, MA).
DuBois, P. (1982) *Centaurs and Amazons: Women and the Pre-History of the Great Chain of Being* (Ann Arbor).
(1988) *Sowing the Body. Psychoanalysis and Ancient Representations of Women* (Chicago).
(1996) "Archaic Bodies-in-Pieces." In Kampen (1996) 55–64.
Eagleton, T. (1996) *Literary Theory. An Introduction*, 2nd edition (Minneapolis).
(2003) *After Theory* (New York).
Ellinghaus, C., *Aristokratische Leitbilder, Demokratische Leitbilder, Kampfdarstellungen a. athenischen Vasen in arch. u. fruhkl. Zeit* (Munster, 1997).
Else, G. F. (1957) "The Origin of ΤΡΑΓΩΔΙΑ." *Hermes* 85: 17–46.
Fantham, E., et al. (1994) *Women in the Classical World. Image and Text* (Oxford).
Faraone, C. (2003) "Playing the Bear and Fawn for Artemis. Female Initiation of Substitute Sacrifice?" In Dodd and Faraone (2003) 43–68.
Ferrari, G. (1987) "Menelas." *JHS* 107: 180–2.
(1990) "Figures of Speech: The Picture of Aidos." *Métis* 5: 185–204.
(1995) "Heracles, Pisistratus and the Panathenaia." *Métis* 9/10: 219–26.

(2002) *Figures of Speech. Men and Maidens in Ancient Greece* (Chicago).
(2003) "What Kind of Rite of Passage was the Ancient Greek Wedding?" In Dodd and Faraone (2003) 27–42.
Fish, S. (2004) "Theory's Hope." *Critical Inquiry* 30 (Winter 2004) 374–8.
Fittschen, K. (1970) "Zur Herakles-Nessos Sage." *Gymnasium* 77: 161–71.
Fletcher, M. and G. R. Lock (1991) *Digging Numbers. Elementary Statistics for Archaeologists*, Oxford University Committee for Archaeology Monograph 33 (Oxford).
Foley, H. P., ed. (1981) *Reflections of Women in Antiquity* (New York).
Frede, D. (1992) "The Cognitive Role of *Phantasia* in Aristotle." In M. C. Nussbaum and A. O. Rorty, eds. *Essays on Aristotle's* De Anima (Oxford) 279–96.
Frontisi-Ducroux, F. (1995) *Du masque au visage. Aspects de l'identité en Grèce ancienne* (Paris).
(1996) "Eros, Desire, and the Gaze." In Kampen (1996) 81–100.
Frost, F. J. (1990) "Peisistratos, the Cults, and the Unification of Attica." *Ancient World* 21: 3–9.
(1994) "Aspects of Early Athenian Citizenship." In Boegehold and Scafuro (1994) 45–56.
Gadamer, H.-G. (1985) *Truth and Method* (New York).
Garland, R. (1985) *The Greek Way of Death* (Ithaca, New York).
Gay, P. (1976) *Art and Act. On Causes in History – Manet, Gropius, Mondrian* (New York).
Geertz, C. (1973) *The Interpretation of Cultures* (New York).
(1983) *Local Knowledge: Further Essays in Interpretive Anthropology* (New York).
Ghiron-Bistagne, P. (1976) *Recherches sur les Acteurs dans la Grèce antique* (Paris).
Gill, D. W. (1994) "Positivism, Pots and Long-Distance Trade." In Morris, ed. (1994) 99–107.
Ginge, B. (1988) "A New Evaluation of the Origins of Tyrrhenian Pottery: Etruscan Precursors of Pontic Ceramics." In Christiansen and Melander (1988) 201–10.
Goldhill, S. (1990) "The Great Dionysia and Civic Ideology." In. J. Winkler and F. I. Zeitlin, eds., Nothing to Do with Dionysos? Athenian Drama in Its Social Context (Princeton) 97–129.
Goldhill, S. and R. Osborne, eds. (1999) *Performance and Culture and Athenian Democracy* (Cambridge).
Gordon, P. (2002) "Some Unseen Monster. Rereading Lucretius on Sex." In D. Frederick, ed. *The Roman Gaze. Vision, Power, and the Body* (Baltimore) 86–109.
Graef, B. and F. Langlotz (1925) *Die antiken Vasen von der Akropolis zu Athen*, vol. 1 (Berlin).
(1931) *Die antiken Vasen von der Akropolis zu Athen*, vol. 2 (Berlin).
Graf, F. (1996) "*Pompai* in Greece. Some Considerations about Space and Ritual in the Greek *Polis*." In Hägg (1996) 55–65.
Greenblatt, S. (1980) *Renaissance Self-Fashioning. From More to Shakespeare* (Chicago).
Hägg, R., ed. (1996) *The Role of Religion in the Early Greek Polis. Proceedings of the Third International Seminar on Ancient Greek cult, organized by the Swedish Institute at Athens, 16–18 October* 1992, Skrifter utgivna av Svenska Institutet i Athen 14 (Stockholm).
Hall, J. M. (1997) *Ethnic Identity in Greek Antiquity* (Cambridge).
(2003) "'Culture' or 'Cultures'? Hellenism in the Late Sixth Century." In Dougherty and Kurke (2003) 23–34.
Hamdorf, F. W. (1990) "Musik und Symposion." In Vierneisel and Kaeser (1990) 238–46.
Hannestad, L. (1988) "The Athenian Potter and the Home Market." In Christiansen and Melander (1988) 222–30.
(1989) Athenian Pottery in Etruria c. 550–470 BC." *Acta Archeologica* 59: 113–30.
(1999) "The Reception of Attic Pottery by the Indigenous Peoples of Italy: The Evidence from Funerary Contexts." In Crielaard, Stissi, and van Wijngaarden (1999) 303–18.
Hardwick, L. (1990) "Ancient Amazons – Heroes, Outsiders or Women?" *Greece and Rome* 37: 14–30.

Harootunian, H. "Theory's Empire: Reflections on a Vocation for *Critical Inquiry*." *Critical Inquiry* 30 (Winter 2004): 396–402.
Haspels, C. H. E. (1936) *Athenian Black-Figure Lekythoi* (Paris).
Hawley, R. and B. Levick, eds. (1995) *Women in Antiquity. New Assessments* (London/New York).
Heesen, P. (1996) *The J. L. Theodor Collection of Attic Black-Figure Vases* (Amsterdam).
Hoesch, N. (1990) "Die schöne Frau, der schöne Knabe." In Vierneisel and Kaeser (1990) 142–5.
Hoffmann, H. (1988) "The Cicada on the Omphalos. An Iconological Excursion." *Antiquity* 62: 744–9.
(1989) "Rhyta and Kantharoi in Greek Ritual." *Greek Vases in the J. Paul Getty Museum* 4: 131–66.
(1994) "The Riddle of the Sphinx: A Case Study in Athenian Immortality Symbolism." In Morris (1994) 71–80.
Hofstetter, E. (1990) *Sirenen im archaischen und klassischen Griechenland* (Würzburg).
Hopper, R. J. (1961) " 'Plain,' 'Shore,' and 'Hill' in Early Athens." *Annual of the British School at Athens* 56: 189–219.
Houby-Nielsen, S. (1995) " 'Burial Language' in Archaic and Classical Kerameikos." *Proceedings of the Danish Institute at Athens* 1: 129–91.
(1996) "Women and the Formation of the Athenian State. The Evidence of Burial Customs." *Métis* 11: 233–60.
Hurwit, J. M. (1985) *The Art and Culture of Early Greece, 1100–480 BC.* (Ithaca).
(1999) *The Athenian Acropolis. History, Mythology, and Archaeology from the Neolithic Era to the Present* (Cambridge).
Hutchinson, G. O. (2001) *Greek Lyric Poetry. A Commentary on Selected Larger Pieces* (Oxford).
Isler, H. P. (1970) *Acheloos. Eine Monographie* (Berne).
Isler-Kerényi, C. (1969) *Nike. Der Typus der laufenden Flügelfrau in archaischer Zeit* (Zürich).
Jay, M. (1993) *Downcast Eyes. The Denigration of Vision in Twentieth-Century French Thought* (Berkeley/Los Angeles).
Jenkins, I. (1983) "Is There Life after Marriage? A Study of the Abduction Motif in Vase Paintings of the Athenian Wedding Ceremony." *Bulletin of the Institute of Classical Studies of the University of London* 30: 137–45.
Johnston, A. W. (1979) *Trademarks on Greek Vases* (Warminster).
(1984) "The Development of Amphora Shapes, Symposium and Shipping." In Brijder, ed. (1984) 208–11.
(1991) "Greek Vases in the Marketplace." In Rasmussen and Spivey (1991) 203–31.
Junker, K. (2002) "Symposiongeschirr oder Totengefässe?" *AntK* 45: 3–26.
(2003) *Pseudo-Homerica. Kunst und Epos im spätarchaischen Athens*, Berliner Winckelmannsprogramm 141 (Berlin).
Junker, K., ed. (1999) *Aus Mythos und Lebenswelt. Griechische Vasen aus der Sammlung der Universität Mainz* (Worms).
Just, R. (1989) *Women in Athenian Law and Life* (London/New York).
Kaeser, B. (1990) "Zuschauerfiguren." In Vierneisel and Kaeser (1990) 151–6.
Kampen, N. B., ed. (1996) *Sexuality in Ancient Art. Near East, Egypt, Greece, and Italy* (Cambridge).
Kavoulaki, A. (1999) "Processional Performance and the Democratic Polis." In Goldhill and Osborne (1999) 293–320.
Keuls, E. (1985) *The Reign of the Phallus Sexual Politics in Ancient Athens* (New York).
Kluiver, J. (1992) "The 'Tyrrhenian Group.' Its Origin and the Neck-Amphorae in the Netherlands and Belgium." *BABesch* 67: 73–109.

(1995) "Early 'Tyrrhenian': Prometheus Painter, Timiades Painter, Goltyr Painter." *BABesch* 70: 55–103.
(1996) "The Five Later 'Tyrrhenian' Painters." *BABesch* 71: 1–58.
Kirk, G. S., J. E. Raven, and M. S. Schofield (1983) *The Presocratic Philosophers. A Critical History with a Selection of Texts*, 2nd edition (Cambridge).
Knigge, U. (1976) *Kerameikos. Ergebnisse der Ausgrabungen, IX: Der Südhügel* (Berlin).
Knittlmayer, B. (1997) *Die Attische Demokratie und ihre Helden, Darstellungen des trojanischen Sagenkreises im 6. und fruhen 5. Jh.v.Chr.* (Heidelberg).
Kolb, F. (1977) "Die Bau-, Religions- und Kulturpolitik der Peisistratiden." *JdI* 92: 99–138.
Konstan, D. (2001) "To Hellenikon ethnos: Ethnicity and the Construction of Ancient Greek Identity." In I. Malkin, ed. (2001) *Ancient Perceptions of Greek Ethnicity* (Washington, DC/Cambridge, MA) 29–50.
Korte-Konte, S. (1979) "ΟΙ ΘΕΑΤΕΣ ΣΤΙΣ ΗΑΡΑΣΤΑΣΕΙΣ ΑΘΛΩΝ ΚΑ Ι ΑΓΩΝΩΝ ΣΤΗΝ ΑΡΧΑΙΑ ΕΛΛΗΝΙΚΗ ΤΕΧΝΗ," *Epistemonike Epteris Philosophikes Scholes Thessalonike* 18: 163–205.
Kowalzig, B. (2004) "Changing Choral Worlds: Song-Dance and Society in Athens and Beyond." In Murray and Wilson (2004) 39–65.
Kreutzer, B. (1998) *Die attisch schwarzfigurige Keramik aus dem Heraion von Samos*. Samos, XXII (Bonn).
Kunze-Götte, E., K. Tancke, and K. Vierneisel (1999) *Kerameikos, Ergebnisse der Ausgrabungen, VII.2: Die Nekropole von der Mitte des 6. bis zum Ende des 5. Jahrhunderts* (Munich).
Kurke, L. (1999) *Coins, Bodies, Games, and Gold. The Politics of Meaning in Archaic Greece* (Princeton).
Kurtz, D. C. (1975) *Athenian White Lekythoi: Patterns and Painters* (Oxford).
Kurtz, D. C. and J. Boardman (1971) *Greek Burial Customs* (Ithaca).
Kyle, D. G. (1987) *Athletics in Ancient Athens* (Leiden).
(1992) "The Panathenaic Games: Sacred and Civic Athletics." In Neils (1992) 77–102.
Lacan, J. (1968) *The Language of the Self. The Function of Language in Psychoanalysis*, A. Wilden, tr. (Baltimore).
(1977) *Écrits. A. Selection*, A. Sheridan, tr. (New York).
(1978) *The Four Fundamental Concepts of Psychoanalysis*, A. Sheridan, tr., The Seminar of Jacques Lacan XI (New York).
Laks, A. (1999) "Soul, Sensation, and Thought." In A. A. Long, ed. *The Cambridge Companion to Early Greek Philosophy* (Cambridge).
Lambropoulou, V. (1995) "Some Pythagorean Female Virtues." In Hawley and Levick (1995) 122–34.
Landels, J. G. (1999) *Music in Ancient Greece and Rome* (London/New York).
Langlotz, E. (1957) "Von Sinngehalt attischer Vasenbilder." In *Robert Boehringer. Eine Freundesgabe* (Tübingen) 397–421.
Lardinois, A. (2001) "Keening Sappho. Female Speech Genres in Sappho's Poetry." In Lardinois, A. and L. McClure, eds. *Making Silence Speak. Women's Voices in Greek Literature and Society* (Princeton) 75–92.
Lavelle, B. M. (1993) *The Sorrow and the Pity. A Prolegomenon to a History of Athens under the Peisistratids, c. 560–510 BC.* (Stuttgart).
Lewis, S. (2002) *The Athenian Woman. An Iconographic Handbook* (London/New York).
Lindberg, D. C. (1976) *Theories of Vision from al-Kindi to Kepler* (Chicago).
Lissarrague, F. (1990) *The Aesthetics of the Greek Banquet. Images of Wine and Ritual* (Un Flot d'Images), A. Szegedy-Maszak, tr. (Princeton).
(1996) "Images dans la Cité." *Metis* 9/10: 237–42.

(1999) "Publicity and Performance: *Kalos* inscriptions in Attic Vase-painting." In Goldhill and Osborne (1999) 359–73.
Lloyd, G. E. R. (1970) *Early Greek Science. Thales to Aristotle* (New York).
(1987) *The Revolutions of Wisdom. Studies in the Claims and Practices of Ancient Greek Science* (Berkeley/Los Angeles).
Lonsdale, S. (1993) *Dance and Ritual Play in Greek Religion* (Baltimore).
Loraux, N. (1993) *The Children of Athena. Athenian Ideas about Citizenship and the Division between the Sexes*, C. Levine, tr. (Princeton).
(1998) *Mothers in Mourning*, C. Pache, tr. (Ithaca).
Mackay, E. A. (2002) "The Evocation of Emotional Response in Early Greek Poetry and Painting." In I. Worthington and J. M. Foley, eds. *Epea and Grammata. Oral and Written Communication in Ancient Greece*, Orality and Literacy in Ancient Greece, 4 (Leiden) 55–69.
Manville, P. B. (1990) *The Origins of Citizenship in Ancient Athens* (Princeton).
(1994) "Toward a New Paradigm of Athenian Citizenship." In Boegehold and Scafuro (1994) 34–44.
Martin, R. P. (2003) "The Pipes Are Brawling: Conceptualizing Musical Performance in Athens." In Dougherty and Kurke (2003) 153–80.
Marx, P. A. (2003) "Athena on Early Panathenaic Amphoras." *AntK* 46: 14–29.
Matheson Burke, S. and J. J. Pollitt (1975) *Greek Vases at Yale* (New Haven).
Maul-Mandelartz, E. (1990) *Griechische Reiterdarstellungen in agonistischem Zusammenhang* (Frankfurt).
McClure, L. (1999) *Spoken like a Woman. Speech and Gender in Athenian Drama* (Princeton).
McGlew, J. F. (1993) *Tyranny and Political Culture in Ancient Greece* (Ithaca).
McNiven, T. J. (1982) *Gestures in Attic Vase Painting: Use and Meaning, 550–450 BC*, diss. (Ann Arbor).
(2000) "Behaving Like an Other: Telltale Gestures in Athenian Vase Painting." In Cohen (2000) 71–97.
Mehren, M. von (2001) "Two Groups of Attic Amphorae as Export Ware for Etruria: The So-Called Tyrrhenian Group and 'Nikosthenic Amphora'." In Scheffer, ed. (2001) 45–53.
Mitchell, W. J. T. (2004) "Medium Theory: Preface to the 2003 *Critical Inquiry* Symposium." *Critical Inquiry* 30 (Winter 2004) 324–35.
Mommsen, H. (2002) "Siegreiche Gespannpferde." *AntK* 45: 27–39.
Moon, W. G. and L. Berge (1979) *Greek Vase-Painting in Midwestern Collections* (Chicago).
Moore, M. B. (1997) *Attic Red-Figured and White Ground Pottery*, The Athenian Agora 30 (Princeton).
Moore, M. B. and M. A. Philippides (1986) *Attic Black-figure Pottery*, The Athenian Agora 23 (Princeton).
Morris, I. (1994) "Archaeologies of Greece." In Morris, ed. (1994) 8–47.
(2000) *Archaeology as Cultural History. Words and Things in Iron Age Greece* (Oxford).
Morris, I., ed. (1994) *Classical Greece: Ancient Histories and Modern Archaeologies* (Cambridge).
Mulvey, L. (1975) "Visual Pleasure and Narrative Cinema." *Screen* 16.3: 6–18.
Murray, O. (1993) *Early Greece*, 2nd edition (Cambridge, MA).
Murray, O., ed. (1990) *Sympotica: A Symposium on the Symposium* (Oxford).
Murray, O. and S. Price, eds. (1990) *The Greek City from Homer to Alexander* (Oxford).
Murray, P. and P. Wilson, eds. (2004) *Music and the Muses. The Culture of 'Mousike' in the Classical Athenian City* (Oxford).
Naerebout, F. G. (1997) *Attractive Performances. Ancient Greek Dance: Three Preliminary Studies* (Amsterdam).

Neer, R. T. (2002) *Style and Politics in Athenian Vase-Painting. The Craft of Democracy, ca. 530–460 B.C.E.* (Cambridge).

(2004) "Reaction and Response." *Critical Inquiry* 30 (Winter 2004) 472–6.

Neils, J. (1992) *Goddess and Polis. The Panathenaic Festival in Ancient Athens* (Hanover, NH/Princeton).

(2001) *The Parthenon Frieze* (Cambridge).

Neumann, G. (1965) *Gesten und Gebärden in der griechischen Kunst* (Berlin).

Nevett, L. C. (1999) *House and Society in the Ancient Greek World* (Cambridge).

Oakley, J. H., W. D. E. Coulson, and O. Palagia, eds. (1997) *Athenian Potters and Painters. The Conference Proceedings* (Oxford).

Oakley, J. H. and R. H. Sinos (1993) *The Wedding in Ancient Athens* (Madison).

Ober, J. (1994) "Revolution Matters: Democracy as Demotic Action (A Response to Kurt A. Raaflaub)." In Coulsen (1994) 67–86.

Osborne, R. (1991) "Whose Image and Superscription is This?" *Arion*, ser. 3, 1.2: 255–75.

(1994) "Archaeology, the Salaminioi, and the Politics of Sacred Space in Archaic Attica." In Alcock and Osborne (1994) 143–60.

(1996a) *Greece in the Making, 1200–479 B.C.* (London).

(1996b) "Pots, Trade and the Archaic Greek Economy." *Antiquity* 70: 31–44.

(1998) *Archaic and Classical Greek Art* (Oxford).

Papadopoulos, J. K. (2003) *Ceramicus Redivivus. The Early Iron Age Potters' Field in the Area of the Classical Athenian Agora* (Athens).

Patterson, C. B. (1991) "Marriage and the Married Woman in Athenian Law." In Pomeroy (1991) 48–72.

Percy, W. A., III (1996) *Pederasty and Pedagogy in Archaic Greece* (Urbana/Chicago).

Pfisterer-Haas, S. (1990) "Jugendliche Reiter." In Vierneisel and Kaeser (1990) 126–9.

Pickard-Cambridge, A. (1968) *The Dramatic Festivals of Athens*, 2nd edition (Oxford).

Pingiatoglou, S. (1994) "Rituelle Frauenlage auf schwarzfigurigen attischen Vases." *AM* 109: 39–51.

Plantzos, D. (1997) "Crystals and Lenses in the Graeco-Roman World." *AJA* 101: 451–64.

Poliakoff, M. B. (1987) *Combat Sports in the Ancient World. Competition, Violence, and Culture* (New Haven/London).

Polignac, F. de (1995) *Cults, Territory, and the Origins of the Greek City-State*, J. Lloyd, tr. (Chicago).

Pollitt, J. J. (1985) "Early Classical Greek Art in a Platonic Universe." In C. G. Boulter, ed. *Greek Art. Archaic into Classical. A Symposium Held at the University of Cincinnati, April 2–3, 1982* (Leiden) 96–112.

Pomeroy, S. B. (1975) *Goddesses, Whores, Wives, and Slaves. Women in Classical Antiquity* (New York).

(1995) "Women's Identity and the Family in the Classical *Polis*." In Hawley and Levick (1995) 111–121.

(2002) *Spartan Women* (Oxford).

Pomeroy, S. B., ed. (1991) *Women's History and Ancient History* (Chapel Hill/London).

Poovey, M. (2004) "For What It's Worth . . ." *Critical Inquiry* 30 (Winter 2004) 429–33.

Poursat, J.-M. (1968) "Les représentations de danse armée dans la céramique attique." *Bulletin de correspondance hellénique* 92: 550–615.

Raaflaub, K. A. (1994a) "Power in the Hands of the People: Foundations of Athenian Democracy." In Coulsen (1994) 31–66.

(1994b) "The Thetes and Democracy (A Response of Josiah Ober)." In Coulsen (1994) 87–103.

Rasmussen, T. (1991) "Corinth and the Orientalising Phenomenon." In Rasmussen and Spivey (1991) 57–78.

Rasmussen, T. and N. Spivey, eds. (1991) *Looking at Greek Vases* (Cambridge).

Reed, N. (1987) "The Euandria Competition at the Panathenaia Reconsidered." *Ancient World* 15: 59–64.

Reeder, E., ed. (1995) *Pandora. Women in Classical Greece* (Princeton).

Reinholdt, C. (1994) "ΝΟΣΤΟΣ ΟΔΥΣΣΗΙ oder Vita humana?" *Opuscula atheniensia* 20: 163–77.

Reinsberg, C. (1989) *Ehe, Hetärentum und Knabe im antiken Griechenland* (Munich).

Reusser, C. (2002) *Vasen für Etrurien. Verbreitung und Funktionen attischer Keramik im Etrurien des 6. und 5. Jahrhunderts vor Christus* (Zürich).

Rhomiopoulou, K. (1988) "The Panathenaic Festival." In Tzachou-Alexandri (1988) 38–43.

Ridgway, B. S. (1992) "Images of Athena on the Acropolis." In Neils (1992) 119–42.

Robertson, N. (1992) *Festivals and Legends: The Formation of Greek Cities in the Light of Public Ritual* (Toronto).

Robinson, D. M. (1932) "Illustrations of Aeschylus' Choephoroi and of a Satyr-Play on Hydrias by the Niobid Painter." *AJA* 36: 401–7.

Rosivach, V. J. (1987) "Autochthony and the Athenians." *Classical Quarterly* 37: 294–306.

Ronchi, V. (1957) *Optics. The Science of Vision*, E. Rosen, tr. (New York).

Rosati, R. (1989) *La Ceramica Attica nel mediterraneo. Analisi computerizzata della diffusione le fasi iniziali (630–560 a.C.)* (Bologna).

Rose, J. (1986) *Sexuality in the Field of Vision* (London).

Rouet, P. (2001) *Approaches to the Study of Attic Vases. Beazley and Pottier*, Liz Nash, tr. (Oxford).

Rutherford, I. (2004) "Song-Dance and the State-Pilgrimage at Athens." In Murray and Wilson (2004) 67–90.

Sahlins, M. (1981) *Historical Metaphors and Mythical Realities* (Ann Arbor).

Salomé, M.-R. (1980) *Code pour l'analyse des représentations figurées sur les vases grecs* (Paris).

Schauenburg, K. (1973) "Parisurteil und Nessosabenteuer auf attischen Vases hocharchaischer Zeit." *Aachener Kunstblätter* 44: 15–42.

Scheffer, C. (1988) "Workshop and Trade Patterns in Athenian Black-Figure." In Christiansen and Melander (1988) 536–46.

(2001) "Gods on Athenian Vases: Their Function in the Archaic and Classical Periods." In Scheffer, ed. (2001) 127–37.

Scheffer, C., ed. (2001) *Ceramics in Context. Proceedings of the Internordic Colloquium on Ancient Pottery held at Stockholm, 13–15 June 1997*. Acta Universitatis Stockholmiensis. Stockholm Studies in Classical Archaeology 12 (Stockholm).

Scheibler, I. (1983) *Griechische Töpferkunst. Herstellung, Handel und Gebrauch der antiken Tongefäße* (Munich).

(1987) "Bild und Gefäss. Zur ikonographischen und funktionalen Bedeutung der attischen Bildfeldamphoren." *JdI* 102: 57–118.

(1988) "Die Kuroi des Amasis-Malers." In Christiansen and Melander (1988) 547–57.

(2000) "Attische Skyphoi für attische Feste." *AntK* 43: 17–43.

Schmaltz, B. and M. Söldner (2003) *Griechische Keramik im kulturellen Kontext. Akten des Internationalen Vasen-Symposions in Kiel vom 24.–28.9.2001 veranstaltet durch das Archäologische Institut der Christian-Albrechts-Universität zu Kiel* (Münster).

Schmitt Pantel, P. (1997) *La Cité au Banquet: Histoire des repas publics dans les cités grecques*, 2nd printing, Collection École Française de Rome, 157 (Rome).

Schnapp, A. (1989) "Eros the Hunter." In Bérard (1989) 71–87.

Seagal, C. (1985) "Archaic Choral Lyric." In P. E. Easterling and B. M. W. Knox, eds. *The Cambridge History of Classical Literature*, vol. 1: Greek Literature (Cambridge) 124–160.
Shanks, M. (1999) *Art and the Greek City State. An Interpretive Archaeology* (Cambridge).
Shapiro, H. A. (1981) "Courtship Scenes in Attic Vase-Painting." *AJA* 85: 133–43.
(1984) "Herakles and Kyknos." *AJA* 88: 523–9.
(1989) *Art and Cult under the Tyrants in Athens* (Mainz).
(1990) "Old and New Heroes. Narrative, Composition, and Subject in Attic Black-Figure." *ClAnt* 9: 114–48.
(1991) "The Iconography of Mourning in Athenian Art" *AJA* 95: 629–56.
(1992) "Mousikoi Agones: Music and Poetry at the Panathenaia." In Neils (1992) 53–76.
(1996) "Cults of Solonian Athens." In Hägg (1996) 127–33.
(1997) "Correlating Shape and Subject: The Case of the Archaic Pelike." In Oakley, Coulson, and Palagia, eds. (1997) 63–70.
(1998) "Hipparchos and the Rhapsodes." In Dougherty and Kurke (1998) 92–107.
Shapiro, H. A., C. A. Picón, and G. D. Scott, III, eds. (1995) *Greek Vases in the San Antonio Museum of Art* (San Antonio).
Shear, T. L., Jr. (1978) "Tyrants and Buildings in Archaic Athens." In T. L. Shear, Jr., ed. *Athens Comes of Age: From Solon to Salamis* (Princeton) 1–19.
Simon, E. (1983) *Festivals of Attica. An Archaeological Commentary* (Madison).
Simon, G. (1988) *Le Regard, l'être et l'apparence dans l'optique de l'antiquité* (Paris).
Sinos, R. H. (1998) "Divine Selection: Epiphany and Politics in Archaic Greece." In Dougherty and Kurke (1998) 73–91.
Skinner, M. B. (1993) "Woman and Language in Archaic Greece." In N. S. Rabinowitz and A. Richlin, eds. *Feminist Theory and the Classics* (New York/London) 125–44.
Small, J. P. (1994) "Scholars, Etruscans, and Attic Painted Vases." *Journal of Roman Archaeology* 7: 34–58.
Smith, T. J. (2000) "Dancing Spaces and Dining Place: Archaic Komasts at the Symposion." In Tsetskhladze, Prag, and Snodgrass (2000) 309–19.
Snodgrass, A. M. (1979) "Poet and Painter in 8th Century Greece." *Proceedings of the Cambridge Philological Society* 205: 118–30.
(1980a) *Archaic Greece. The Age of Experiment* (Berkeley).
(1980b) "Towards the Interpretation of the Geometric Figure-Scenes." *AM* 95: 51–8.
(1987) *An Archaeology of Greece. The Present and Future Scope of a Discipline*, Sather Classical Lectures 53 (Berkeley).
Sourvinou-Inwood, C. (1988) *Studies in Girls' Transitions: Aspects of the Arkteia and Age Representation in Attic Iconography* (Athens).
(2003) *Tragedy and Athenian Religion* (Lanham, MD).
Sparkes, B. A. (1996) *The Red and the Black. Studies in Greek Pottery* (London/New York).
Spivey, N. (1991) "Greek Vases in Etruria." In Rasmussen and Spivey (1991) 131–50.
Stahl, M. (1987) *Aristokraten und Tyrannen im archaischen Athen* (Stuttgart).
Stansbury-O'Donnell, M. D. (1999) *Pictorial Narrative in Ancient Greek Art* (Cambridge).
Stehle, E. (1997) *Performance and Gender in Ancient Greece* (Princeton).
Stehle, E. and A. Day. (1996) "Women Looking at Women. Women's Ritual and Temple Sculpture." In Kampen (1996) 101–116.
Steiner, A. (1993) "The Meaning of Repetition. Visual Redundancy on Archaic Athenian Vases." *Mitteilungen des Deutschen Archäologischen Instituts, Athenische Abteilung* 108: 197–219.
(1997) "Illustrious Repetitions: Visual Redundancy in Exekias and his Followers." In Oakley, J. H., Coulson, W. D. E., and Palagia, O., eds. *Athenian Potters and Painters. The Conference Proceedings* (Oxford) 157–70.

(2002) "Private and Public: Links between *Symposion* and *Syssition* in Fifth-Century Athens." *ClAnt* 21: 347–79.
(2004) "The Alkmene Hydrias and Vase Painting in Late-Sixth-Century Athens." *Hesperia* 73: 427–63.
Steiner, D. T. (1998) "Moving Images: Fifth-Century Victory Monuments and the Athlete's Allure." *ClAnt* 17: 123–49.
(2001) *Images in Mind. Statues in Archaic and Classical Greek Literature and Thought* (Princeton).
Stewart, A. (1990) *Greek Sculpture. An Exploration* (New Haven).
(1995) "Rape?" In Reeder (1995) 74–90.
(1996) "Reflections." In Kampen (1996) 136–54.
(1997) *Art, Desire and the Body in Ancient Greece* (Cambridge).
Stissi, V. (1999) "Production, Circulation and Consumption of Archaic Greek Pottery (Sixth and Early Fifth Centuries BC)." In Crielaard, Stissi, and van Wijngaarden (1999) 83–113.
(2003) "From Catalogue to Cultural Context: Bringing Life to Greek Sanctuary Pottery." In Schmaltz and Söldner (2003) 77–9.
Stratton, G. M. (1917) *Theophrastus and the Greek Physiological Psychology before Aristotle* (London/New York).
Sutton, R. F., Jr. (2000) "The Good, the Base, and the Ugly: The Drunken Orgy in Attic Vase Painting and the Athenian Self." In Cohen (2000) 180–202.
Svenbro, J. (1993) *Phrasikleia. An Anthropology of Reading in Ancient Greece*, J. Lloyd, tr. (Ithaca).
Tsetskhladze, G. R., A. J. N. W. Prag, and A. M. Snodgrass, eds. (2000) *Periplous. Papers on Classical Art and Archaeology Presented to Sir John Boardman* (London).
Tuna-Nörling, Y. (1995) *Die attisch-schwarzfigurige Keramik und der attische Keramikexport nach Kleinasien. Die Ausgrabungen von Alt-Smyrna und Pitane.* Istanbuler Forschungen 41 (Tübingen).
(1997) "Attic Black-Figure Export to the East: The "Tyrrhenian Group" in Ionia." In Oakley, Coulson, and Palagia (1997) 435–46.
Tyrrel, W. B. (1984) *Amazons. A Study in Athenian Mythmaking* (Baltimore/London).
Tzachou-Alexandri, O., ed. (1988) *Mind and Body: Athletic Contests in Ancient Greece* (Athens).
Uhlenbrock, J. P. (1986) *Herakles. Passage of the Hero through 1000 Years of Classical Art.* (New Rochelle/New York/Annandale-on-Hudson, NY).
Ure, P. N. (1927) *Sixth & Fifth Century Pottery from Excavations Made at Rhitsona by R. M. Burrows in 1909* (Oxford).
Vedder, U. (1990) "Wettkämpfe." In Vierneisel and Kaeser 130–3.
Vermeule, E. T. (1979) *Aspects of Death in Early Greek Art and Poetry* (Berkeley).
Vian, F. (1945) "Le combat d'Héracles et de Kyknos d'après les documents figurés du VIe et du Ve siècle." *Revue des études anciennes* 47: 5–32.
Vidal-Naquet, P. (1986) *The Black Hunter. Forms of Thought and Forms of Society in the Greek World*, A. Szegedy-Maszak, tr. (Baltimore).
Vierneisel, K. and B. Kaeser, eds. (1990) *Kunst der Schale, Kultur der Trinkens* (Munich).
Walker, S. (1983) "Women and Housing in Classical Greece: The Archaeological Evidence." In A. Cameron and A. Kuhrt, eds. *Images of Women in Antiquity* (Detroit) 81–91.
Wallace, R. W. (1994) "Solonian Democracy." In Coulsen (1994) 11–29.
Waterfield, R. (2000) *The First Philosophers. The Presocratics and the Sophists* (Oxford).
Wescoat, B. D. (1986) *Poets and Heroes. Scenes of the Trojan War*, Emory University Museum of Art and Archaeology (Atlanta).

Wees, H. van (1997) "Greeks Bearing Arms. The State, the Leisure Class, and the Display of Weapons in Archaic Greece." In N. Fischer and H. van Wees, eds. *Archaic Greece. New Approaches and New Evidence* (Swansea) 333–78.
West. M. L. (1992) *Ancient Greek Music* (Oxford).
Wheeler, E. L. (1982) "*Hoplomachia* and Greek Dances in Arms." *Greek, Roman and Byzantine Studies* 23: 223–33.
Whitley, J. (2001) *The Archaeology of Ancient Greece* (Cambridge).
Wickersham, J. M. (1991) "Myth and Identity in the Archaic Polis." In D. C. Pozzi and J. M. Wickersham, eds. *Myth and the Polis* (Ithaca) 1–15.
Williams, D. (1980) "Ajax, Odysseus and the Arms of Achilles." *Antike Kunst* 23: 137–45.
Winkler, J. J. (1990) "The Ephebes' Song: *Tragoidia* and *Polis*." In J. J. Winkler and F. I. Zeitlin, eds. *Nothing to Do with Dionysos? Athenian Drama in its Social Context* (Princeton) 20–62.

INDEX